Tokyo Tarareba Girls volume 3 is a work of fiction. Names, characters, places, and incidents are the products of the author's imagination or are used fictitiously. Any resemblance to actual events, locales, or persons, living or dead, is entirely coincidental.

A Kodansha Comics Trade Paperback Original.

Published in the United States by Kodansha Comics,
an imprint of Kodansha USA Publishing, LLC, New York.

Publication rights for this English edition arranged through Kodansha Ltd., Tokyo.

First published in Japan in 2015 by Kodansha Ltd., Tokyo, as *Tokyo Tarareba Musume* volume 3.

ISBN 978-1-63236-687-0

Printed in the United States of America.

www.kodanshacomics.com

9 8 7 6 5 4 3 2 1

Translation: Steven LeCroy
Lettering: Rina Mapa and Paige Pumphrey
Editing: Sarah Tilson and Lauren Scanlan
YKS Services LLC/SKY Japan, INC.
Kodansha Comics Edition Cover Design: Phil Balsman

In love, there are no save points.

ヲタクに恋は難しい

WOTAKOI:
LOVE IS HARD FOR OTAKU

by FUJITA

Narumi has had it rough: Every boyfriend she's had dumped her once they found out she was an otaku, so she's gone to great lengths to hide it. At her new job, she bumps into Hirotaka, her childhood friend and fellow otaku. When Hirotaka almost gets her secret outed at work, she comes up with a plan to keep him quiet. But he comes up with a counter-proposal: Why doesn't she just date him instead?

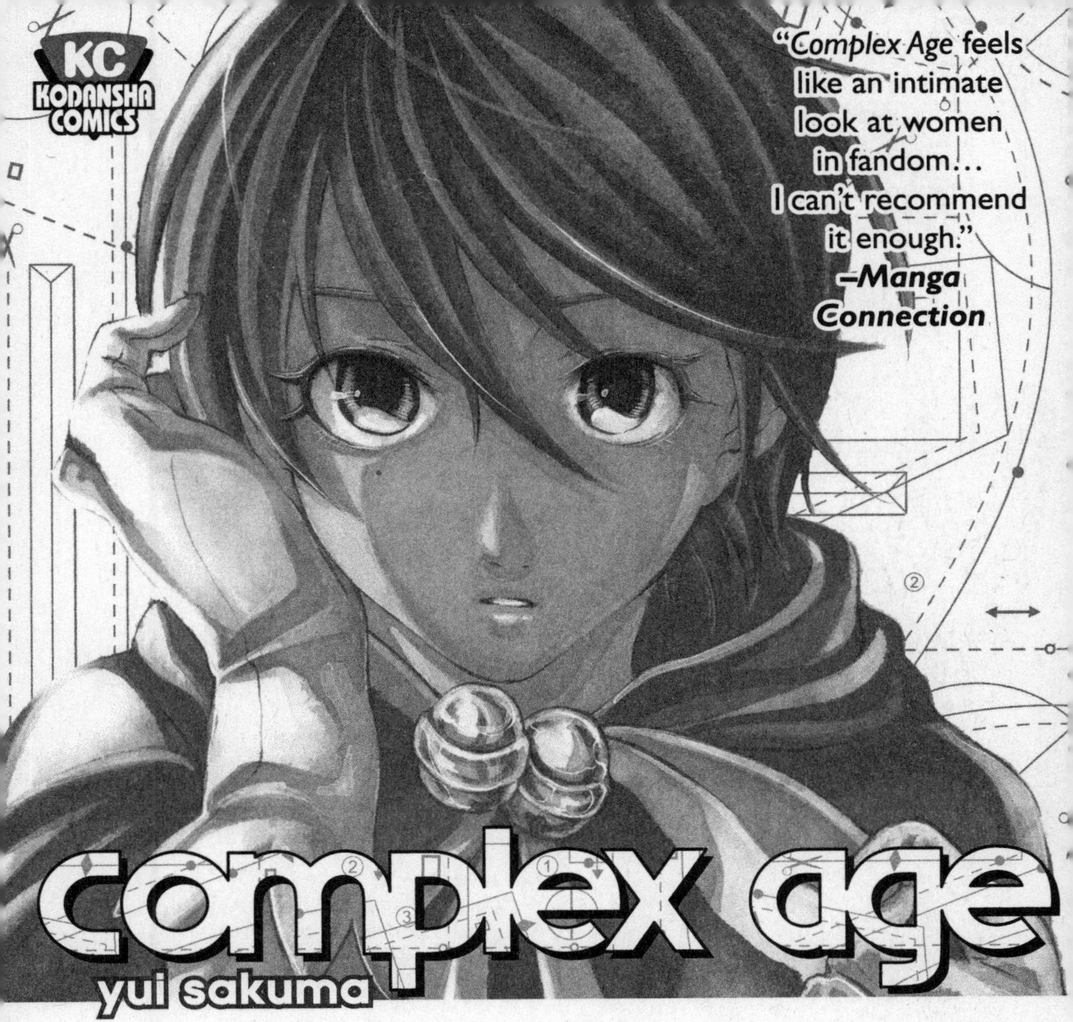
KC
KODANSHA COMICS
"Complex Age feels like an intimate look at women in fandom… I can't recommend it enough."
–Manga Connection
complex age
yui sakuma

26-year-old Nagisa Kataura has a secret. Transforming into her favorite anime and manga characters is her passion in life, and she's earned great respect amongst her fellow cospayers.

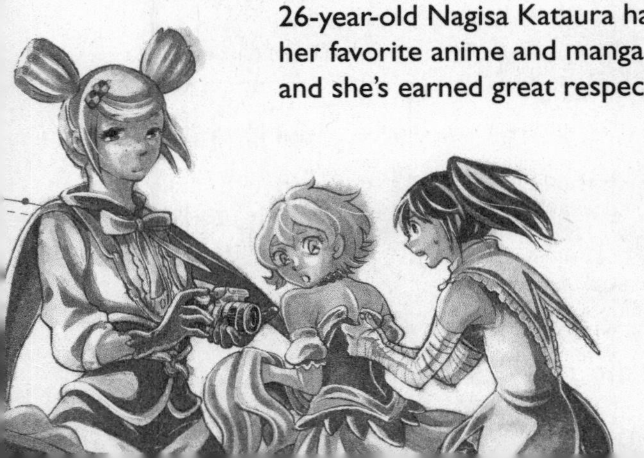

But to the rest of society, her hobby is a silly fantasy. As demands from both her office job and cosplaying begin to increase, she may one day have to make a tough choice—what's more important to her, cosplay or being "normal"?

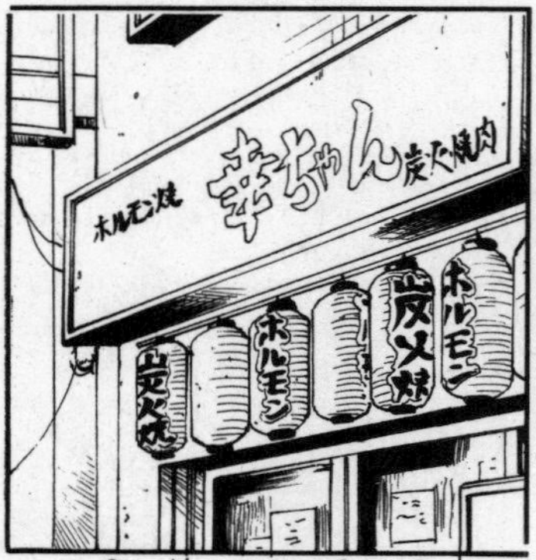

Sign: Horumonyaki Shinchan

***Horumonyaki*, page 112**

Horumonyaki is the Japanese name for "offal," or parts of beef or pork not often eaten. This can include hearts, tripe, intestine, uterus, etc. Restaurants specializing in *horumonyaki* are places to grill these pieces (and often other cuts of beef or pork), which are delicious.

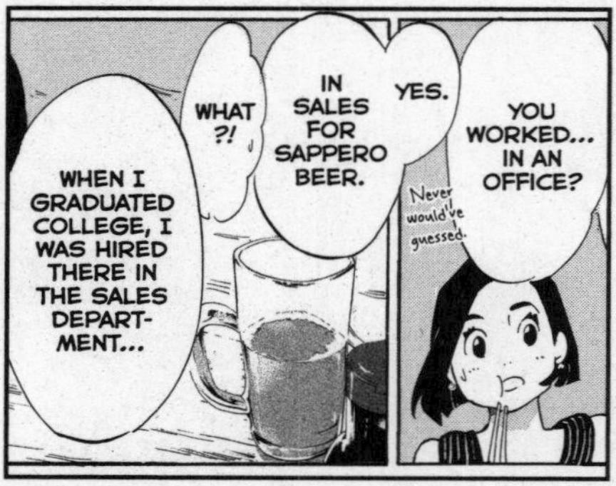
YOU WORKED... IN AN OFFICE?
Never would've guessed.
YES.
IN SALES FOR SAPPERO BEER.
WHAT ?!
WHEN I GRADUATED COLLEGE, I WAS HIRED THERE IN THE SALES DEPARTMENT...

Sappero Beer, page 113

In order to avoid copyright issues, sometimes mangaka will change the names of famous brands by one letter. In this case, a Sappero might be a stand-in for a more famous beer from the far northern island in Japan.

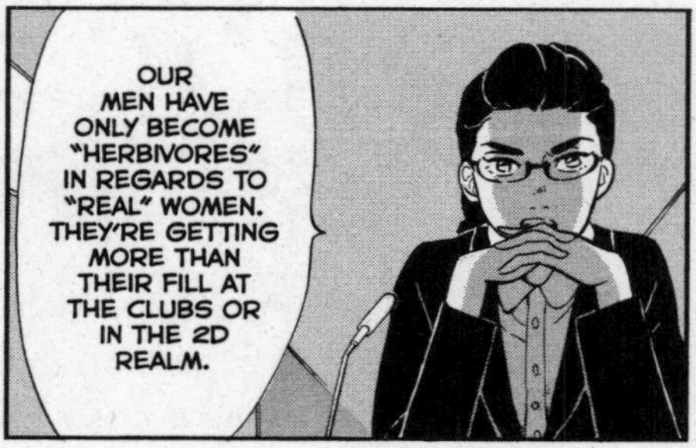
OUR MEN HAVE ONLY BECOME "HERBIVORES" IN REGARDS TO "REAL" WOMEN. THEY'RE GETTING MORE THAN THEIR FILL AT THE CLUBS OR IN THE 2D REALM.

Herbivore men, page 121

Herbivore men (*soushoku-kei danshi*) is a term used in Japan to describe men who are uninterested in aggressively pursuing relationships, love, and/or sex. These men are sometimes blamed for the declining birth rate in Japan. Their counterparts, carnivore women, are women who *do* aggressively pursue relationships, love, and/or sex.

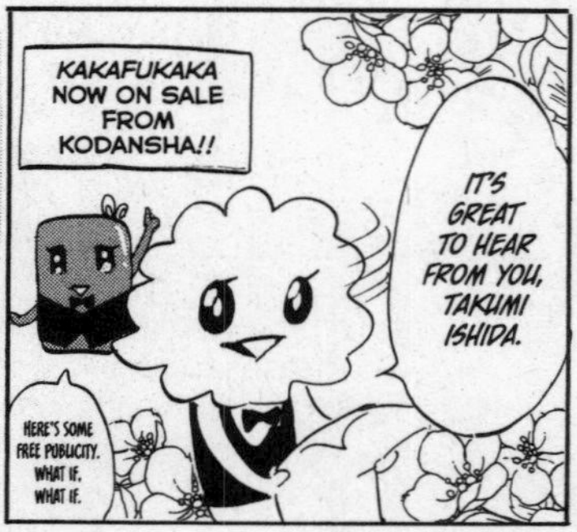
IT'S GREAT TO HEAR FROM YOU, TAKUMI ISHIDA.
KAKAFUKAKA NOW ON SALE FROM KODANSHA!!
HERE'S SOME FREE PUBLICITY. WHAT IF, WHAT IF.

***Kakafukaka* and Takumi Ishida, page 164**

Takumi Ishida is another Kodansha author, who just came out with a new work, *Kakafukaka*, about a young woman who gets reunited with a former flame. Takumi Ishida and Akiko Higashimura are friends as well as colleagues.

TOKYO TARAREBA GIRLS

3

AKIKO HIGASHIMURA

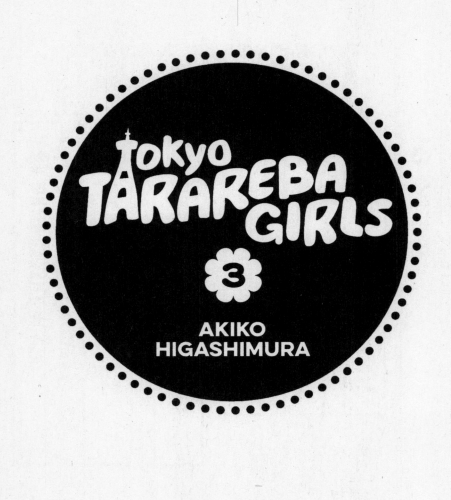

TODAY'S RECOMMENDATIONS

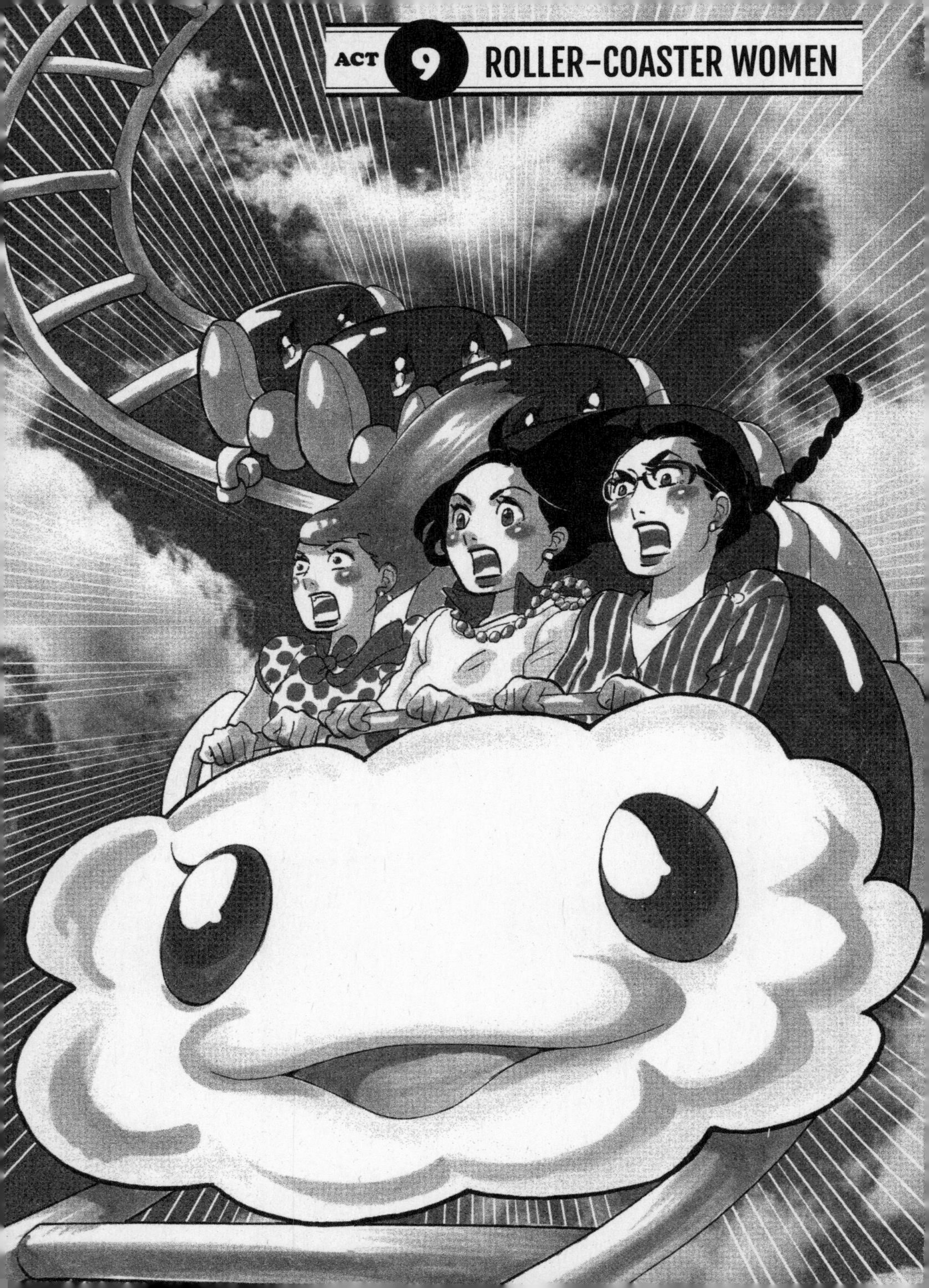
ACT 9 ROLLER-COASTER WOMEN

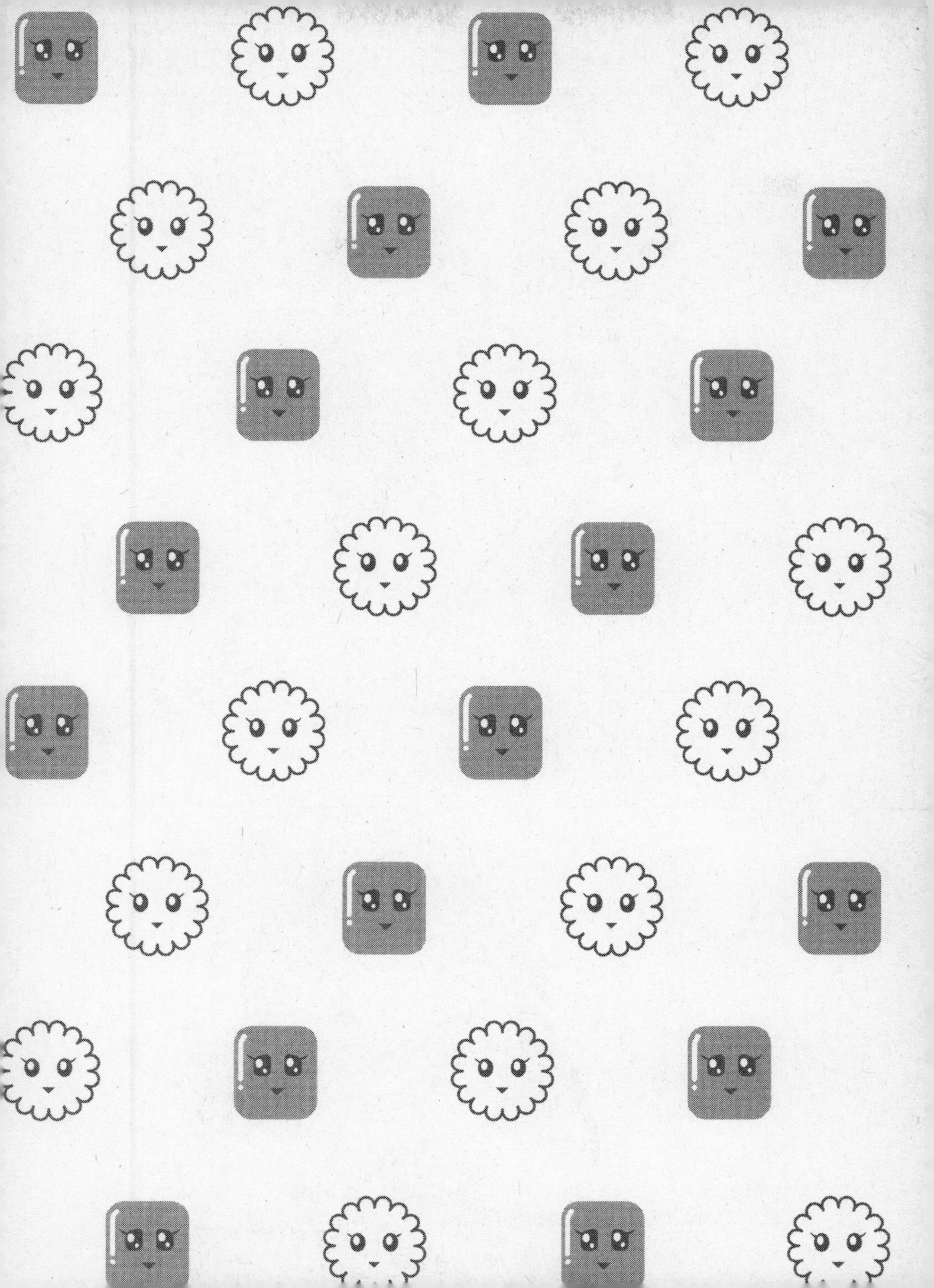

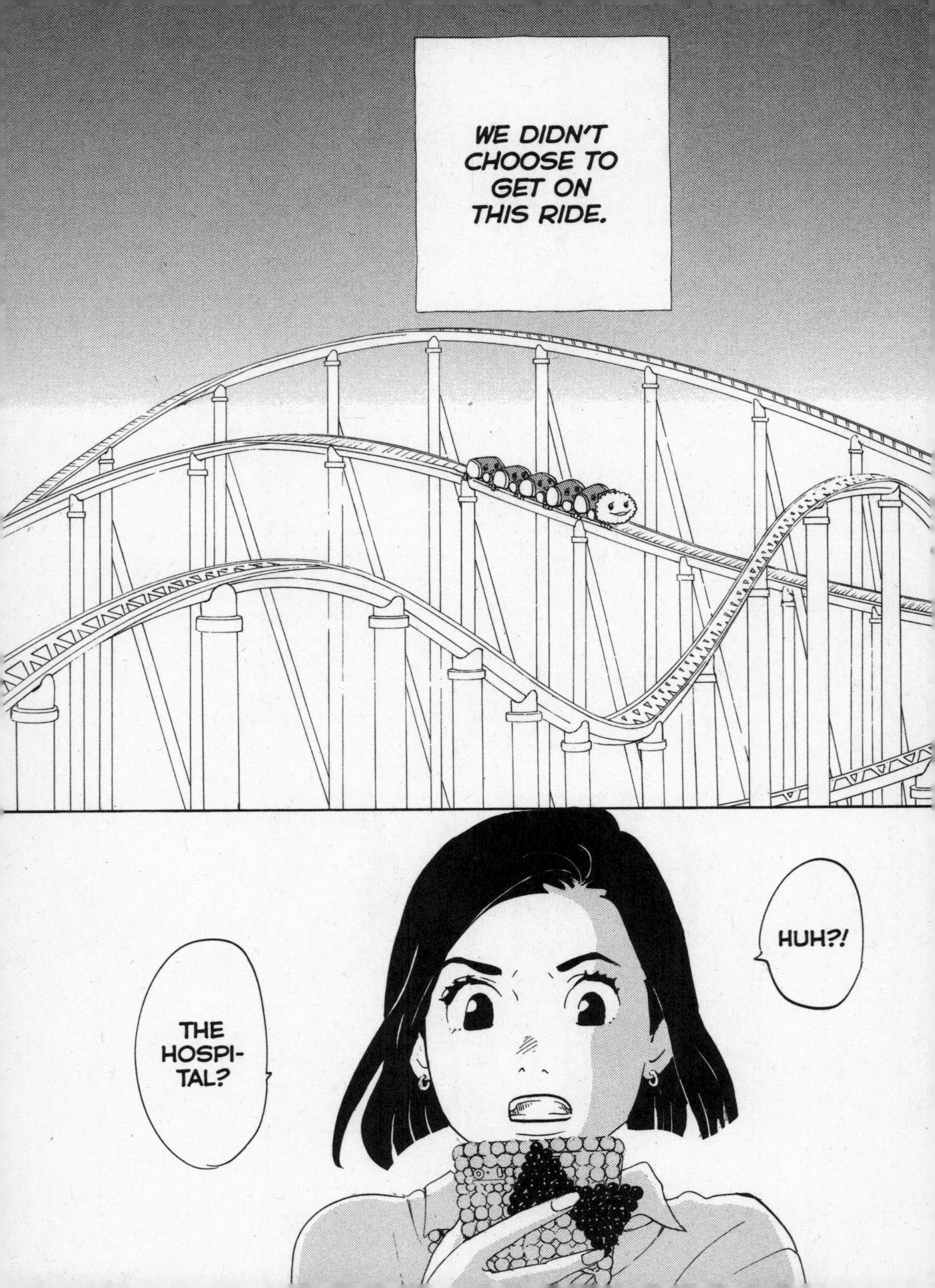
WE DIDN'T CHOOSE TO GET ON THIS RIDE.
HUH?!
THE HOSPI-TAL?

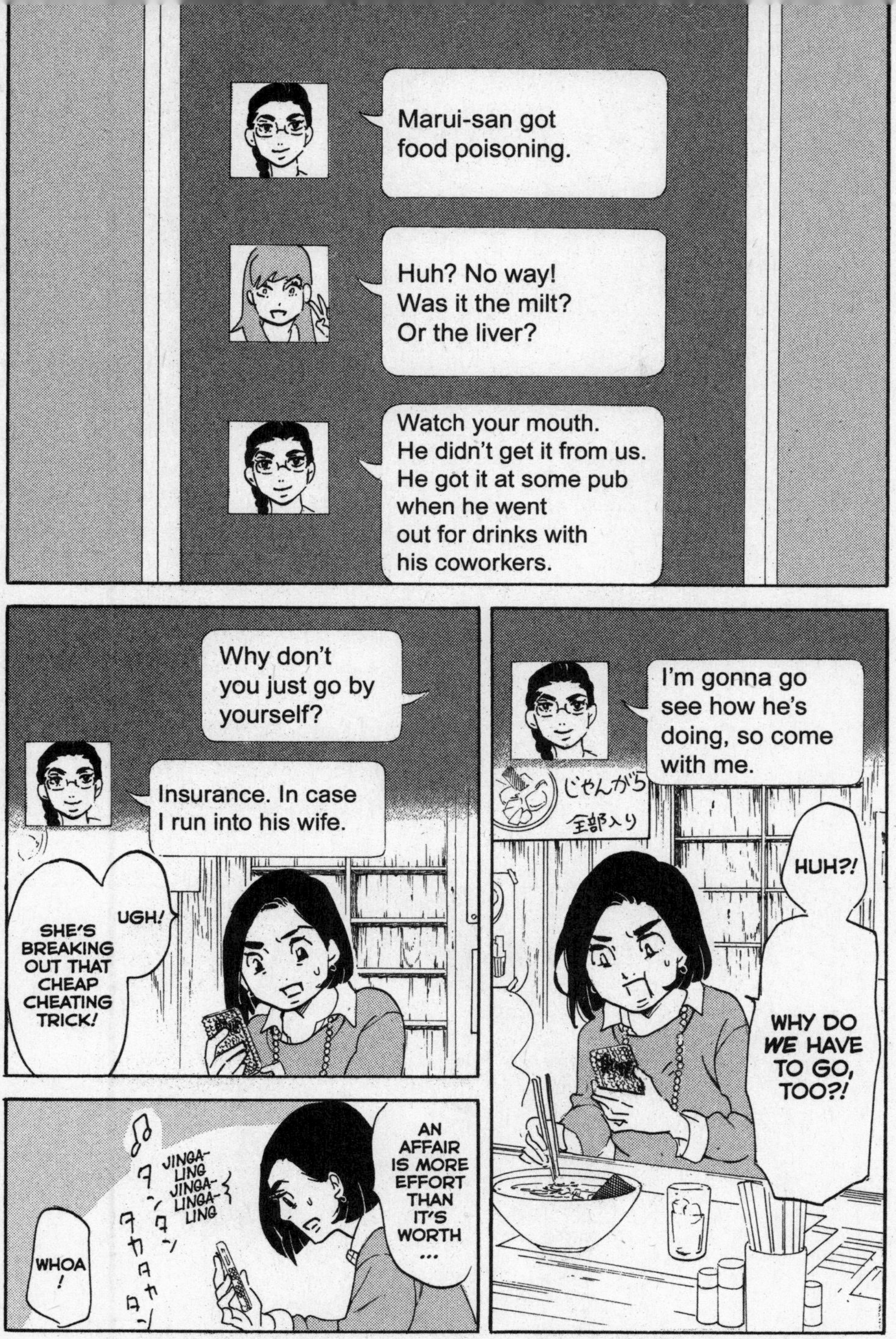

Marui-san got food poisoning.
Huh? No way! Was it the milt? Or the liver?
Watch your mouth. He didn't get it from us. He got it at some pub when he went out for drinks with his coworkers.
I'm gonna go see how he's doing, so come with me.
じゃんがら
全部入り
HUH?!
WHY DO WE HAVE TO GO, TOO?!
Why don't you just go by yourself?
Insurance. In case I run into his wife.
UGH!
SHE'S BREAKING OUT THAT CHEAP CHEATING TRICK!
AN AFFAIR IS MORE EFFORT THAN IT'S WORTH...
JINGA-LING JINGA-LINGA-LING
WHOA!

Sign: Jangara with Everything!

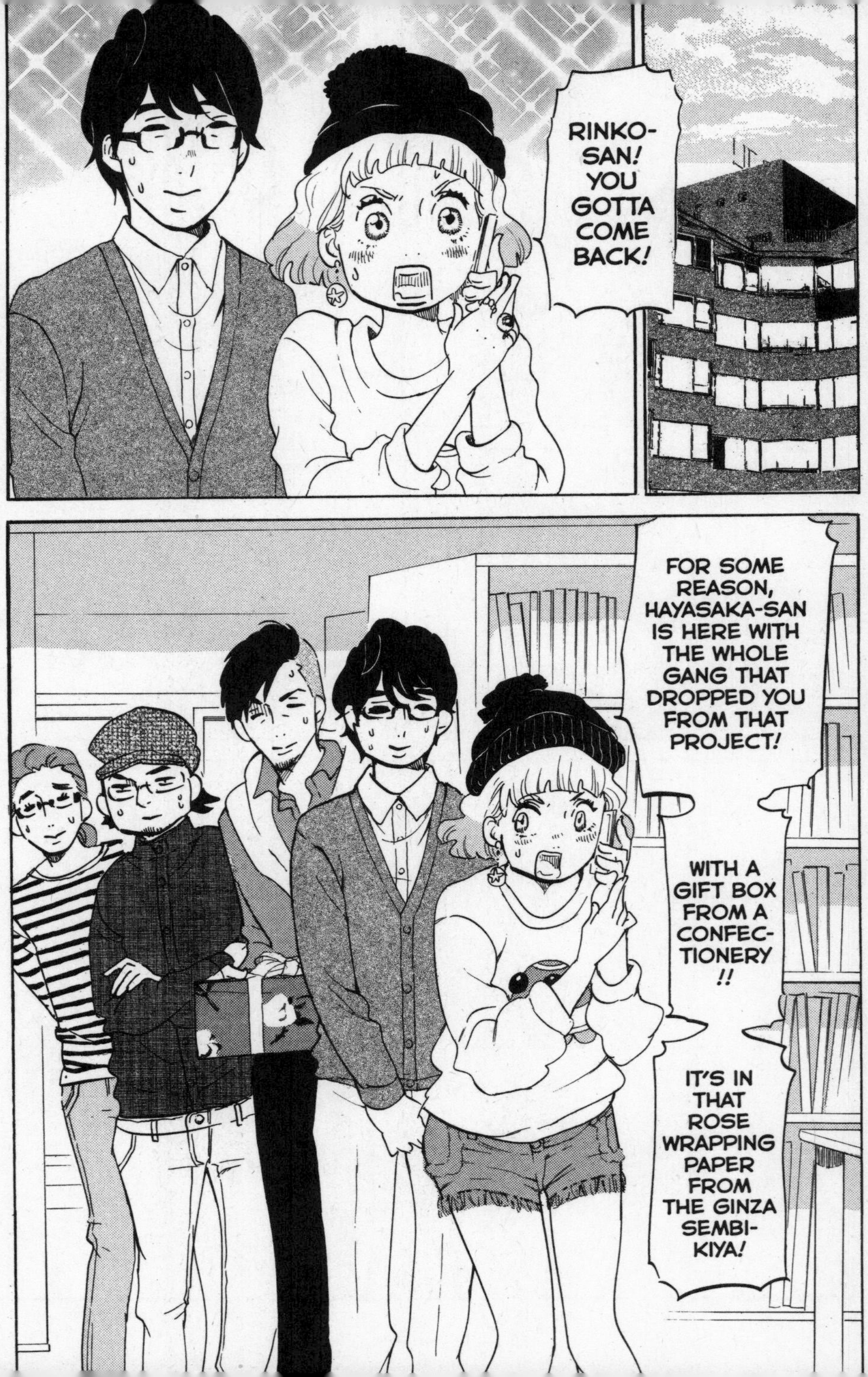
RINKO-SAN! YOU GOTTA COME BACK!
FOR SOME REASON, HAYASAKA-SAN IS HERE WITH THE WHOLE GANG THAT DROPPED YOU FROM THAT PROJECT!
WITH A GIFT BOX FROM A CONFECTIONERY!!
IT'S IN THAT ROSE WRAPPING PAPER FROM THE GINZA SEMBIKIYA!

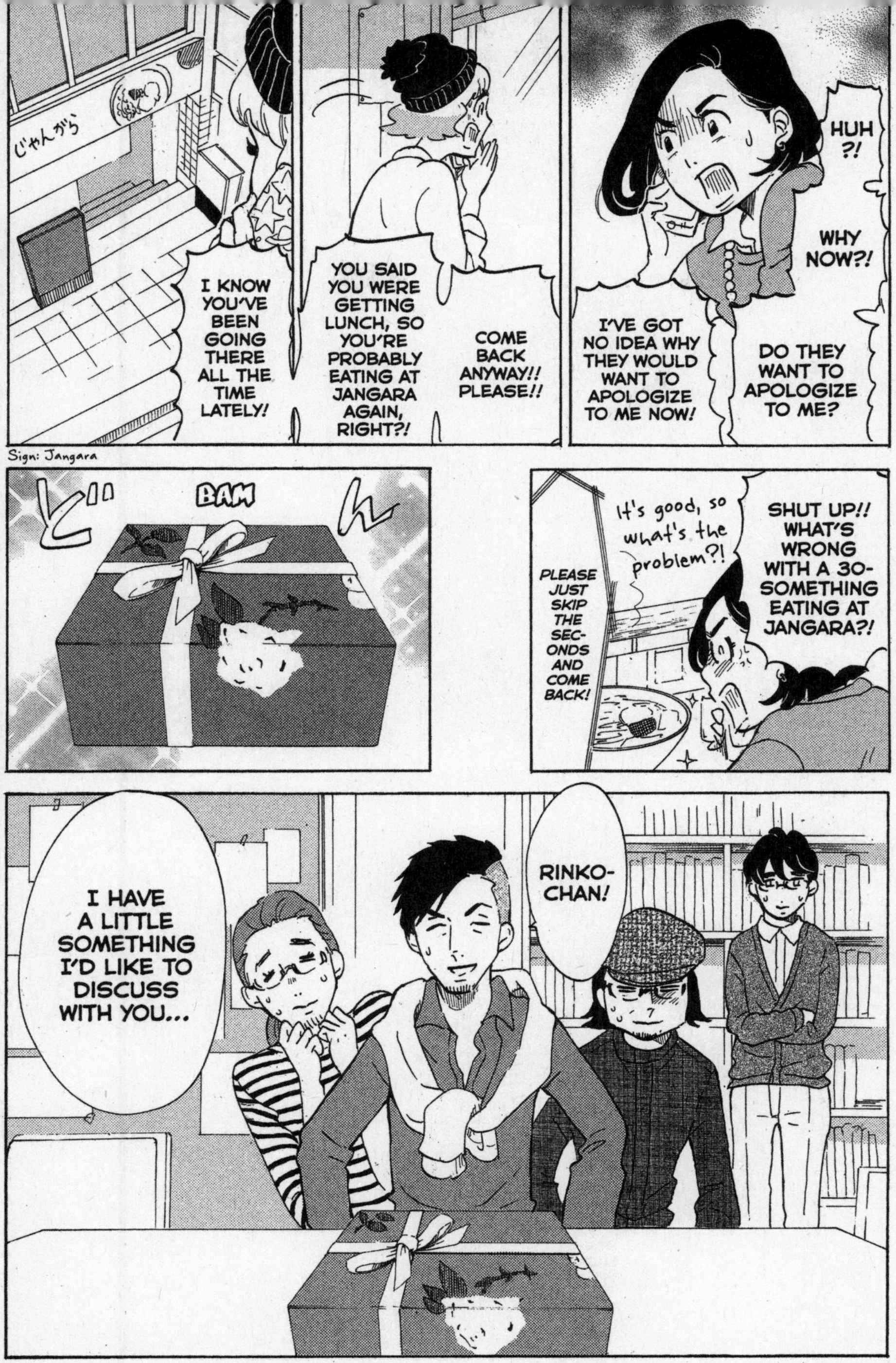
HUH?!
WHY NOW?!
DO THEY WANT TO APOLOGIZE TO ME?
I'VE GOT NO IDEA WHY THEY WOULD WANT TO APOLOGIZE TO ME NOW!
COME BACK ANYWAY!! PLEASE!!
YOU SAID YOU WERE GETTING LUNCH, SO YOU'RE PROBABLY EATING AT JANGARA AGAIN, RIGHT?!
じゃんがら
I KNOW YOU'VE BEEN GOING THERE ALL THE TIME LATELY!
SHUT UP!! WHAT'S WRONG WITH A 30-SOMETHING EATING AT JANGARA?!
It's good, so what's the problem?!
PLEASE JUST SKIP THE SEC-ONDS AND COME BACK!
ど
BAM
ん
RINKO-CHAN!
I HAVE A LITTLE SOMETHING I'D LIKE TO DISCUSS WITH YOU...
Sign: Jangara

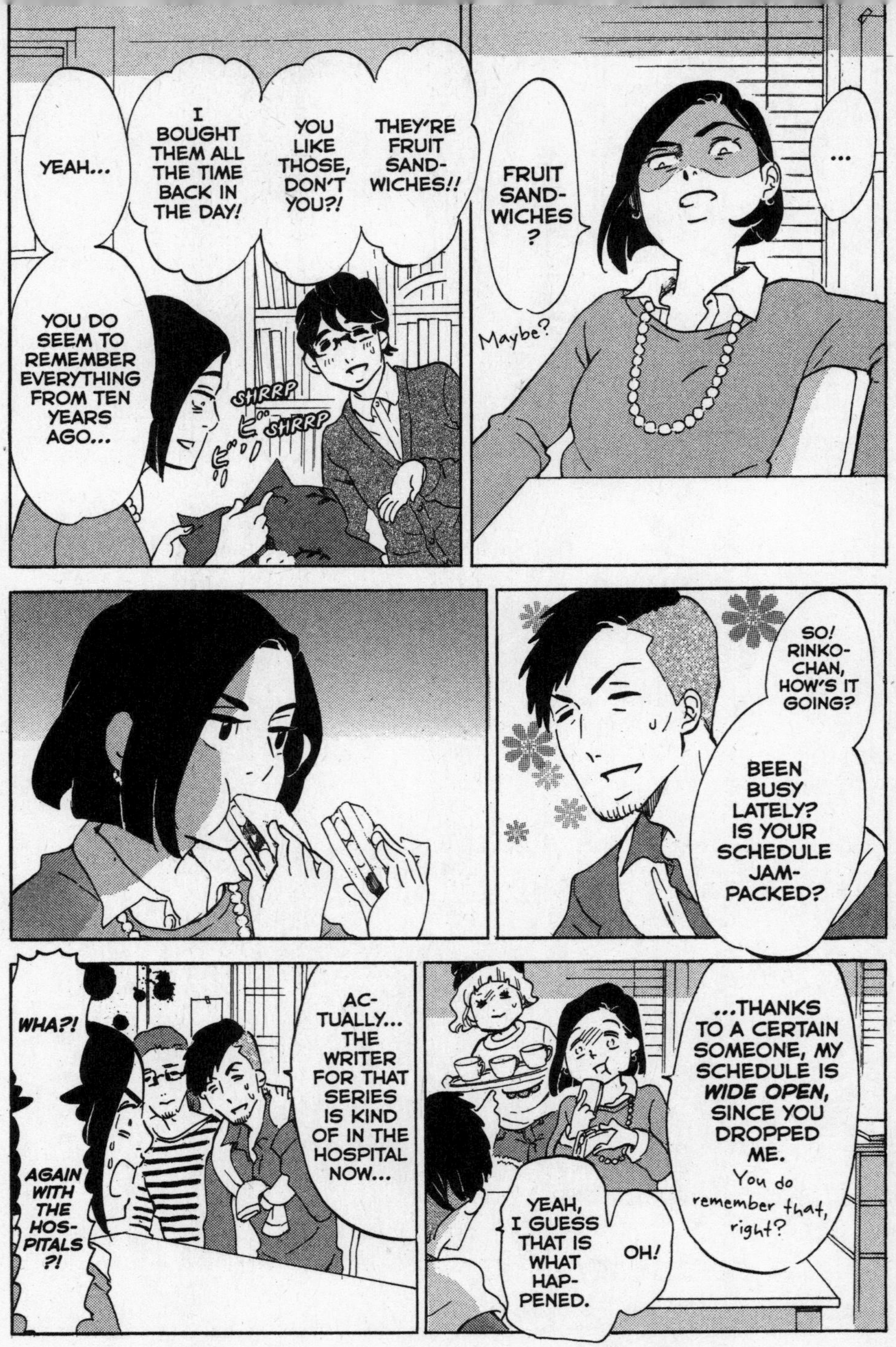
...
FRUIT SANDWICHES?
Maybe?
THEY'RE FRUIT SANDWICHES!!
YOU LIKE THOSE, DON'T YOU?!
I BOUGHT THEM ALL THE TIME BACK IN THE DAY!
YEAH...
YOU DO SEEM TO REMEMBER EVERYTHING FROM TEN YEARS AGO...
SHRRP
SHRRP
SO! RINKO-CHAN, HOW'S IT GOING?
BEEN BUSY LATELY? IS YOUR SCHEDULE JAM-PACKED?
...THANKS TO A CERTAIN SOMEONE, MY SCHEDULE IS *WIDE OPEN*, SINCE YOU DROPPED ME.
You do remember that, right?
OH!
YEAH, I GUESS THAT IS WHAT HAPPENED.
ACTUALLY... THE WRITER FOR THAT SERIES IS KIND OF IN THE HOSPITAL NOW...
WHA?!
AGAIN WITH THE HOSPITALS?!

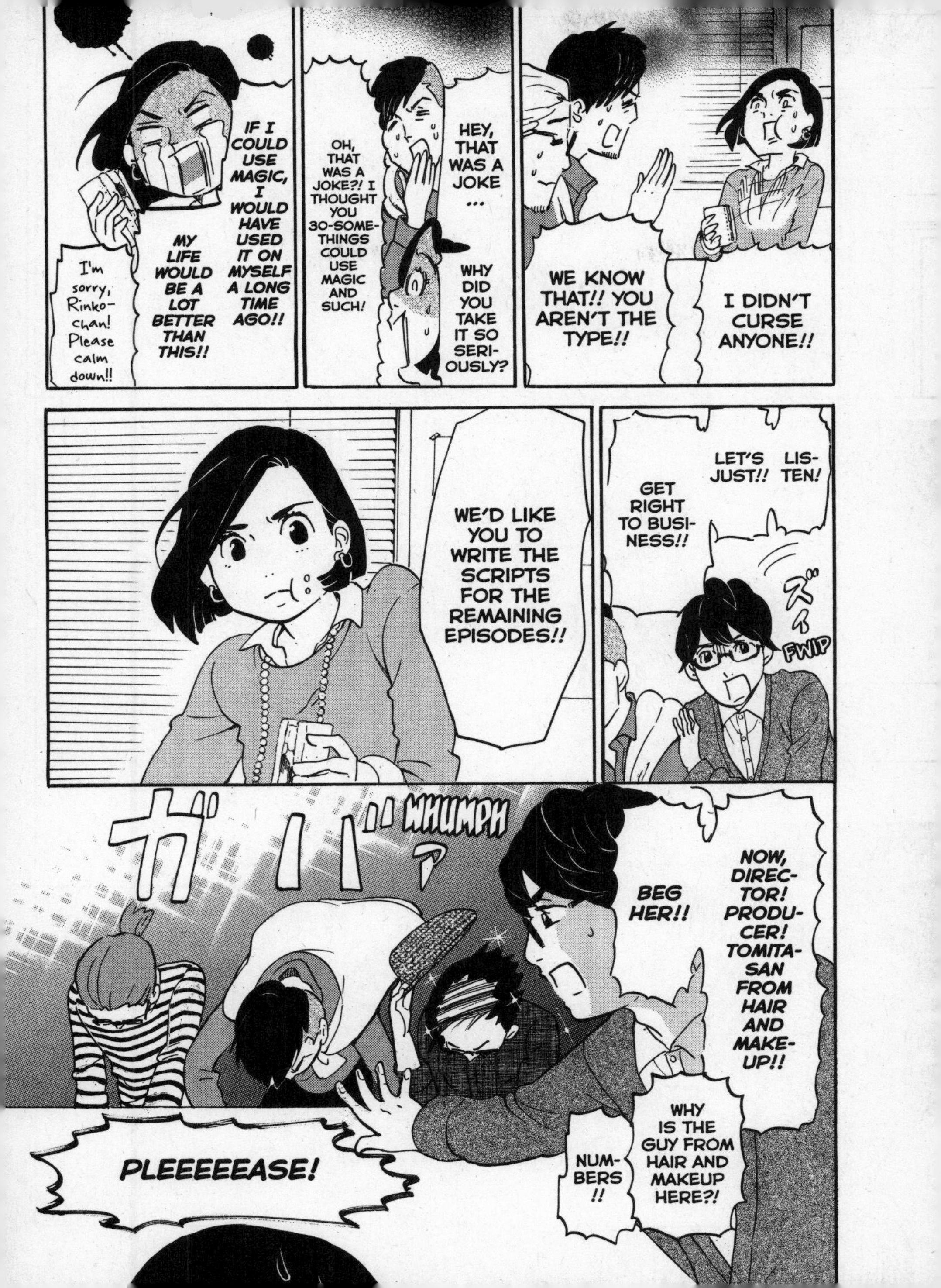
I DIDN'T CURSE ANYONE!!
WE KNOW THAT!! YOU AREN'T THE TYPE!!
HEY, THAT WAS A JOKE ...
WHY DID YOU TAKE IT SO SERIOUSLY?
OH, THAT WAS A JOKE?! I THOUGHT YOU 30-SOME-THINGS COULD USE MAGIC AND SUCH!
IF I COULD USE MAGIC, I WOULD HAVE USED IT ON MYSELF A LONG TIME AGO!!
MY LIFE WOULD BE A LOT BETTER THAN THIS!!
I'm sorry, Rinko-chan! Please calm down!!
LIS-TEN!
LET'S JUST!!
GET RIGHT TO BUSINESS!!
ズイ FWIP
WE'D LIKE YOU TO WRITE THE SCRIPTS FOR THE REMAINING EPISODES!!
NOW, DIRECTOR! PRODUCER! TOMITA-SAN FROM HAIR AND MAKEUP!!
BEG HER!!
ガバァ WHUMPH
WHY IS THE GUY FROM HAIR AND MAKEUP HERE?!
NUMBERS!!
PLEEEEEEASE!

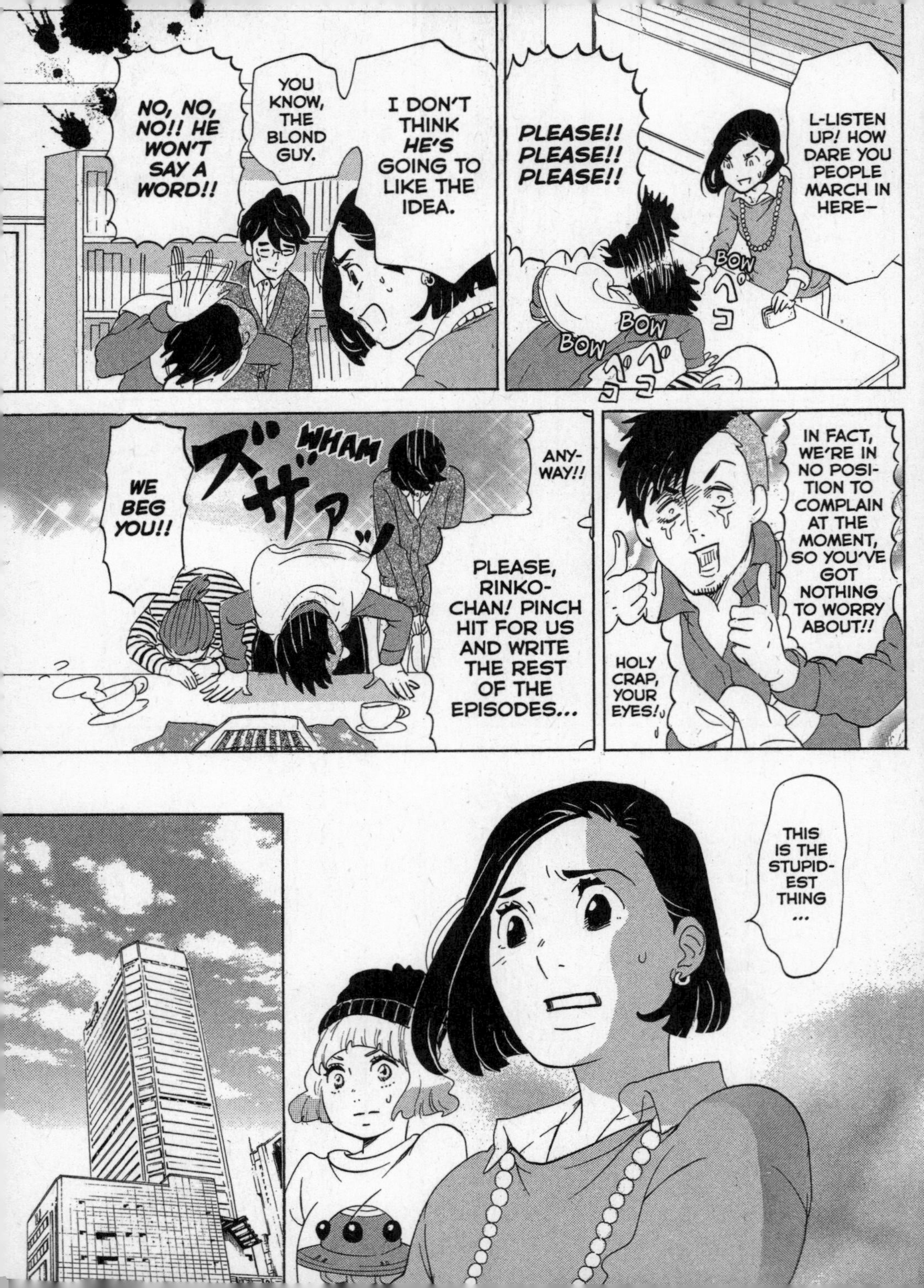
L-LISTEN UP! HOW DARE YOU PEOPLE MARCH IN HERE—
PLEASE!! PLEASE!! PLEASE!!
BOW
BOW
BOW
I DON'T THINK HE'S GOING TO LIKE THE IDEA.
YOU KNOW, THE BLOND GUY.
NO, NO, NO!! HE WON'T SAY A WORD!!
IN FACT, WE'RE IN NO POSI-TION TO COMPLAIN AT THE MOMENT, SO YOU'VE GOT NOTHING TO WORRY ABOUT!!
HOLY CRAP, YOUR EYES!
ANY-WAY!!
PLEASE, RINKO-CHAN! PINCH HIT FOR US AND WRITE THE REST OF THE EPISODES...
WHAM
ズザァッ
WE BEG YOU!!
THIS IS THE STUPID-EST THING ...

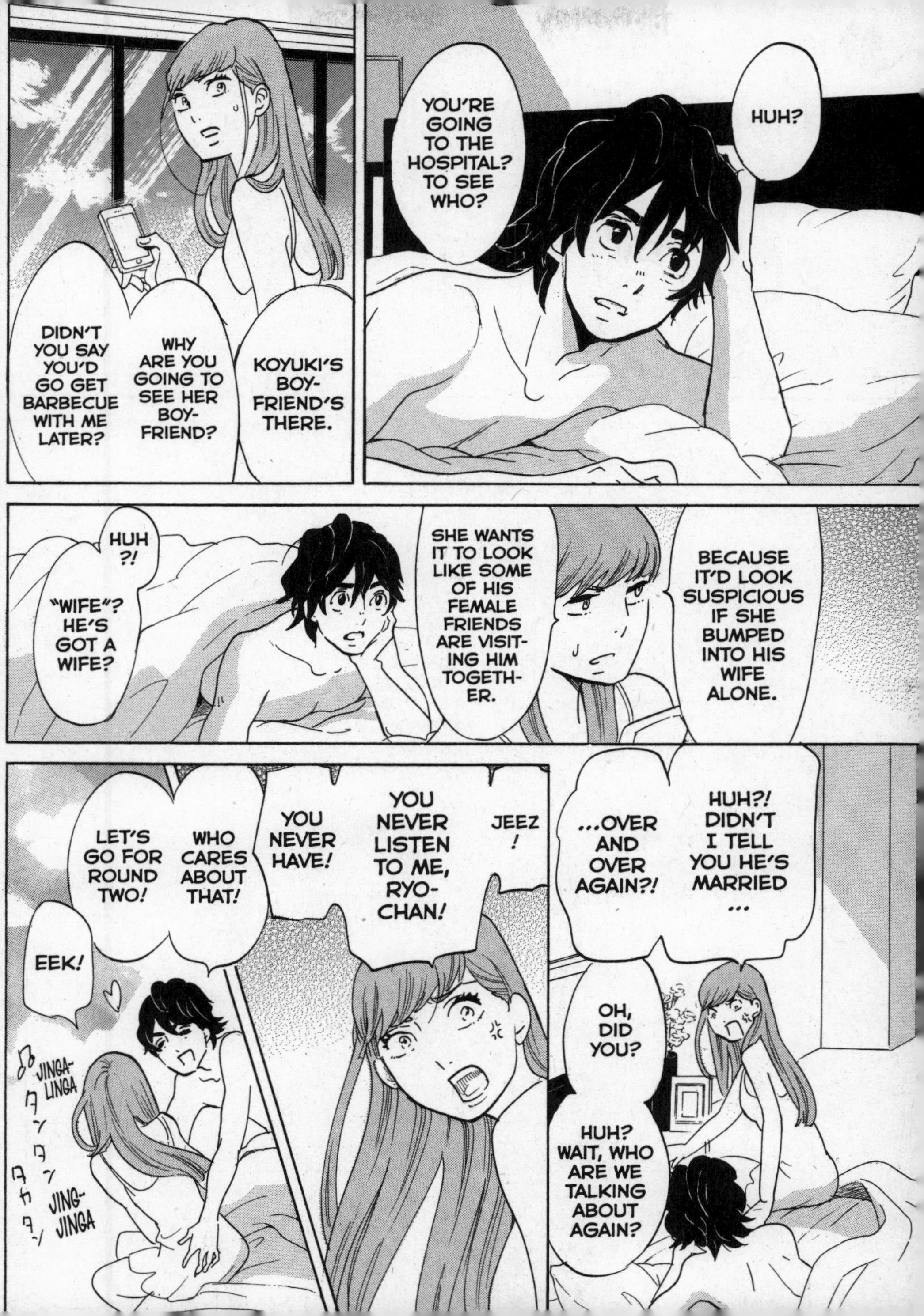
HUH?
YOU'RE GOING TO THE HOSPITAL? TO SEE WHO?
KOYUKI'S BOY-FRIEND'S THERE.
WHY ARE YOU GOING TO SEE HER BOY-FRIEND?
DIDN'T YOU SAY YOU'D GO GET BARBECUE WITH ME LATER?
BECAUSE IT'D LOOK SUSPICIOUS IF SHE BUMPED INTO HIS WIFE ALONE.
SHE WANTS IT TO LOOK LIKE SOME OF HIS FEMALE FRIENDS ARE VISIT-ING HIM TOGETH-ER.
HUH?!
"WIFE"? HE'S GOT A WIFE?
HUH?! DIDN'T I TELL YOU HE'S MARRIED...
...OVER AND OVER AGAIN?!
OH, DID YOU?
HUH? WAIT, WHO ARE WE TALKING ABOUT AGAIN?
JEEZ!
YOU NEVER LISTEN TO ME, RYO-CHAN!
YOU NEVER HAVE!
WHO CARES ABOUT THAT!
LET'S GO FOR ROUND TWO!
EEK!
JINGA-LINGA
JING-JINGA

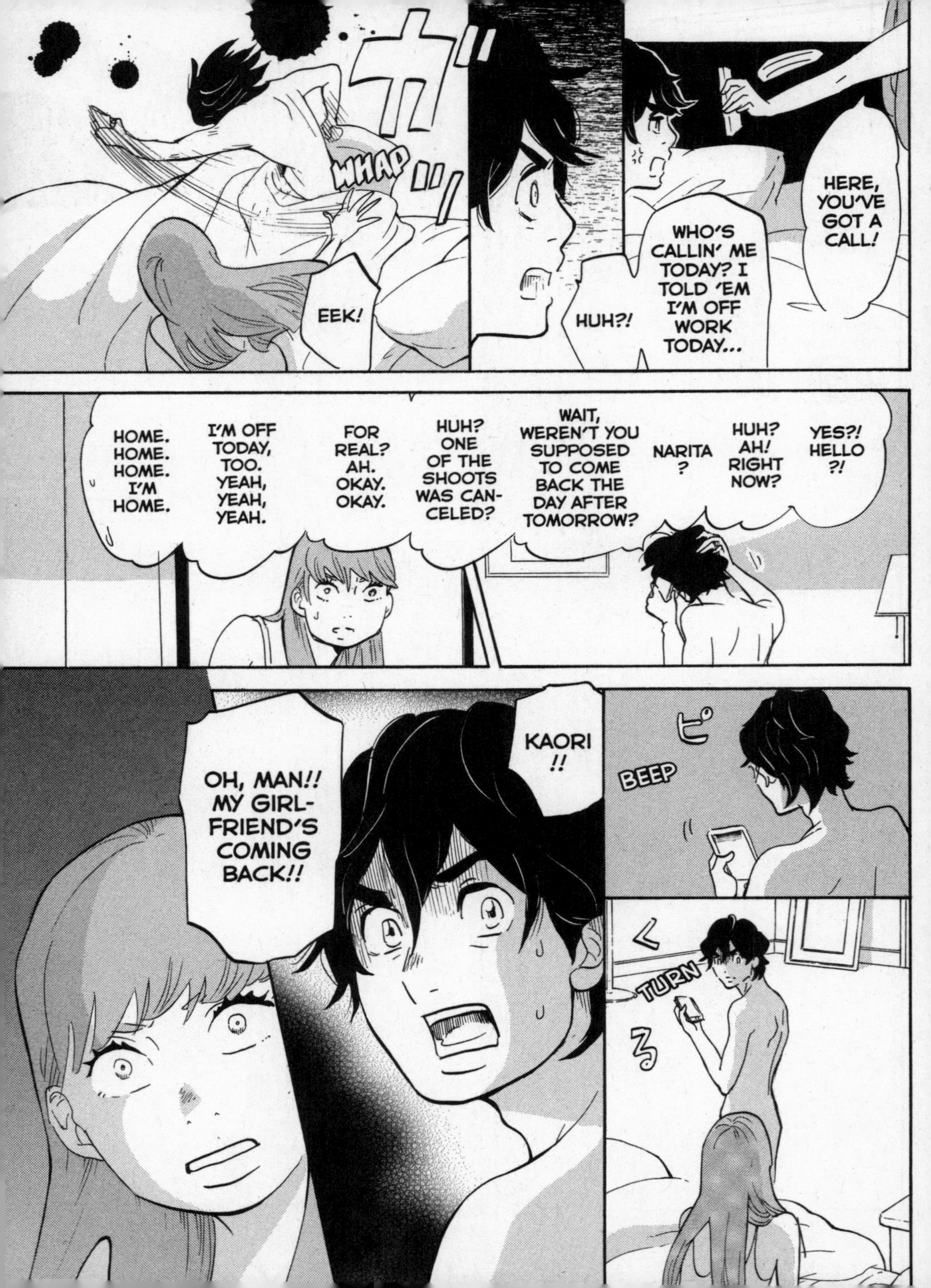
HERE, YOU'VE GOT A CALL!
WHO'S CALLIN' ME TODAY? I TOLD 'EM I'M OFF WORK TODAY...
HUH?!
WHAP!!
EEK!
YES?! HELLO ?!
HUH? AH! RIGHT NOW?
NARITA ?
WAIT, WEREN'T YOU SUPPOSED TO COME BACK THE DAY AFTER TOMORROW?
HUH? ONE OF THE SHOOTS WAS CAN-CELED?
FOR REAL? AH. OKAY. OKAY.
I'M OFF TODAY, TOO. YEAH, YEAH, YEAH.
HOME. HOME. HOME. I'M HOME.
ピ
BEEP
く
TURN
る
KAORI !!
OH, MAN!! MY GIRL-FRIEND'S COMING BACK!!

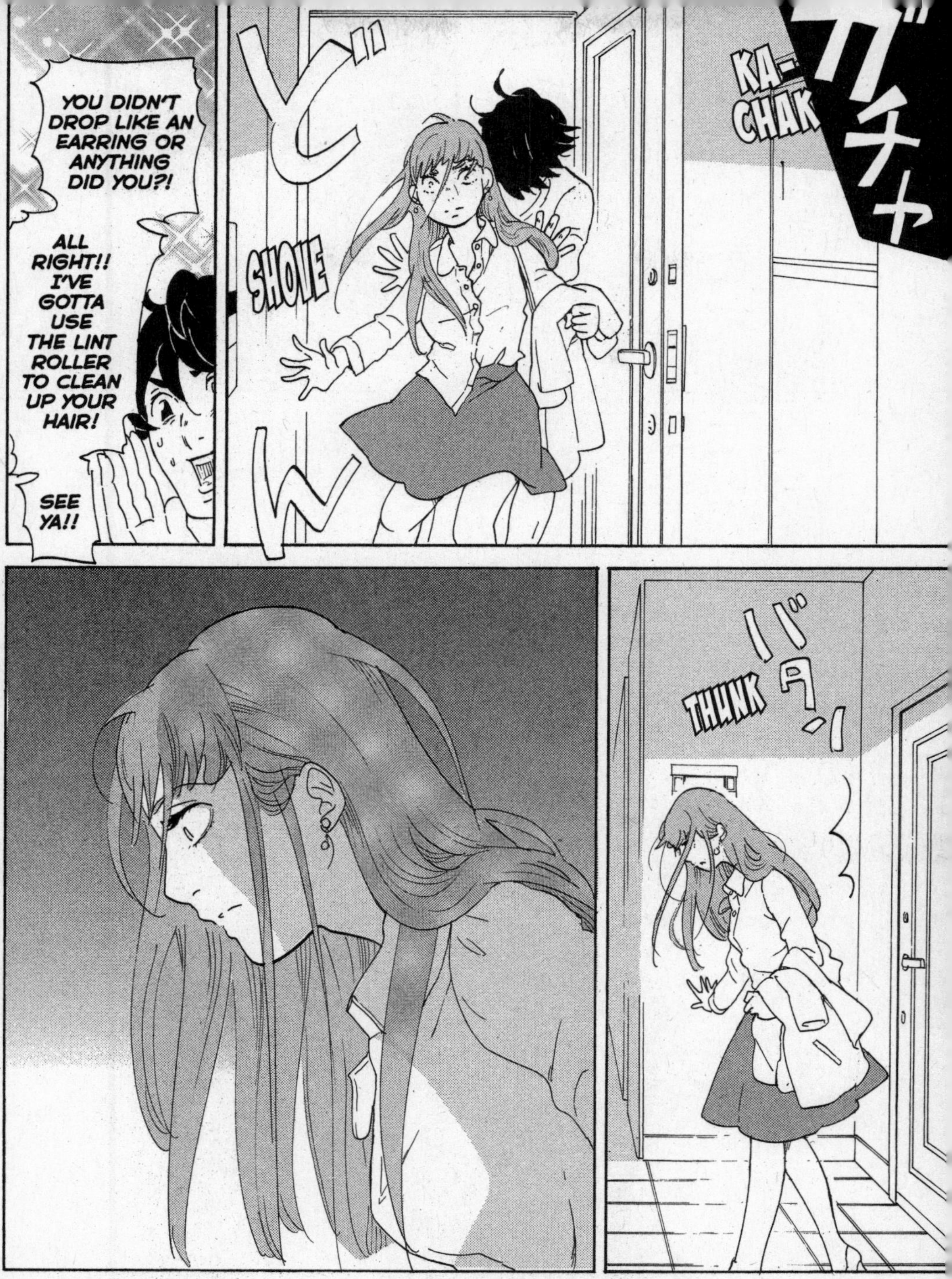
ガチャ
KA-CHAK
SHOVE
YOU DIDN'T DROP LIKE AN EARRING OR ANYTHING DID YOU?!
ALL RIGHT!! I'VE GOTTA USE THE LINT ROLLER TO CLEAN UP YOUR HAIR!
SEE YA!!
THUNK

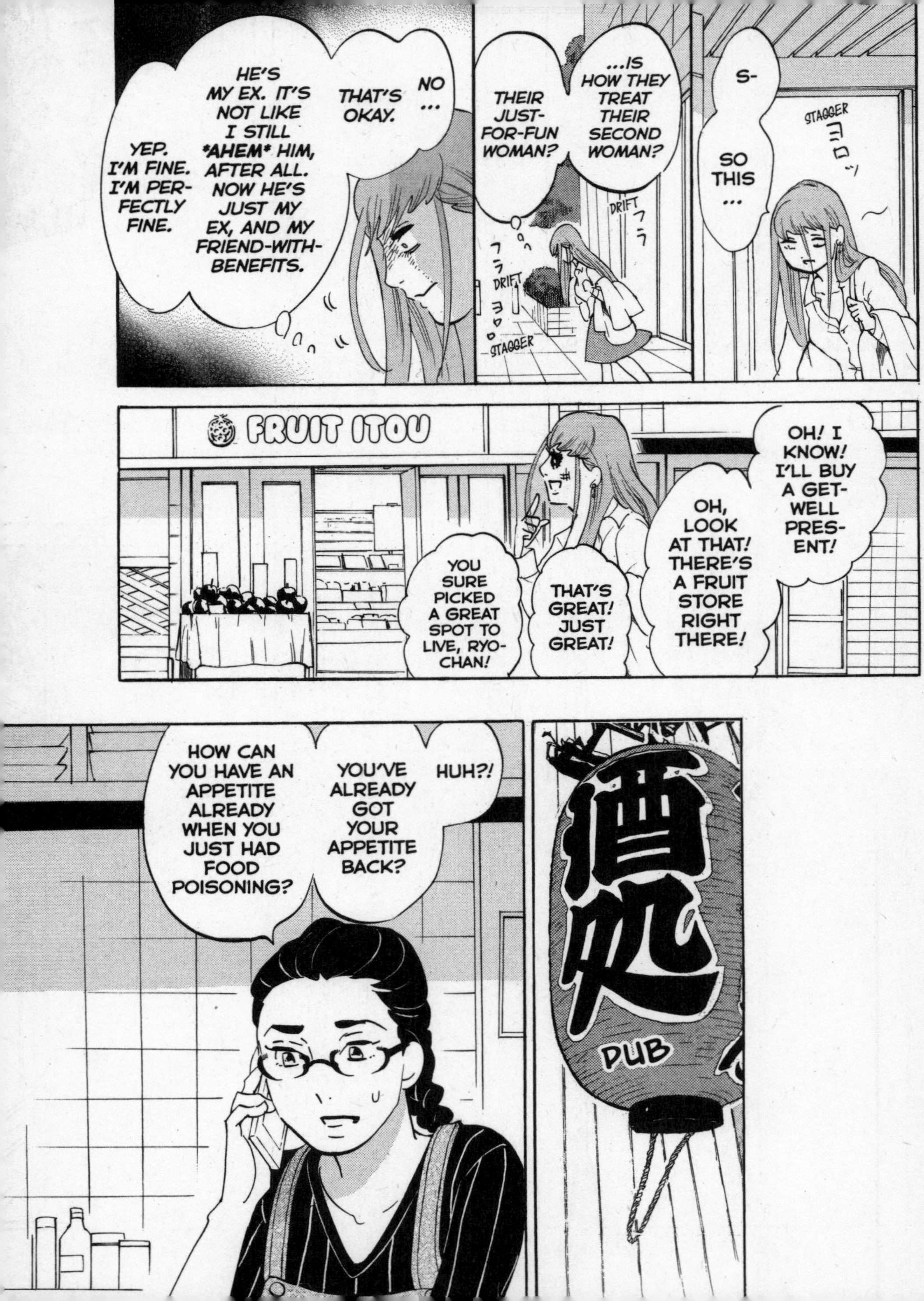
S-
SO THIS ...
STAGGER
ヨロッ
...IS HOW THEY TREAT THEIR SECOND WOMAN?
THEIR JUST-FOR-FUN WOMAN?
DRIFT
フラ
DRIFT
STAGGER
NO ...
THAT'S OKAY.
HE'S MY EX. IT'S NOT LIKE I STILL *AHEM* HIM, AFTER ALL. NOW HE'S JUST MY EX, AND MY FRIEND-WITH-BENEFITS.
YEP. I'M FINE. I'M PERFECTLY FINE.
FRUIT ITOU
OH! I KNOW! I'LL BUY A GET-WELL PRESENT!
OH, LOOK AT THAT! THERE'S A FRUIT STORE RIGHT THERE!
THAT'S GREAT! JUST GREAT!
YOU SURE PICKED A GREAT SPOT TO LIVE, RYO-CHAN!
酒処
PUB
HUH?!
YOU'VE ALREADY GOT YOUR APPETITE BACK?
HOW CAN YOU HAVE AN APPETITE ALREADY WHEN YOU JUST HAD FOOD POISONING?

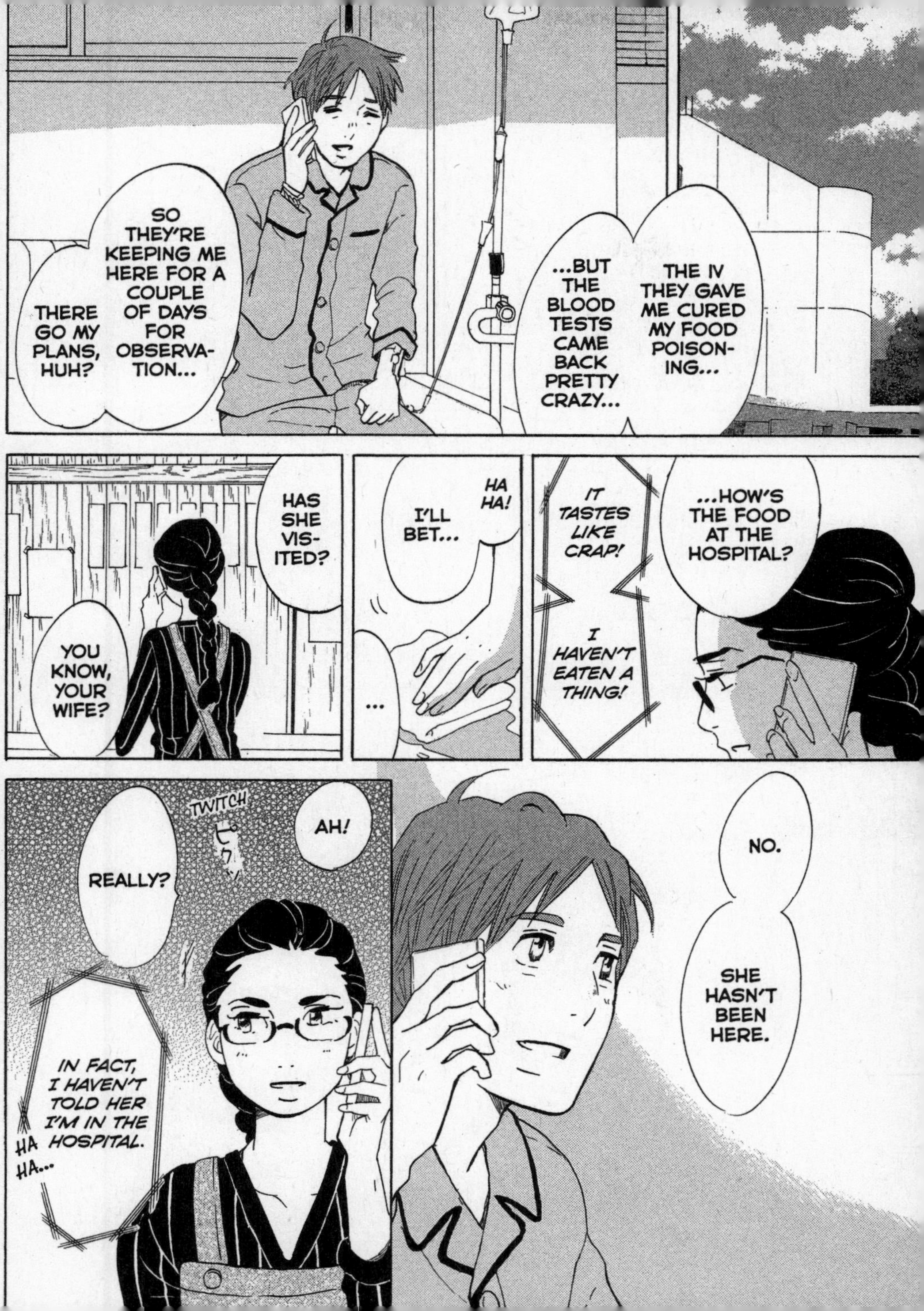
THE IV THEY GAVE ME CURED MY FOOD POISONING...
...BUT THE BLOOD TESTS CAME BACK PRETTY CRAZY...
SO THEY'RE KEEPING ME HERE FOR A COUPLE OF DAYS FOR OBSERVATION...
THERE GO MY PLANS, HUH?
...HOW'S THE FOOD AT THE HOSPITAL?
IT TASTES LIKE CRAP!
I HAVEN'T EATEN A THING!
HA HA!
I'LL BET...
...
HAS SHE VISITED?
YOU KNOW, YOUR WIFE?
NO.
SHE HASN'T BEEN HERE.
AH!
TWITCH
REALLY?
IN FACT, I HAVEN'T TOLD HER I'M IN THE HOSPITAL.
HA HA...

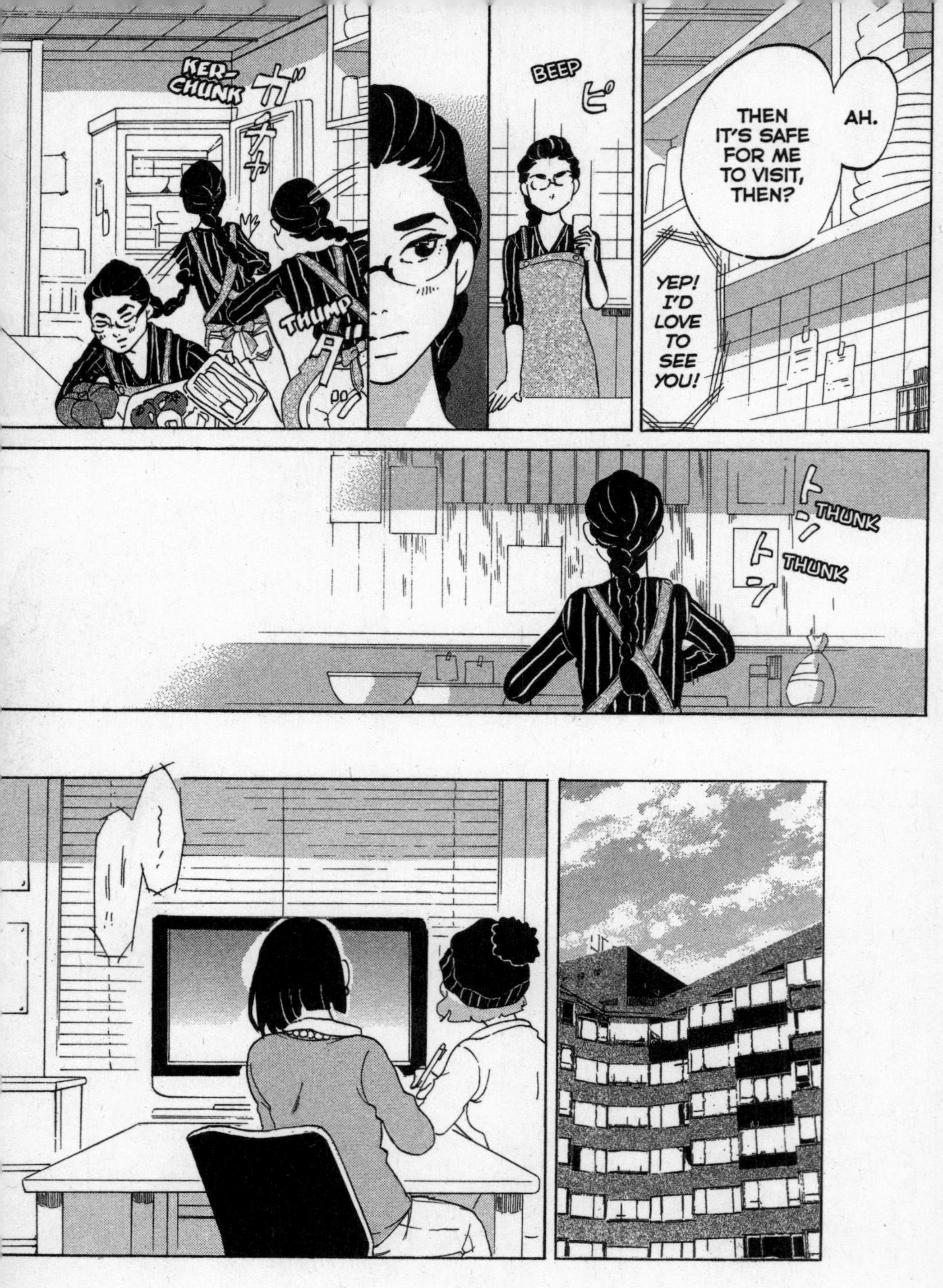
AH.
THEN IT'S SAFE FOR ME TO VISIT, THEN?
YEP! I'D LOVE TO SEE YOU!
BEEP
ピ
KER-CHUNK
ガチャ
THUMP
トン
THUNK
トン
THUNK

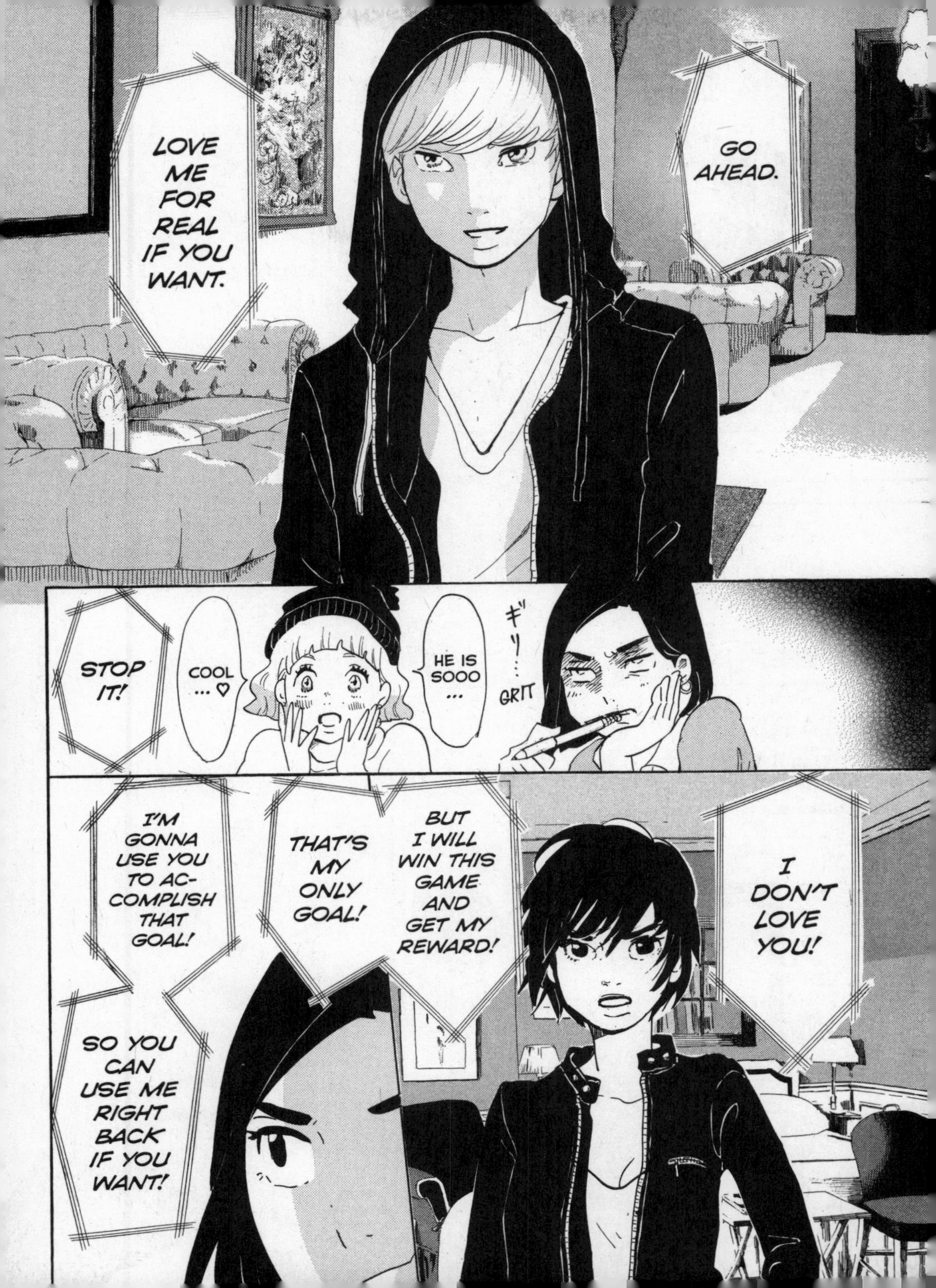
GO AHEAD.
LOVE ME FOR REAL IF YOU WANT.
ギリ… GRIT
HE IS SOOO ...
COOL ... ♡
STOP IT!
I DON'T LOVE YOU!
BUT I WILL WIN THIS GAME AND GET MY REWARD!
THAT'S MY ONLY GOAL!
I'M GONNA USE YOU TO AC-COMPLISH THAT GOAL!
SO YOU CAN USE ME RIGHT BACK IF YOU WANT!

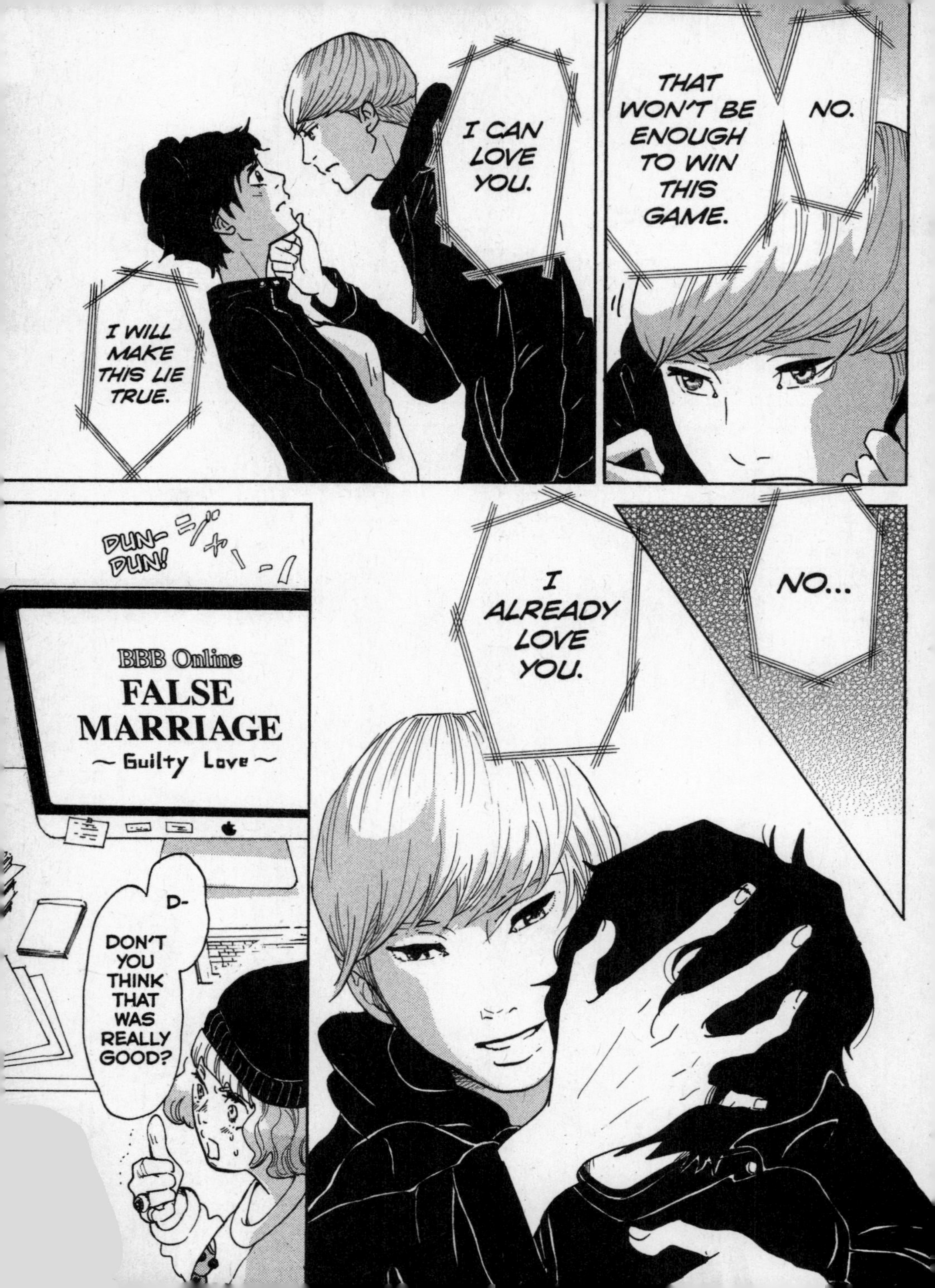
NO.
THAT WON'T BE ENOUGH TO WIN THIS GAME.
I CAN LOVE YOU.
I WILL MAKE THIS LIE TRUE.
NO...
I ALREADY LOVE YOU.
DUN-DUN!
BBB Online
FALSE MARRIAGE
~Guilty Love~
D-
DON'T YOU THINK THAT WAS REALLY GOOD?

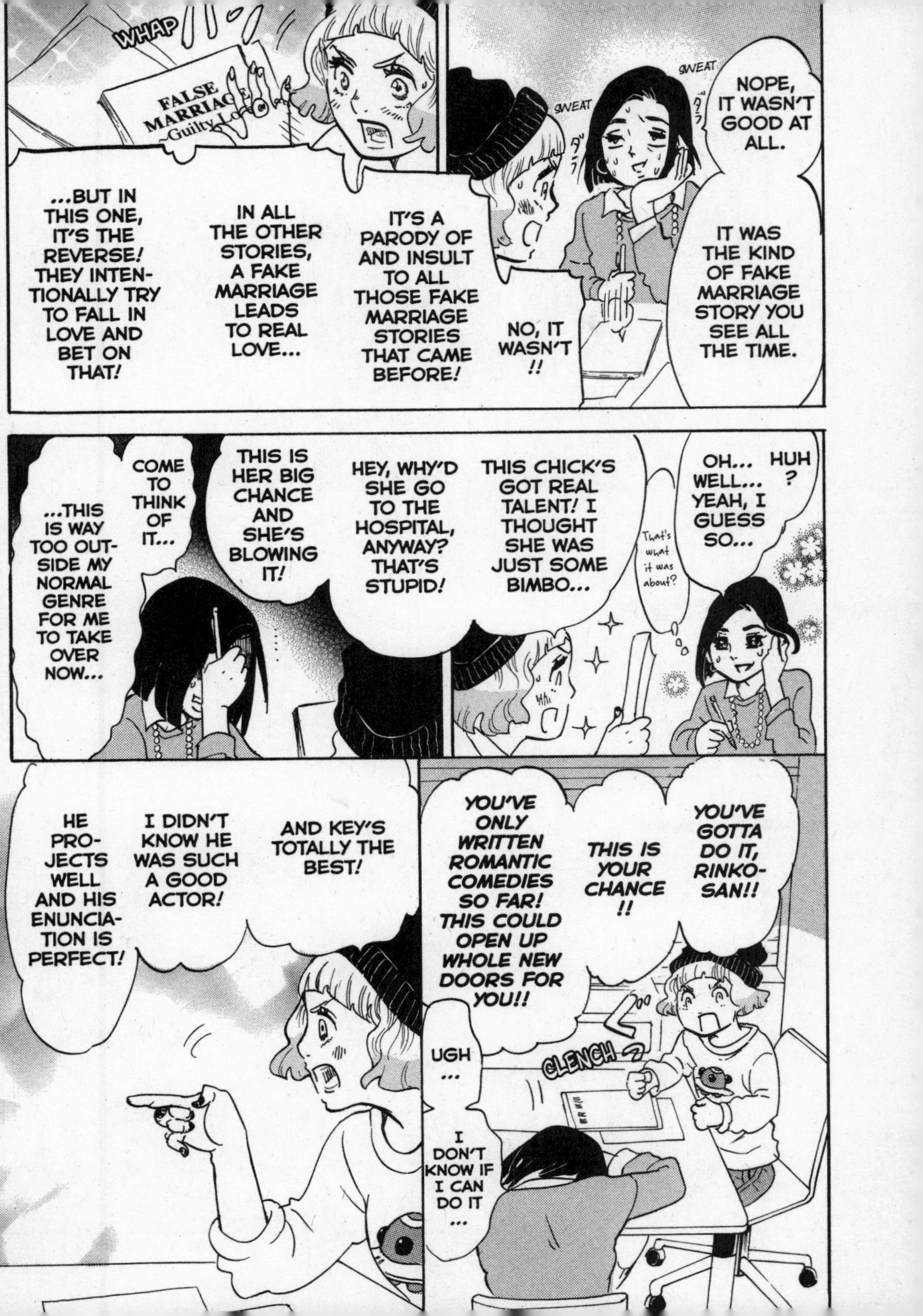

SWEAT
SWEAT
NOPE, IT WASN'T GOOD AT ALL.
IT WAS THE KIND OF FAKE MARRIAGE STORY YOU SEE ALL THE TIME.
NO, IT WASN'T!!
WHAP
FALSE MARRIAGE
Guilty Love
IT'S A PARODY OF AND INSULT TO ALL THOSE FAKE MARRIAGE STORIES THAT CAME BEFORE!
IN ALL THE OTHER STORIES, A FAKE MARRIAGE LEADS TO REAL LOVE...
...BUT IN THIS ONE, IT'S THE REVERSE! THEY INTEN-TIONALLY TRY TO FALL IN LOVE AND BET ON THAT!
HUH?
OH... WELL... YEAH, I GUESS SO...
That's what it was about?
THIS CHICK'S GOT REAL TALENT! I THOUGHT SHE WAS JUST SOME BIMBO...
HEY, WHY'D SHE GO TO THE HOSPITAL, ANYWAY? THAT'S STUPID!
THIS IS HER BIG CHANCE AND SHE'S BLOWING IT!
COME TO THINK OF IT...
...THIS IS WAY TOO OUT-SIDE MY NORMAL GENRE FOR ME TO TAKE OVER NOW...
YOU'VE GOTTA DO IT, RINKO-SAN!!
THIS IS YOUR CHANCE!!
YOU'VE ONLY WRITTEN ROMANTIC COMEDIES SO FAR! THIS COULD OPEN UP WHOLE NEW DOORS FOR YOU!!
CLENCH
UGH...
I DON'T KNOW IF I CAN DO IT...
AND KEY'S TOTALLY THE BEST!
I DIDN'T KNOW HE WAS SUCH A GOOD ACTOR!
HE PRO-JECTS WELL AND HIS ENUNCIA-TION IS PERFECT!

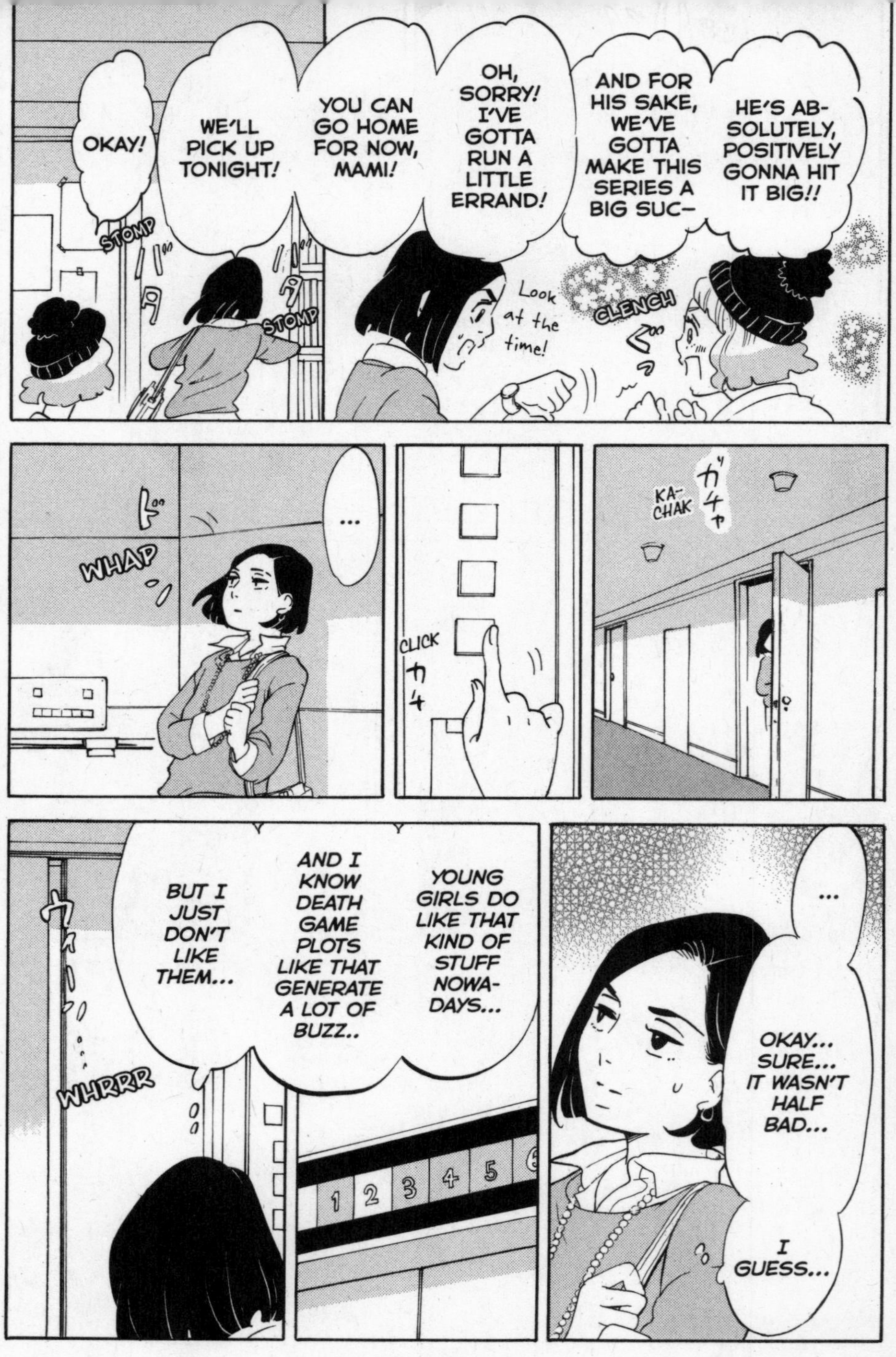
HE'S AB-SOLUTELY, POSITIVELY GONNA HIT IT BIG!!
AND FOR HIS SAKE, WE'VE GOTTA MAKE THIS SERIES A BIG SUC–
CLENCH
OH, SORRY! I'VE GOTTA RUN A LITTLE ERRAND!
Look at the time!
YOU CAN GO HOME FOR NOW, MAMI!
STOMP
WE'LL PICK UP TONIGHT!
STOMP
OKAY!
KA-CHAK
ガチャ
CLICK
カチ
...
WHAP
ド
...
OKAY... SURE... IT WASN'T HALF BAD...
I GUESS...
YOUNG GIRLS DO LIKE THAT KIND OF STUFF NOWA-DAYS...
AND I KNOW DEATH GAME PLOTS LIKE THAT GENERATE A LOT OF BUZZ..
BUT I JUST DON'T LIKE THEM...
WHRRR

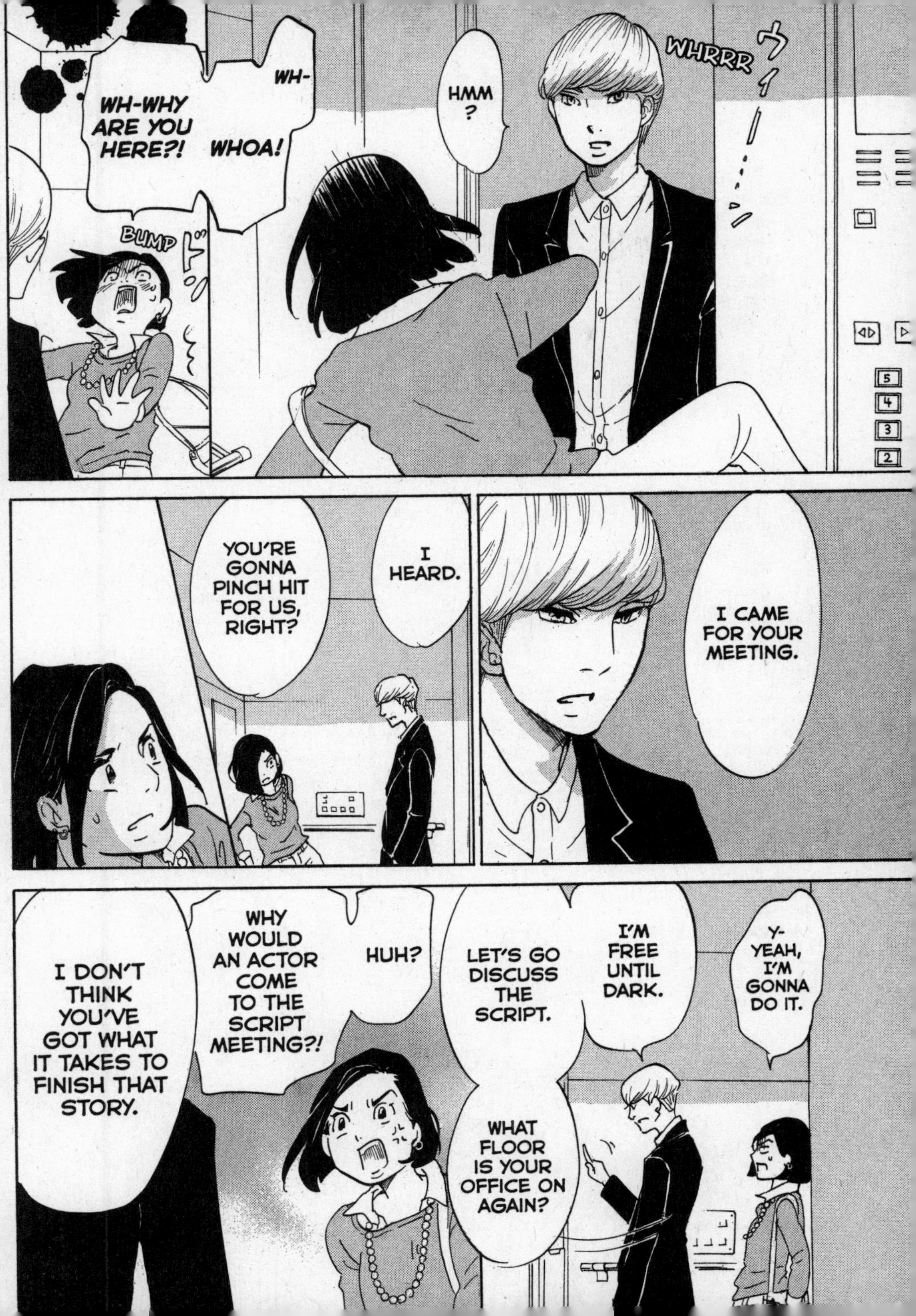
WHRRR
HMM?
WH-
WH-WHY ARE YOU HERE?!
WHOA!
BUMP
I CAME FOR YOUR MEETING.
I HEARD.
YOU'RE GONNA PINCH HIT FOR US, RIGHT?
Y-YEAH, I'M GONNA DO IT.
I'M FREE UNTIL DARK.
LET'S GO DISCUSS THE SCRIPT.
WHAT FLOOR IS YOUR OFFICE ON AGAIN?
HUH?
WHY WOULD AN ACTOR COME TO THE SCRIPT MEETING?!
I DON'T THINK YOU'VE GOT WHAT IT TAKES TO FINISH THAT STORY.

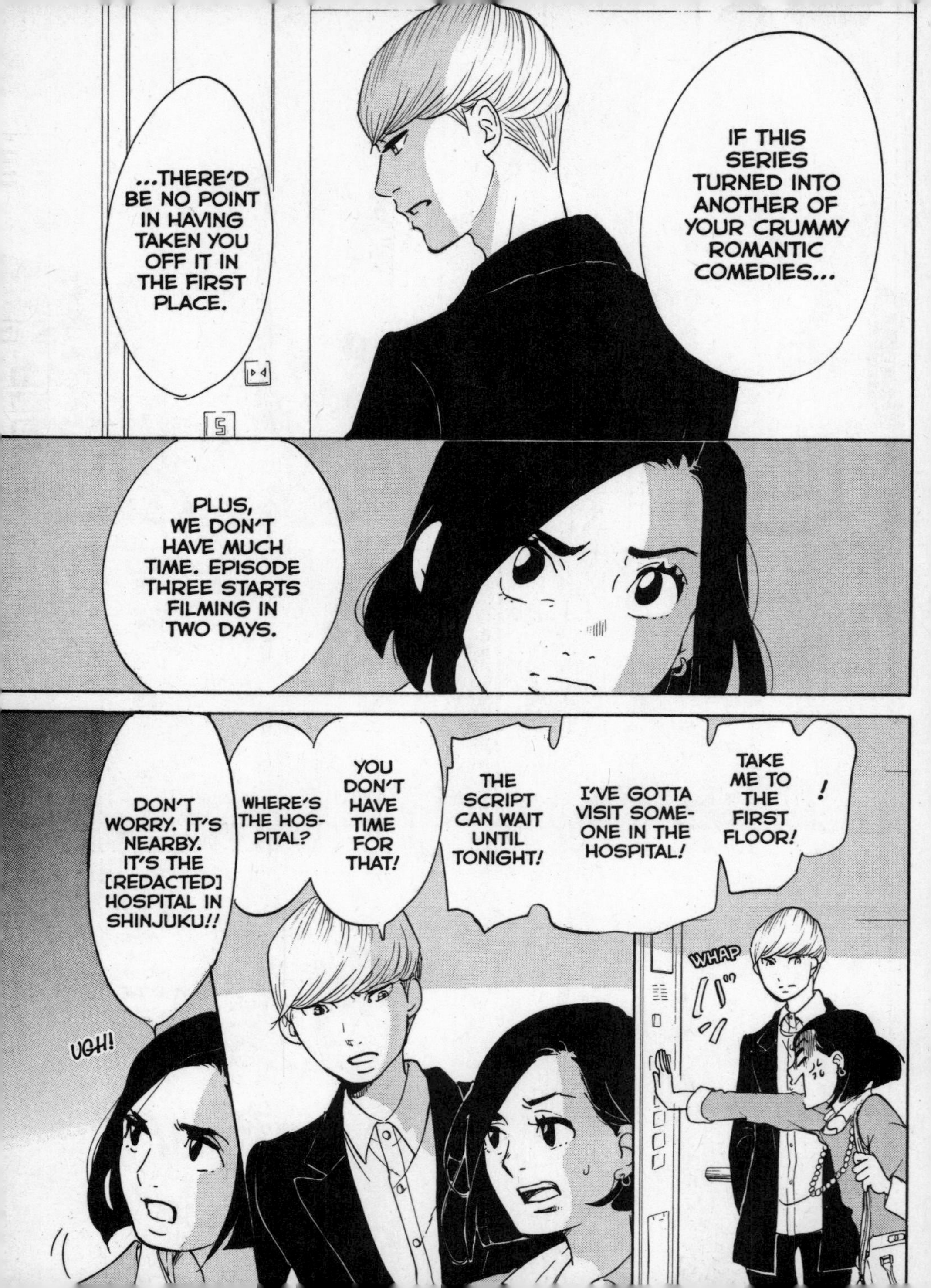
IF THIS SERIES TURNED INTO ANOTHER OF YOUR CRUMMY ROMANTIC COMEDIES...
...THERE'D BE NO POINT IN HAVING TAKEN YOU OFF IT IN THE FIRST PLACE.
PLUS, WE DON'T HAVE MUCH TIME. EPISODE THREE STARTS FILMING IN TWO DAYS.
!
TAKE ME TO THE FIRST FLOOR!
WHAP
I'VE GOTTA VISIT SOME-ONE IN THE HOSPITAL!
THE SCRIPT CAN WAIT UNTIL TONIGHT!
YOU DON'T HAVE TIME FOR THAT!
WHERE'S THE HOS-PITAL?
DON'T WORRY. IT'S NEARBY. IT'S THE [REDACTED] HOSPITAL IN SHINJUKU!!
UGH!

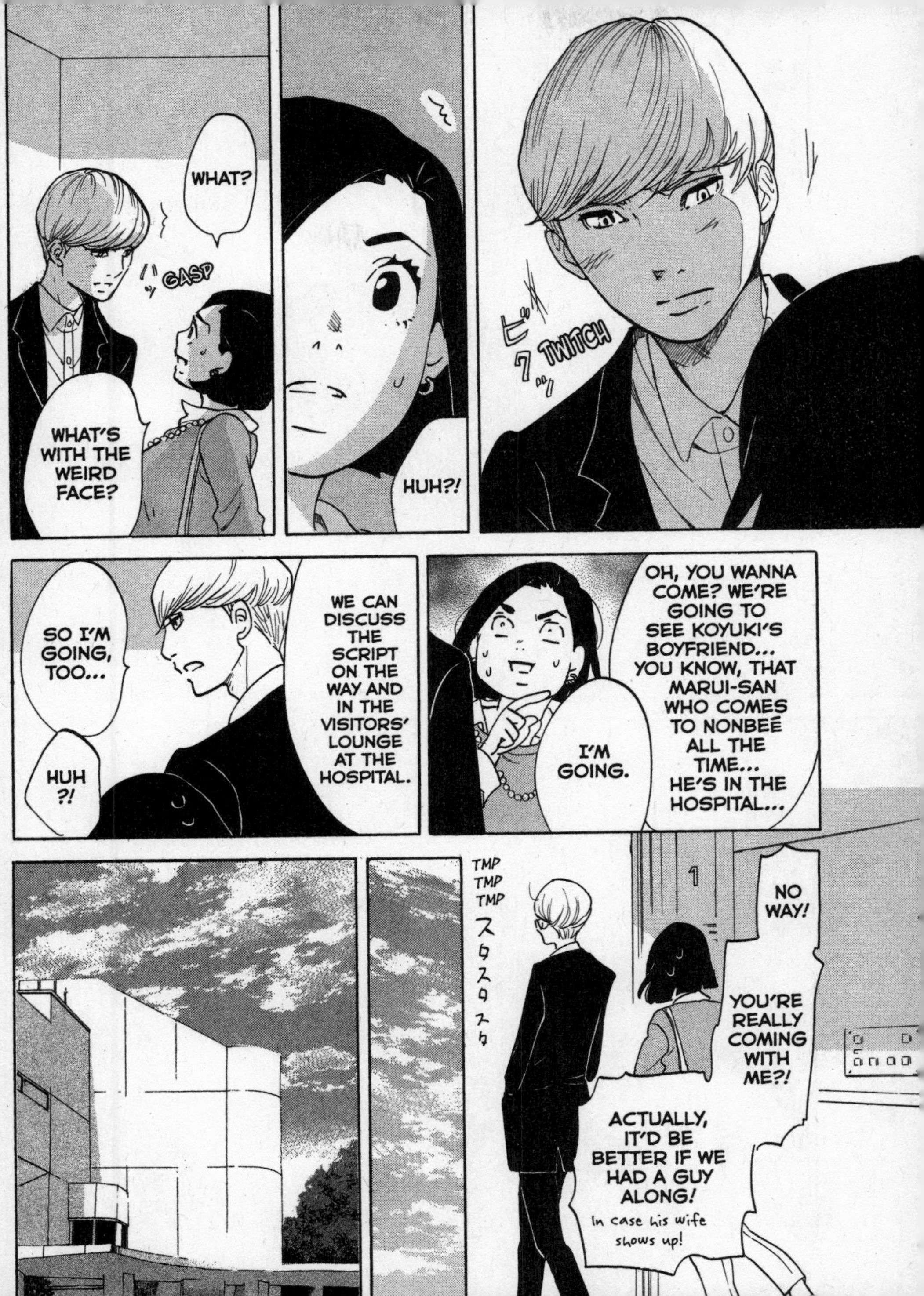
ビクッ
TWITCH
HUH?!
WHAT?
ハッ
GASP
WHAT'S WITH THE WEIRD FACE?
OH, YOU WANNA COME? WE'RE GOING TO SEE KOYUKI'S BOYFRIEND... YOU KNOW, THAT MARUI-SAN WHO COMES TO NONBEÉ ALL THE TIME... HE'S IN THE HOSPITAL...
I'M GOING.
WE CAN DISCUSS THE SCRIPT ON THE WAY AND IN THE VISITORS' LOUNGE AT THE HOSPITAL.
SO I'M GOING, TOO...
HUH?!
NO WAY!
YOU'RE REALLY COMING WITH ME?!
ACTUALLY, IT'D BE BETTER IF WE HAD A GUY ALONG!
In case his wife shows up!
TMP TMP TMP
スタスタスタ

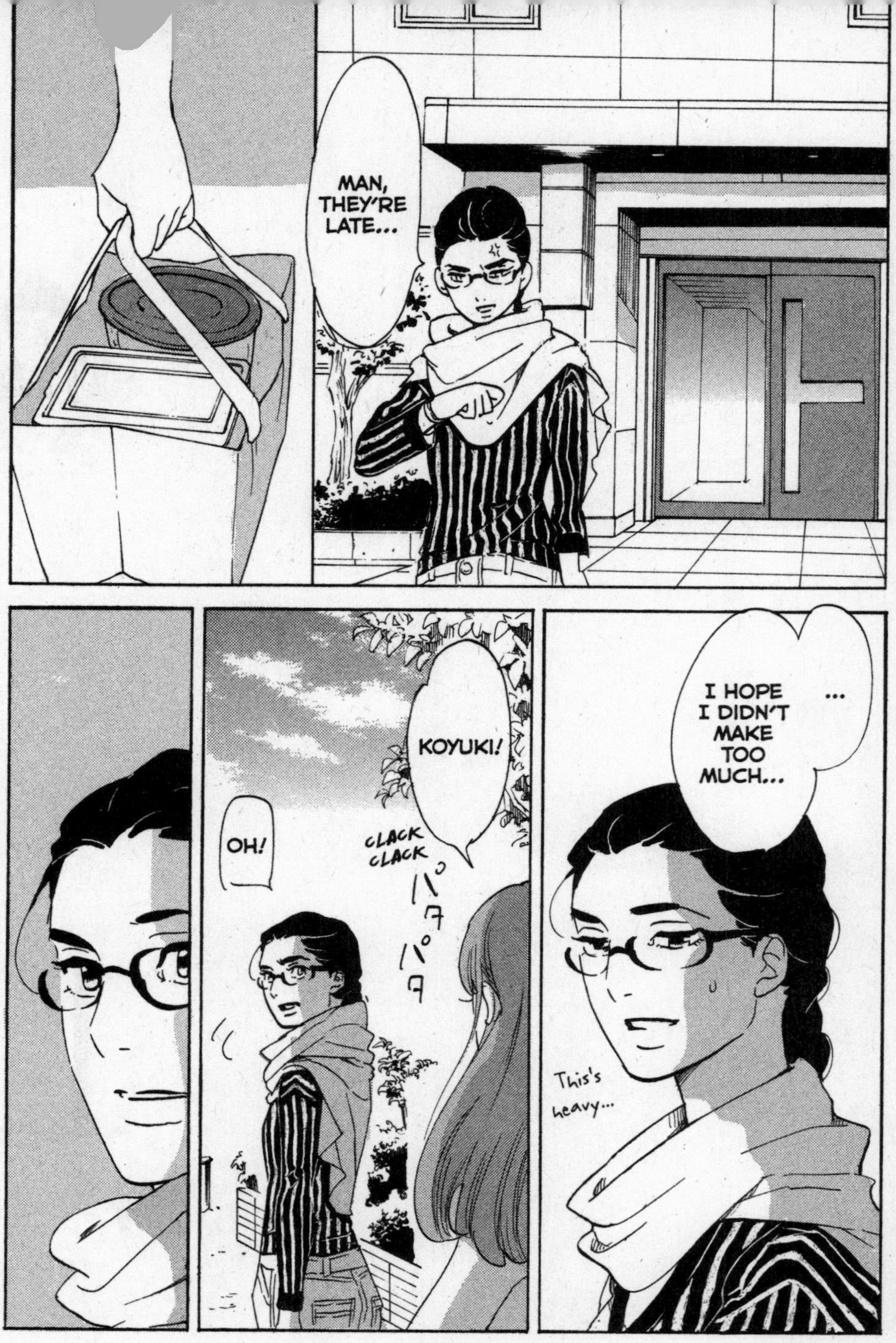
MAN, THEY'RE LATE...
...
I HOPE I DIDN'T MAKE TOO MUCH...
This's heavy...
KOYUKI!
CLACK CLACK
パタパタ
OH!

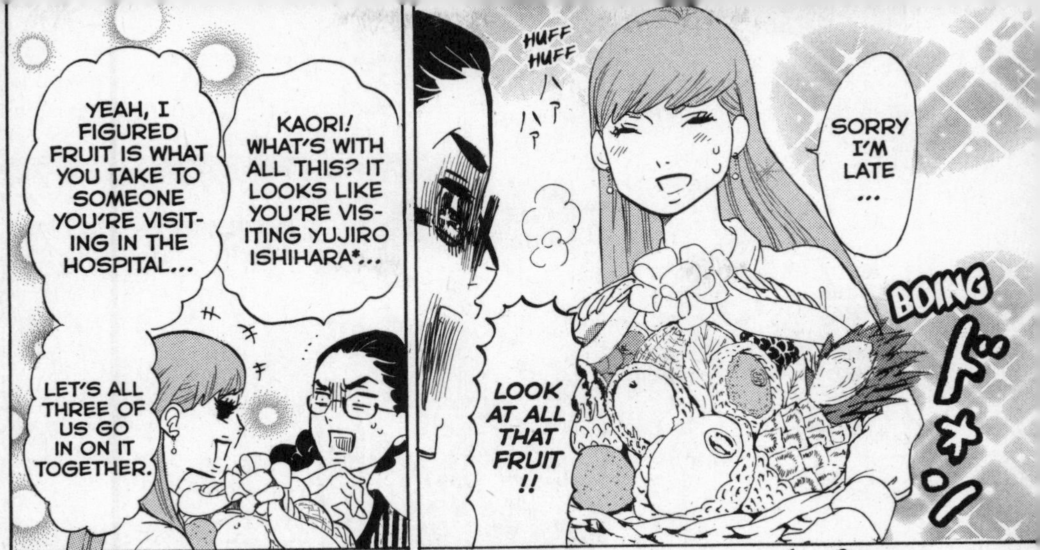
HUFF HUFF
SORRY I'M LATE ...
BOING
LOOK AT ALL THAT FRUIT !!
KAORI! WHAT'S WITH ALL THIS? IT LOOKS LIKE YOU'RE VISITING YUJIRO ISHIHARA*...
YEAH, I FIGURED FRUIT IS WHAT YOU TAKE TO SOMEONE YOU'RE VISITING IN THE HOSPITAL...
LET'S ALL THREE OF US GO IN ON IT TOGETHER.

*An actor who starred in a movie called Crazed Fruit, based on a novel written by his brother.

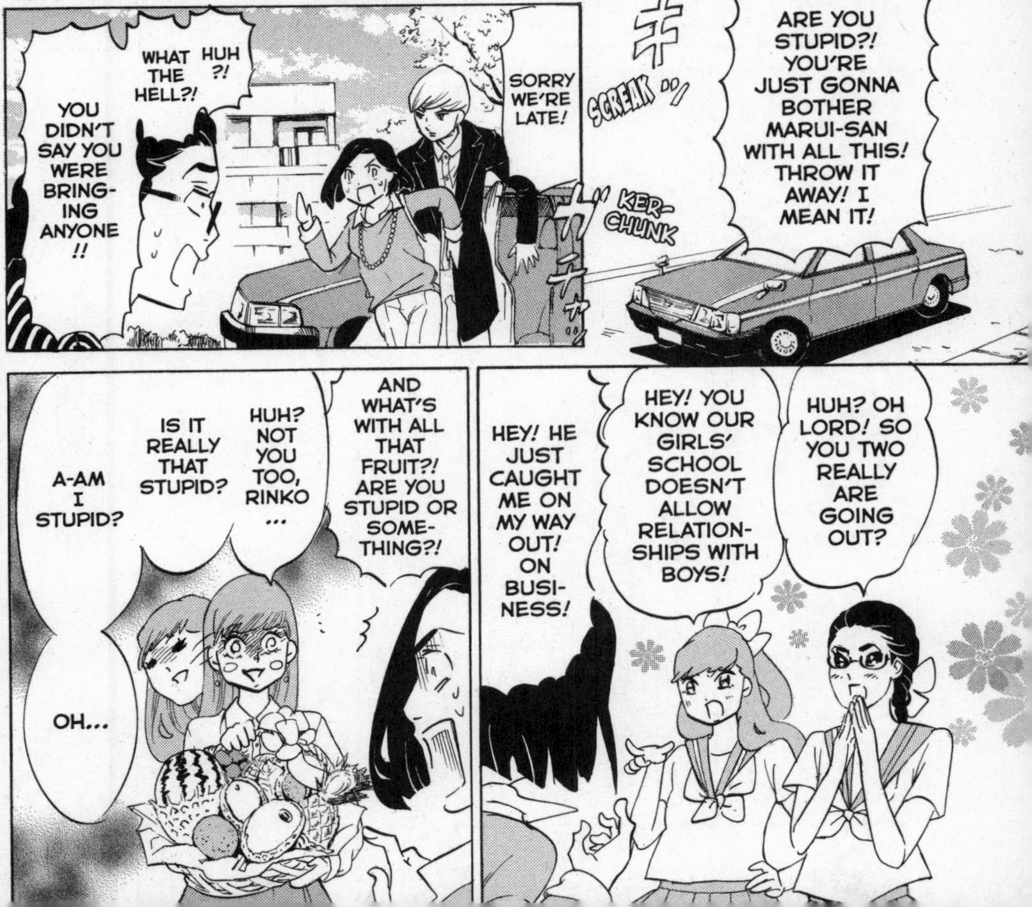
ARE YOU STUPID?! YOU'RE JUST GONNA BOTHER MARUI-SAN WITH ALL THIS! THROW IT AWAY! I MEAN IT!
SCREAK
KER-CHUNK
SORRY WE'RE LATE!
HUH ?!
WHAT THE HELL?!
YOU DIDN'T SAY YOU WERE BRINGING ANYONE !!
HUH? OH LORD! SO YOU TWO REALLY ARE GOING OUT?
HEY! YOU KNOW OUR GIRLS' SCHOOL DOESN'T ALLOW RELATIONSHIPS WITH BOYS!
HEY! HE JUST CAUGHT ME ON MY WAY OUT! ON BUSINESS!
AND WHAT'S WITH ALL THAT FRUIT?! ARE YOU STUPID OR SOMETHING?!
HUH? NOT YOU TOO, RINKO ...
IS IT REALLY THAT STUPID?
A-AM I STUPID?
OH...

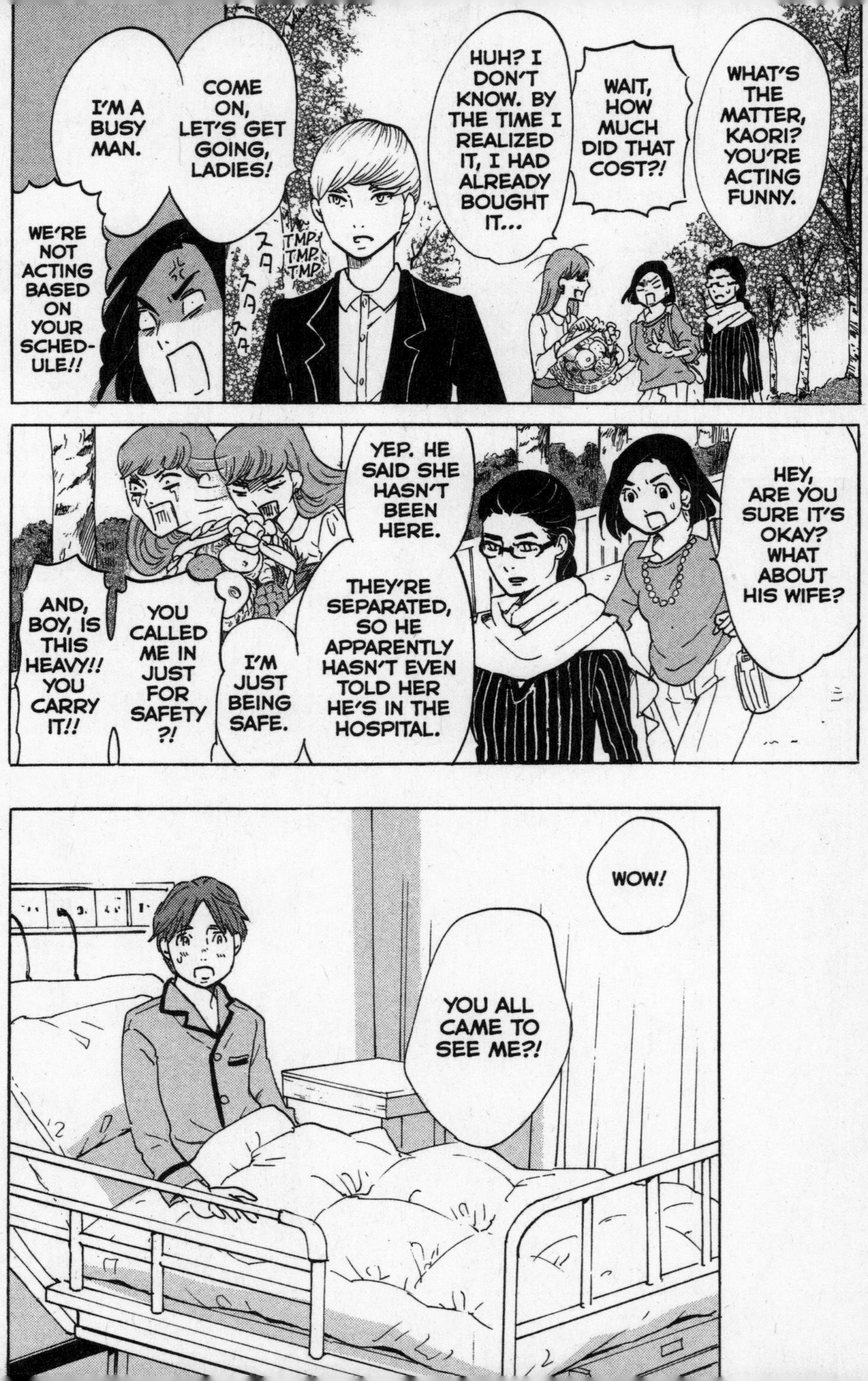
WHAT'S THE MATTER, KAORI? YOU'RE ACTING FUNNY.
WAIT, HOW MUCH DID THAT COST?!
HUH? I DON'T KNOW. BY THE TIME I REALIZED IT, I HAD ALREADY BOUGHT IT...
COME ON, LET'S GET GOING, LADIES!
I'M A BUSY MAN.
TMP TMP TMP
WE'RE NOT ACTING BASED ON YOUR SCHED-ULE!!
HEY, ARE YOU SURE IT'S OKAY? WHAT ABOUT HIS WIFE?
YEP. HE SAID SHE HASN'T BEEN HERE.
THEY'RE SEPARATED, SO HE APPARENTLY HASN'T EVEN TOLD HER HE'S IN THE HOSPITAL.
I'M JUST BEING SAFE.
YOU CALLED ME IN JUST FOR SAFETY?!
AND, BOY, IS THIS HEAVY!! YOU CARRY IT!!
WOW!
YOU ALL CAME TO SEE ME?!

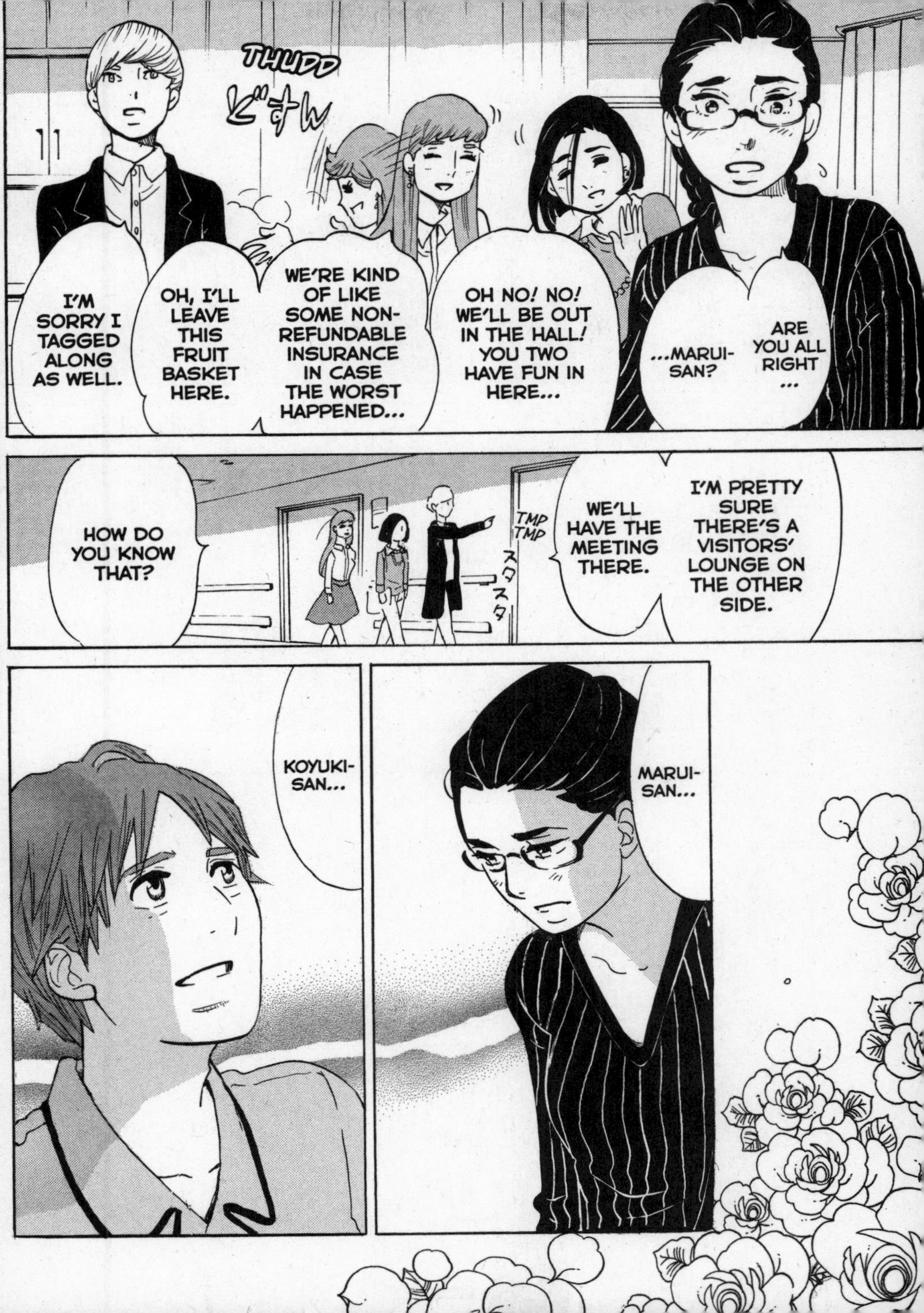

ARE YOU ALL RIGHT ...
...MARUI-SAN?
THUDD
どすん
OH NO! NO! WE'LL BE OUT IN THE HALL! YOU TWO HAVE FUN IN HERE...
WE'RE KIND OF LIKE SOME NON-REFUNDABLE INSURANCE IN CASE THE WORST HAPPENED...
OH, I'LL LEAVE THIS FRUIT BASKET HERE.
I'M SORRY I TAGGED ALONG AS WELL.
I'M PRETTY SURE THERE'S A VISITORS' LOUNGE ON THE OTHER SIDE.
WE'LL HAVE THE MEETING THERE.
TMP TMP
スタスタ
HOW DO YOU KNOW THAT?
MARUI-SAN...
KOYUKI-SAN...

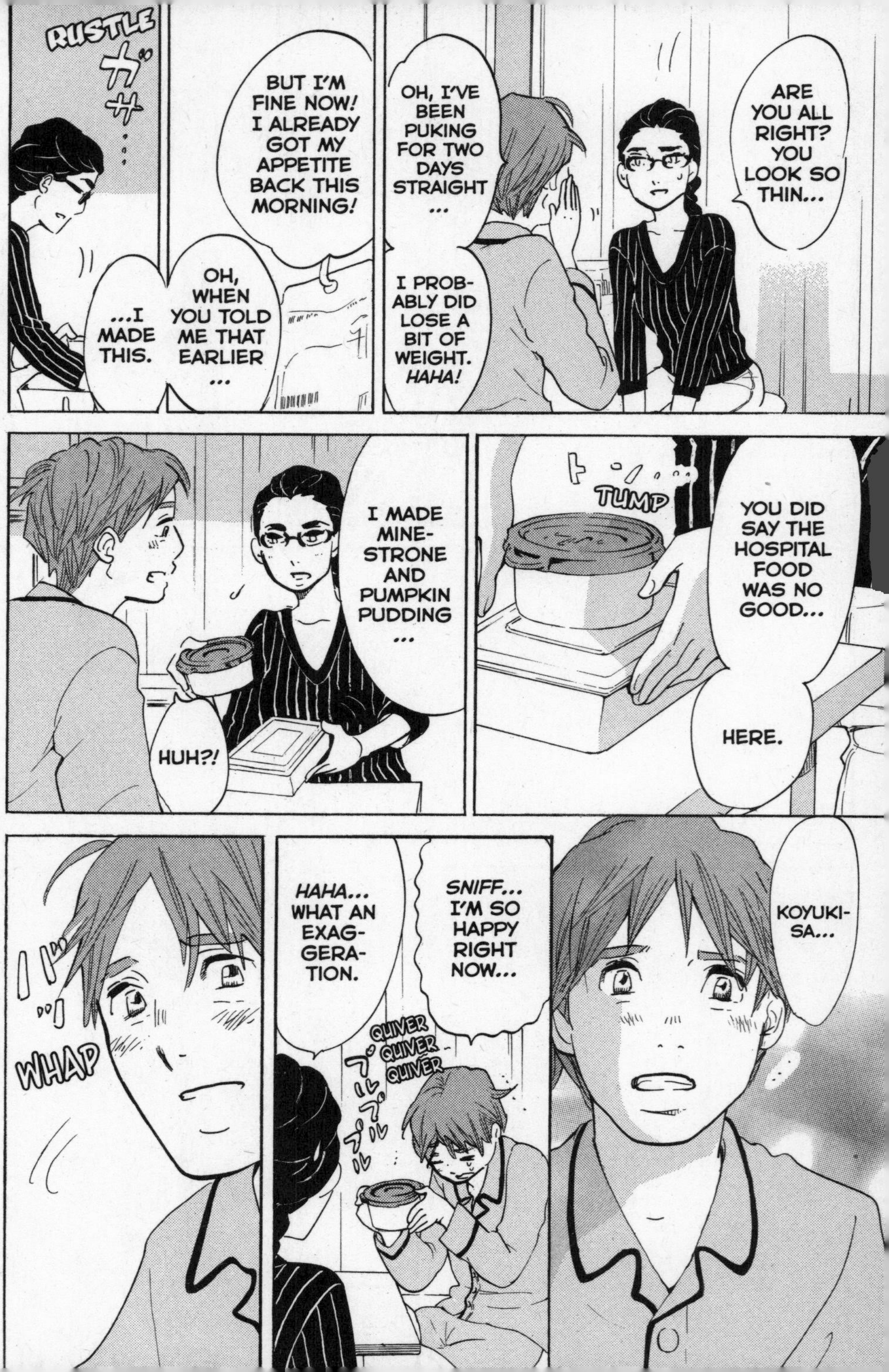
ARE YOU ALL RIGHT? YOU LOOK SO THIN...
OH, I'VE BEEN PUKING FOR TWO DAYS STRAIGHT...
I PROBABLY DID LOSE A BIT OF WEIGHT. HAHA!
BUT I'M FINE NOW! I ALREADY GOT MY APPETITE BACK THIS MORNING!
OH, WHEN YOU TOLD ME THAT EARLIER...
RUSTLE
ガサ…
...I MADE THIS.
TUMP
YOU DID SAY THE HOSPITAL FOOD WAS NO GOOD...
HERE.
I MADE MINE-STRONE AND PUMPKIN PUDDING...
HUH?!
KOYUKI-SA...
SNIFF... I'M SO HAPPY RIGHT NOW...
QUIVER QUIVER QUIVER
プルプル
HAHA... WHAT AN EXAG-GERA-TION.
WHAP

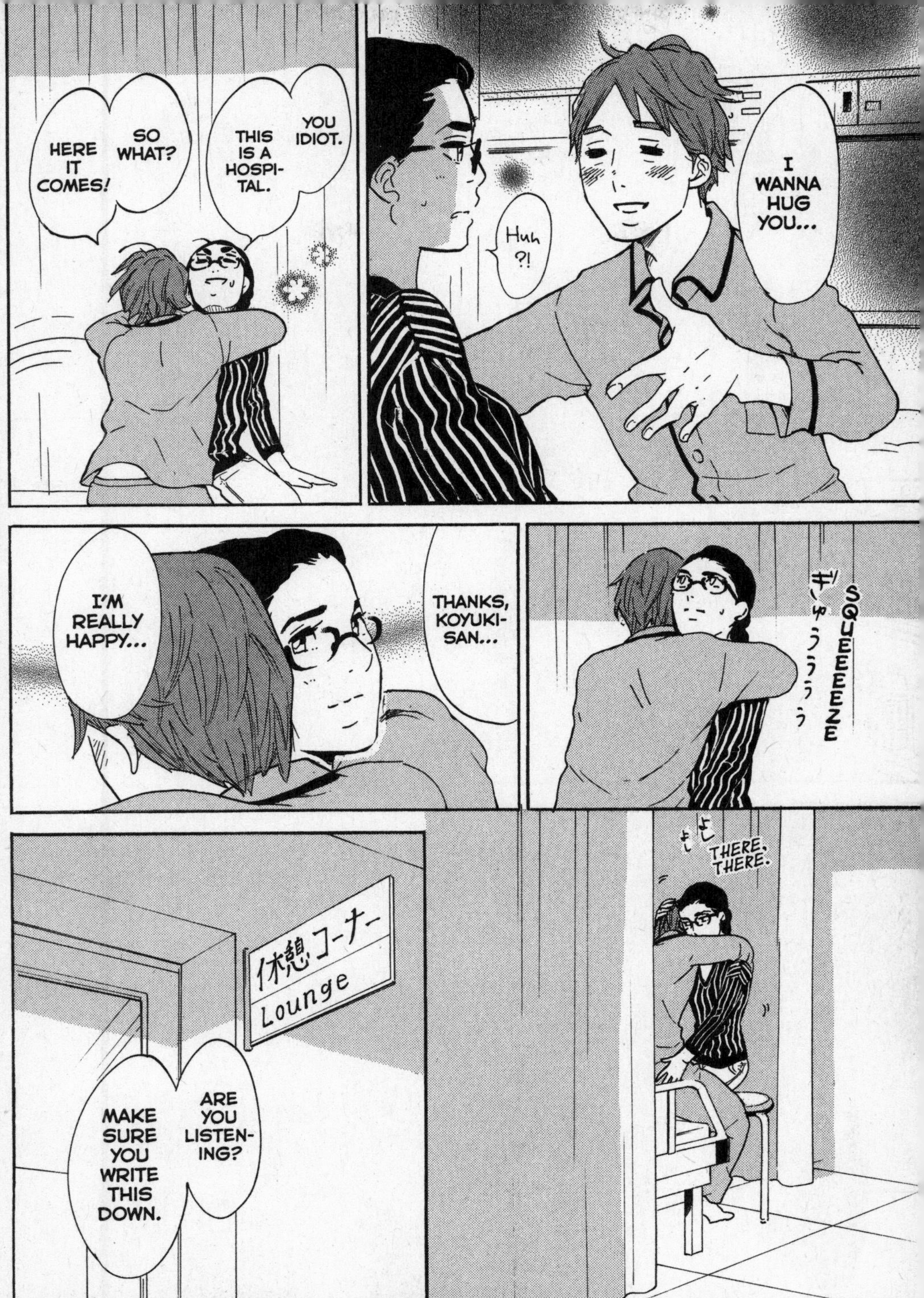
I WANNA HUG YOU...
Huh ?!
YOU IDIOT.
THIS IS A HOSPITAL.
SO WHAT?
HERE IT COMES!
ギュううう
SQUEEEEZE
THANKS, KOYUKI-SAN...
I'M REALLY HAPPY...
よしよし
THERE, THERE.
休憩コーナー
Lounge
ARE YOU LISTENING?
MAKE SURE YOU WRITE THIS DOWN.

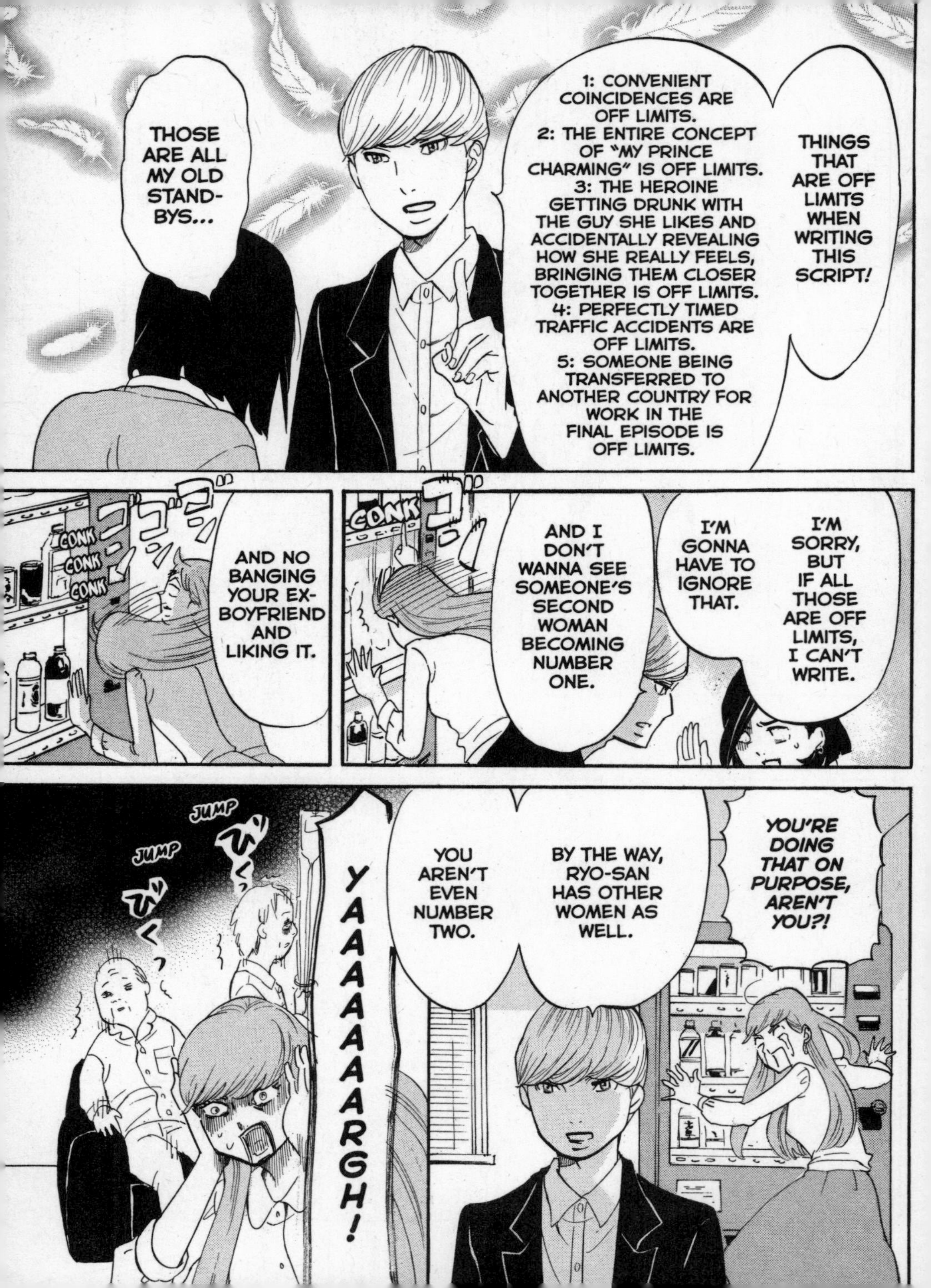
THINGS THAT ARE OFF LIMITS WHEN WRITING THIS SCRIPT!
1: CONVENIENT COINCIDENCES ARE OFF LIMITS. 2: THE ENTIRE CONCEPT OF "MY PRINCE CHARMING" IS OFF LIMITS. 3: THE HEROINE GETTING DRUNK WITH THE GUY SHE LIKES AND ACCIDENTALLY REVEALING HOW SHE REALLY FEELS, BRINGING THEM CLOSER TOGETHER IS OFF LIMITS. 4: PERFECTLY TIMED TRAFFIC ACCIDENTS ARE OFF LIMITS. 5: SOMEONE BEING TRANSFERRED TO ANOTHER COUNTRY FOR WORK IN THE FINAL EPISODE IS OFF LIMITS.
THOSE ARE ALL MY OLD STANDBYS...
I'M SORRY, BUT IF ALL THOSE ARE OFF LIMITS, I CAN'T WRITE.
I'M GONNA HAVE TO IGNORE THAT.
AND I DON'T WANNA SEE SOMEONE'S SECOND WOMAN BECOMING NUMBER ONE.
GONK
AND NO BANGING YOUR EX-BOYFRIEND AND LIKING IT.
GONK
GONK
GONK
YOU'RE DOING THAT ON PURPOSE, AREN'T YOU?!
BY THE WAY, RYO-SAN HAS OTHER WOMEN AS WELL.
YOU AREN'T EVEN NUMBER TWO.
YAAAAAAAAARGH!
JUMP
JUMP

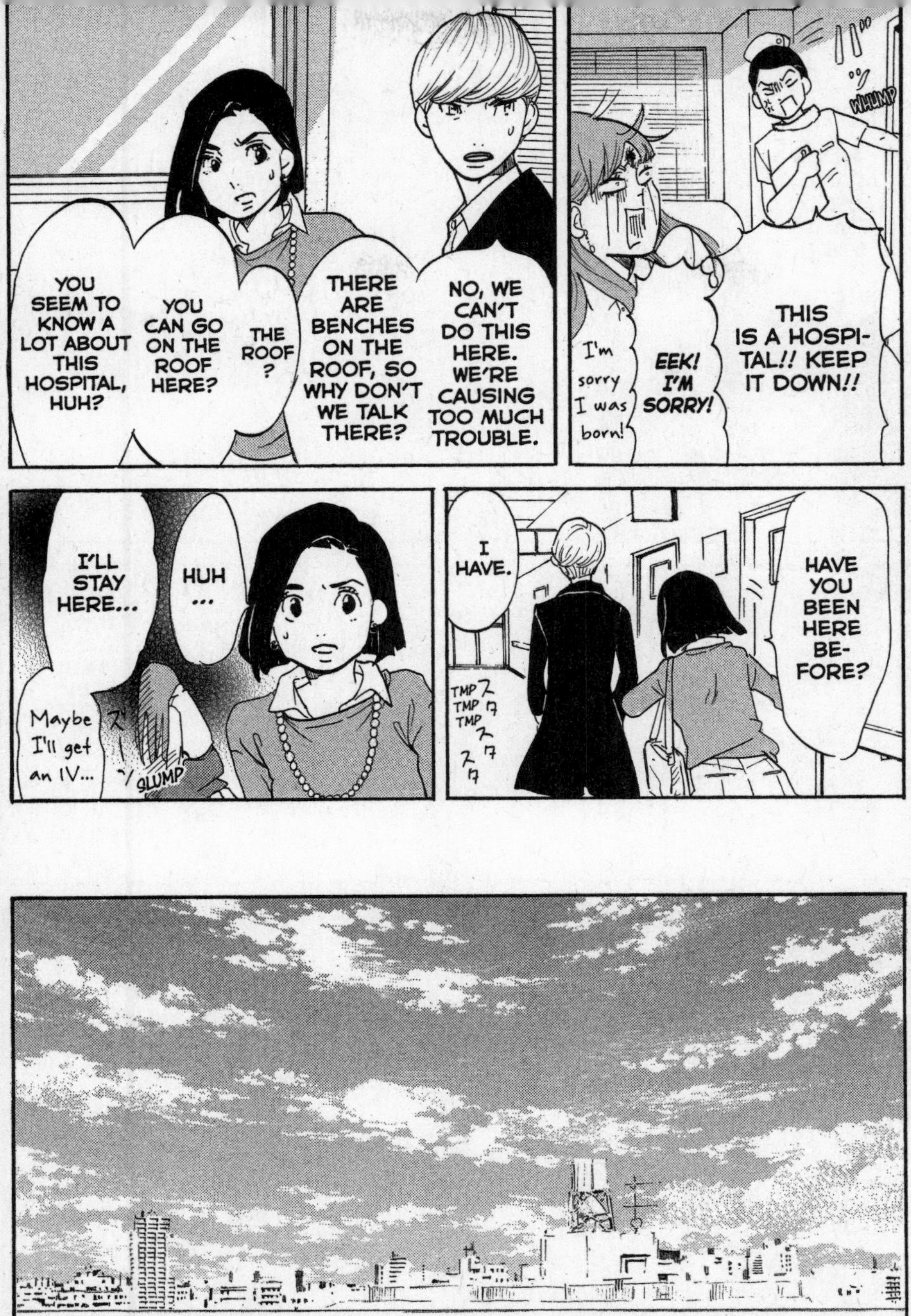
WHUMP
THIS IS A HOSPITAL!! KEEP IT DOWN!!
EEK! I'M SORRY!
I'm sorry I was born!
NO, WE CAN'T DO THIS HERE. WE'RE CAUSING TOO MUCH TROUBLE.
THERE ARE BENCHES ON THE ROOF, SO WHY DON'T WE TALK THERE?
THE ROOF?
YOU CAN GO ON THE ROOF HERE?
YOU SEEM TO KNOW A LOT ABOUT THIS HOSPITAL, HUH?
HAVE YOU BEEN HERE BEFORE?
I HAVE.
TMP TMP TMP
HUH...
I'LL STAY HERE...
SLUMP
Maybe I'll get an IV...

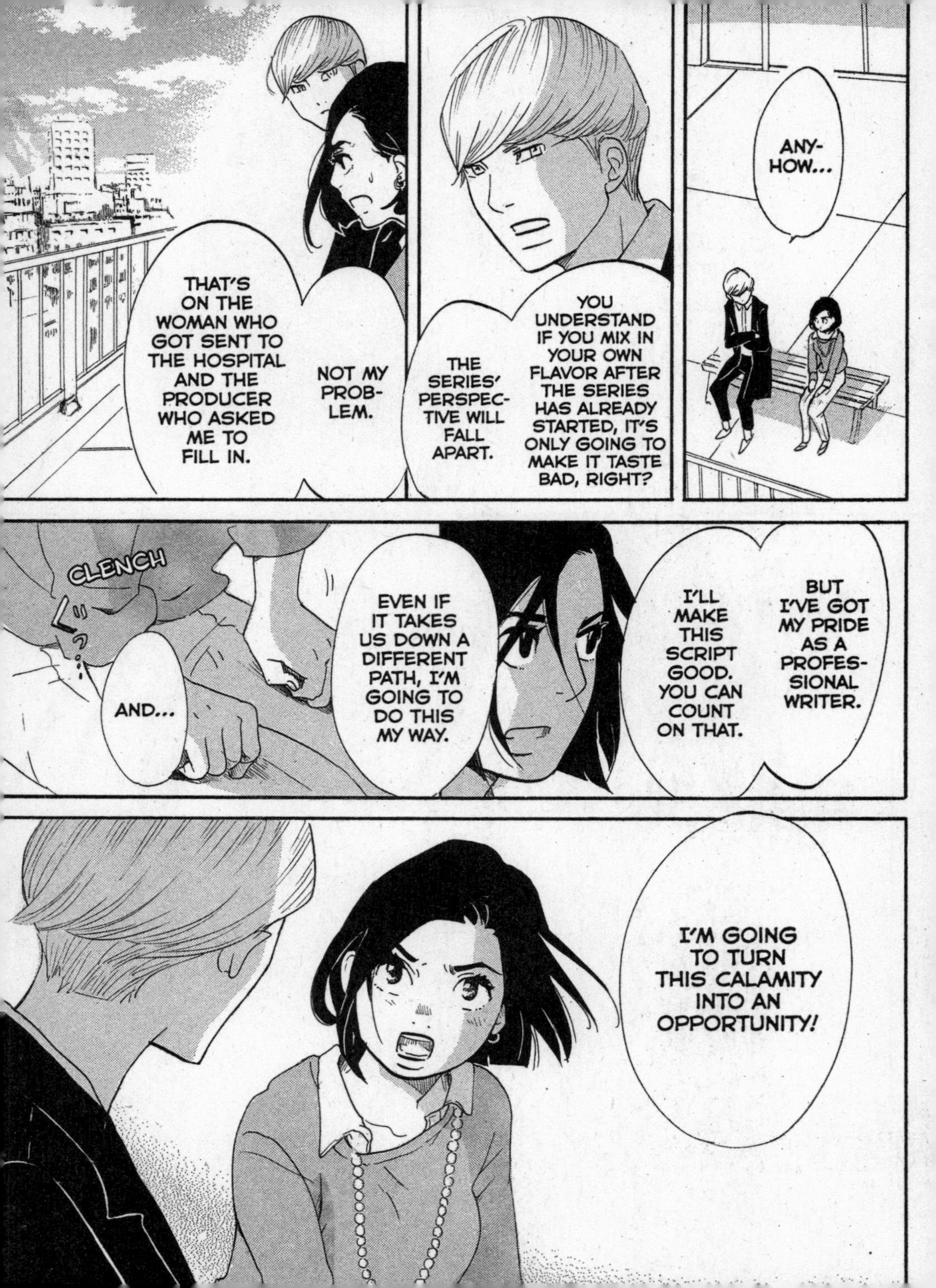
ANY-HOW...
YOU UNDERSTAND IF YOU MIX IN YOUR OWN FLAVOR AFTER THE SERIES HAS ALREADY STARTED, IT'S ONLY GOING TO MAKE IT TASTE BAD, RIGHT?
THE SERIES' PERSPEC-TIVE WILL FALL APART.
NOT MY PROB-LEM.
THAT'S ON THE WOMAN WHO GOT SENT TO THE HOSPITAL AND THE PRODUCER WHO ASKED ME TO FILL IN.
BUT I'VE GOT MY PRIDE AS A PROFES-SIONAL WRITER.
I'LL MAKE THIS SCRIPT GOOD. YOU CAN COUNT ON THAT.
EVEN IF IT TAKES US DOWN A DIFFERENT PATH, I'M GOING TO DO THIS MY WAY.
CLENCH
AND...
I'M GOING TO TURN THIS CALAMITY INTO AN OPPORTUNITY!

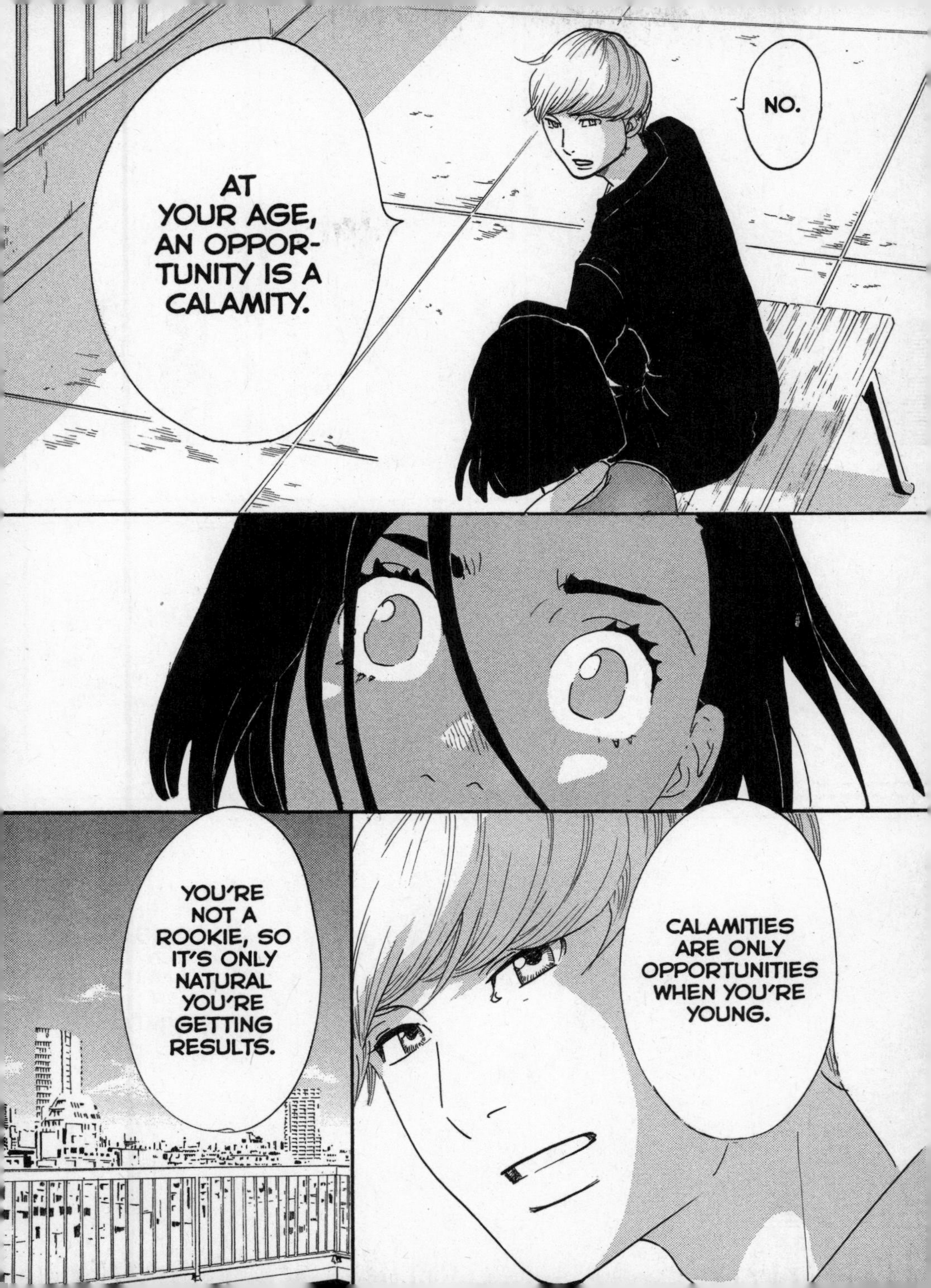
NO.
AT YOUR AGE, AN OPPORTUNITY IS A CALAMITY.
CALAMITIES ARE ONLY OPPORTUNITIES WHEN YOU'RE YOUNG.
YOU'RE NOT A ROOKIE, SO IT'S ONLY NATURAL YOU'RE GETTING RESULTS.

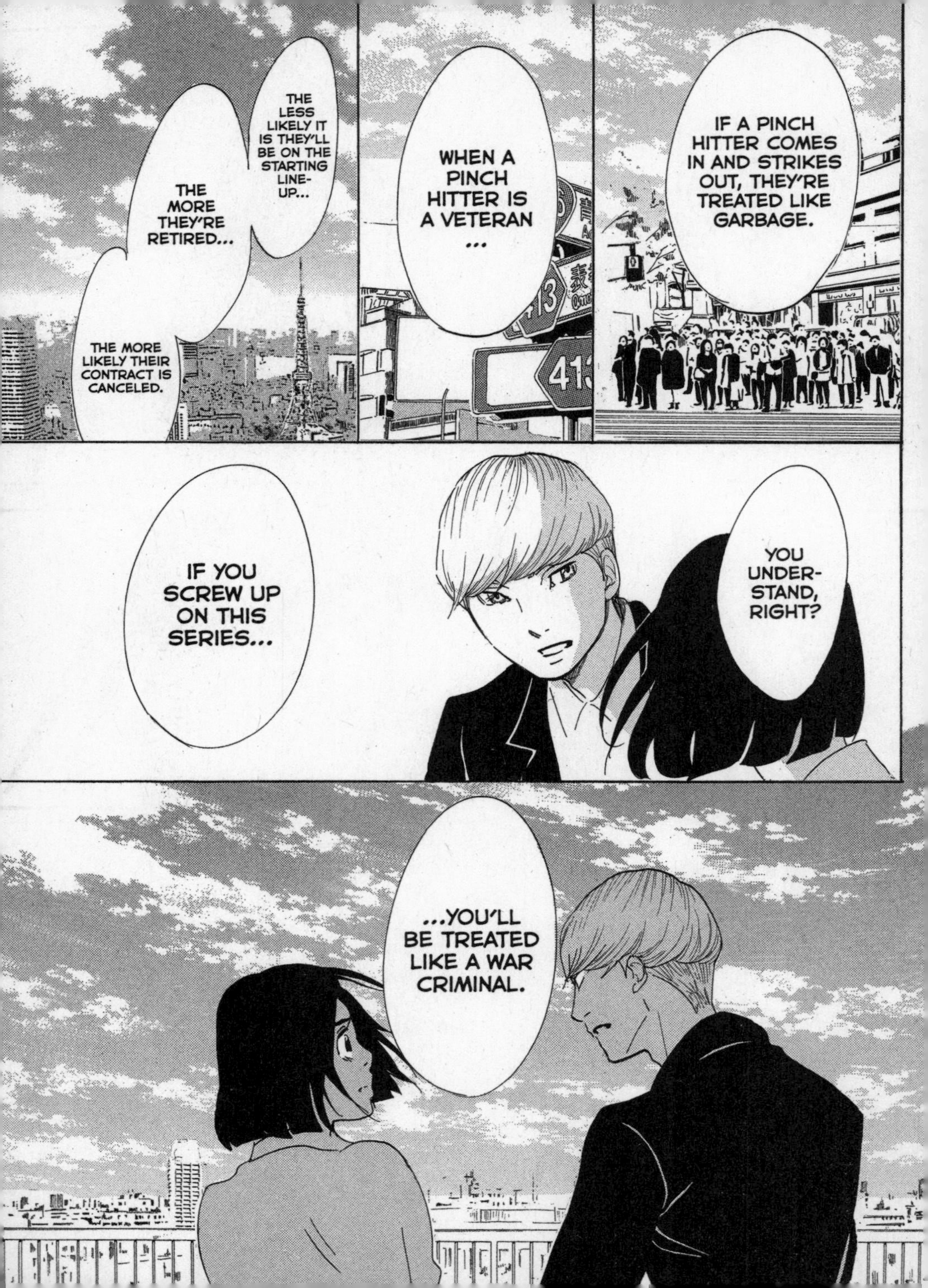
IF A PINCH HITTER COMES IN AND STRIKES OUT, THEY'RE TREATED LIKE GARBAGE.
WHEN A PINCH HITTER IS A VETERAN ...
THE LESS LIKELY IT IS THEY'LL BE ON THE STARTING LINE-UP...
THE MORE THEY'RE RETIRED...
THE MORE LIKELY THEIR CONTRACT IS CANCELED.
YOU UNDER-STAND, RIGHT?
IF YOU SCREW UP ON THIS SERIES...
...YOU'LL BE TREATED LIKE A WAR CRIMINAL.

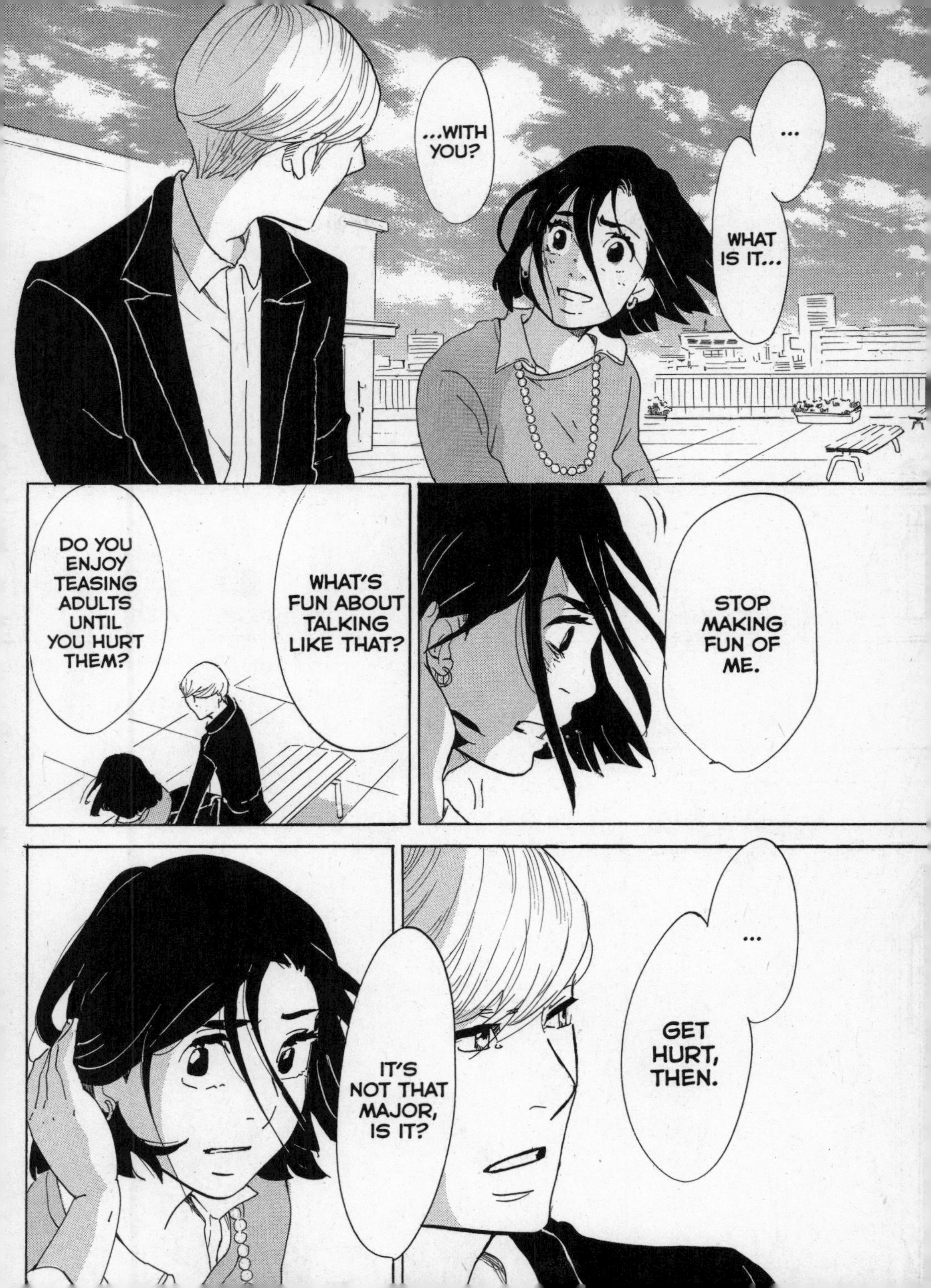
...
WHAT IS IT...
...WITH YOU?
STOP MAKING FUN OF ME.
WHAT'S FUN ABOUT TALKING LIKE THAT?
DO YOU ENJOY TEASING ADULTS UNTIL YOU HURT THEM?
...
GET HURT, THEN.
IT'S NOT THAT MAJOR, IS IT?

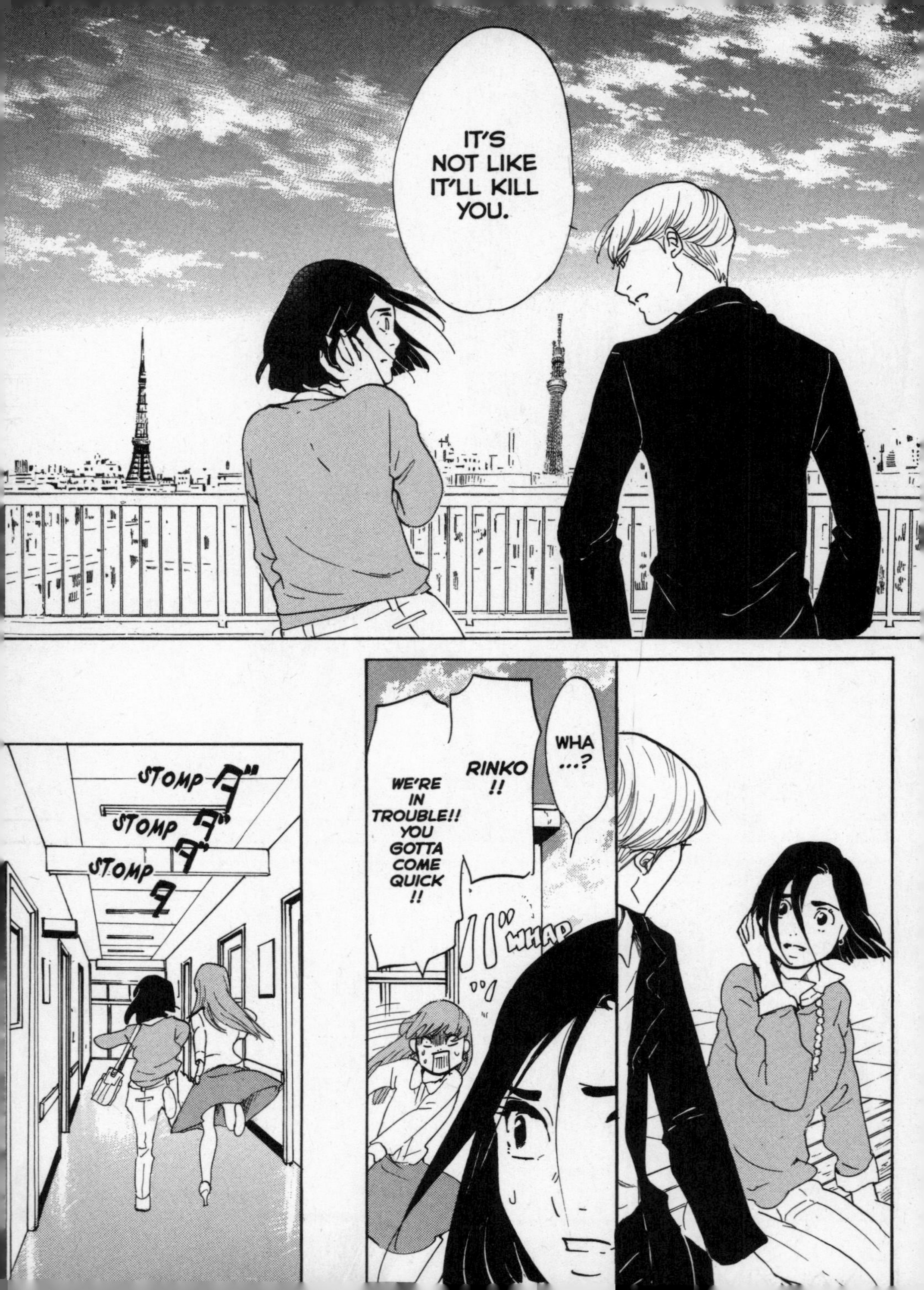
IT'S NOT LIKE IT'LL KILL YOU.
WHA ...?
RINKO !!
WE'RE IN TROUBLE!! YOU GOTTA COME QUICK !!
WHAP
STOMP
STOMP
STOMP

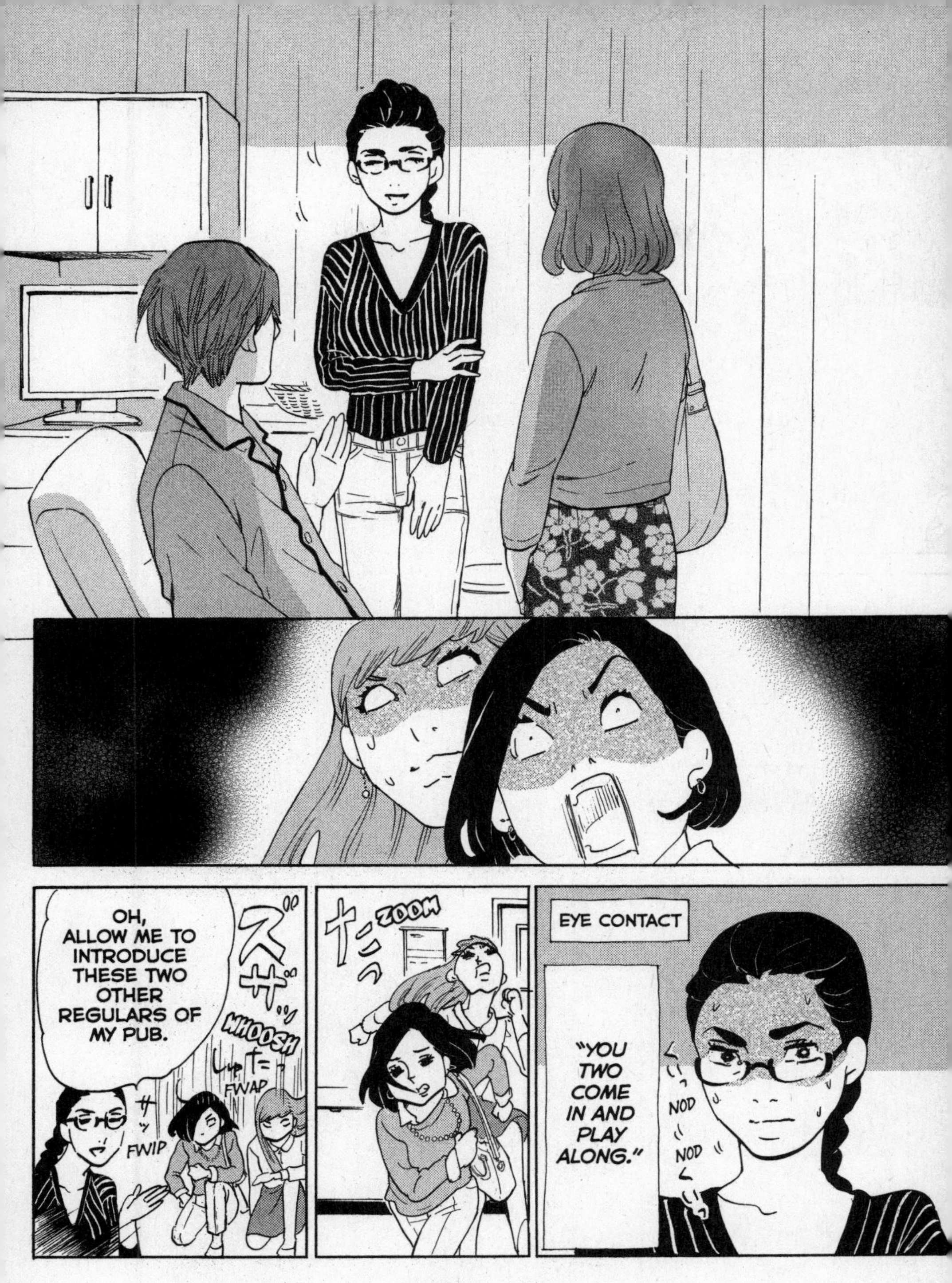
EYE CONTACT
"YOU TWO COME IN AND PLAY ALONG."
NOD
NOD
ZOOM
OH, ALLOW ME TO INTRODUCE THESE TWO OTHER REGULARS OF MY PUB.
WHOOSH
FWAP
FWIP

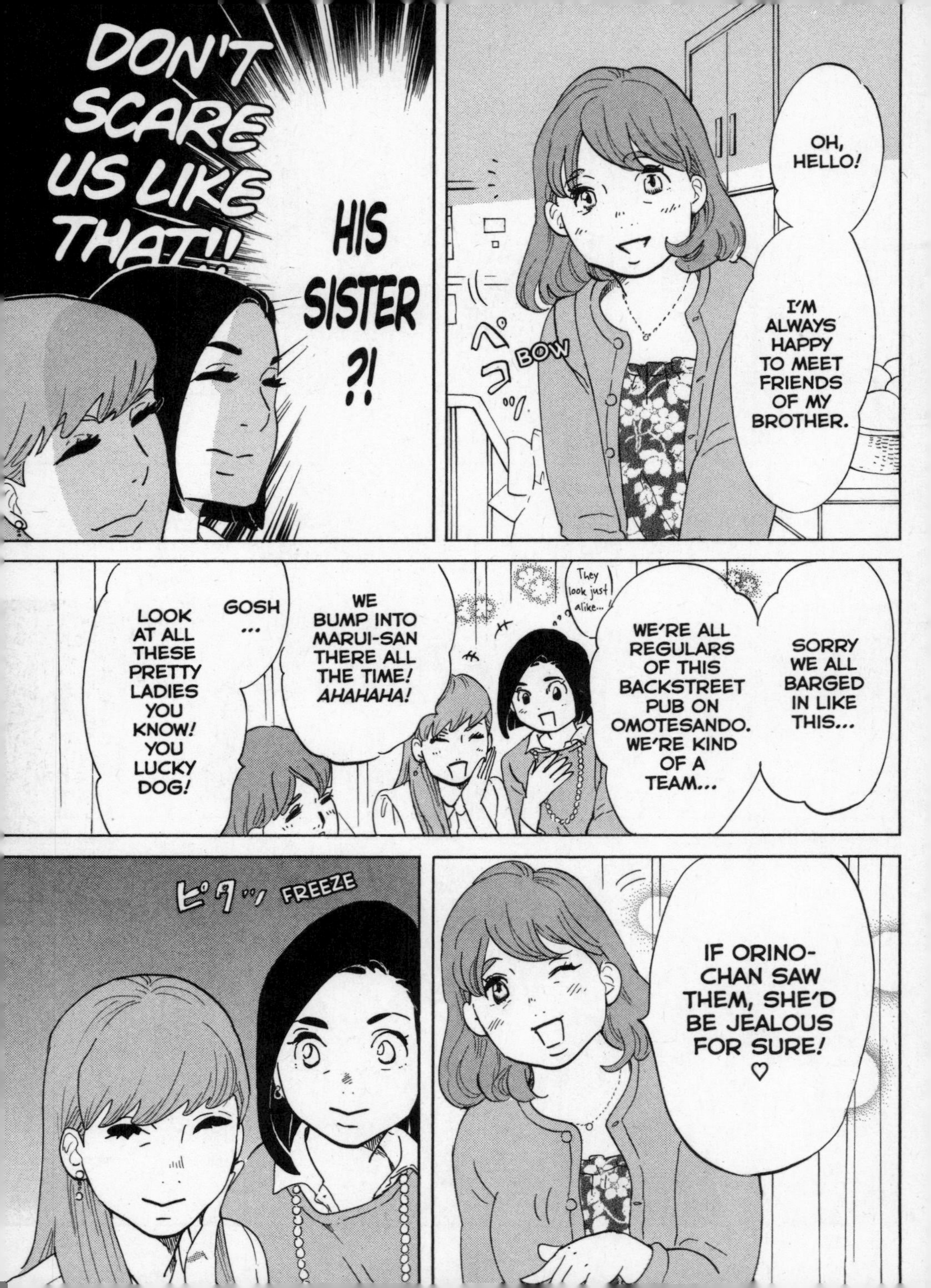
OH, HELLO!
I'M ALWAYS HAPPY TO MEET FRIENDS OF MY BROTHER.
BOW
HIS SISTER ?!
DON'T SCARE US LIKE THAT!!
SORRY WE ALL BARGED IN LIKE THIS...
WE'RE ALL REGULARS OF THIS BACKSTREET PUB ON OMOTESANDO. WE'RE KIND OF A TEAM...
They look just alike...
WE BUMP INTO MARUI-SAN THERE ALL THE TIME! AHAHAHA!
GOSH...
LOOK AT ALL THESE PRETTY LADIES YOU KNOW! YOU LUCKY DOG!
IF ORINO-CHAN SAW THEM, SHE'D BE JEALOUS FOR SURE! ♡
FREEZE

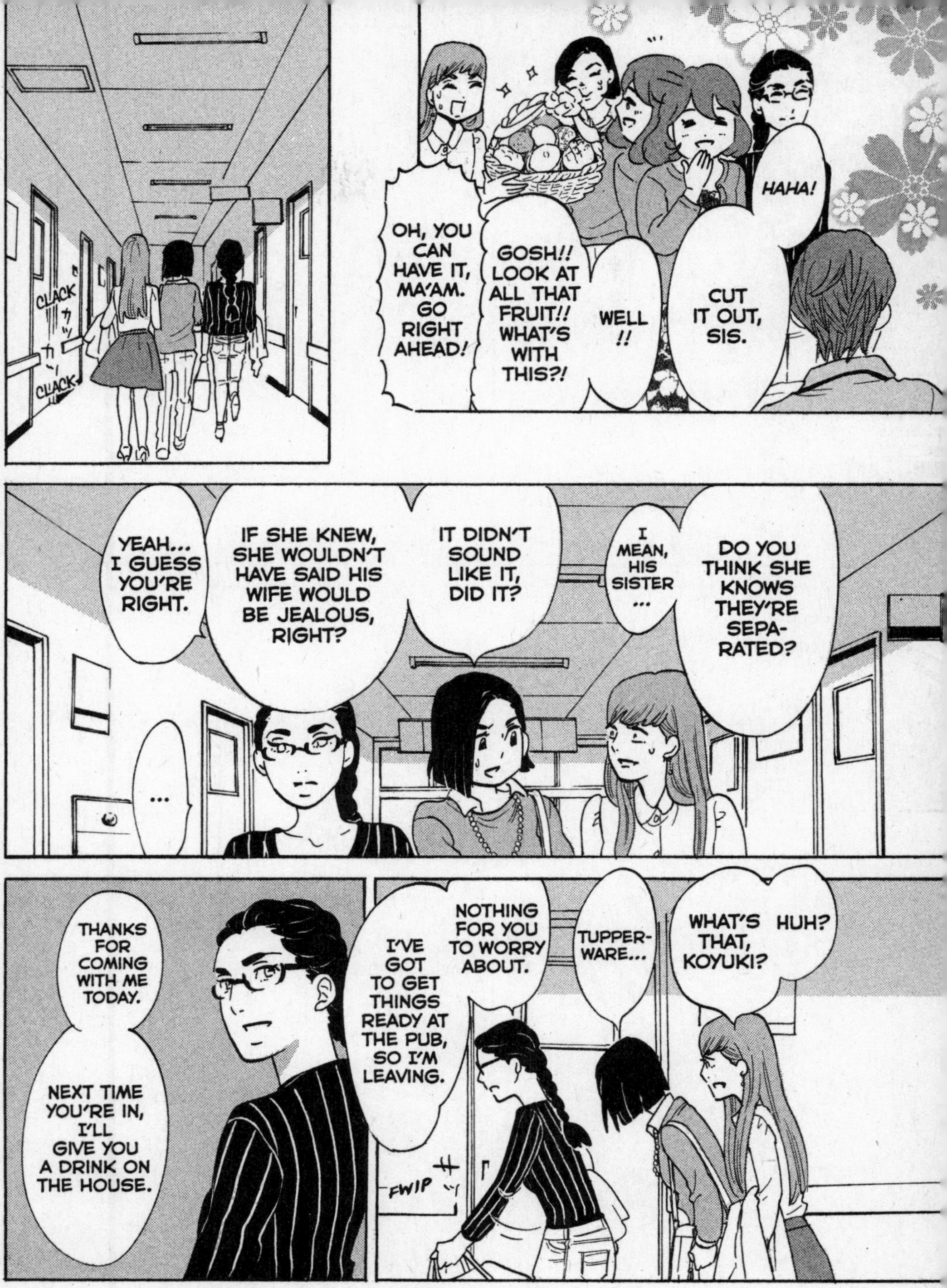
HAHA!
CUT IT OUT, SIS.
WELL!!
GOSH!! LOOK AT ALL THAT FRUIT!! WHAT'S WITH THIS?!
OH, YOU CAN HAVE IT, MA'AM. GO RIGHT AHEAD!
CLACK
CLACK
DO YOU THINK SHE KNOWS THEY'RE SEPARATED?
I MEAN, HIS SISTER...
IT DIDN'T SOUND LIKE IT, DID IT?
IF SHE KNEW, SHE WOULDN'T HAVE SAID HIS WIFE WOULD BE JEALOUS, RIGHT?
YEAH... I GUESS YOU'RE RIGHT.
...
HUH?
WHAT'S THAT, KOYUKI?
TUPPERWARE...
NOTHING FOR YOU TO WORRY ABOUT.
I'VE GOT TO GET THINGS READY AT THE PUB, SO I'M LEAVING.
FWIP
THANKS FOR COMING WITH ME TODAY.
NEXT TIME YOU'RE IN, I'LL GIVE YOU A DRINK ON THE HOUSE.

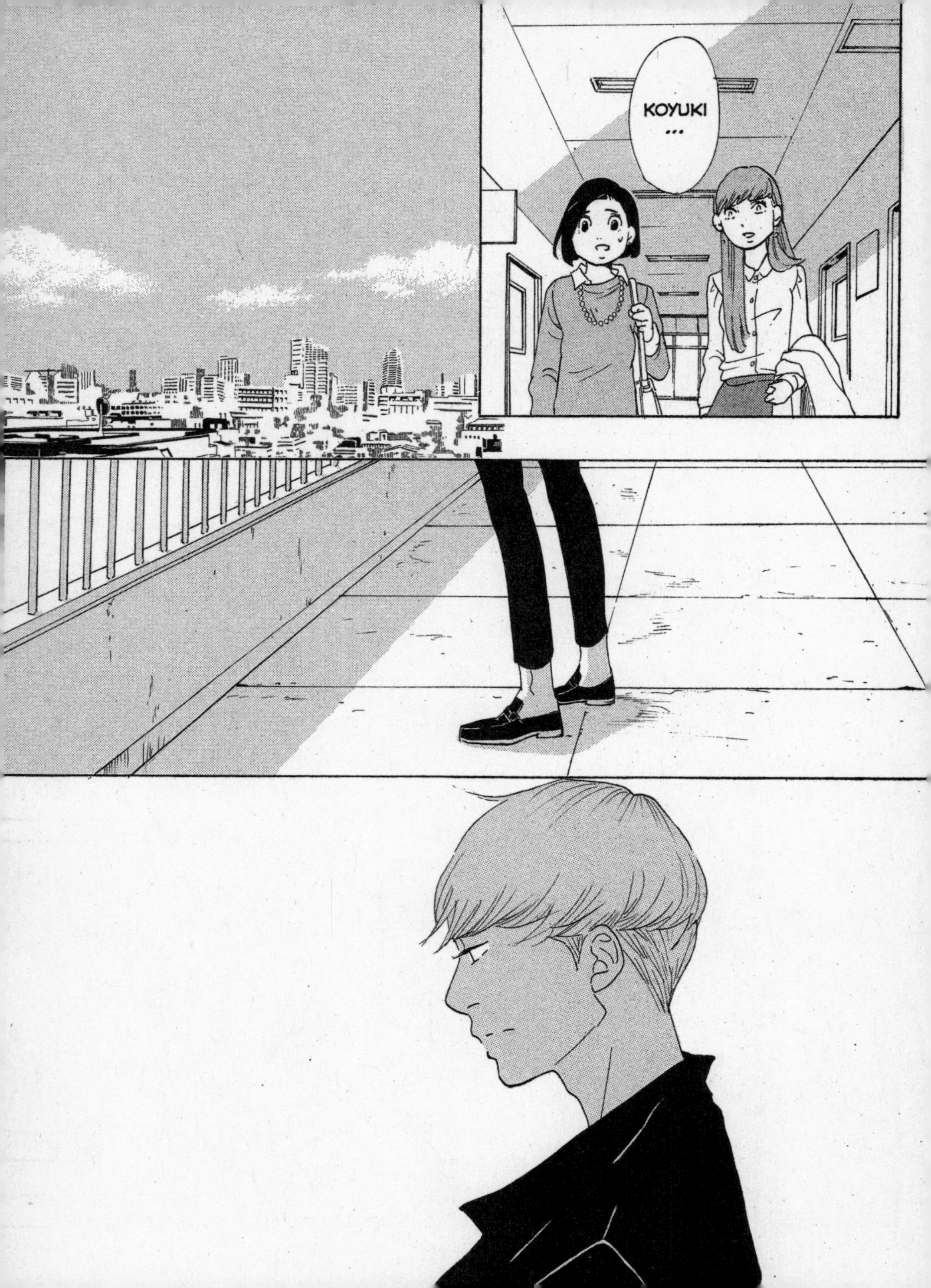
KOYUKI
...

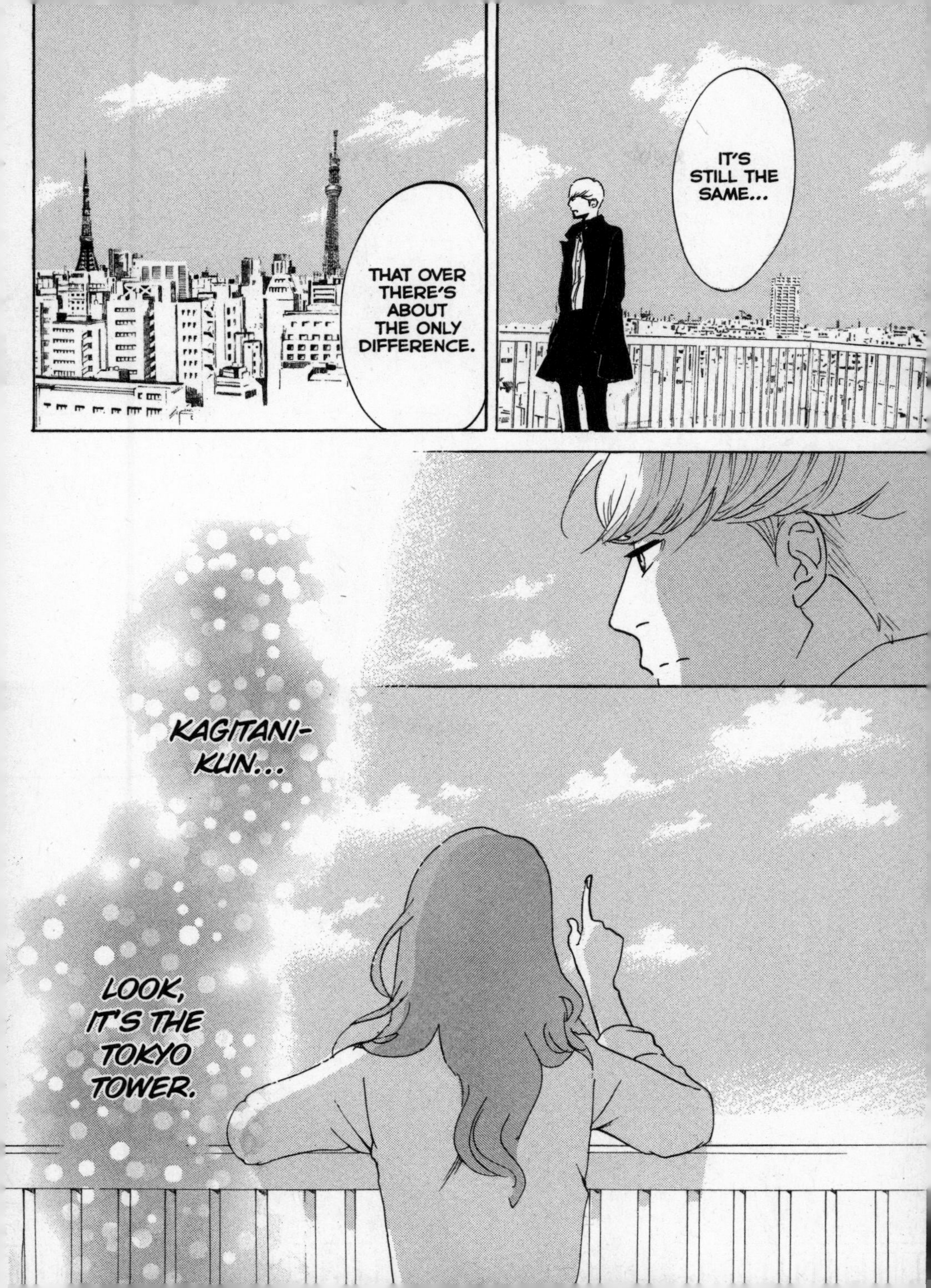
IT'S STILL THE SAME...
THAT OVER THERE'S ABOUT THE ONLY DIFFERENCE.
KAGITANI-KUN...
LOOK, IT'S THE TOKYO TOWER.

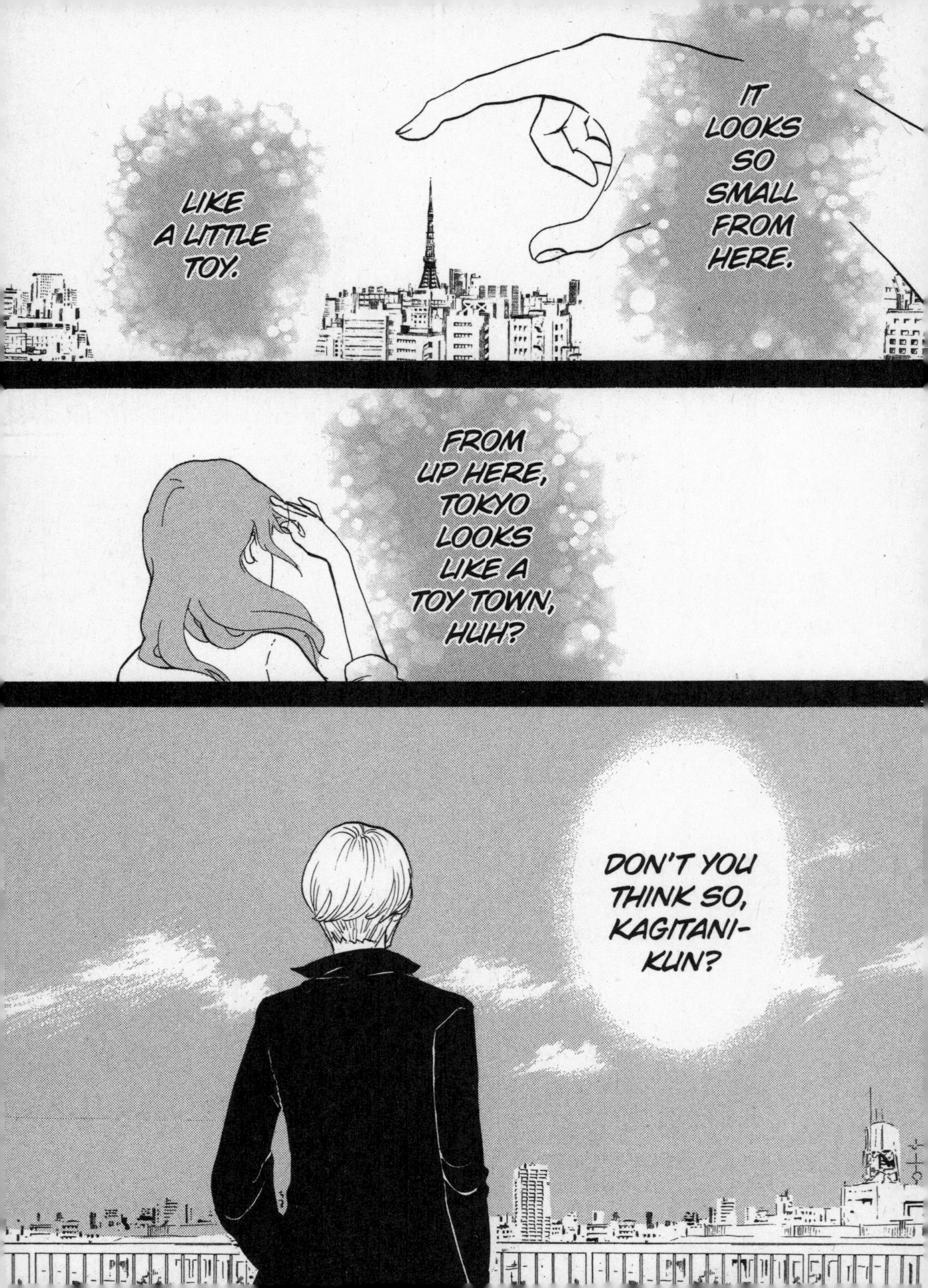
IT LOOKS SO SMALL FROM HERE.
LIKE A LITTLE TOY.
FROM UP HERE, TOKYO LOOKS LIKE A TOY TOWN, HUH?
DON'T YOU THINK SO, KAGITANI-KUN?

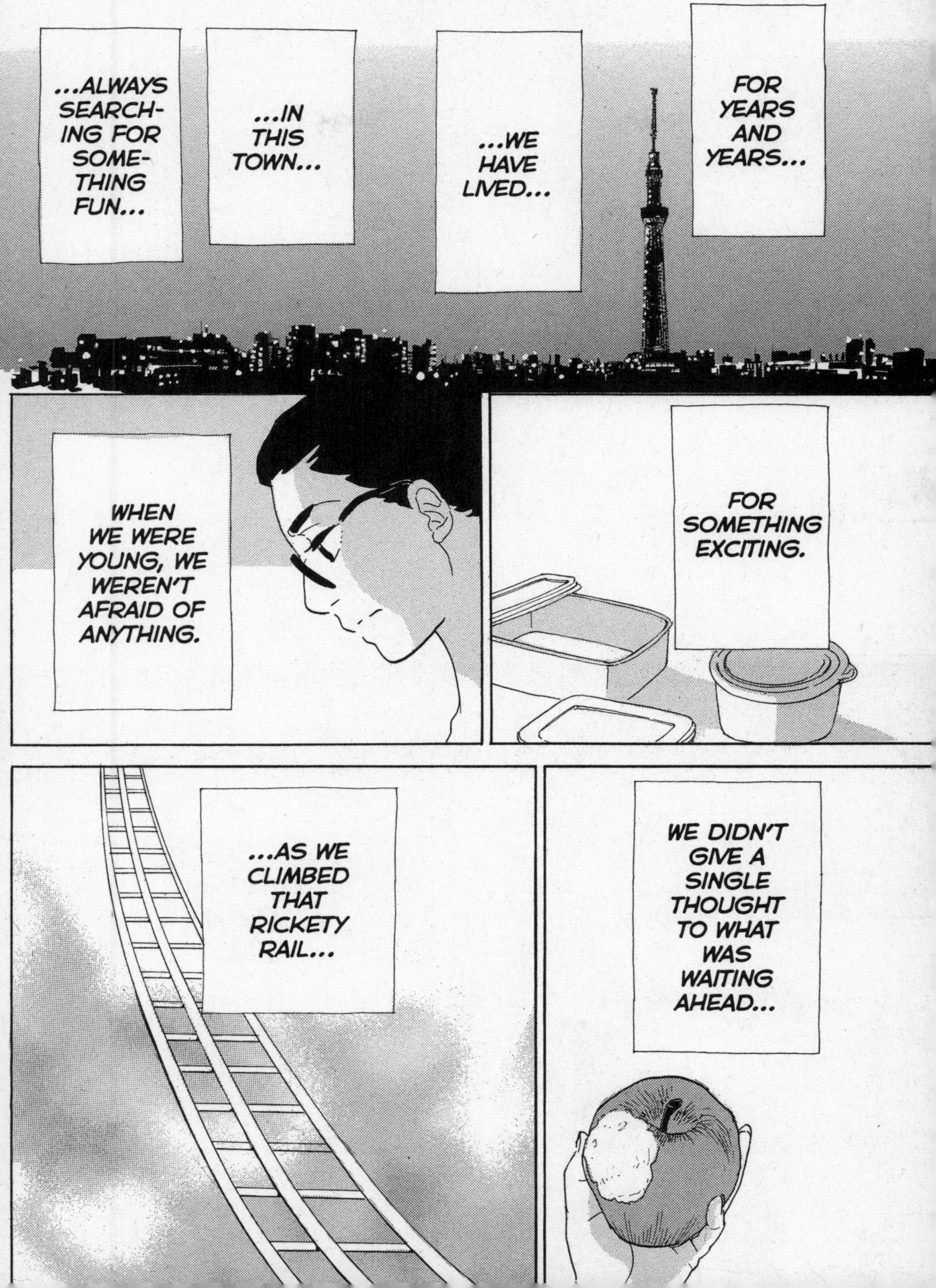
FOR YEARS AND YEARS...
...WE HAVE LIVED...
...IN THIS TOWN...
...ALWAYS SEARCHING FOR SOMETHING FUN...
FOR SOMETHING EXCITING.
WHEN WE WERE YOUNG, WE WEREN'T AFRAID OF ANYTHING.
WE DIDN'T GIVE A SINGLE THOUGHT TO WHAT WAS WAITING AHEAD...
...AS WE CLIMBED THAT RICKETY RAIL...

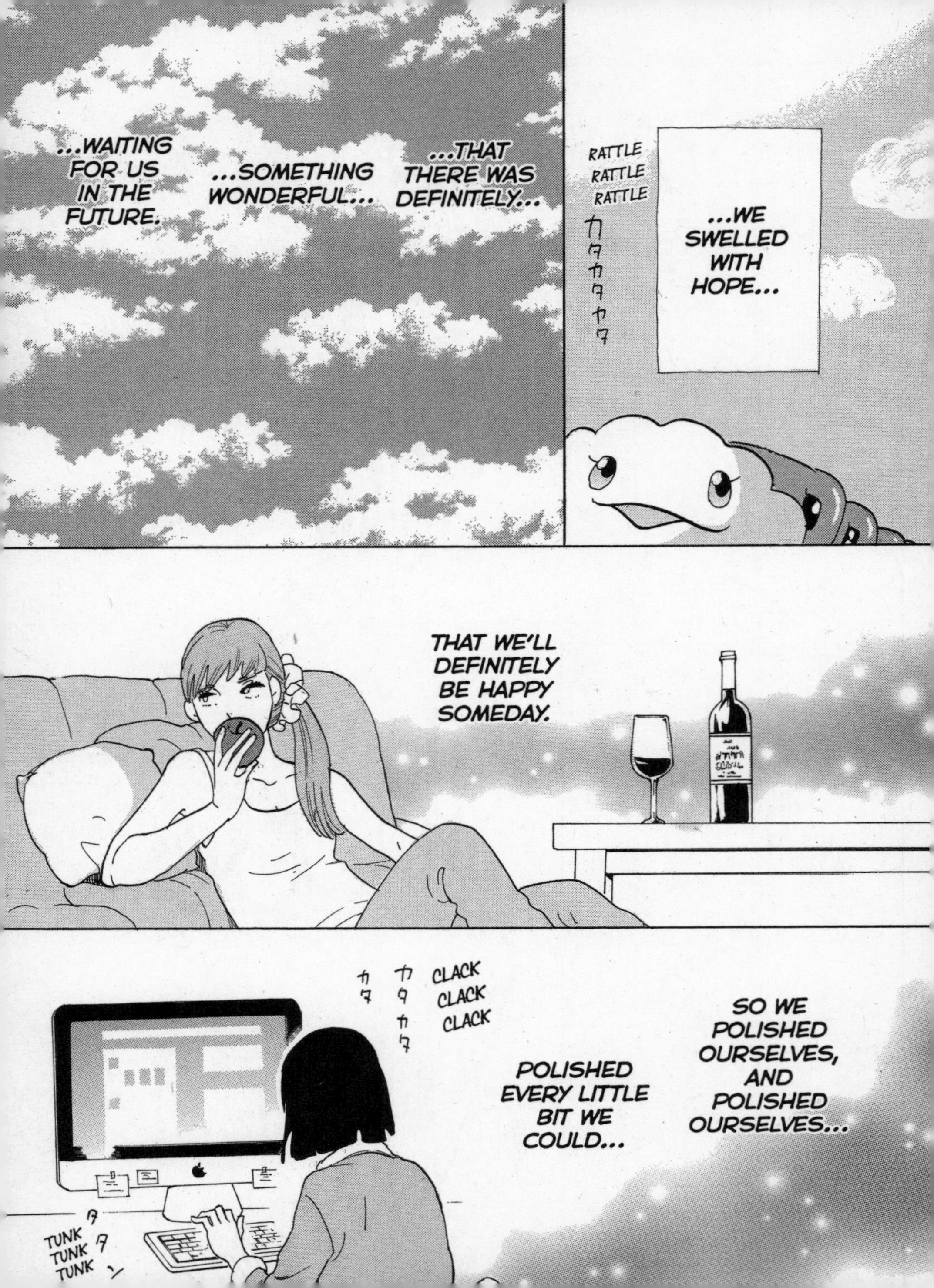
RATTLE RATTLE RATTLE
カタカタカタ
...WE SWELLED WITH HOPE...
...THAT THERE WAS DEFINITELY...
...SOMETHING WONDERFUL...
...WAITING FOR US IN THE FUTURE.
THAT WE'LL DEFINITELY BE HAPPY SOMEDAY.
SO WE POLISHED OURSELVES, AND POLISHED OURSELVES...
POLISHED EVERY LITTLE BIT WE COULD...
CLACK CLACK CLACK
TUNK TUNK TUNK

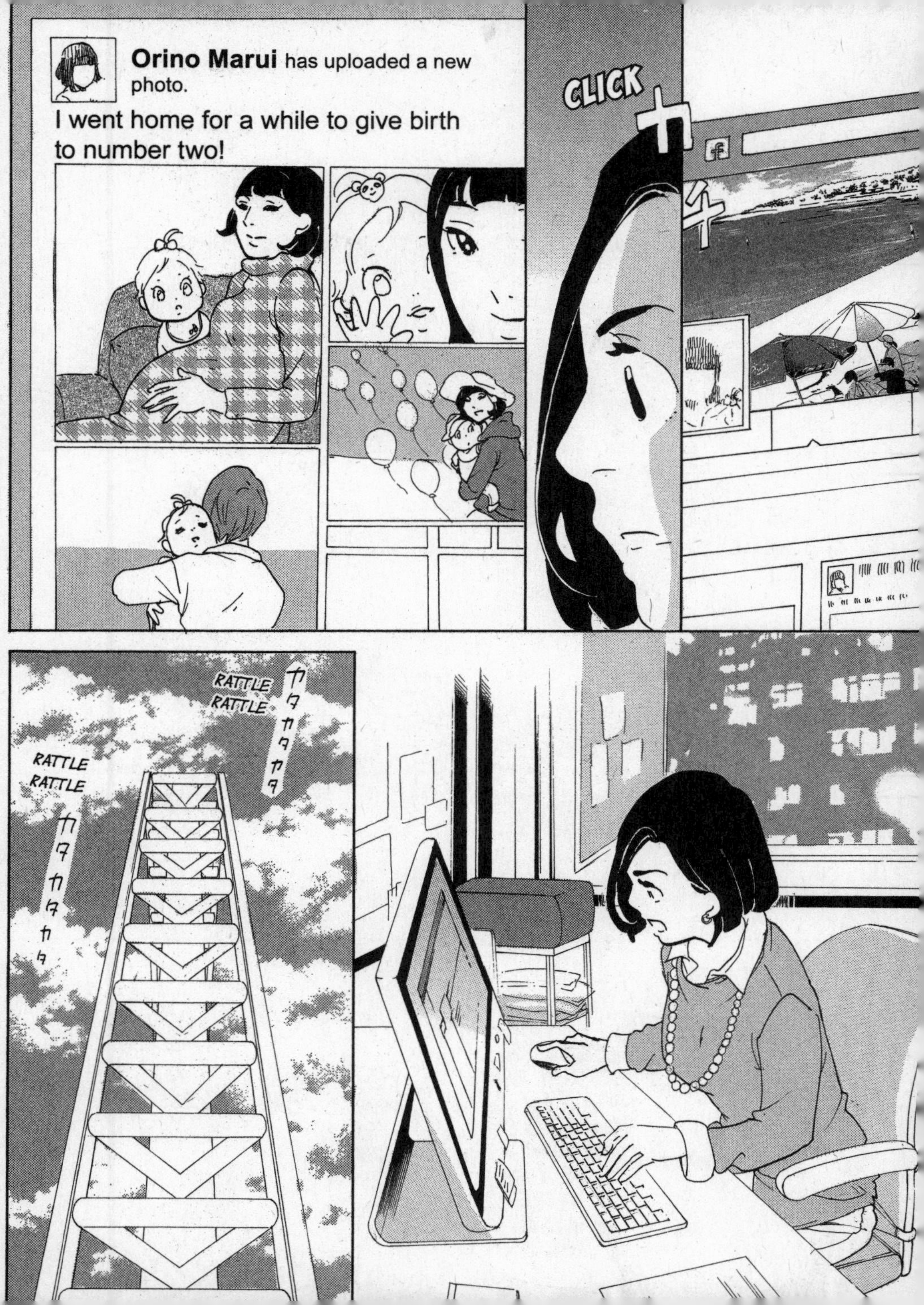
CLICK
Orino Marui has uploaded a new photo.
I went home for a while to give birth to number two!
RATTLE RATTLE
カタカタ
RATTLE RATTLE
カタカタカタ

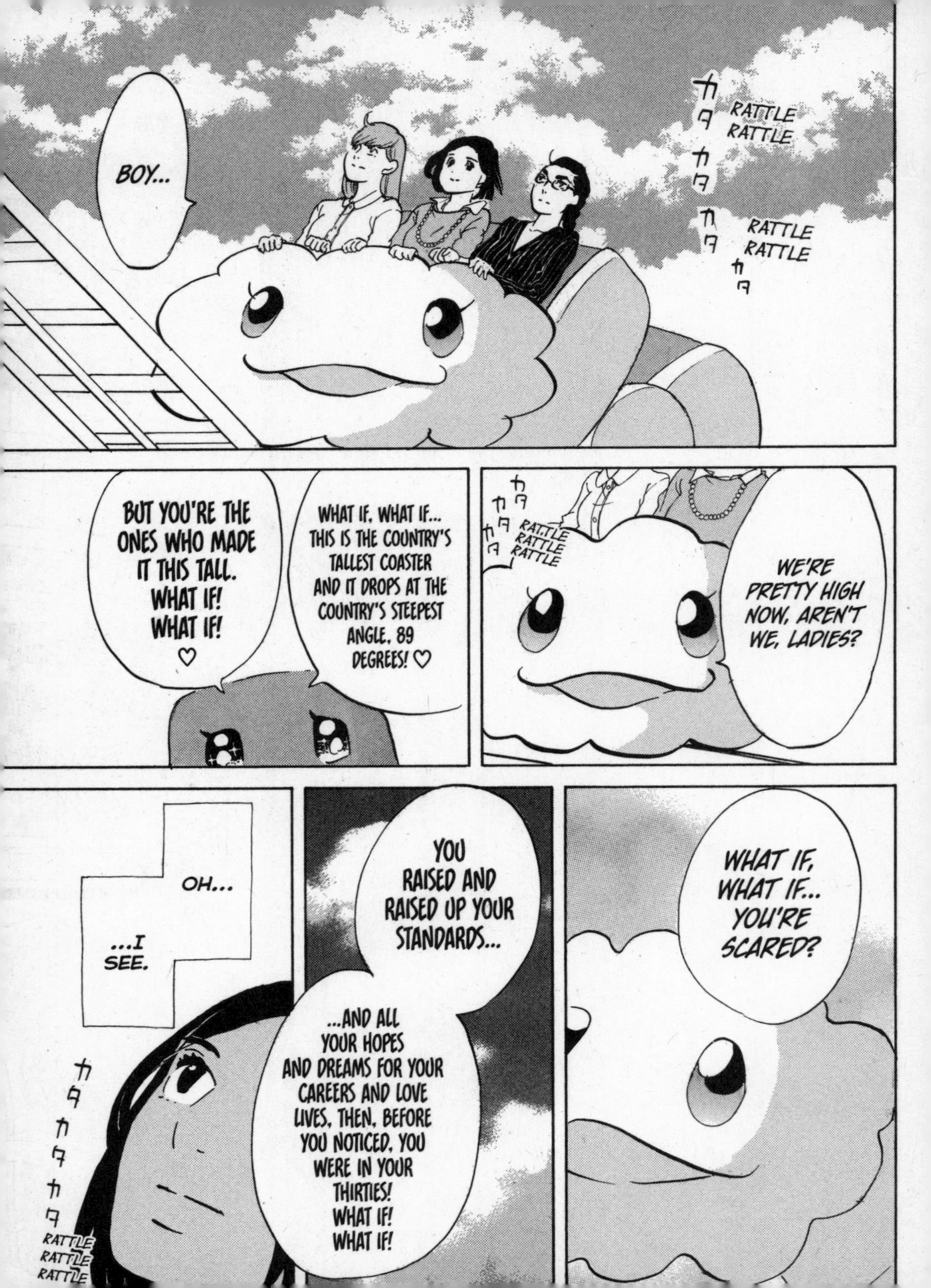
カタカタカタカタ
RATTLE RATTLE
RATTLE RATTLE
BOY...
カタカタカタ
RATTLE RATTLE RATTLE
WE'RE PRETTY HIGH NOW, AREN'T WE, LADIES?
WHAT IF, WHAT IF... THIS IS THE COUNTRY'S TALLEST COASTER AND IT DROPS AT THE COUNTRY'S STEEPEST ANGLE, 89 DEGREES! ♡
BUT YOU'RE THE ONES WHO MADE IT THIS TALL. WHAT IF! WHAT IF! ♡
WHAT IF, WHAT IF... YOU'RE SCARED?
YOU RAISED AND RAISED UP YOUR STANDARDS...
...AND ALL YOUR HOPES AND DREAMS FOR YOUR CAREERS AND LOVE LIVES, THEN, BEFORE YOU NOTICED, YOU WERE IN YOUR THIRTIES! WHAT IF! WHAT IF!
OH...
...I SEE.
カタカタカタ
RATTLE RATTLE RATTLE

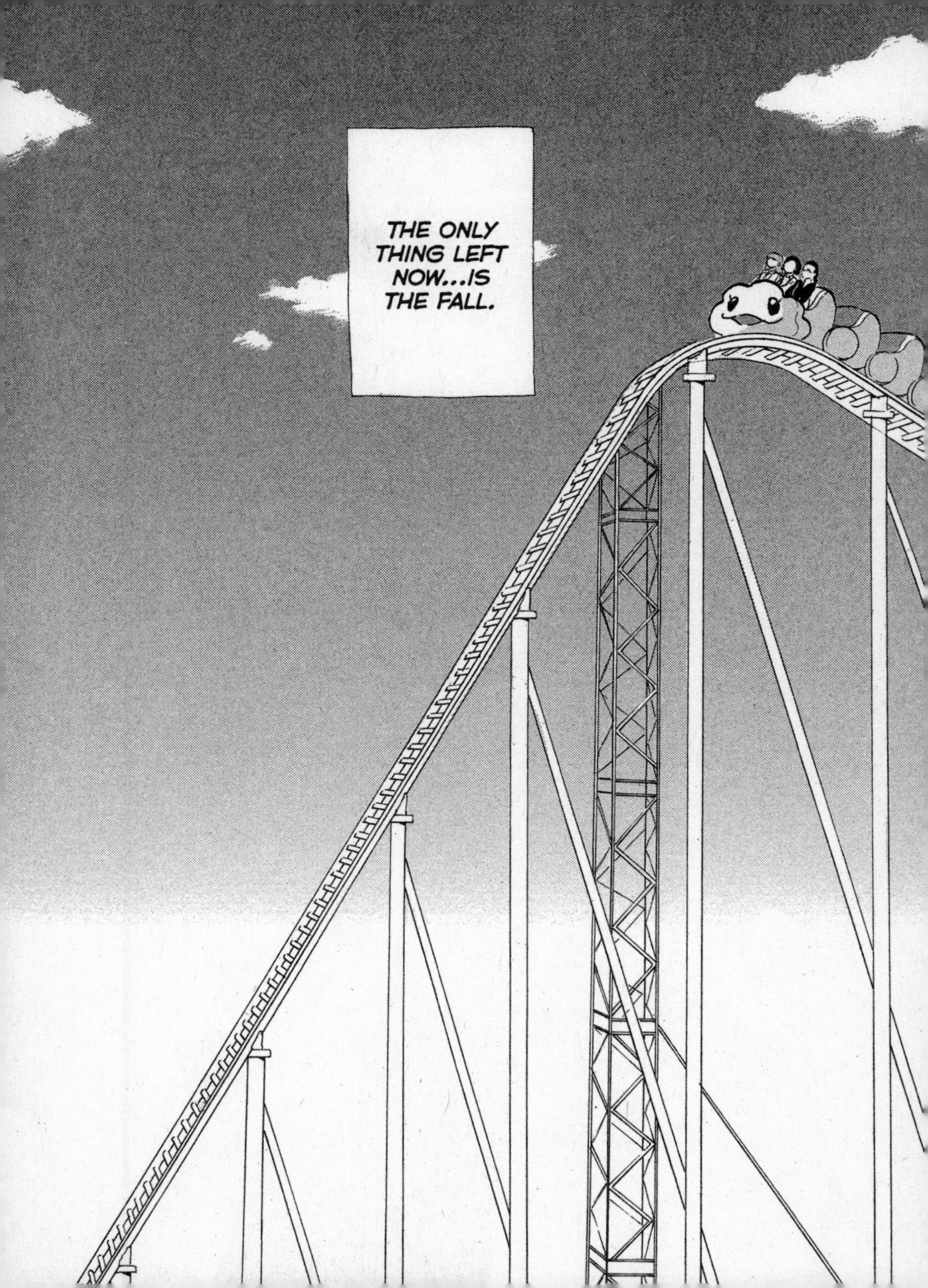
THE ONLY THING LEFT NOW...IS THE FALL.

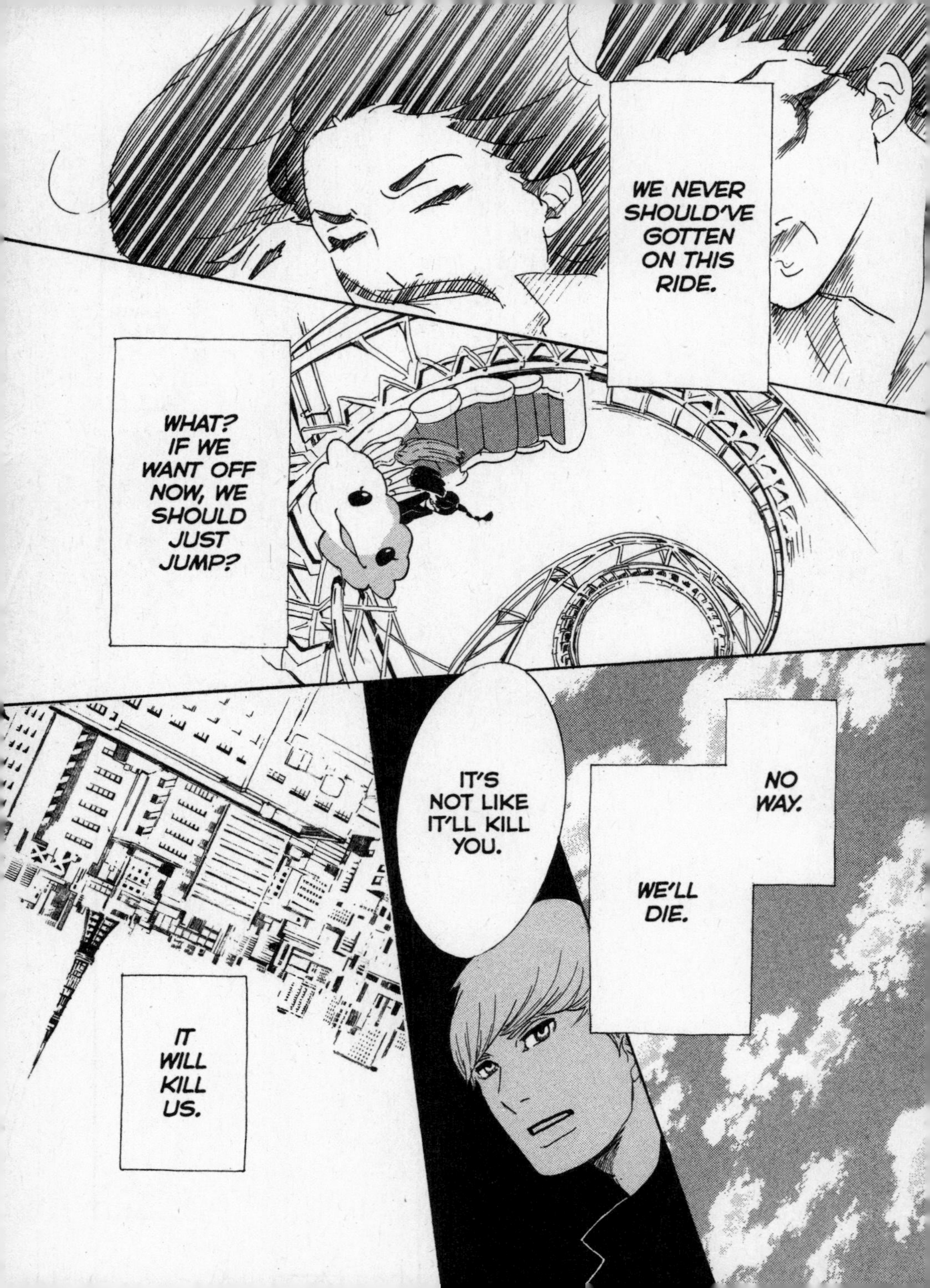
WE NEVER SHOULD'VE GOTTEN ON THIS RIDE.
WHAT? IF WE WANT OFF NOW, WE SHOULD JUST JUMP?
NO WAY.
WE'LL DIE.
IT'S NOT LIKE IT'LL KILL YOU.
IT WILL KILL US.

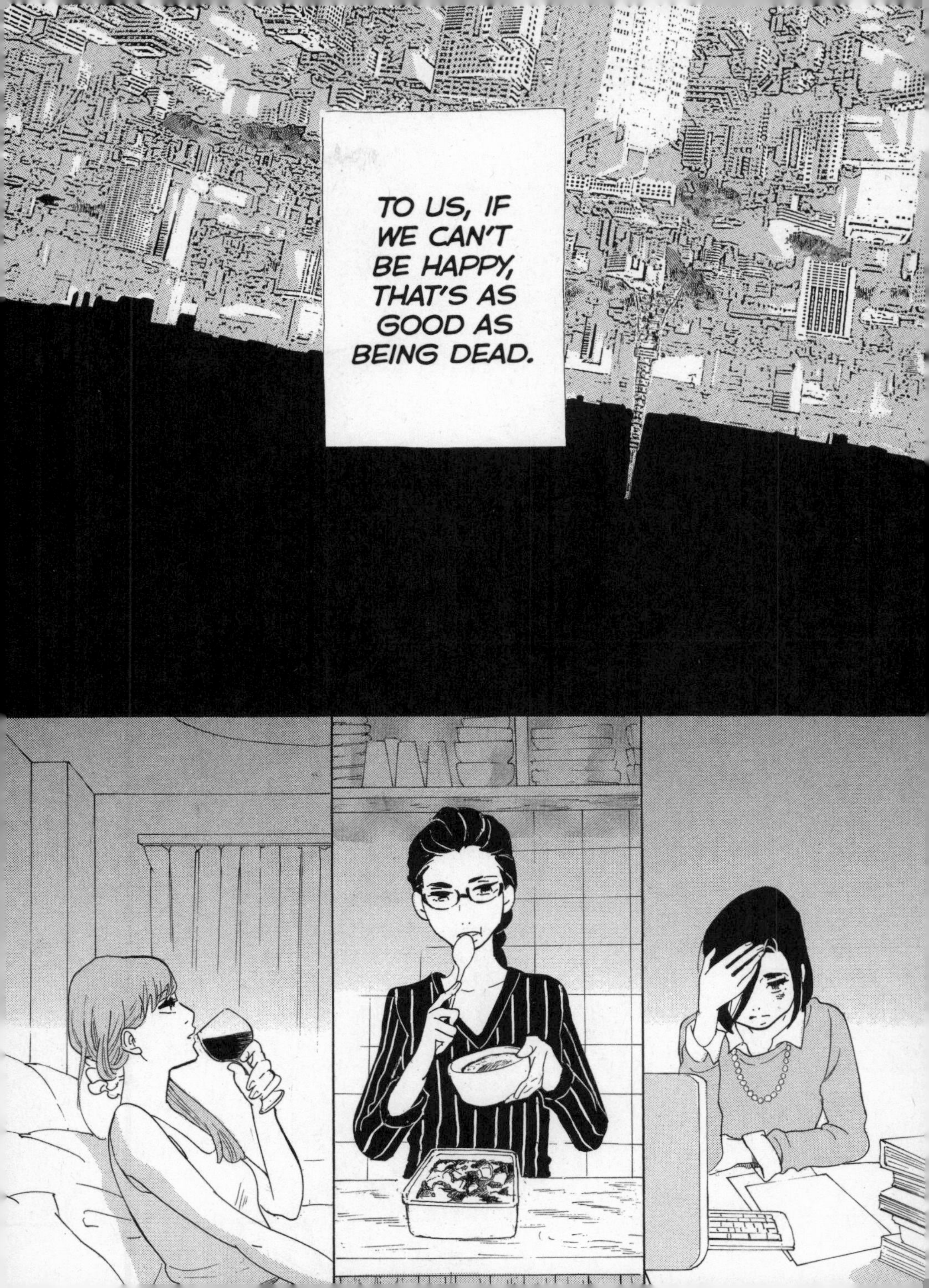
TO US, IF WE CAN'T BE HAPPY, THAT'S AS GOOD AS BEING DEAD.

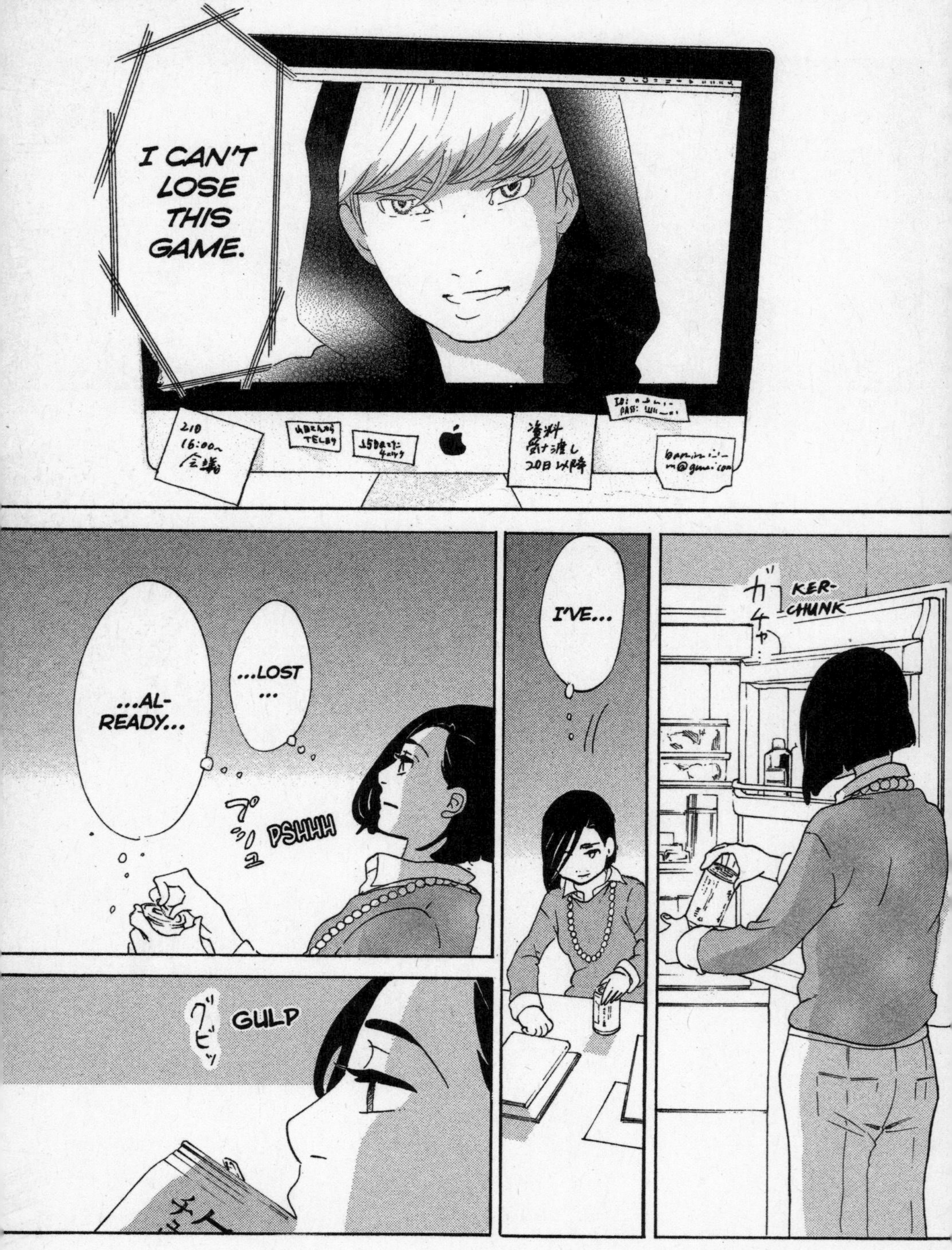
I CAN'T LOSE THIS GAME.
ガチャ
KER-CHUNK
I'VE...
...LOST...
...AL-READY...
プシュ
PSHHH
グビッ
GULP

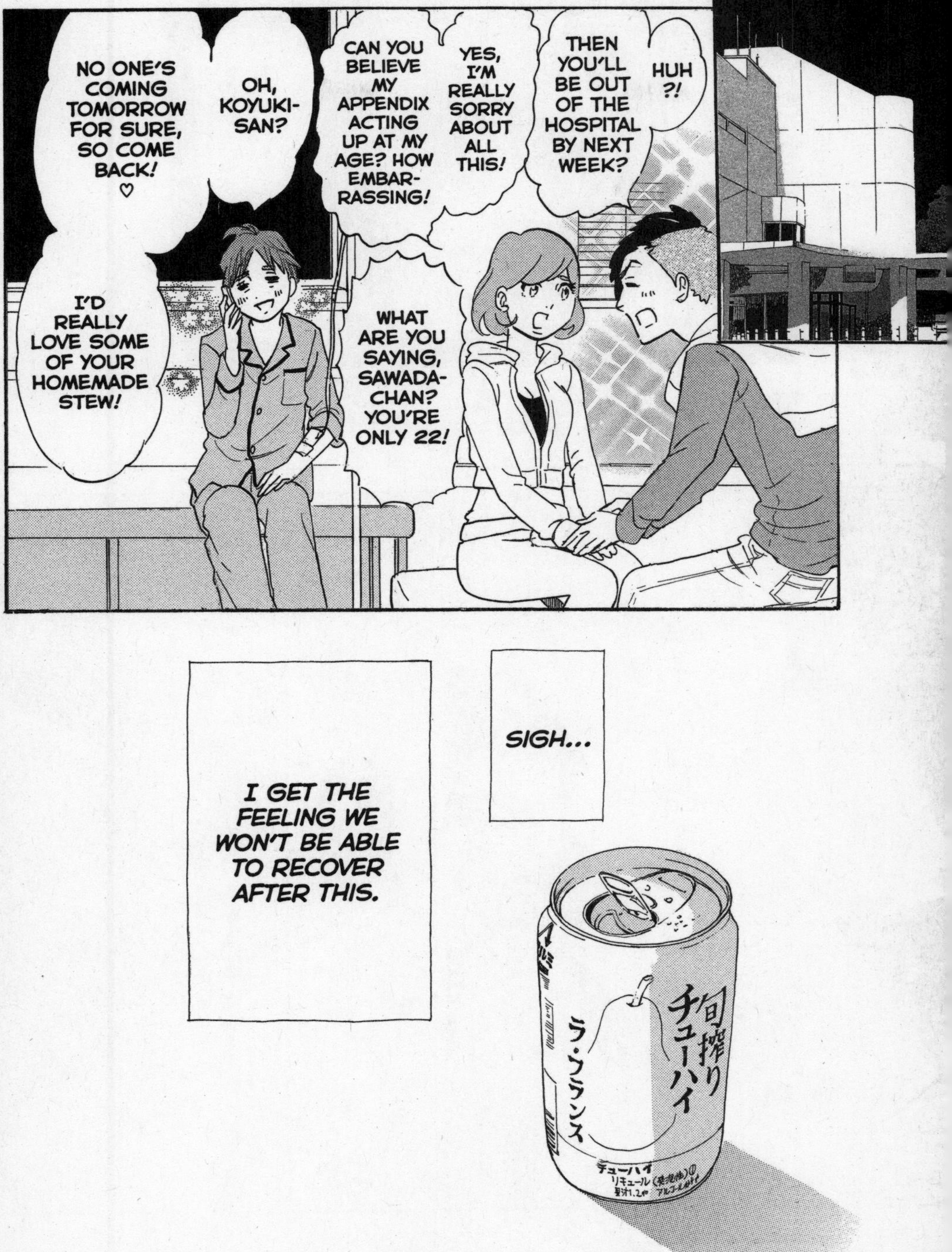
HUH?!
THEN YOU'LL BE OUT OF THE HOSPITAL BY NEXT WEEK?
YES, I'M REALLY SORRY ABOUT ALL THIS!
CAN YOU BELIEVE MY APPENDIX ACTING UP AT MY AGE? HOW EMBAR-RASSING!
WHAT ARE YOU SAYING, SAWADA-CHAN? YOU'RE ONLY 22!
OH, KOYUKI-SAN?
NO ONE'S COMING TOMORROW FOR SURE, SO COME BACK! ♡
I'D REALLY LOVE SOME OF YOUR HOMEMADE STEW!
SIGH...
I GET THE FEELING WE WON'T BE ABLE TO RECOVER AFTER THIS.
旬搾り
チューハイ
ラ・フランス

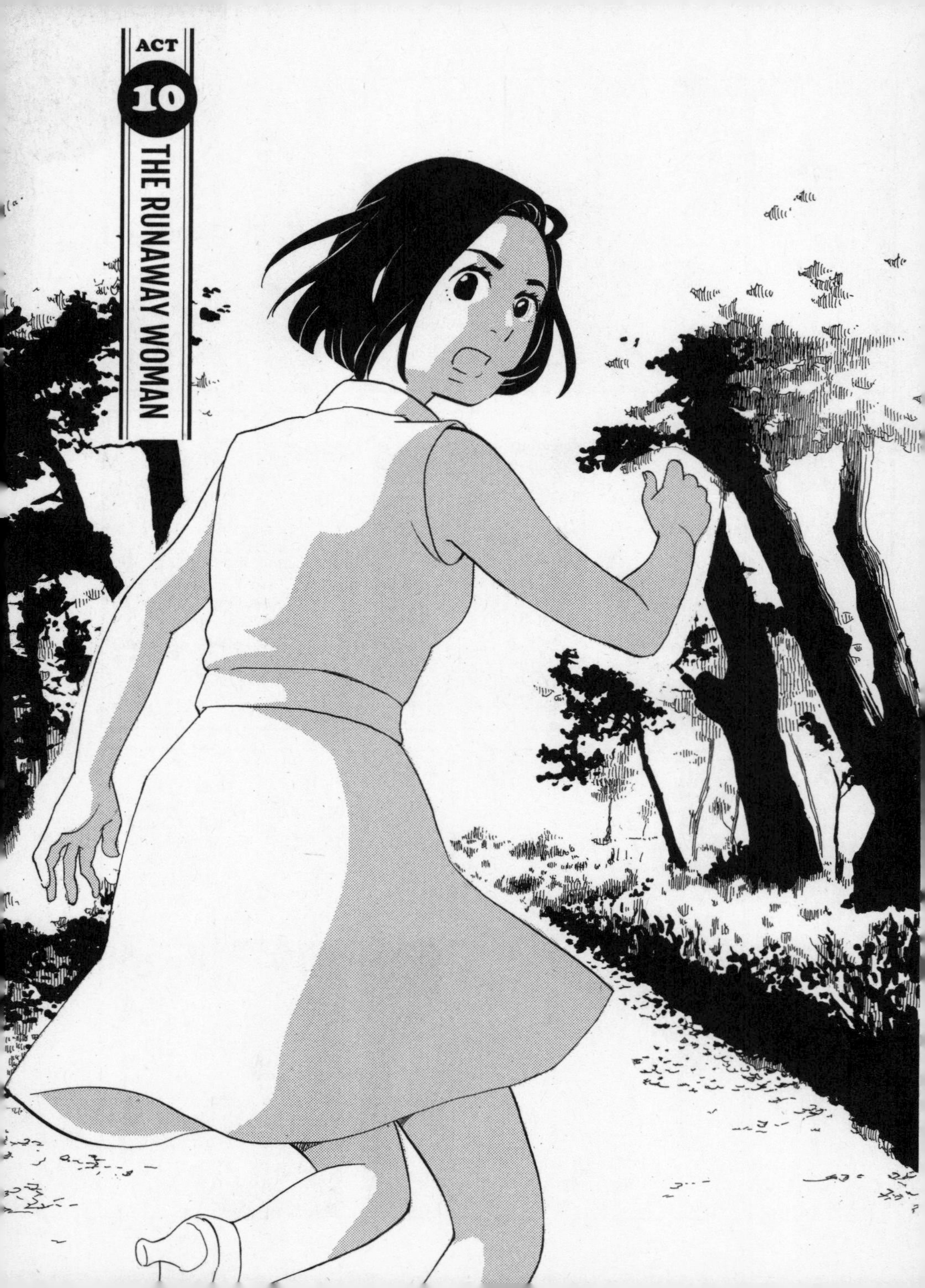
ACT
10
THE RUNAWAY WOMAN

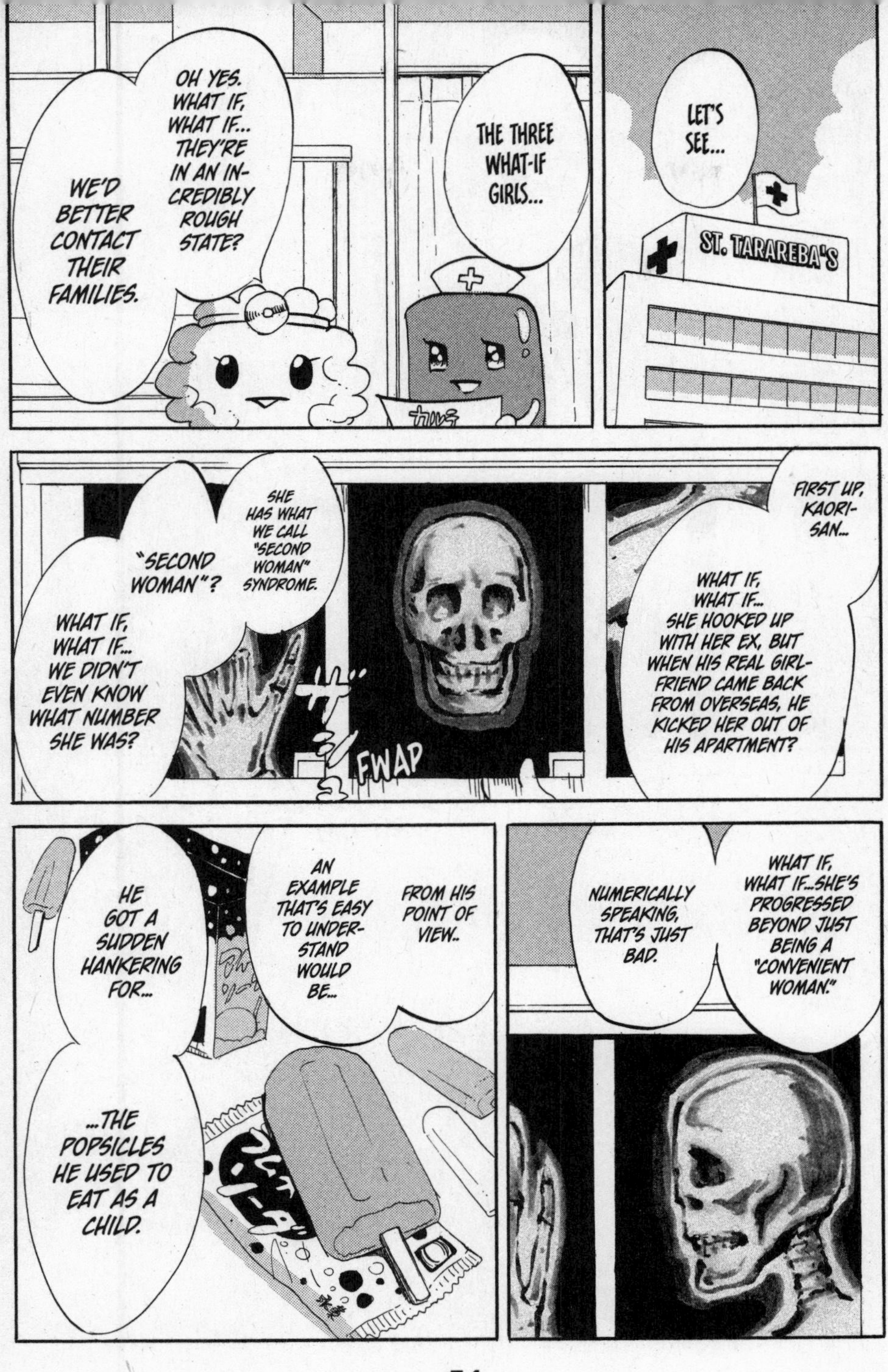
LET'S SEE...
ST. TARAREBA'S
THE THREE WHAT-IF GIRLS...
OH YES. WHAT IF, WHAT IF... THEY'RE IN AN INCREDIBLY ROUGH STATE?
WE'D BETTER CONTACT THEIR FAMILIES.
FIRST UP, KAORI-SAN...
WHAT IF, WHAT IF... SHE HOOKED UP WITH HER EX, BUT WHEN HIS REAL GIRLFRIEND CAME BACK FROM OVERSEAS, HE KICKED HER OUT OF HIS APARTMENT?
SHE HAS WHAT WE CALL "SECOND WOMAN" SYNDROME.
FWAP
"SECOND WOMAN"?
WHAT IF, WHAT IF... WE DIDN'T EVEN KNOW WHAT NUMBER SHE WAS?
WHAT IF, WHAT IF...SHE'S PROGRESSED BEYOND JUST BEING A "CONVENIENT WOMAN."
NUMERICALLY SPEAKING, THAT'S JUST BAD.
FROM HIS POINT OF VIEW..
AN EXAMPLE THAT'S EASY TO UNDERSTAND WOULD BE...
HE GOT A SUDDEN HANKERING FOR...
...THE POPSICLES HE USED TO EAT AS A CHILD.

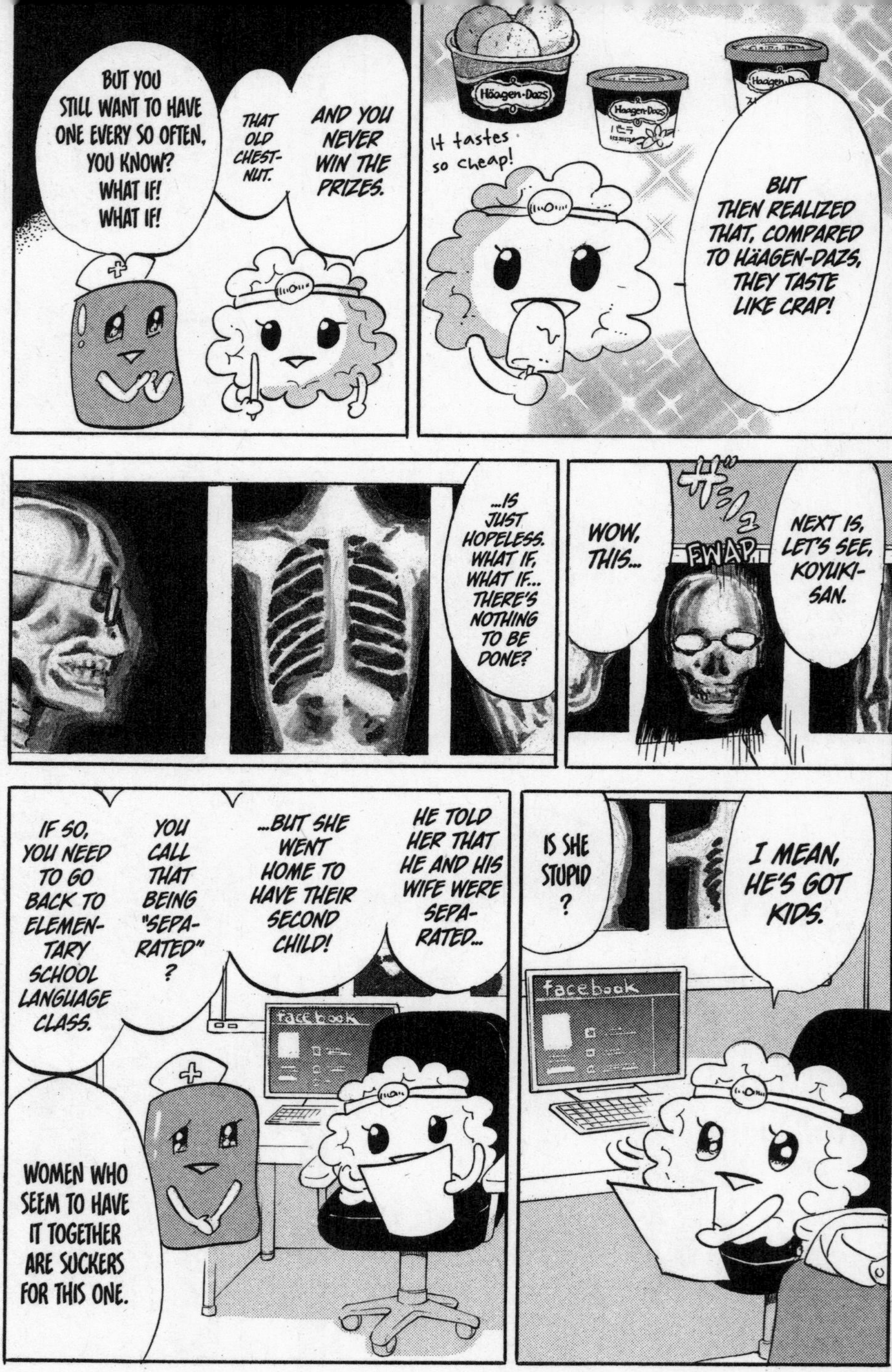
Häagen-Dazs
Häagen-Dazs
Häagen-Dazs
BUT THEN REALIZED THAT, COMPARED TO HÄAGEN-DAZS, THEY TASTE LIKE CRAP!
It tastes so cheap!
AND YOU NEVER WIN THE PRIZES.
THAT OLD CHESTNUT.
BUT YOU STILL WANT TO HAVE ONE EVERY SO OFTEN, YOU KNOW? WHAT IF! WHAT IF!
NEXT IS, LET'S SEE, KOYUKI-SAN.
FWAP
WOW, THIS...
...IS JUST HOPELESS. WHAT IF, WHAT IF... THERE'S NOTHING TO BE DONE?
I MEAN, HE'S GOT KIDS.
IS SHE STUPID?
facebook
HE TOLD HER THAT HE AND HIS WIFE WERE SEPA-RATED...
...BUT SHE WENT HOME TO HAVE THEIR SECOND CHILD!
YOU CALL THAT BEING "SEPA-RATED"?
IF SO, YOU NEED TO GO BACK TO ELEMEN-TARY SCHOOL LANGUAGE CLASS.
facebook
WOMEN WHO SEEM TO HAVE IT TOGETHER ARE SUCKERS FOR THIS ONE.

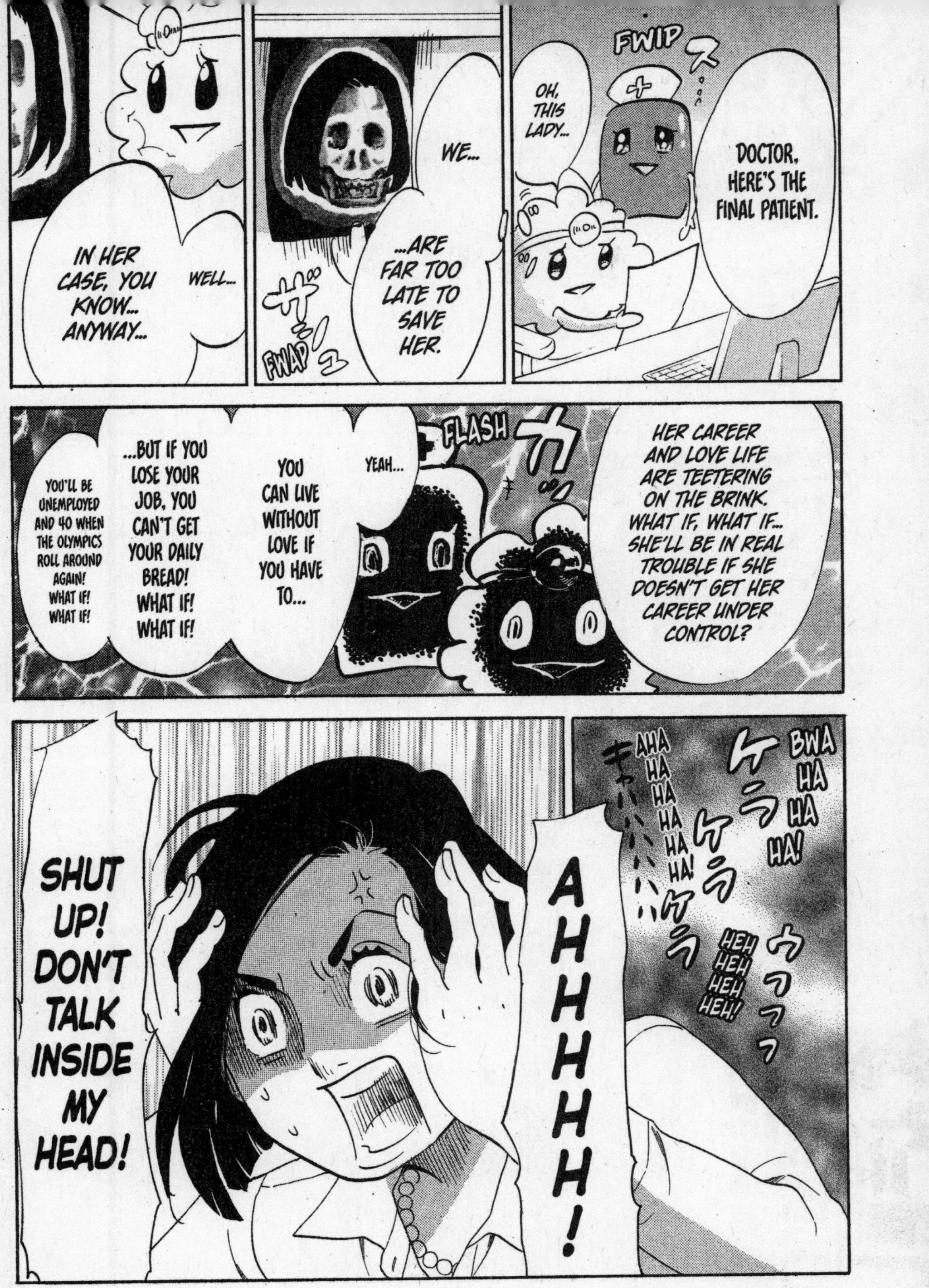
FWIP
DOCTOR, HERE'S THE FINAL PATIENT.
OH, THIS LADY...
WE...
...ARE FAR TOO LATE TO SAVE HER.
FWAP
WELL...
IN HER CASE, YOU KNOW... ANYWAY...
FLASH
HER CAREER AND LOVE LIFE ARE TEETERING ON THE BRINK. WHAT IF, WHAT IF... SHE'LL BE IN REAL TROUBLE IF SHE DOESN'T GET HER CAREER UNDER CONTROL?
YEAH...
YOU CAN LIVE WITHOUT LOVE IF YOU HAVE TO...
...BUT IF YOU LOSE YOUR JOB, YOU CAN'T GET YOUR DAILY BREAD! WHAT IF! WHAT IF!
YOU'LL BE UNEMPLOYED AND 40 WHEN THE OLYMPICS ROLL AROUND AGAIN! WHAT IF! WHAT IF!
BWA HA HA HA HA!
AHA HA HA HA HA HA!
HEH HEH HEH HEH!
AHHHHH!
SHUT UP! DON'T TALK INSIDE MY HEAD!

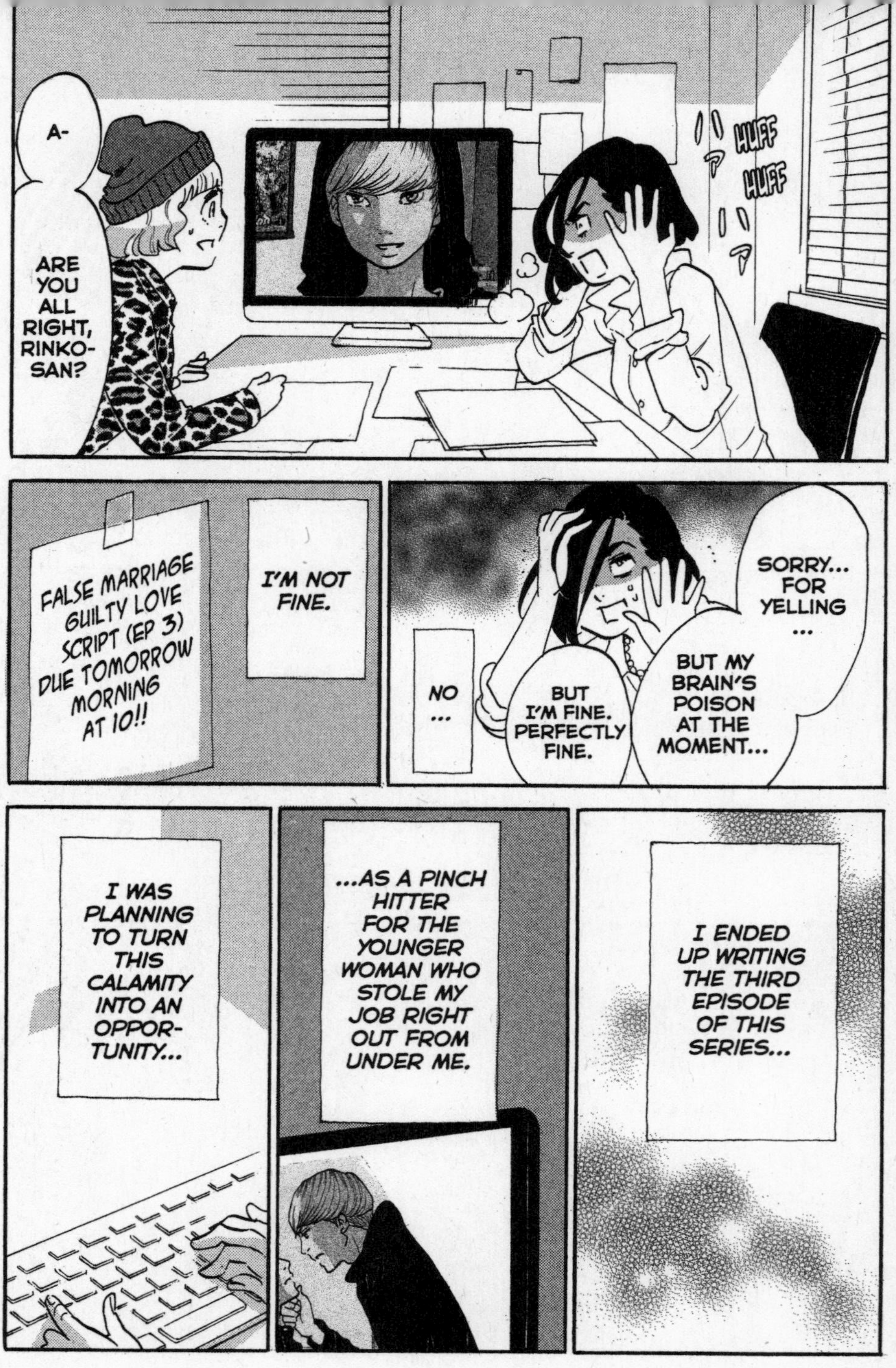
HUFF
HUFF
A-
ARE YOU ALL RIGHT, RINKO-SAN?
SORRY... FOR YELLING ...
BUT MY BRAIN'S POISON AT THE MOMENT...
BUT I'M FINE. PERFECTLY FINE.
NO ...
I'M NOT FINE.
FALSE MARRIAGE GUILTY LOVE SCRIPT (EP 3) DUE TOMORROW MORNING AT 10!!
I ENDED UP WRITING THE THIRD EPISODE OF THIS SERIES...
...AS A PINCH HITTER FOR THE YOUNGER WOMAN WHO STOLE MY JOB RIGHT OUT FROM UNDER ME.
I WAS PLANNING TO TURN THIS CALAMITY INTO AN OPPOR-TUNITY...

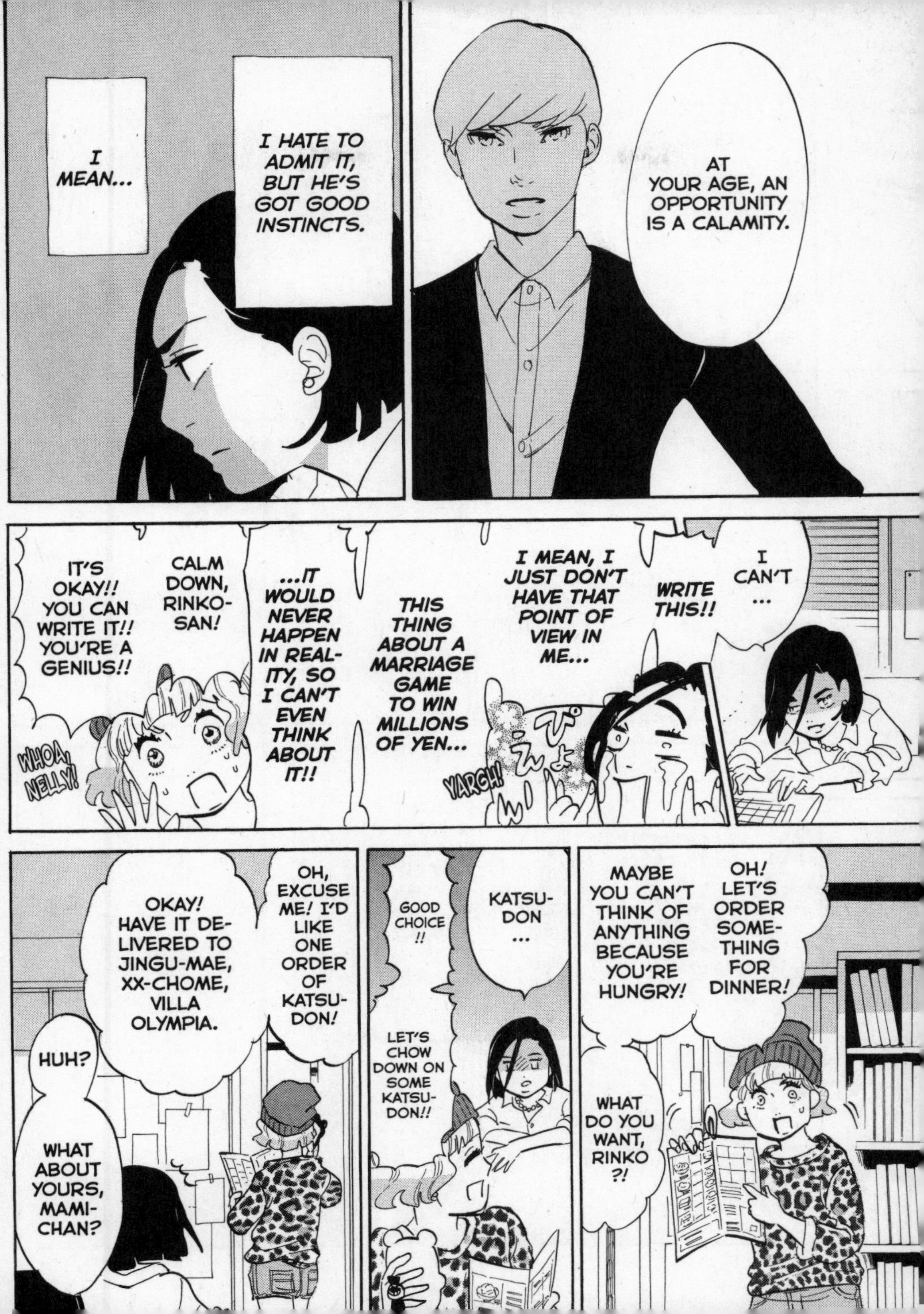
AT YOUR AGE, AN OPPORTUNITY IS A CALAMITY.
I HATE TO ADMIT IT, BUT HE'S GOT GOOD INSTINCTS.
I MEAN...
I CAN'T ...
WRITE THIS!!
I MEAN, I JUST DON'T HAVE THAT POINT OF VIEW IN ME...
THIS THING ABOUT A MARRIAGE GAME TO WIN MILLIONS OF YEN...
...IT WOULD NEVER HAPPEN IN REALITY, SO I CAN'T EVEN THINK ABOUT IT!!
YARGH!
CALM DOWN, RINKO-SAN!
IT'S OKAY!! YOU CAN WRITE IT!! YOU'RE A GENIUS!!
WHOA, NELLY!
OH! LET'S ORDER SOMETHING FOR DINNER!
MAYBE YOU CAN'T THINK OF ANYTHING BECAUSE YOU'RE HUNGRY!
WHAT DO YOU WANT, RINKO?!
KATSU-DON ...
GOOD CHOICE !!
LET'S CHOW DOWN ON SOME KATSU-DON!!
OH, EXCUSE ME! I'D LIKE ONE ORDER OF KATSU-DON!
OKAY! HAVE IT DELIVERED TO JINGU-MAE, XX-CHOME, VILLA OLYMPIA.
HUH?
WHAT ABOUT YOURS, MAMI-CHAN?

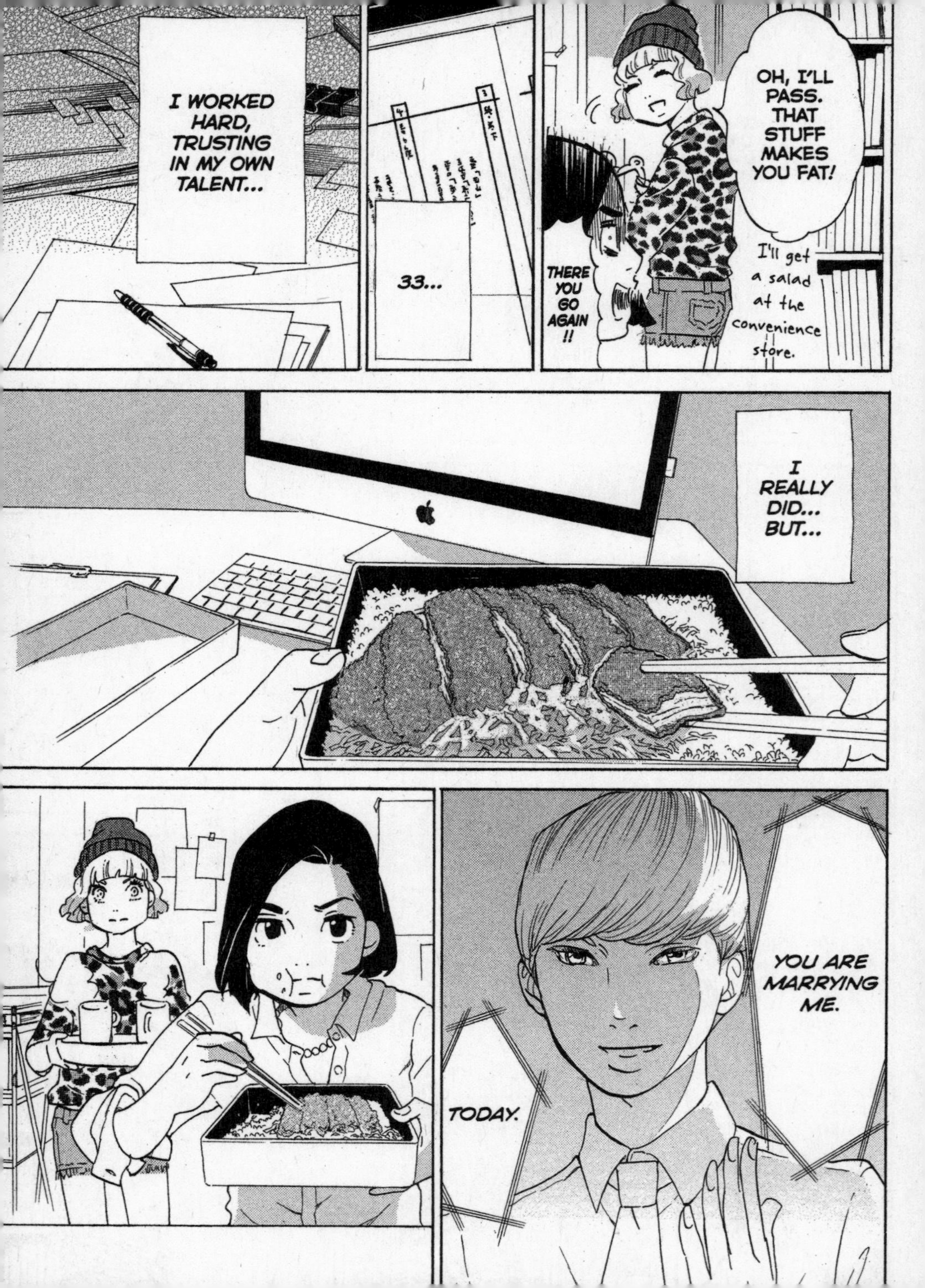
OH, I'LL PASS. THAT STUFF MAKES YOU FAT!
I'll get a salad at the convenience store.
THERE YOU GO AGAIN!!
33...
I WORKED HARD, TRUSTING IN MY OWN TALENT...
I REALLY DID... BUT...
YOU ARE MARRYING ME.
TODAY.

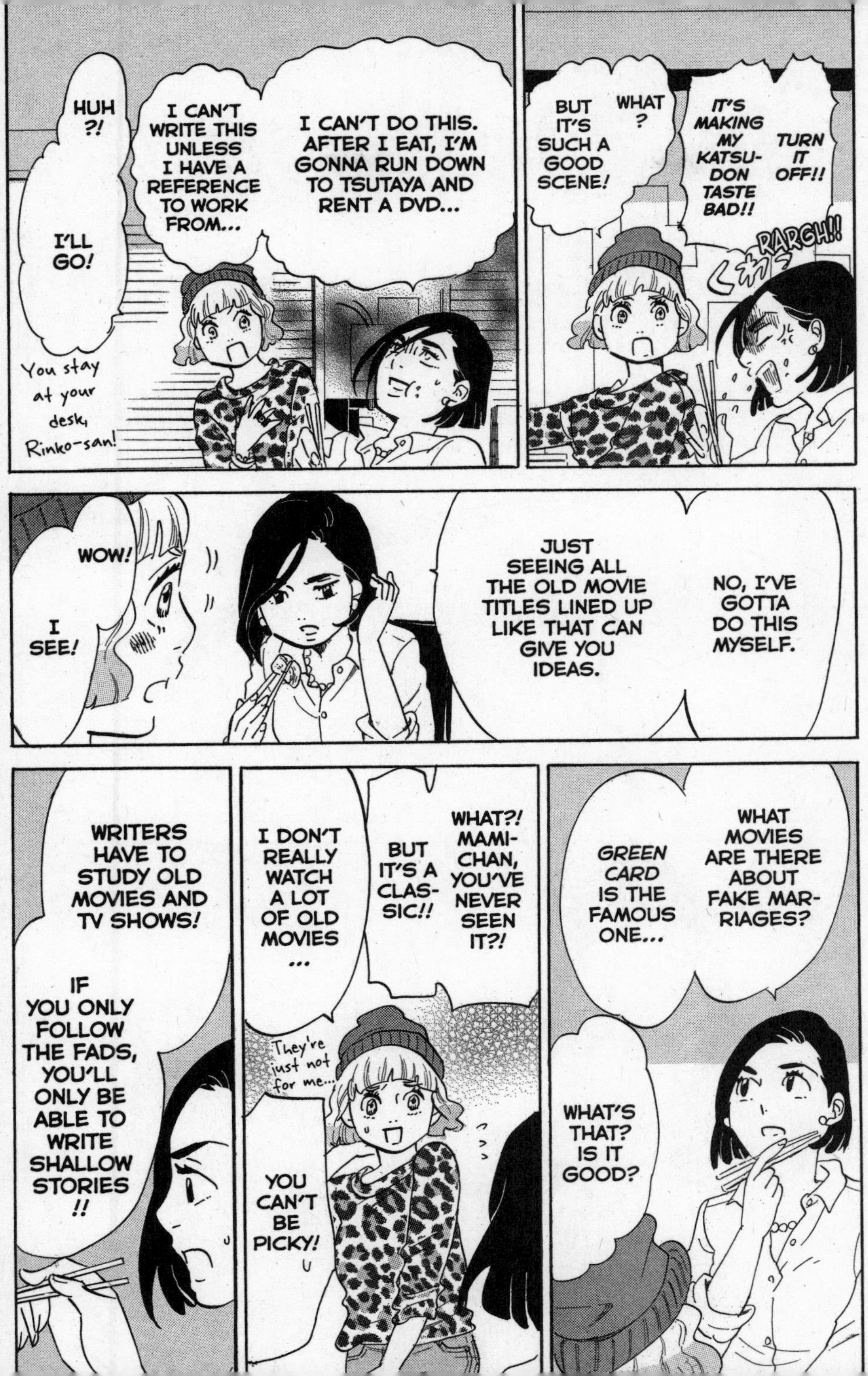
TURN IT OFF!!
IT'S MAKING MY KATSU-DON TASTE BAD!!
RARGH!!
WHAT?
BUT IT'S SUCH A GOOD SCENE!
I CAN'T DO THIS. AFTER I EAT, I'M GONNA RUN DOWN TO TSUTAYA AND RENT A DVD...
I CAN'T WRITE THIS UNLESS I HAVE A REFERENCE TO WORK FROM...
HUH?!
I'LL GO!
You stay at your desk, Rinko-san!
NO, I'VE GOTTA DO THIS MYSELF.
JUST SEEING ALL THE OLD MOVIE TITLES LINED UP LIKE THAT CAN GIVE YOU IDEAS.
WOW!
I SEE!
WHAT MOVIES ARE THERE ABOUT FAKE MAR-RIAGES?
GREEN CARD IS THE FAMOUS ONE...
WHAT'S THAT? IS IT GOOD?
WHAT?! MAMI-CHAN, YOU'VE NEVER SEEN IT?!
BUT IT'S A CLAS-SIC!!
I DON'T REALLY WATCH A LOT OF OLD MOVIES...
They're just not for me...
YOU CAN'T BE PICKY!
WRITERS HAVE TO STUDY OLD MOVIES AND TV SHOWS!
IF YOU ONLY FOLLOW THE FADS, YOU'LL ONLY BE ABLE TO WRITE SHALLOW STORIES!!

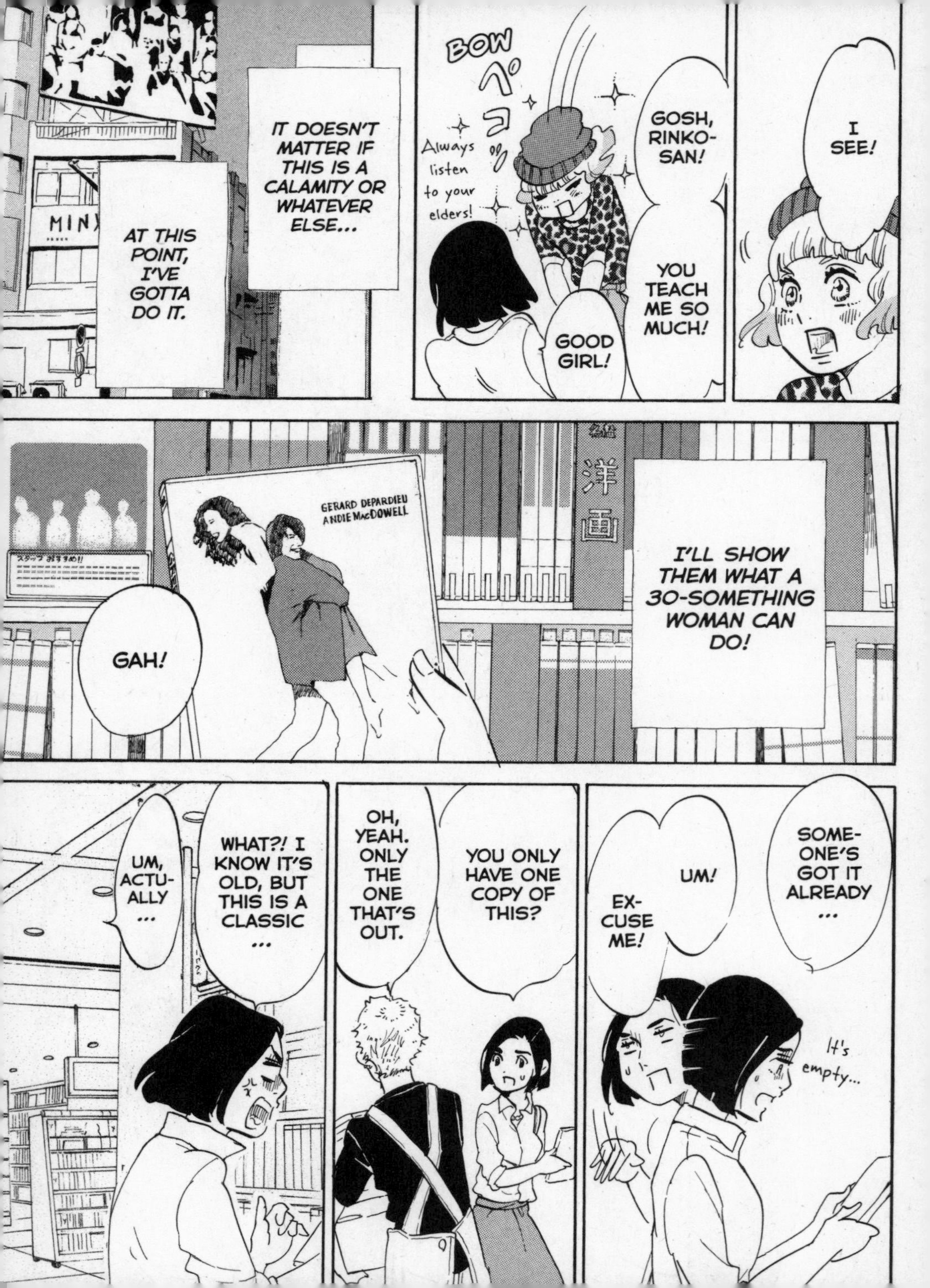
I SEE!
BOW
ペコ
GOSH, RINKO-SAN!
YOU TEACH ME SO MUCH!
Always listen to your elders!
GOOD GIRL!
IT DOESN'T MATTER IF THIS IS A CALAMITY OR WHATEVER ELSE...
AT THIS POINT, I'VE GOTTA DO IT.
MINX
I'LL SHOW THEM WHAT A 30-SOMETHING WOMAN CAN DO!
洋画
GERARD DEPARDIEU
ANDIE MacDOWELL
スタッフ おすすめ!!
GAH!
SOME-ONE'S GOT IT ALREADY...
It's empty...
UM!
EX-CUSE ME!
YOU ONLY HAVE ONE COPY OF THIS?
OH, YEAH. ONLY THE ONE THAT'S OUT.
WHAT?! I KNOW IT'S OLD, BUT THIS IS A CLASSIC...
UM, ACTUALLY...

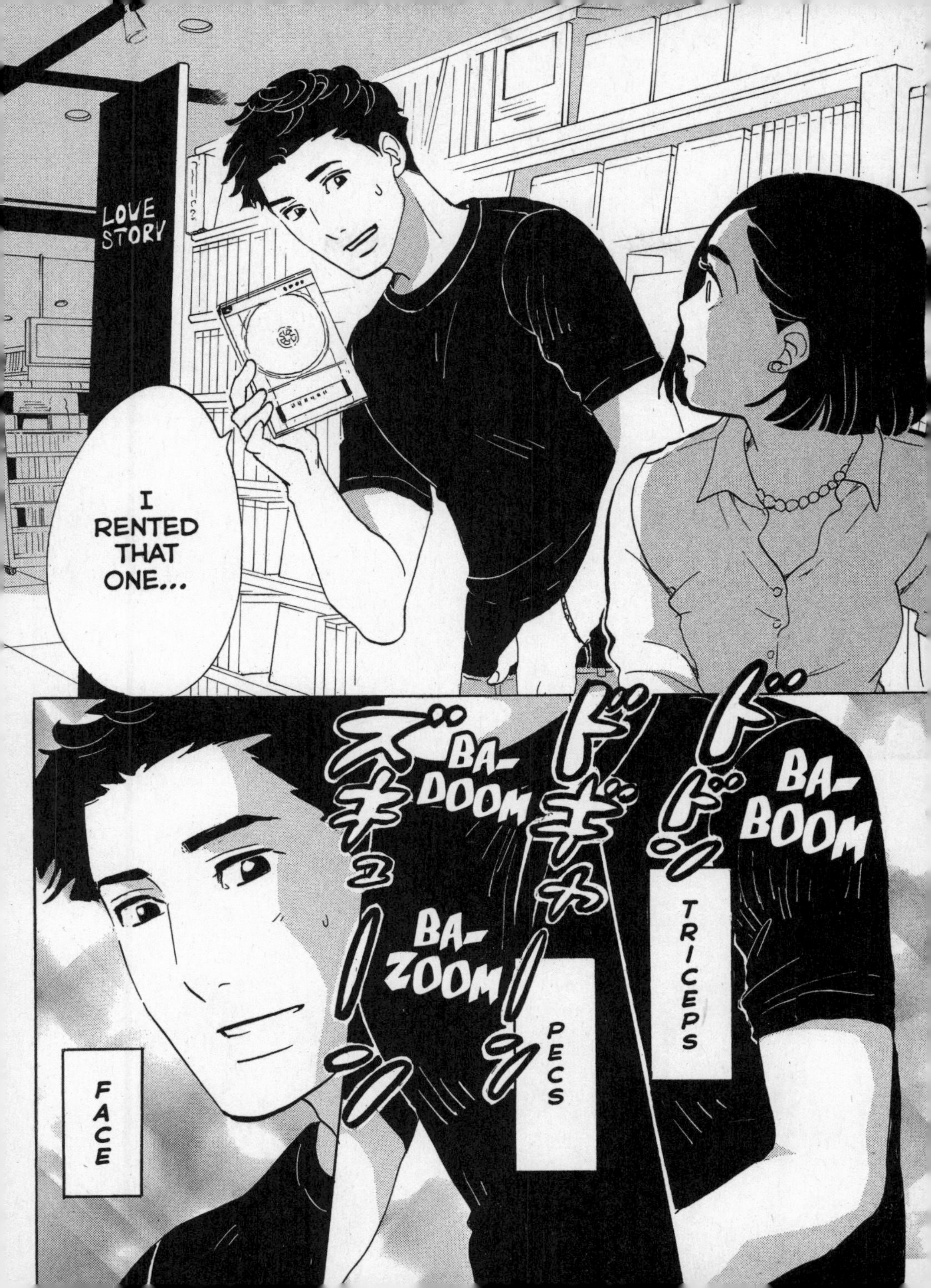
LOVE STORY
I RENTED THAT ONE...
BA-BOOM
TRICEPS
BA-ZOOM
PECS
BA-DOOM
FACE

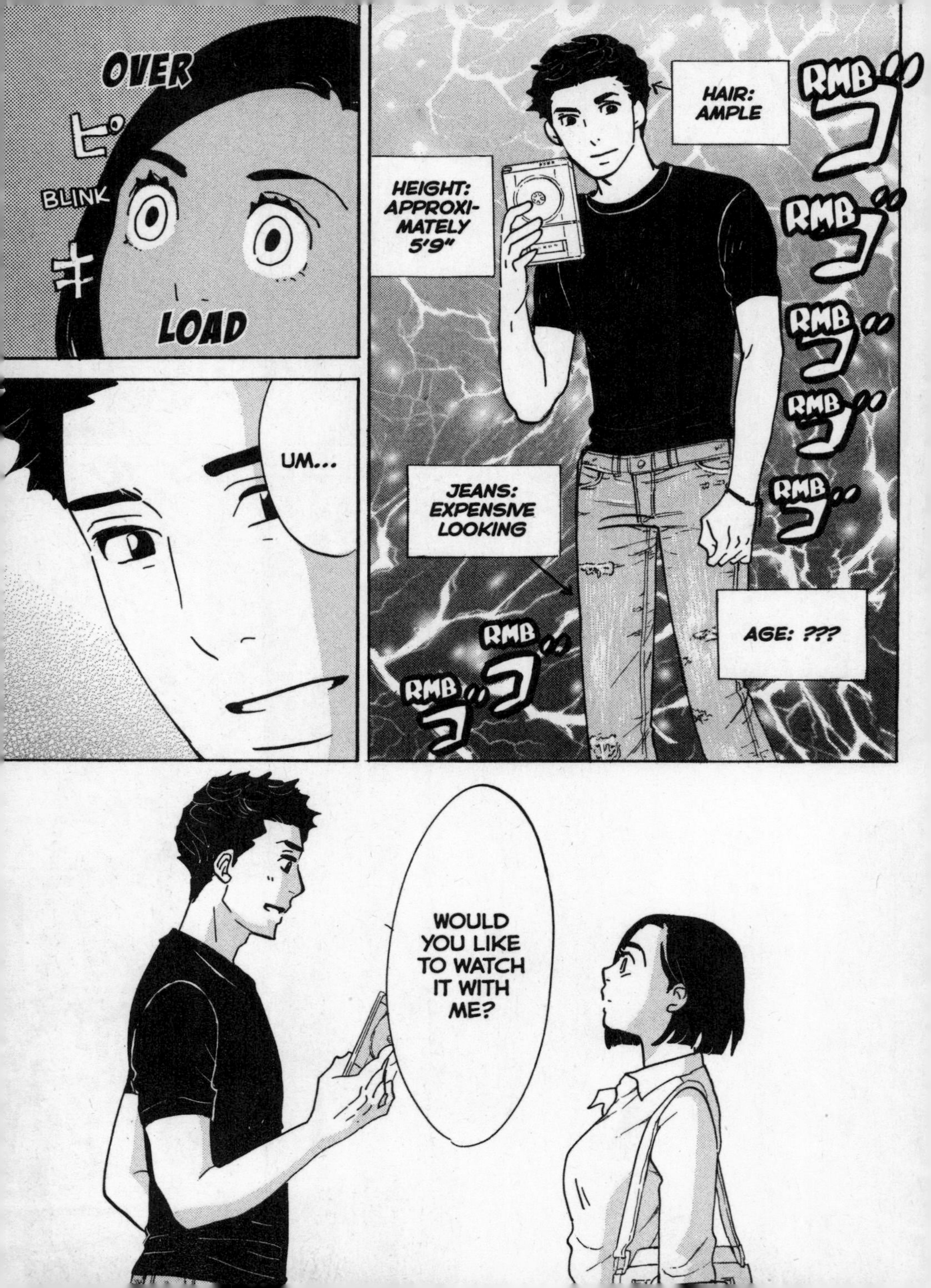
HAIR: AMPLE
RMB ゴ
RMB ゴ
HEIGHT: APPROXIMATELY 5'9"
RMB ゴ
RMB ゴ
RMB ゴ
JEANS: EXPENSIVE LOOKING
AGE: ???
RMB ゴ
RMB ゴ
OVER
ピ
BLINK
キ
LOAD
UM...
WOULD YOU LIKE TO WATCH IT WITH ME?

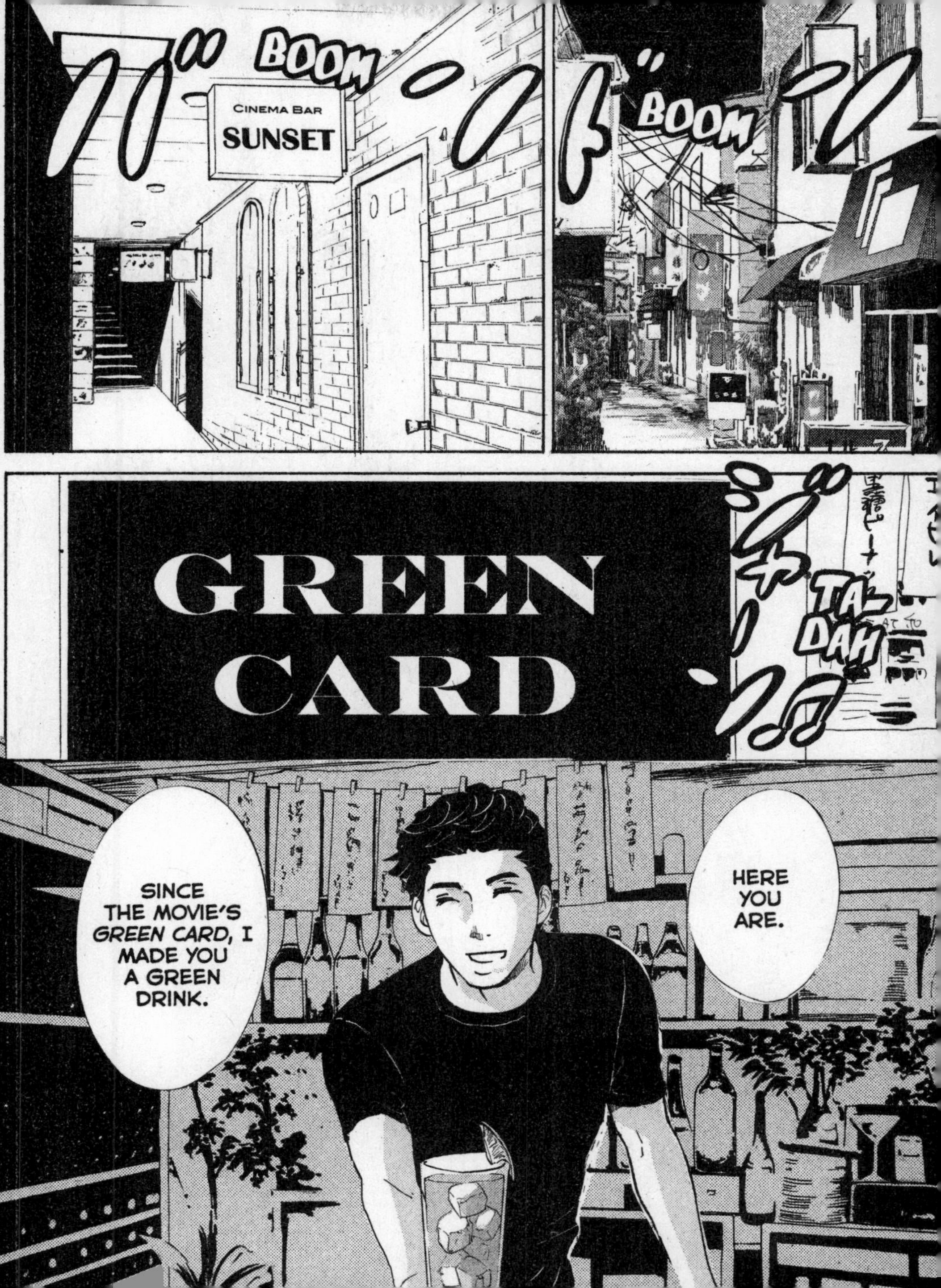
BOOM
CINEMA BAR
SUNSET
BOOM
TA-DAH
GREEN CARD
HERE YOU ARE.
SINCE THE MOVIE'S *GREEN CARD*, I MADE YOU A GREEN DRINK.

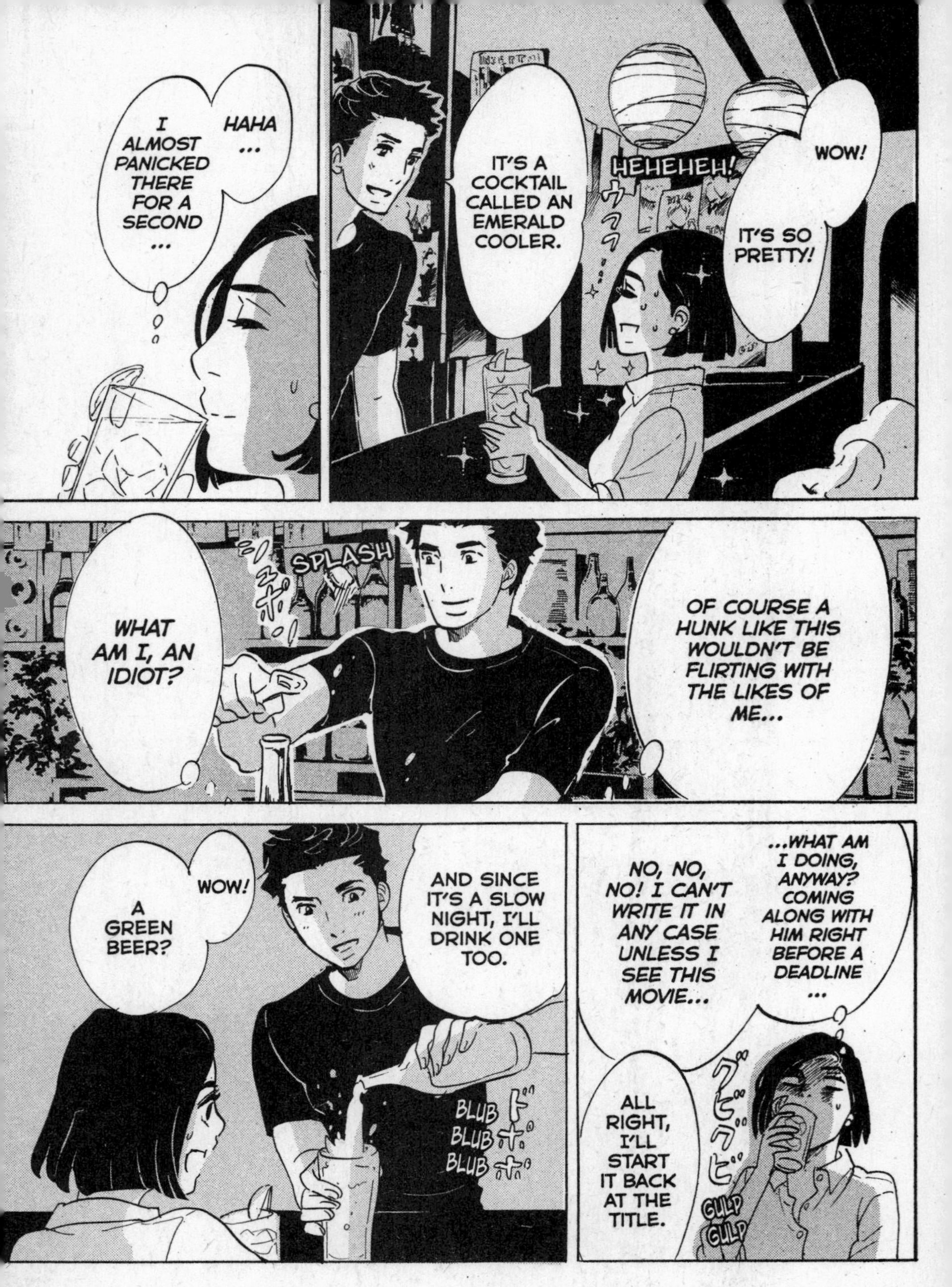
WOW!
IT'S SO PRETTY!
HEHEHEH!
IT'S A COCKTAIL CALLED AN EMERALD COOLER.
HAHA ...
I ALMOST PANICKED THERE FOR A SECOND ...
OF COURSE A HUNK LIKE THIS WOULDN'T BE FLIRTING WITH THE LIKES OF ME...
SPLASH
WHAT AM I, AN IDIOT?
...WHAT AM I DOING, ANYWAY? COMING ALONG WITH HIM RIGHT BEFORE A DEADLINE ...
NO, NO, NO! I CAN'T WRITE IT IN ANY CASE UNLESS I SEE THIS MOVIE...
GULP GULP
ALL RIGHT, I'LL START IT BACK AT THE TITLE.
AND SINCE IT'S A SLOW NIGHT, I'LL DRINK ONE TOO.
WOW!
A GREEN BEER?
BLUB BLUB BLUB

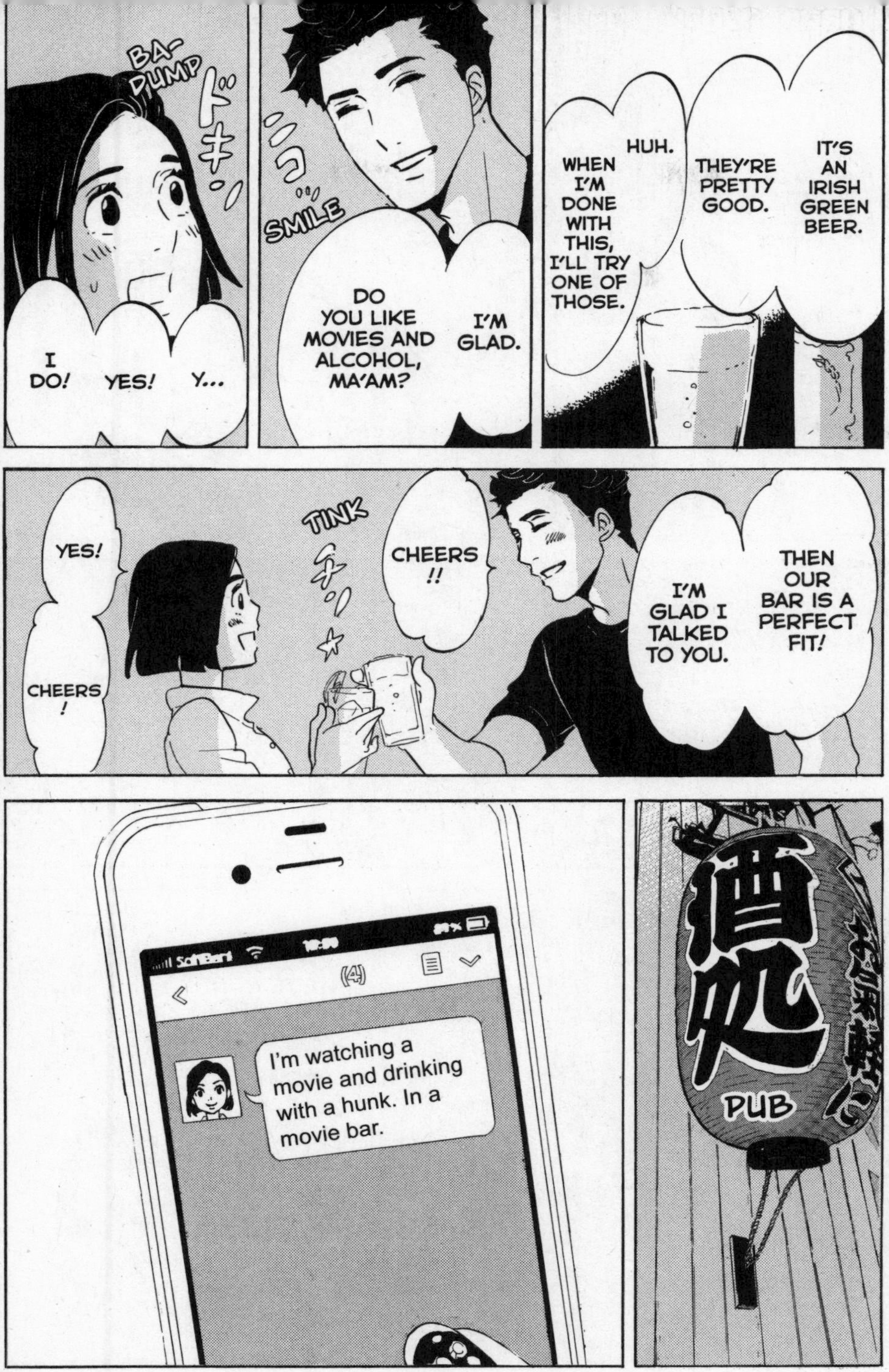
IT'S AN IRISH GREEN BEER.
THEY'RE PRETTY GOOD.
HUH.
WHEN I'M DONE WITH THIS, I'LL TRY ONE OF THOSE.
ニコッ
SMILE
I'M GLAD.
DO YOU LIKE MOVIES AND ALCOHOL, MA'AM?
ドキッ
BA-DUMP
Y...
YES!
I DO!
THEN OUR BAR IS A PERFECT FIT!
I'M GLAD I TALKED TO YOU.
CHEERS !!
TINK
YES!
CHEERS !
酒処
PUB
(4)
I'm watching a movie and drinking with a hunk. In a movie bar.

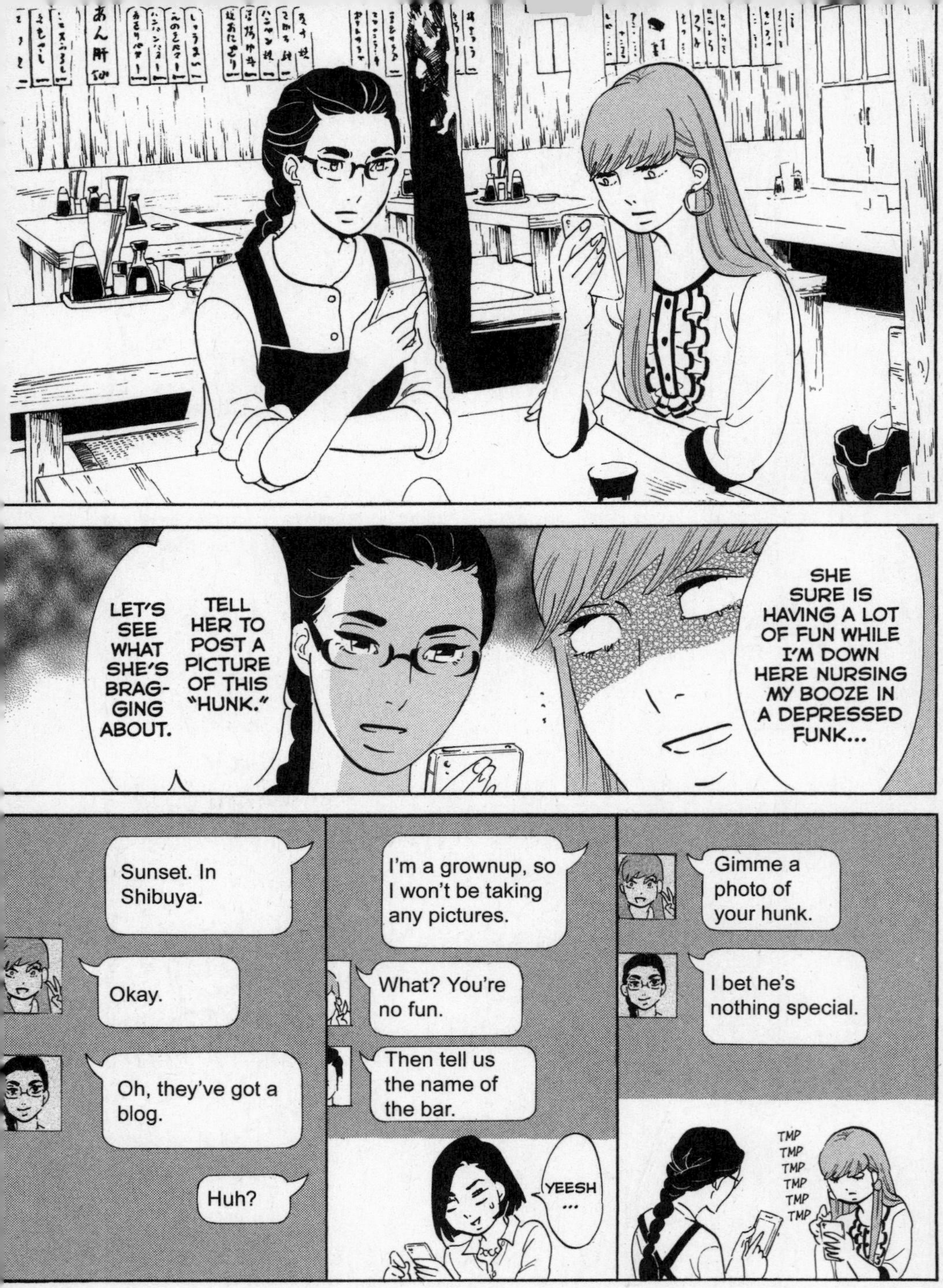
SHE SURE IS HAVING A LOT OF FUN WHILE I'M DOWN HERE NURSING MY BOOZE IN A DEPRESSED FUNK...
LET'S SEE WHAT SHE'S BRAG-GING ABOUT. TELL HER TO POST A PICTURE OF THIS "HUNK."
Gimme a photo of your hunk.
I bet he's nothing special.
TMP
TMP
TMP
TMP
TMP
TMP
I'm a grownup, so I won't be taking any pictures.
What? You're no fun.
Then tell us the name of the bar.
YEESH...
Sunset. In Shibuya.
Okay.
Oh, they've got a blog.
Huh?

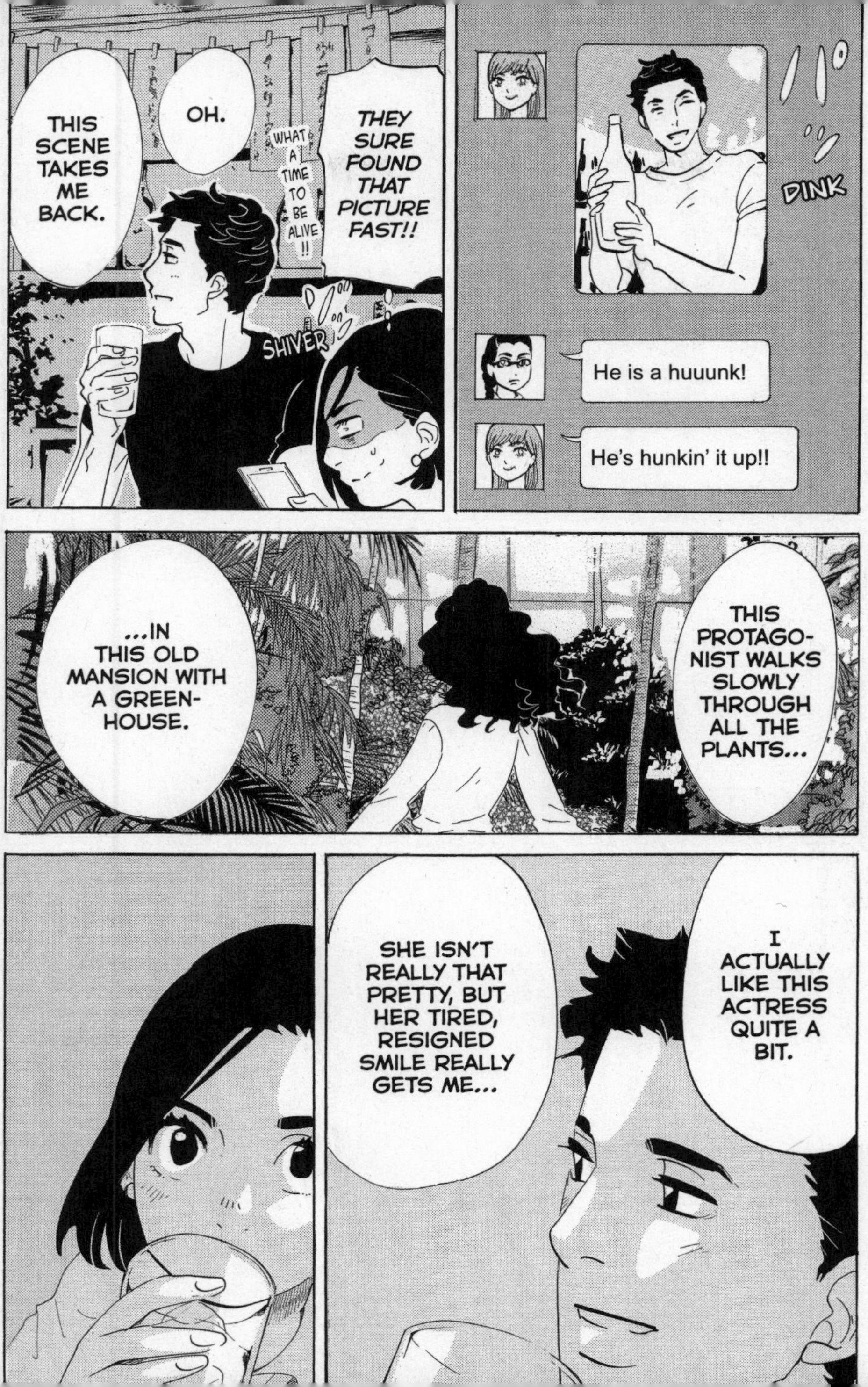
DINK
He is a huuunk!
He's hunkin' it up!!
THEY SURE FOUND THAT PICTURE FAST!!
WHAT A TIME TO BE ALIVE!!
OH.
THIS SCENE TAKES ME BACK.
SHIVER
THIS PROTAGO-NIST WALKS SLOWLY THROUGH ALL THE PLANTS...
...IN THIS OLD MANSION WITH A GREEN-HOUSE.
I ACTUALLY LIKE THIS ACTRESS QUITE A BIT.
SHE ISN'T REALLY THAT PRETTY, BUT HER TIRED, RESIGNED SMILE REALLY GETS ME...

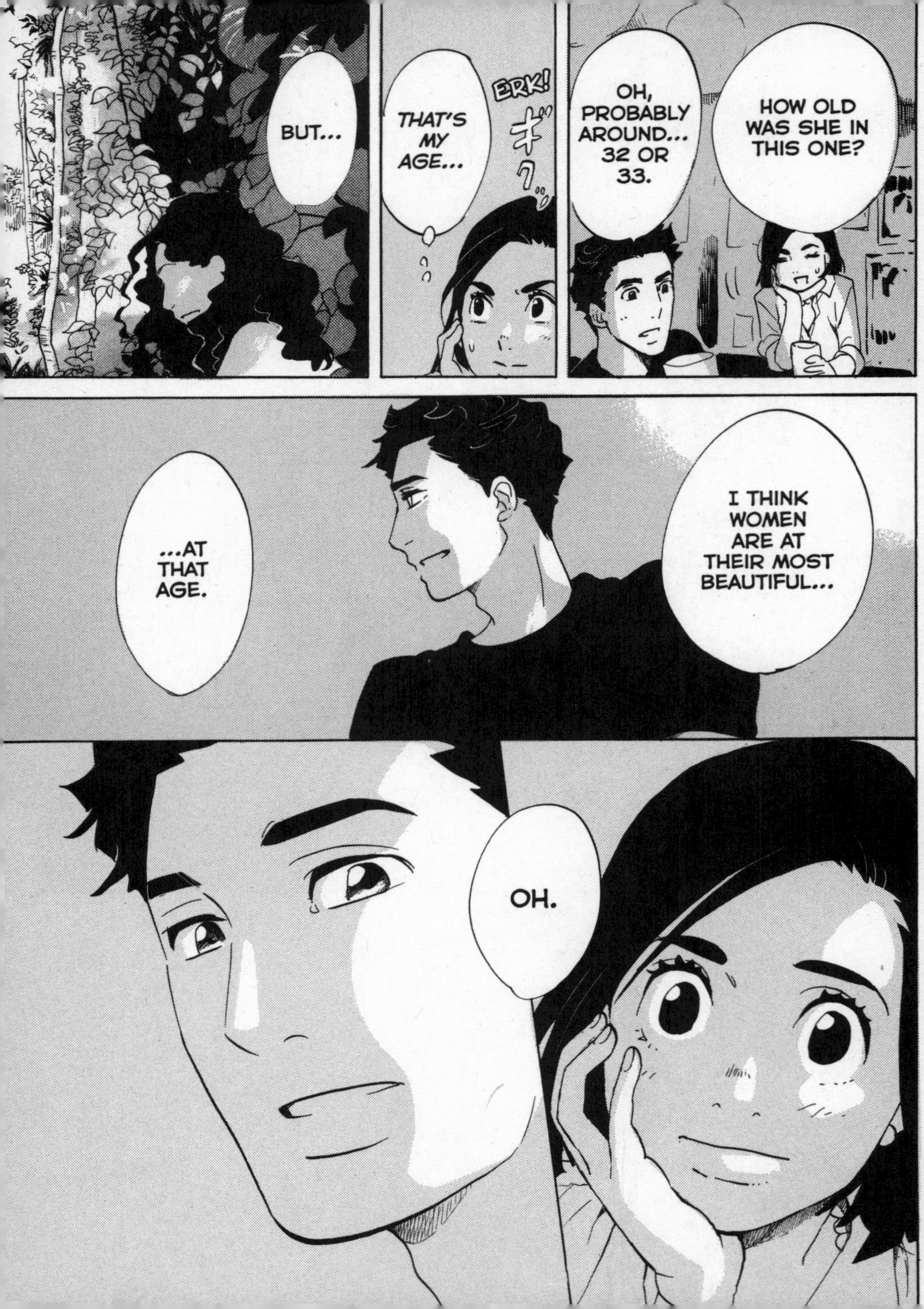
HOW OLD WAS SHE IN THIS ONE?
OH, PROBABLY AROUND... 32 OR 33.
ERK!
ギク
THAT'S MY AGE...
BUT...
I THINK WOMEN ARE AT THEIR MOST BEAUTIFUL...
...AT THAT AGE.
OH.

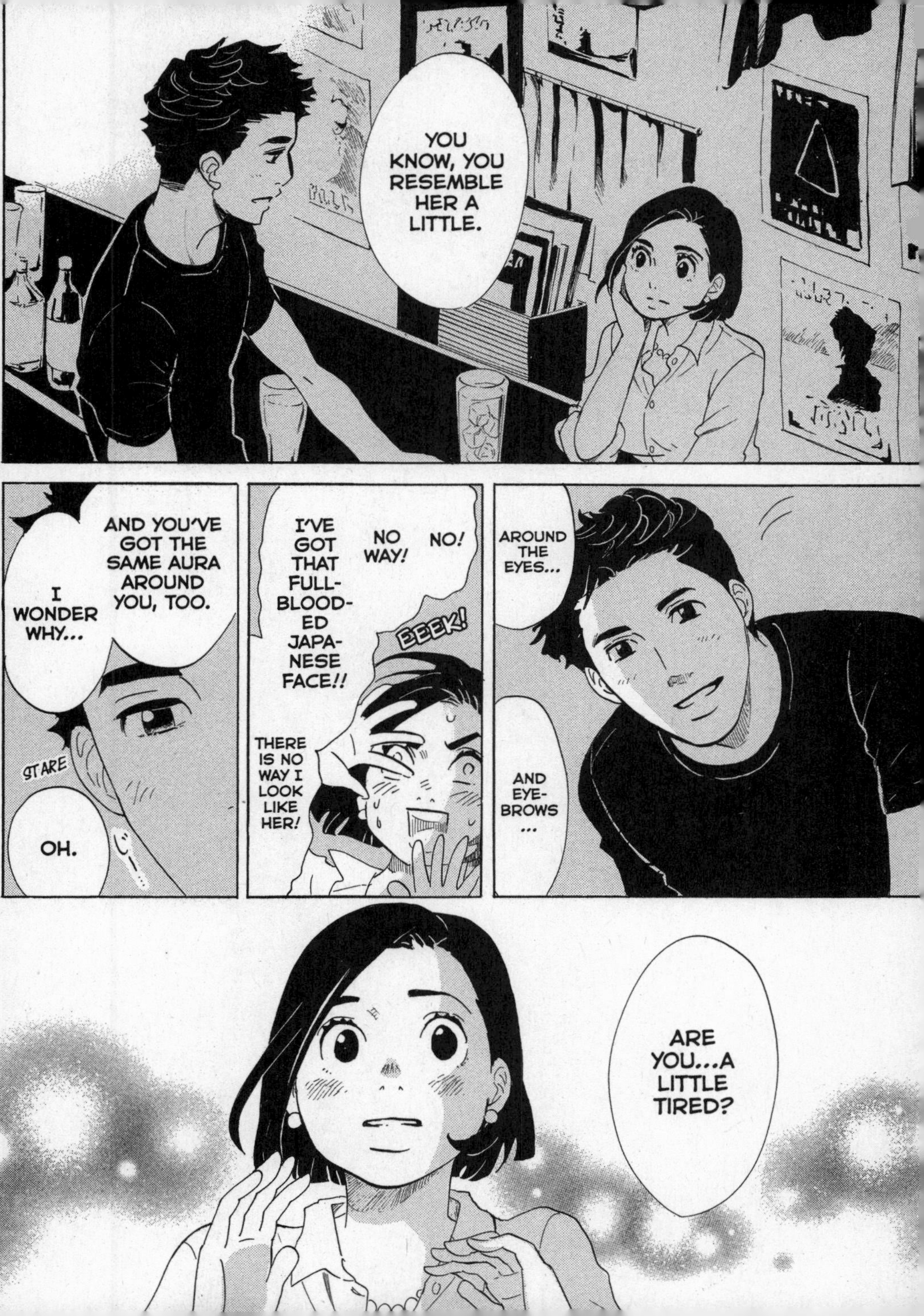
YOU KNOW, YOU RESEMBLE HER A LITTLE.
AROUND THE EYES...
AND EYE-BROWS...
NO!
NO WAY!
I'VE GOT THAT FULL-BLOODED JAPANESE FACE!!
EEEK!
THERE IS NO WAY I LOOK LIKE HER!
AND YOU'VE GOT THE SAME AURA AROUND YOU, TOO.
I WONDER WHY...
STARE
じー…
OH.
ARE YOU...A LITTLE TIRED?

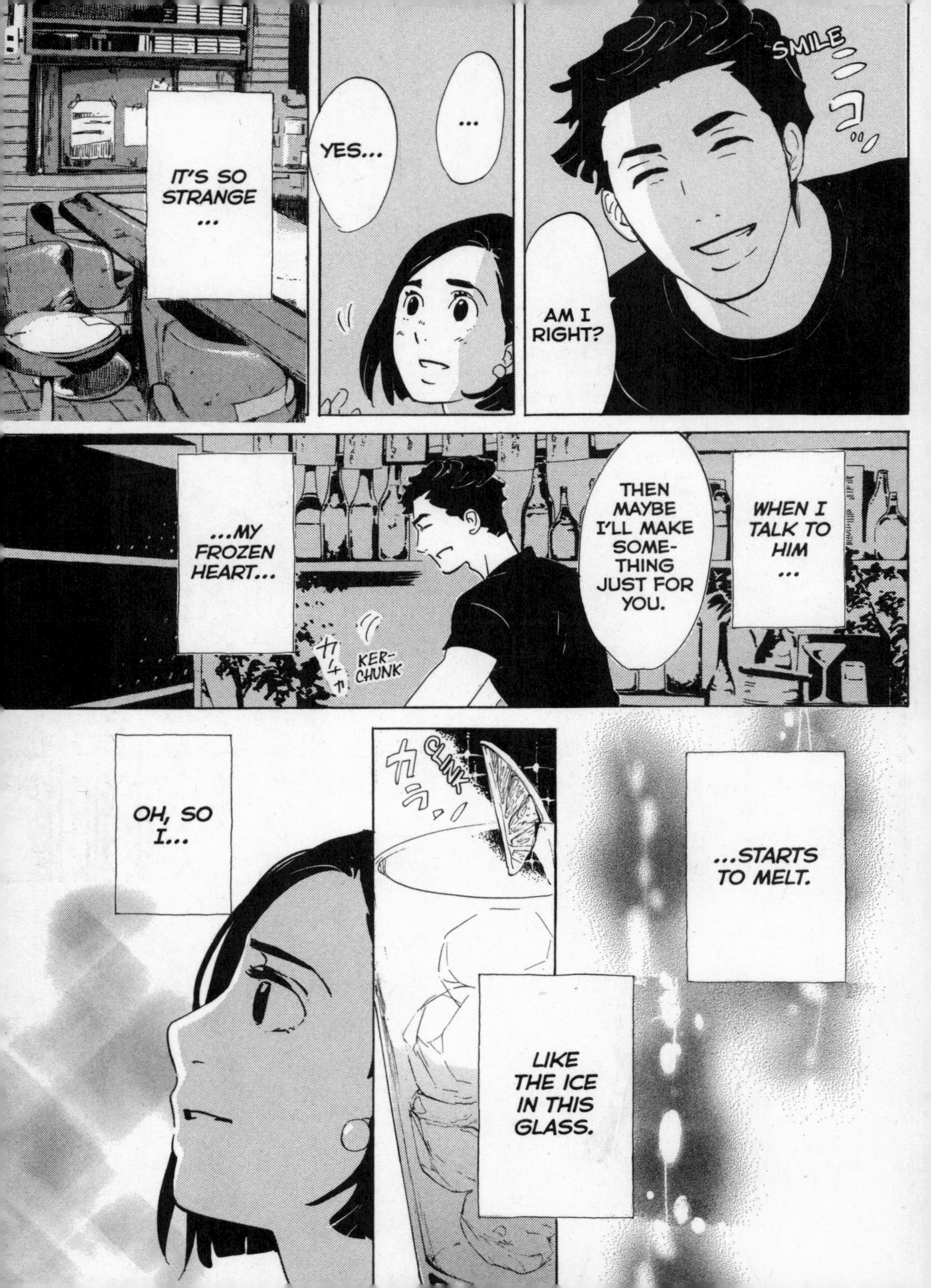
SMILE
AM I RIGHT?
...
YES...
IT'S SO STRANGE...
WHEN I TALK TO HIM...
THEN MAYBE I'LL MAKE SOMETHING JUST FOR YOU.
KER-CHUNK
...MY FROZEN HEART...
...STARTS TO MELT.
LIKE THE ICE IN THIS GLASS.
CLINK
OH, SO I...

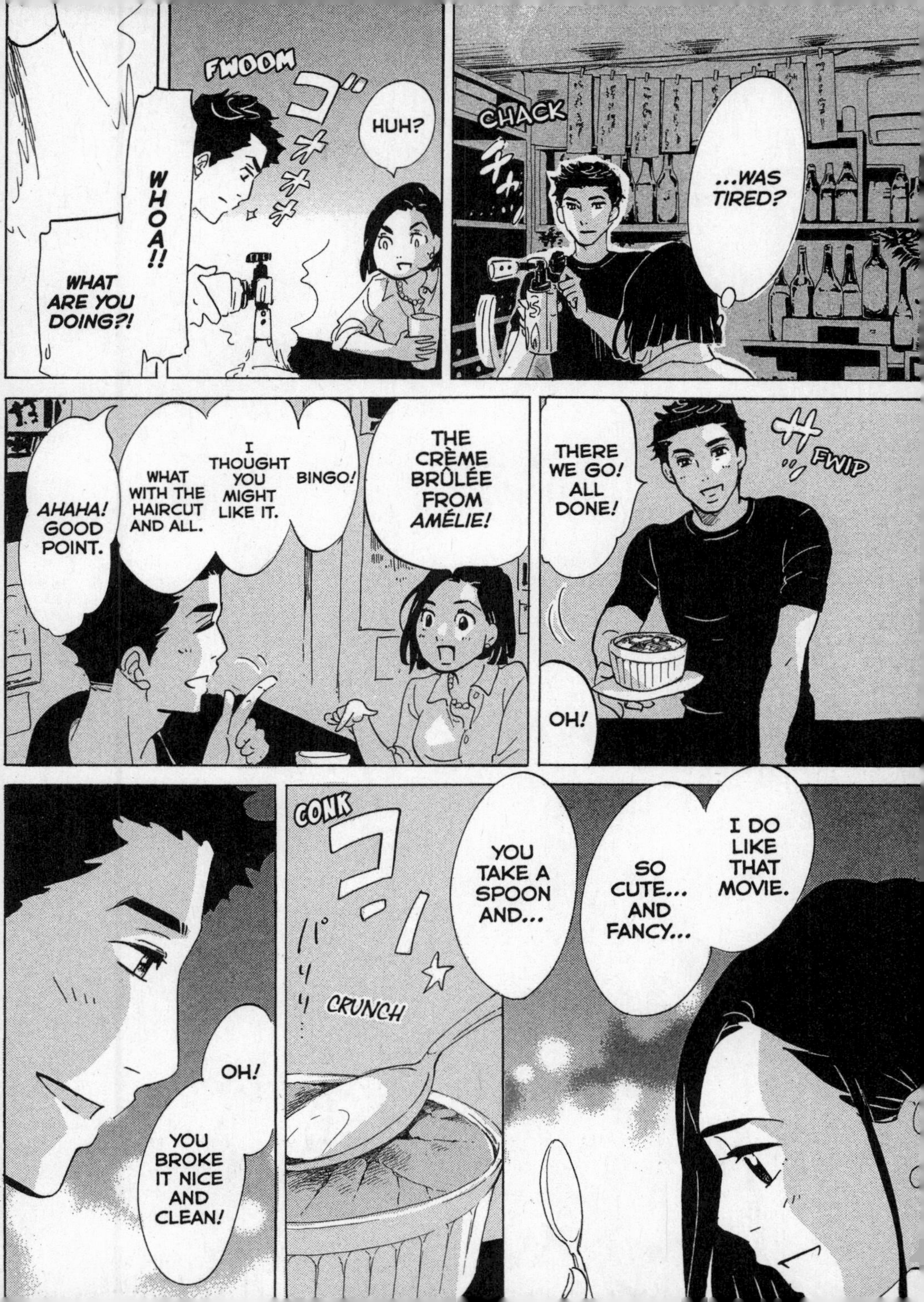
CHACK
...WAS TIRED?
HUH?
FWOOM
WHOA!!
WHAT ARE YOU DOING?!
FWIP
THERE WE GO! ALL DONE!
OH!
THE CRÈME BRÛLÉE FROM AMÉLIE!
BINGO!
I THOUGHT YOU MIGHT LIKE IT.
WHAT WITH THE HAIRCUT AND ALL.
AHAHA! GOOD POINT.
I DO LIKE THAT MOVIE.
SO CUTE... AND FANCY...
YOU TAKE A SPOON AND...
CONK
CRUNCH
OH!
YOU BROKE IT NICE AND CLEAN!

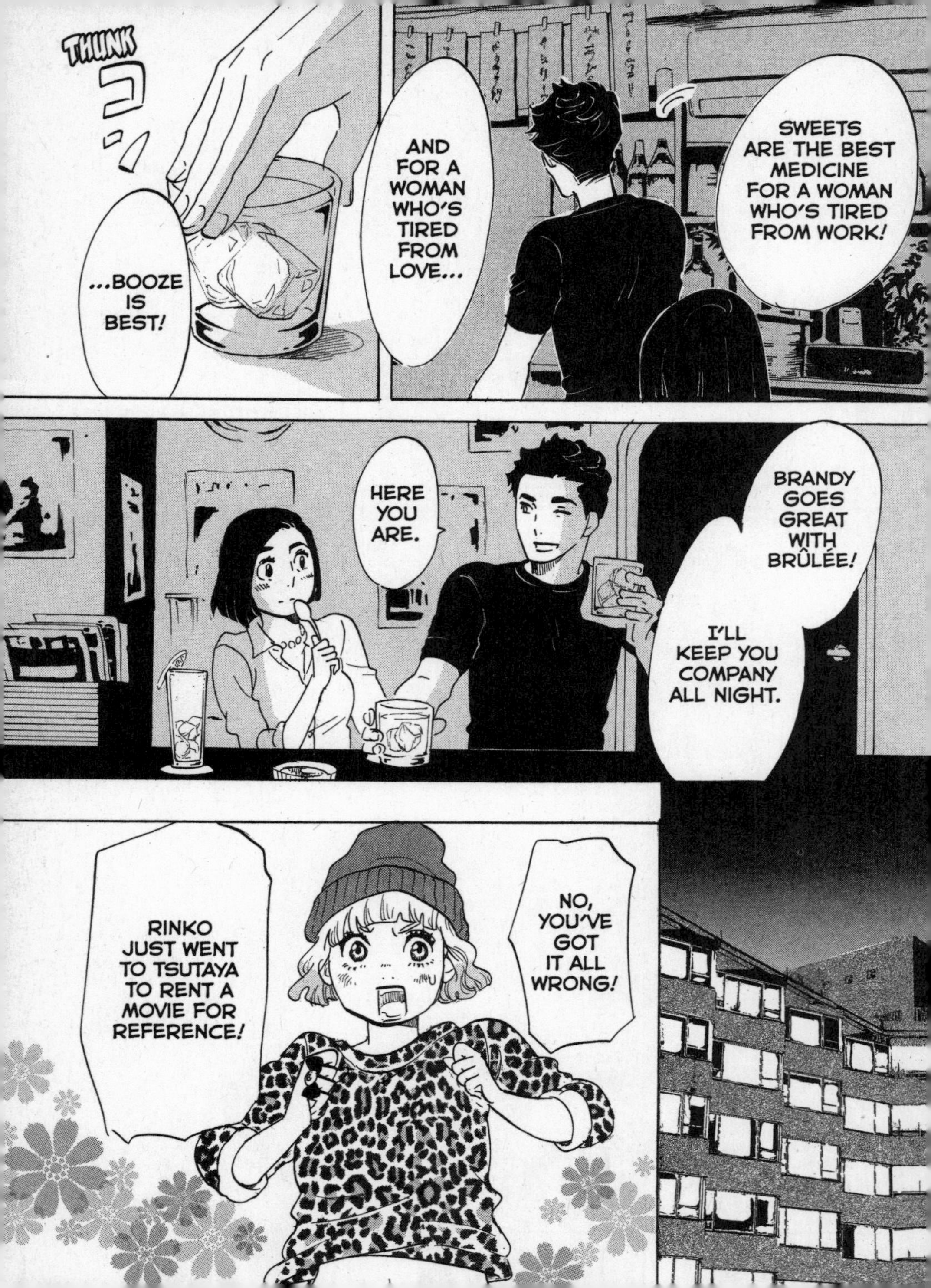
SWEETS ARE THE BEST MEDICINE FOR A WOMAN WHO'S TIRED FROM WORK!
AND FOR A WOMAN WHO'S TIRED FROM LOVE...
THUNK
...BOOZE IS BEST!
BRANDY GOES GREAT WITH BRÛLÉE!
I'LL KEEP YOU COMPANY ALL NIGHT.
HERE YOU ARE.
NO, YOU'VE GOT IT ALL WRONG!
RINKO JUST WENT TO TSUTAYA TO RENT A MOVIE FOR REFERENCE!

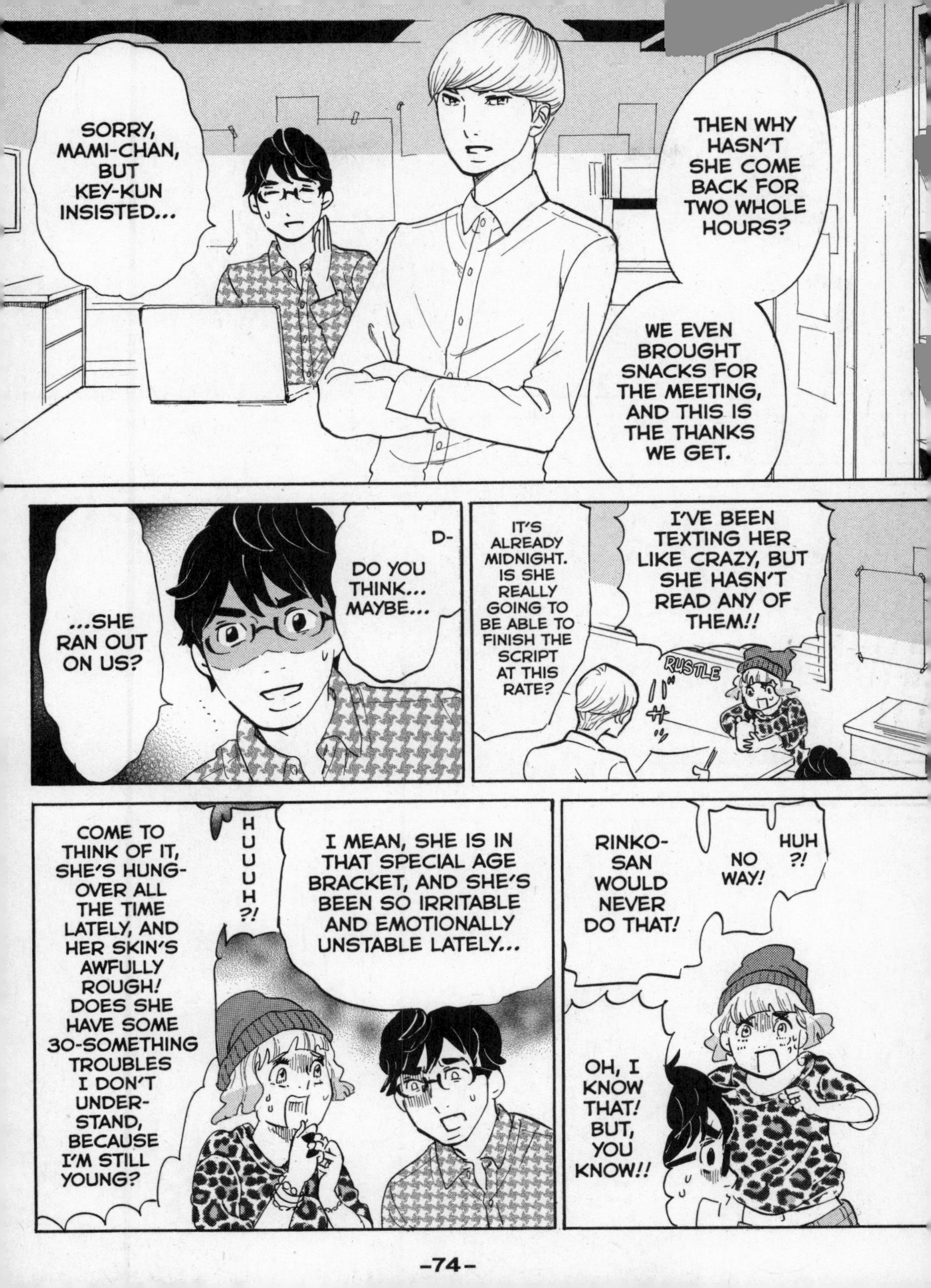
THEN WHY HASN'T SHE COME BACK FOR TWO WHOLE HOURS?
WE EVEN BROUGHT SNACKS FOR THE MEETING, AND THIS IS THE THANKS WE GET.
SORRY, MAMI-CHAN, BUT KEY-KUN INSISTED...
I'VE BEEN TEXTING HER LIKE CRAZY, BUT SHE HASN'T READ ANY OF THEM!!
IT'S ALREADY MIDNIGHT. IS SHE REALLY GOING TO BE ABLE TO FINISH THE SCRIPT AT THIS RATE?
RUSTLE
D-
DO YOU THINK... MAYBE...
...SHE RAN OUT ON US?
HUH ?!
NO WAY!
RINKO-SAN WOULD NEVER DO THAT!
OH, I KNOW THAT! BUT, YOU KNOW!!
HUUUUH?!
I MEAN, SHE IS IN THAT SPECIAL AGE BRACKET, AND SHE'S BEEN SO IRRITABLE AND EMOTIONALLY UNSTABLE LATELY...
COME TO THINK OF IT, SHE'S HUNG-OVER ALL THE TIME LATELY, AND HER SKIN'S AWFULLY ROUGH! DOES SHE HAVE SOME 30-SOMETHING TROUBLES I DON'T UNDER-STAND, BECAUSE I'M STILL YOUNG?

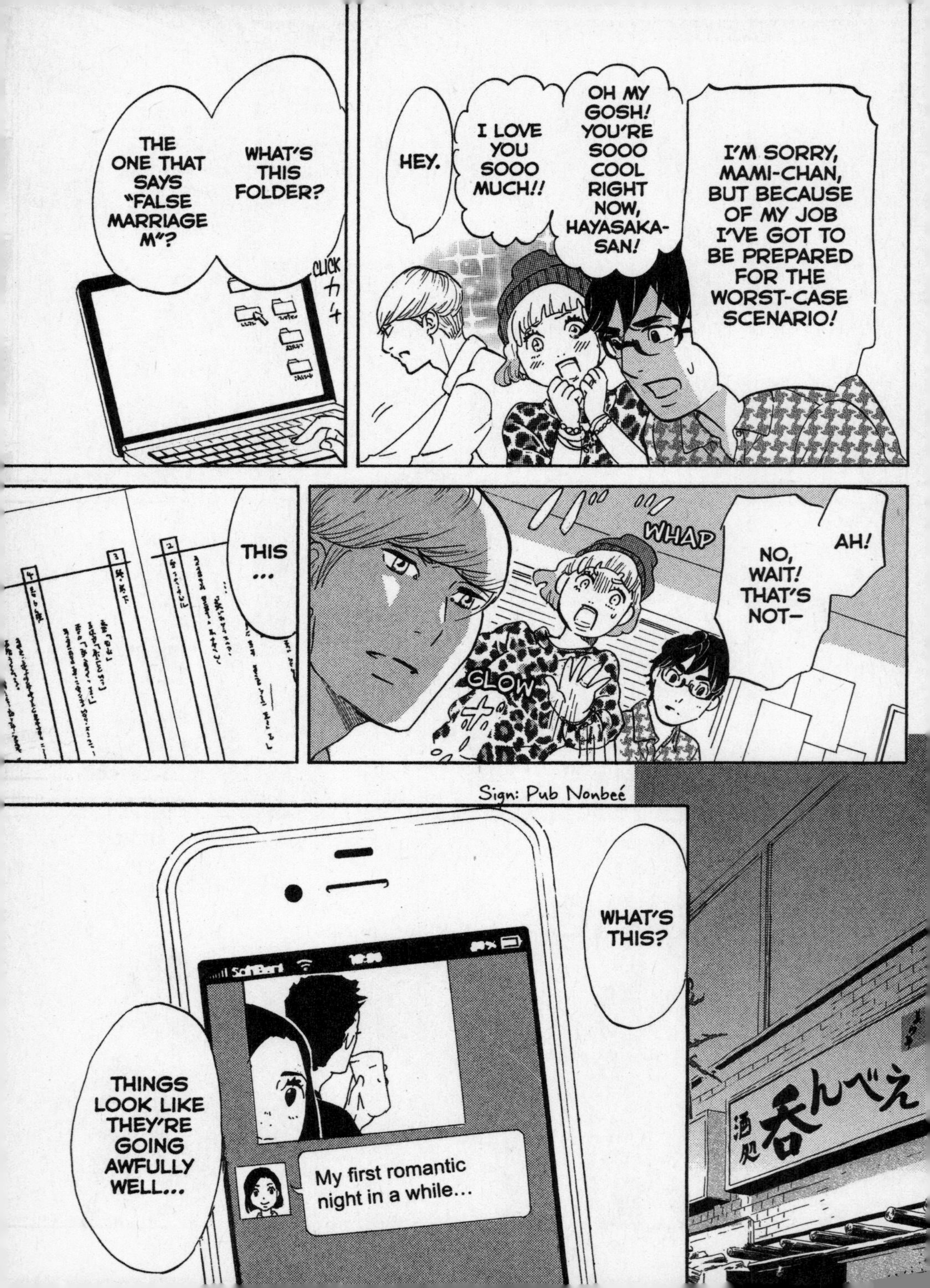
I'M SORRY, MAMI-CHAN, BUT BECAUSE OF MY JOB I'VE GOT TO BE PREPARED FOR THE WORST-CASE SCENARIO!
OH MY GOSH! YOU'RE SOOO COOL RIGHT NOW, HAYASAKA-SAN!
I LOVE YOU SOOO MUCH!!
HEY.
WHAT'S THIS FOLDER?
THE ONE THAT SAYS "FALSE MARRIAGE M"?
CLICK
AH!
NO, WAIT! THAT'S NOT–
WHAP
GLOW
THIS...
Sign: Pub Nonbeé
WHAT'S THIS?
THINGS LOOK LIKE THEY'RE GOING AWFULLY WELL...
My first romantic night in a while...

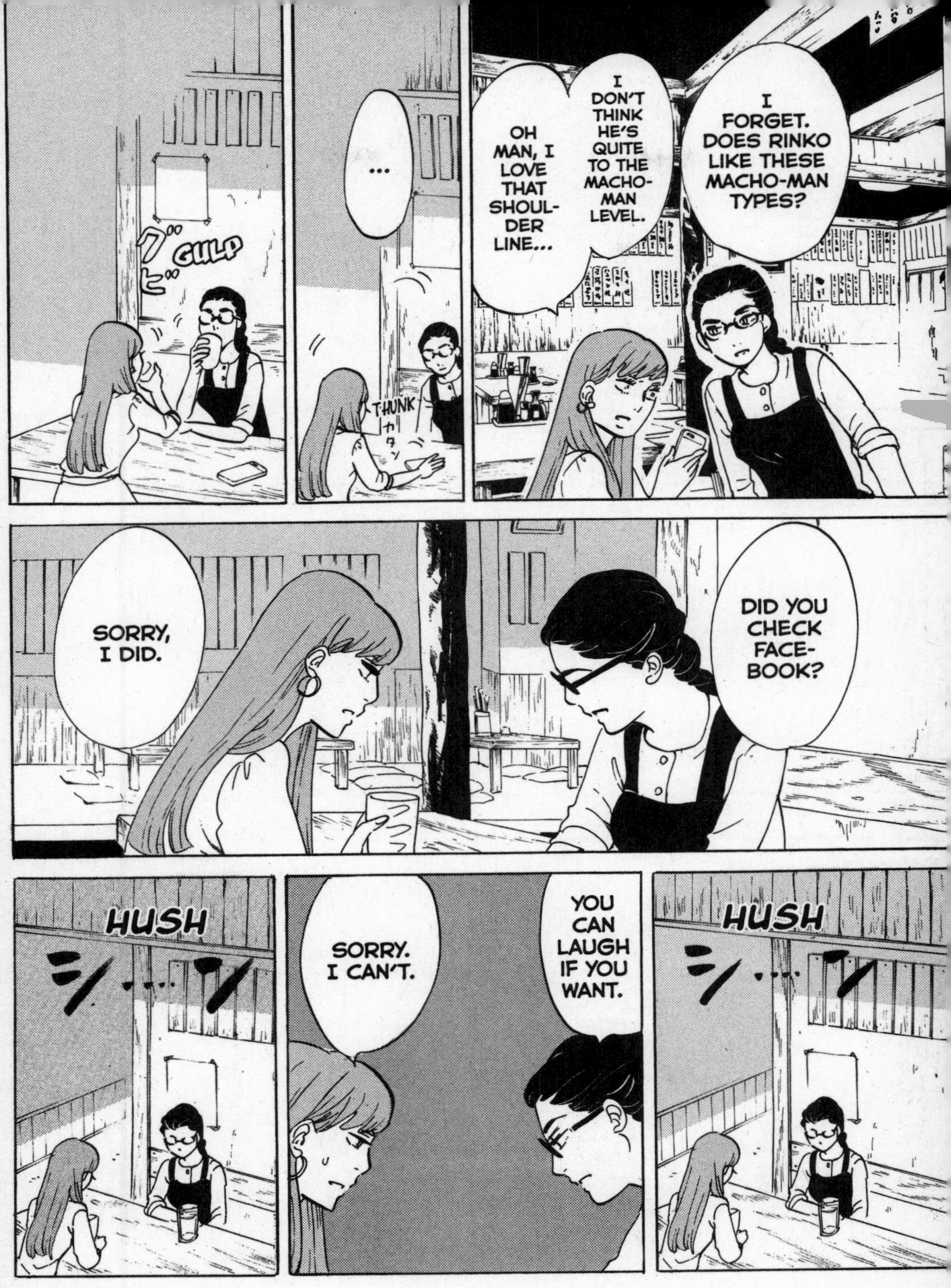
I FORGET. DOES RINKO LIKE THESE MACHO-MAN TYPES?
I DON'T THINK HE'S QUITE TO THE MACHO-MAN LEVEL.
OH MAN, I LOVE THAT SHOULDER LINE...
...
THUNK
カタン
GULP
DID YOU CHECK FACE-BOOK?
SORRY, I DID.
HUSH
YOU CAN LAUGH IF YOU WANT.
SORRY. I CAN'T.
HUSH

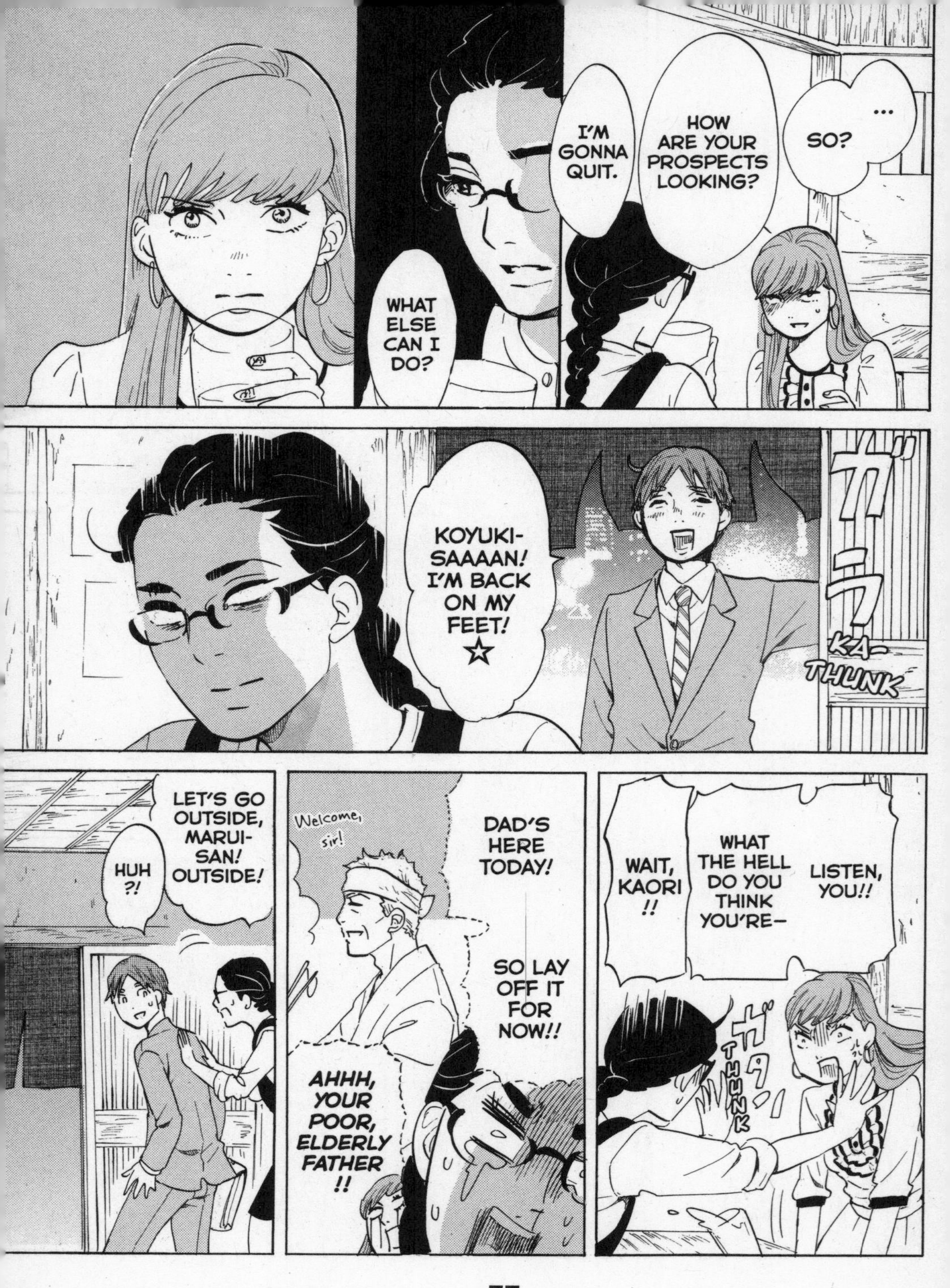
... SO?
HOW ARE YOUR PROSPECTS LOOKING?
I'M GONNA QUIT.
WHAT ELSE CAN I DO?
ガラ
KA-THUNK
KOYUKI-SAAAAN! I'M BACK ON MY FEET! ☆
LISTEN, YOU!!
WHAT THE HELL DO YOU THINK YOU'RE—
WAIT, KAORI !!
ガタ
THUNK
DAD'S HERE TODAY!
SO LAY OFF IT FOR NOW!!
Welcome, sir!
AHHH, YOUR POOR, ELDERLY FATHER !!
LET'S GO OUTSIDE, MARUI-SAN! OUTSIDE!
HUH ?!

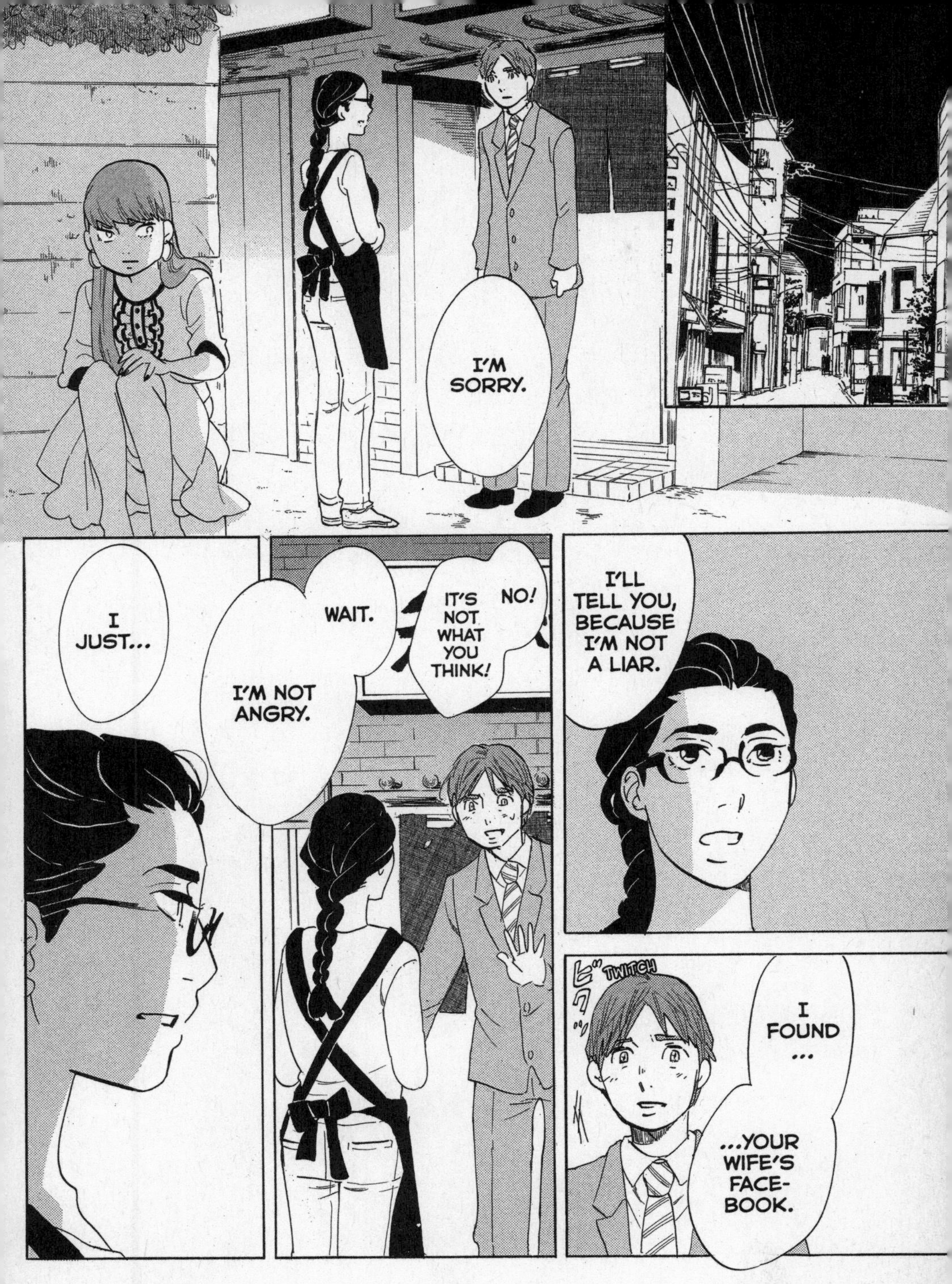
I'M SORRY.
I'LL TELL YOU, BECAUSE I'M NOT A LIAR.
ビクッ
TWITCH
I FOUND ...
...YOUR WIFE'S FACE-BOOK.
NO!
IT'S NOT WHAT YOU THINK!
WAIT.
I'M NOT ANGRY.
I JUST...

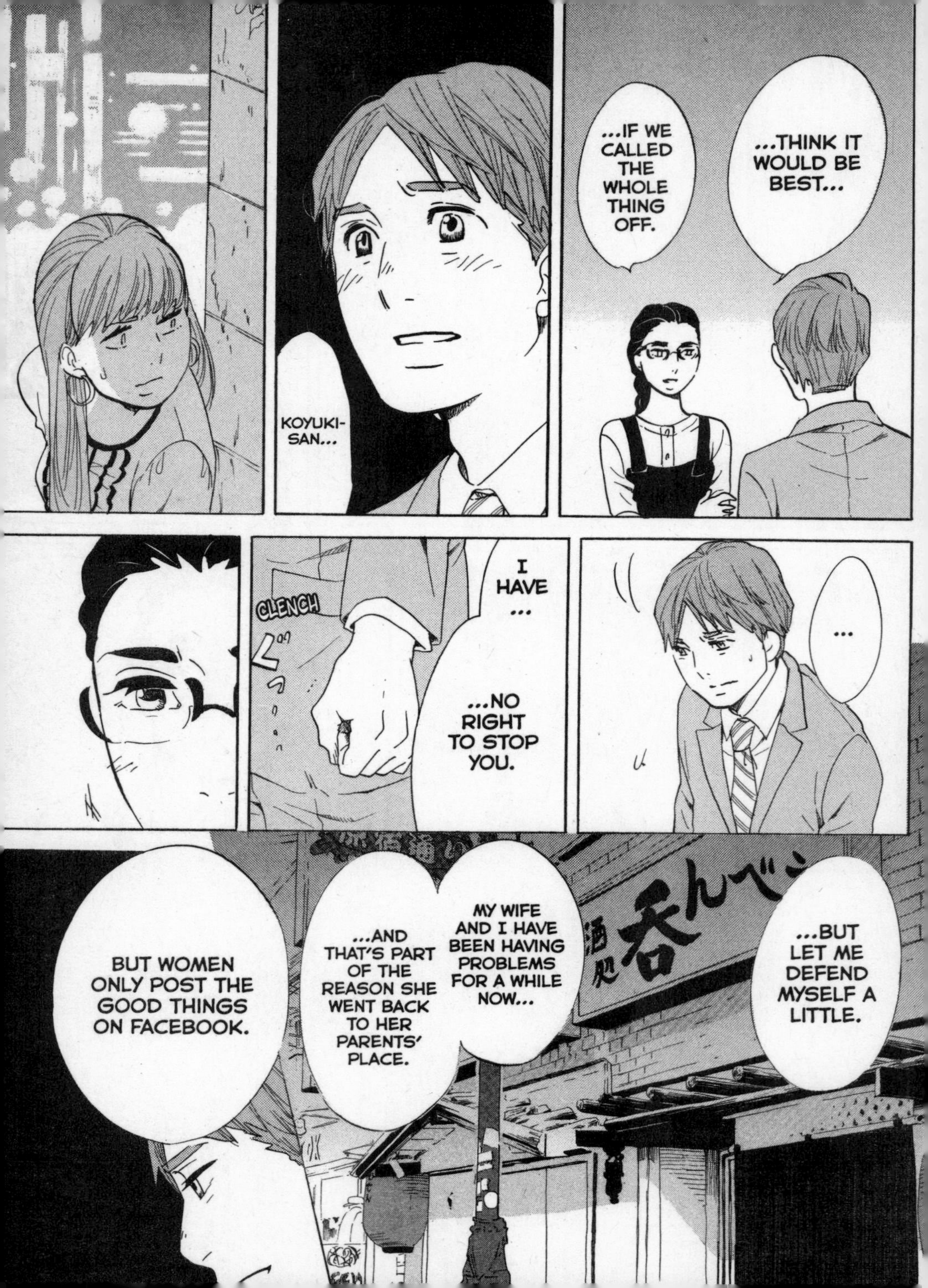
...THINK IT WOULD BE BEST...
...IF WE CALLED THE WHOLE THING OFF.
KOYUKI-SAN...
...
I HAVE...
...NO RIGHT TO STOP YOU.
CLENCH
...BUT LET ME DEFEND MYSELF A LITTLE.
MY WIFE AND I HAVE BEEN HAVING PROBLEMS FOR A WHILE NOW...
...AND THAT'S PART OF THE REASON SHE WENT BACK TO HER PARENTS' PLACE.
BUT WOMEN ONLY POST THE GOOD THINGS ON FACEBOOK.

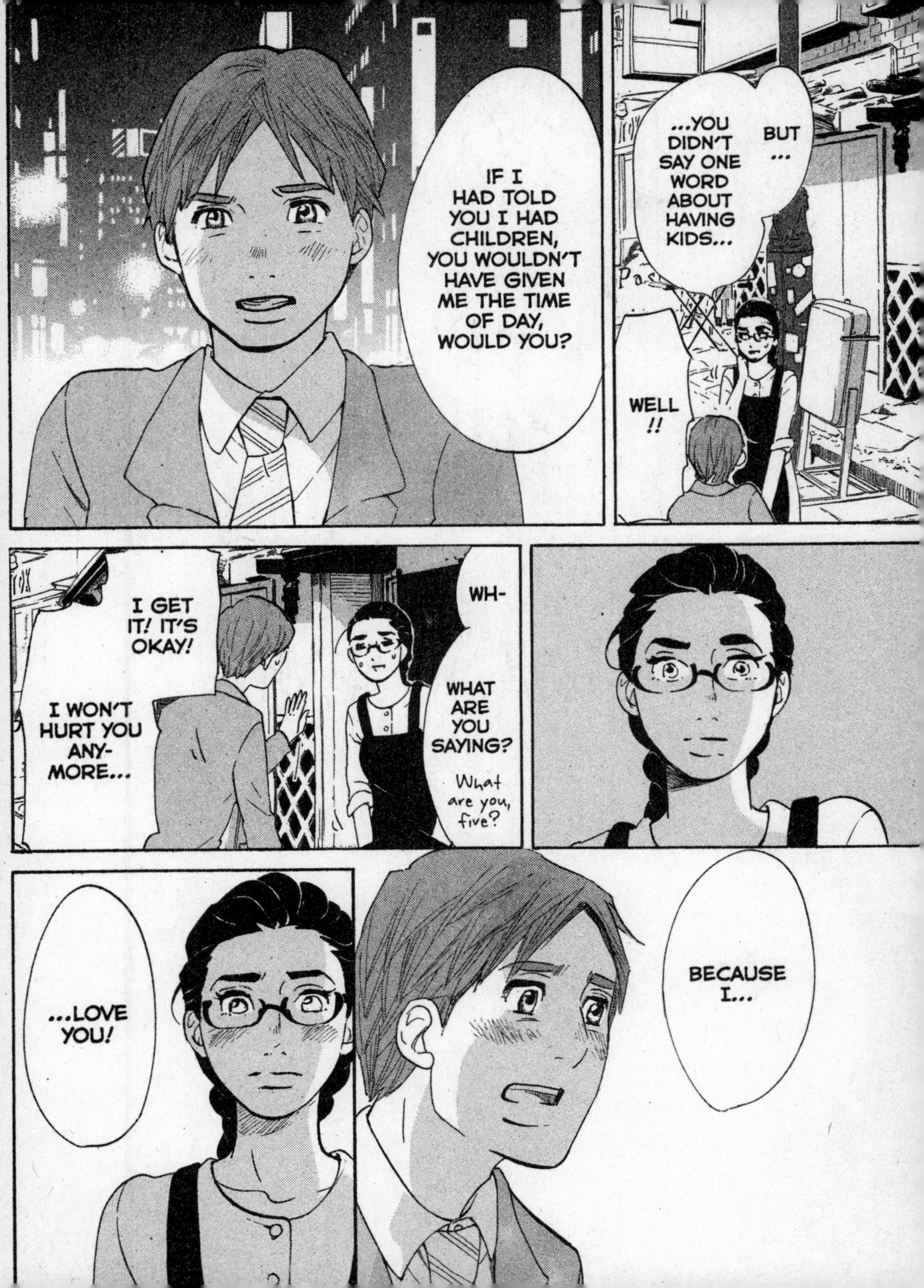
BUT ...
...YOU DIDN'T SAY ONE WORD ABOUT HAVING KIDS...
WELL !!
IF I HAD TOLD YOU I HAD CHILDREN, YOU WOULDN'T HAVE GIVEN ME THE TIME OF DAY, WOULD YOU?
WH-
WHAT ARE YOU SAYING?
What are you, five?
I GET IT! IT'S OKAY!
I WON'T HURT YOU ANY-MORE...
BECAUSE I...
...LOVE YOU!

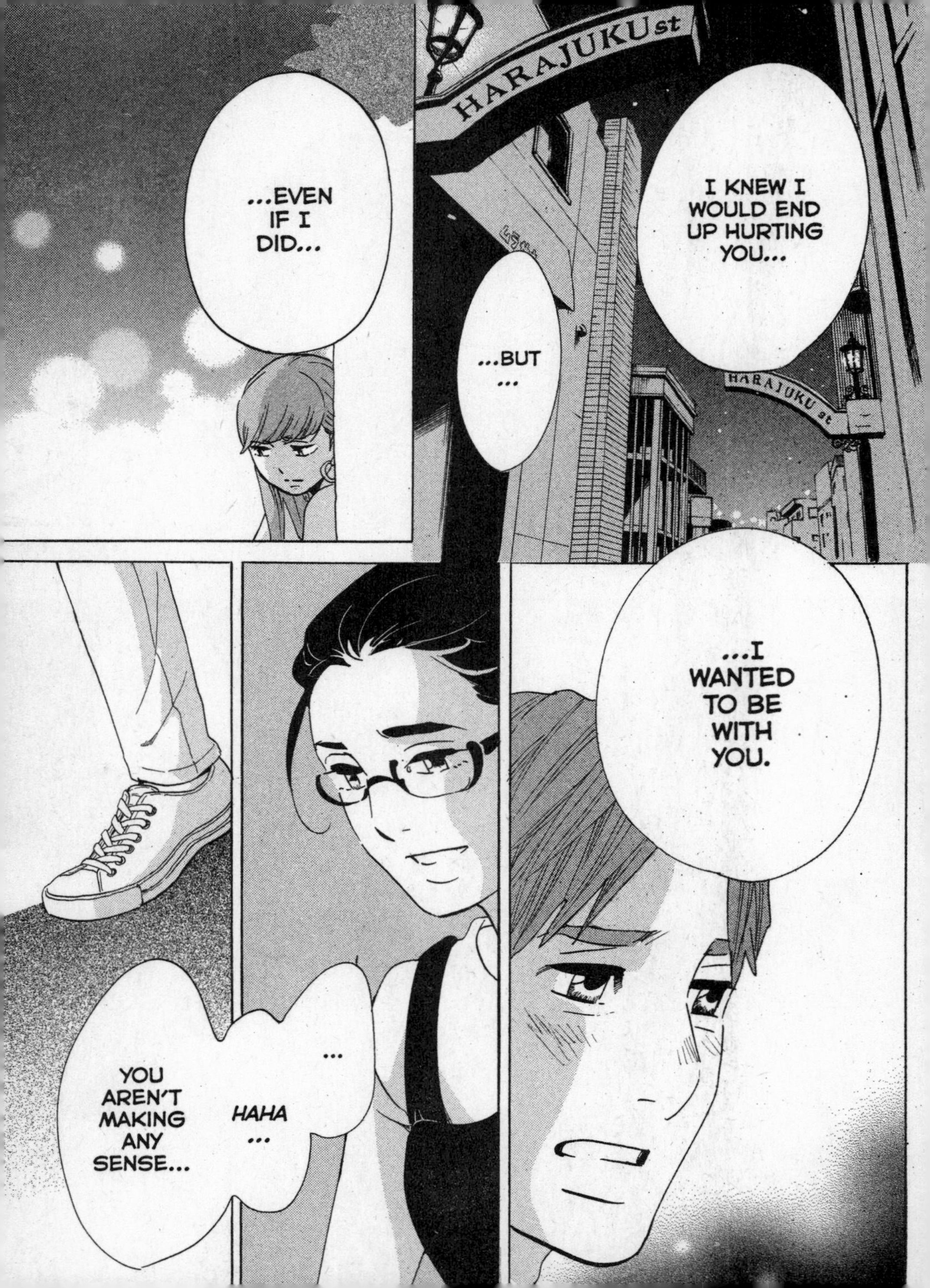
HARAJUKU st
I KNEW I WOULD END UP HURTING YOU...
...BUT ...
HARAJUKU st
...EVEN IF I DID...
...I WANTED TO BE WITH YOU.
...
HAHA ...
YOU AREN'T MAKING ANY SENSE...

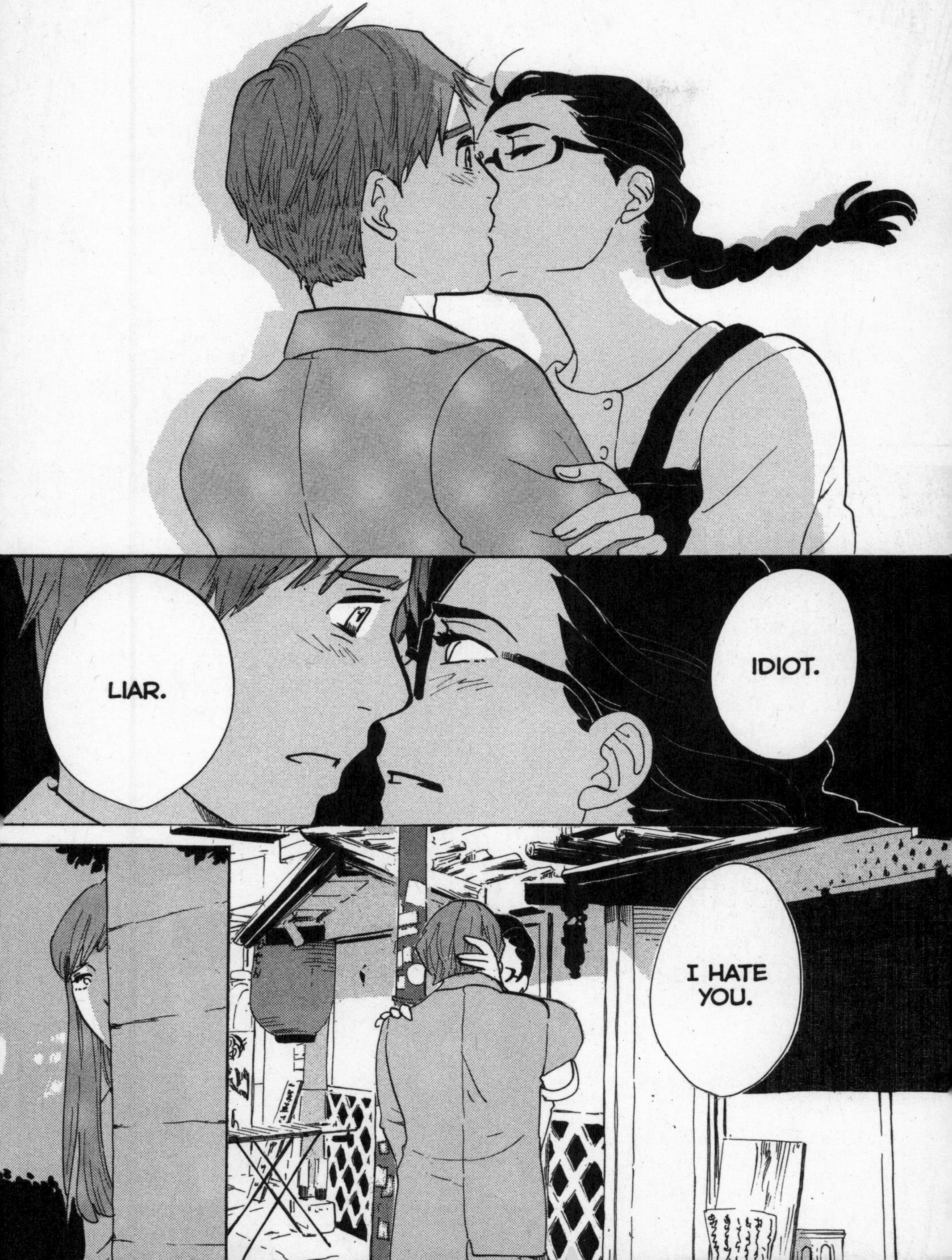
IDIOT.
LIAR.
I HATE YOU.

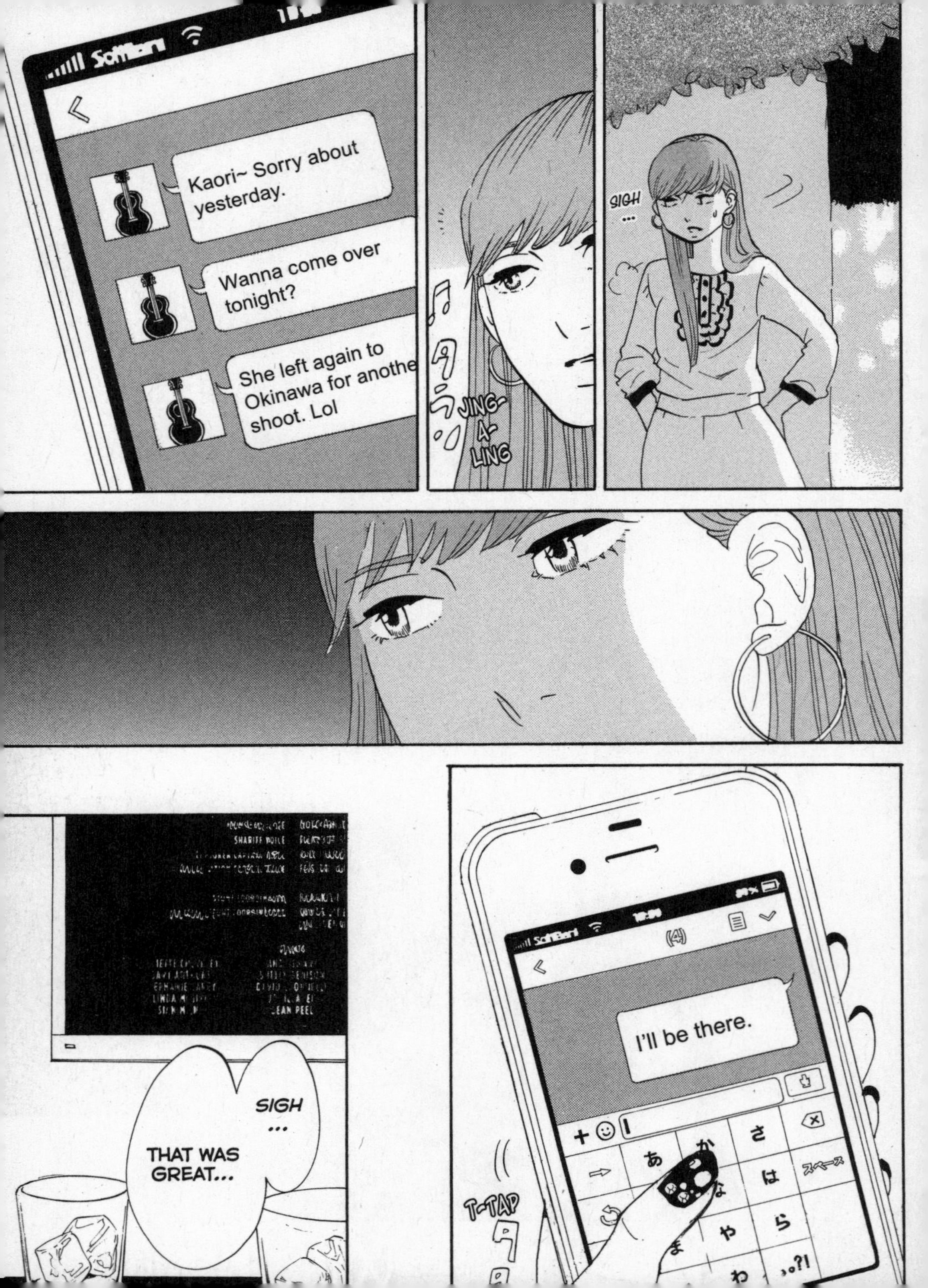
SIGH ...
JING-A-LING
Kaori~ Sorry about yesterday.
Wanna come over tonight?
She left again to Okinawa for anothe
shoot. Lol
I'll be there.
T-TAP
SIGH ...
THAT WAS GREAT...

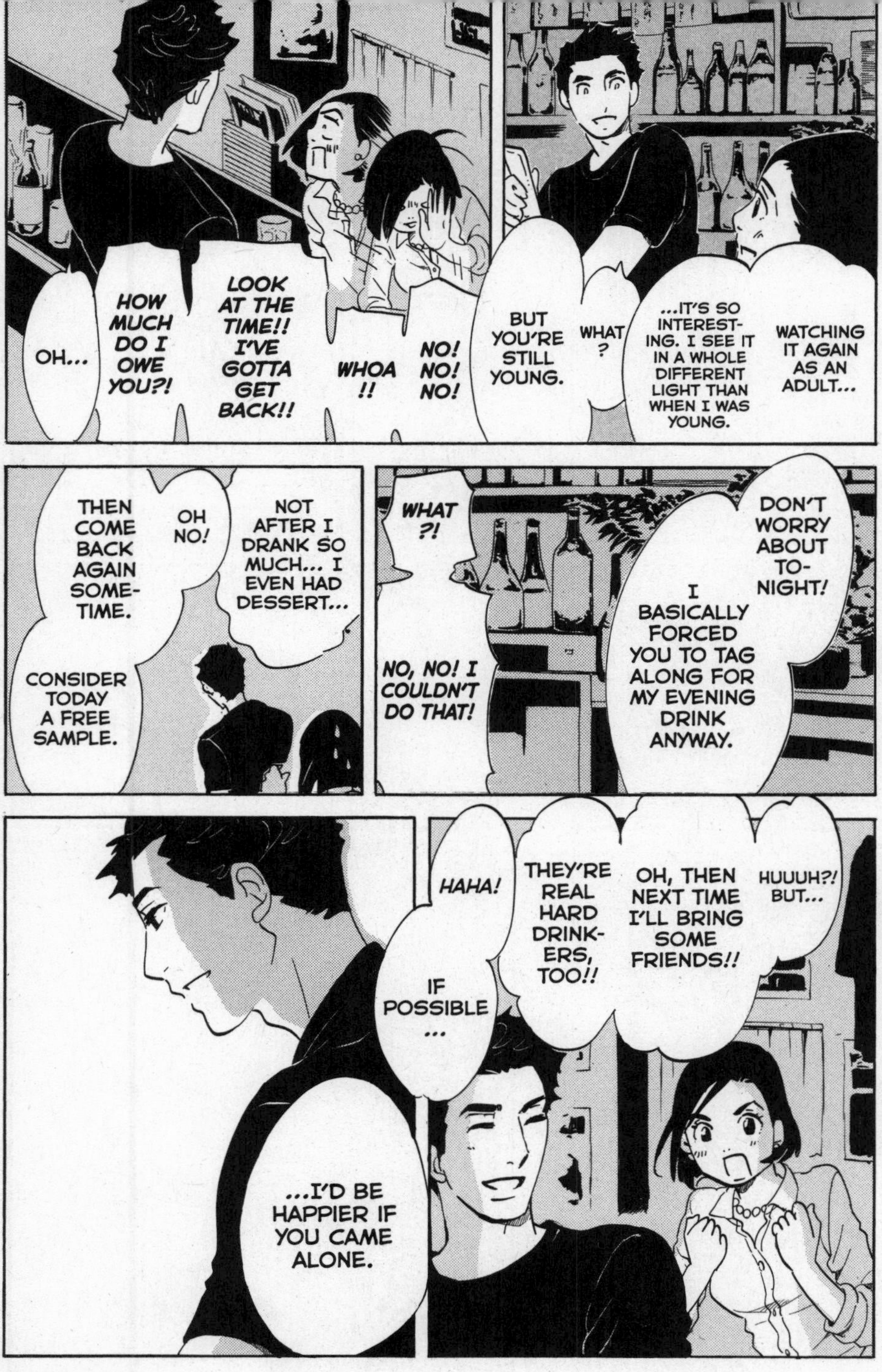
WATCHING IT AGAIN AS AN ADULT...
...IT'S SO INTEREST-ING. I SEE IT IN A WHOLE DIFFERENT LIGHT THAN WHEN I WAS YOUNG.
WHAT?
BUT YOU'RE STILL YOUNG.
NO! NO! NO!
WHOA!!
LOOK AT THE TIME!! I'VE GOTTA GET BACK!!
HOW MUCH DO I OWE YOU?!
OH...
DON'T WORRY ABOUT TO-NIGHT!
I BASICALLY FORCED YOU TO TAG ALONG FOR MY EVENING DRINK ANYWAY.
WHAT?!
NO, NO! I COULDN'T DO THAT!
NOT AFTER I DRANK SO MUCH... I EVEN HAD DESSERT...
OH NO!
THEN COME BACK AGAIN SOME-TIME.
CONSIDER TODAY A FREE SAMPLE.
HUUUH?! BUT...
OH, THEN NEXT TIME I'LL BRING SOME FRIENDS!!
THEY'RE REAL HARD DRINK-ERS, TOO!!
HAHA!
IF POSSIBLE...
...I'D BE HAPPIER IF YOU CAME ALONE.

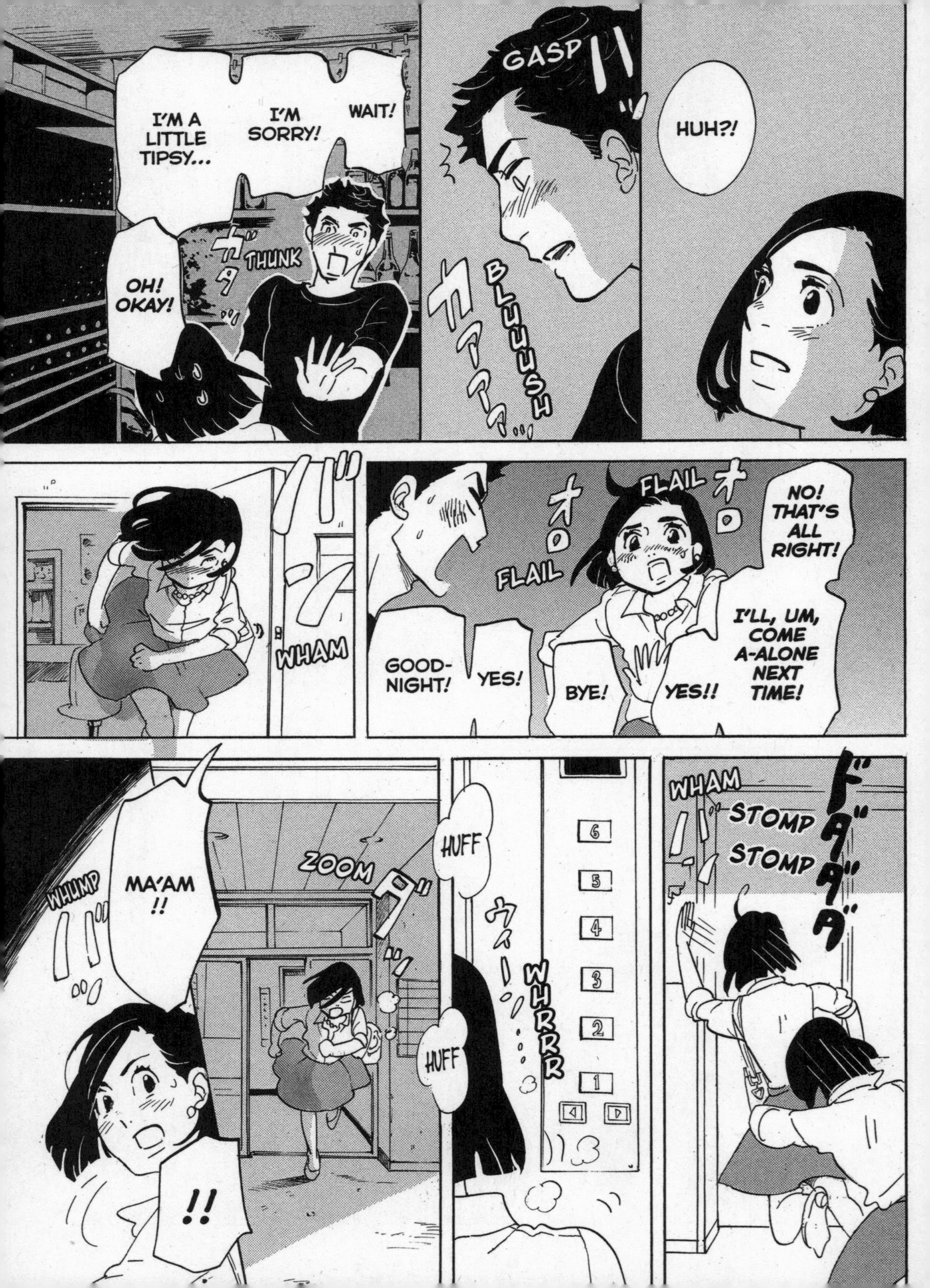
HUH?!
GASP
BLUUUSH
WAIT!
I'M SORRY!
I'M A LITTLE TIPSY...
THUNK
OH! OKAY!
FLAIL
NO! THAT'S ALL RIGHT!
FLAIL
I'LL, UM, COME A-ALONE NEXT TIME!
YES!!
BYE!
YES!
GOOD-NIGHT!
WHAM
WHAM
STOMP
STOMP
HUFF
HUFF
WHRRR
MA'AM !!
ZOOM
WHUMP
!!

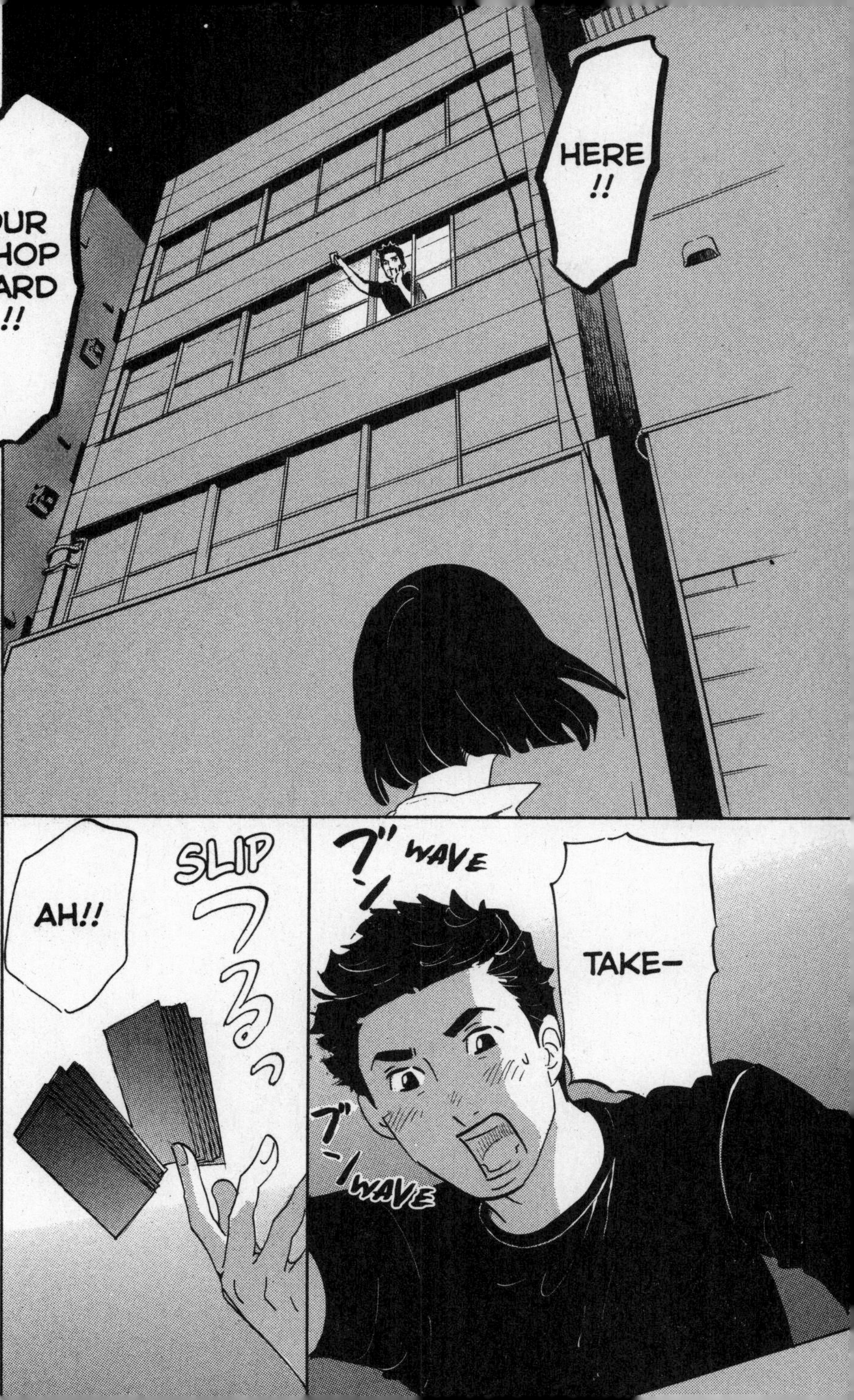
HERE!!
OUR SHOP CARD!!
WAVE
TAKE-
WAVE
SLIP
つるっ
AH!!

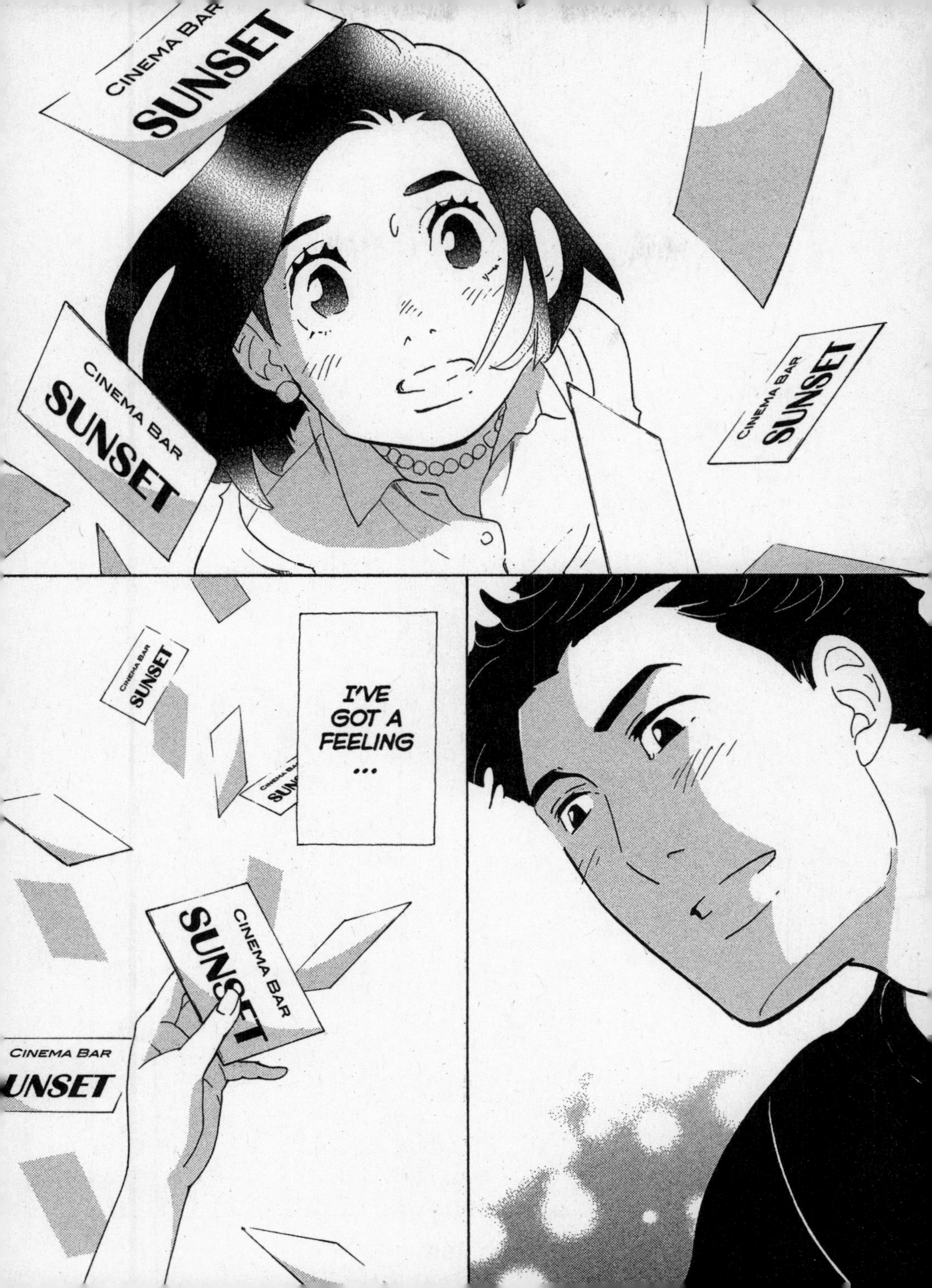
CINEMA BAR
SUNSET
CINEMA BAR
SUNSET
CINEMA BAR
SUNSET
I'VE GOT A FEELING ...
CINEMA BAR
SUNSET
CINEMA BAR
SUNSET

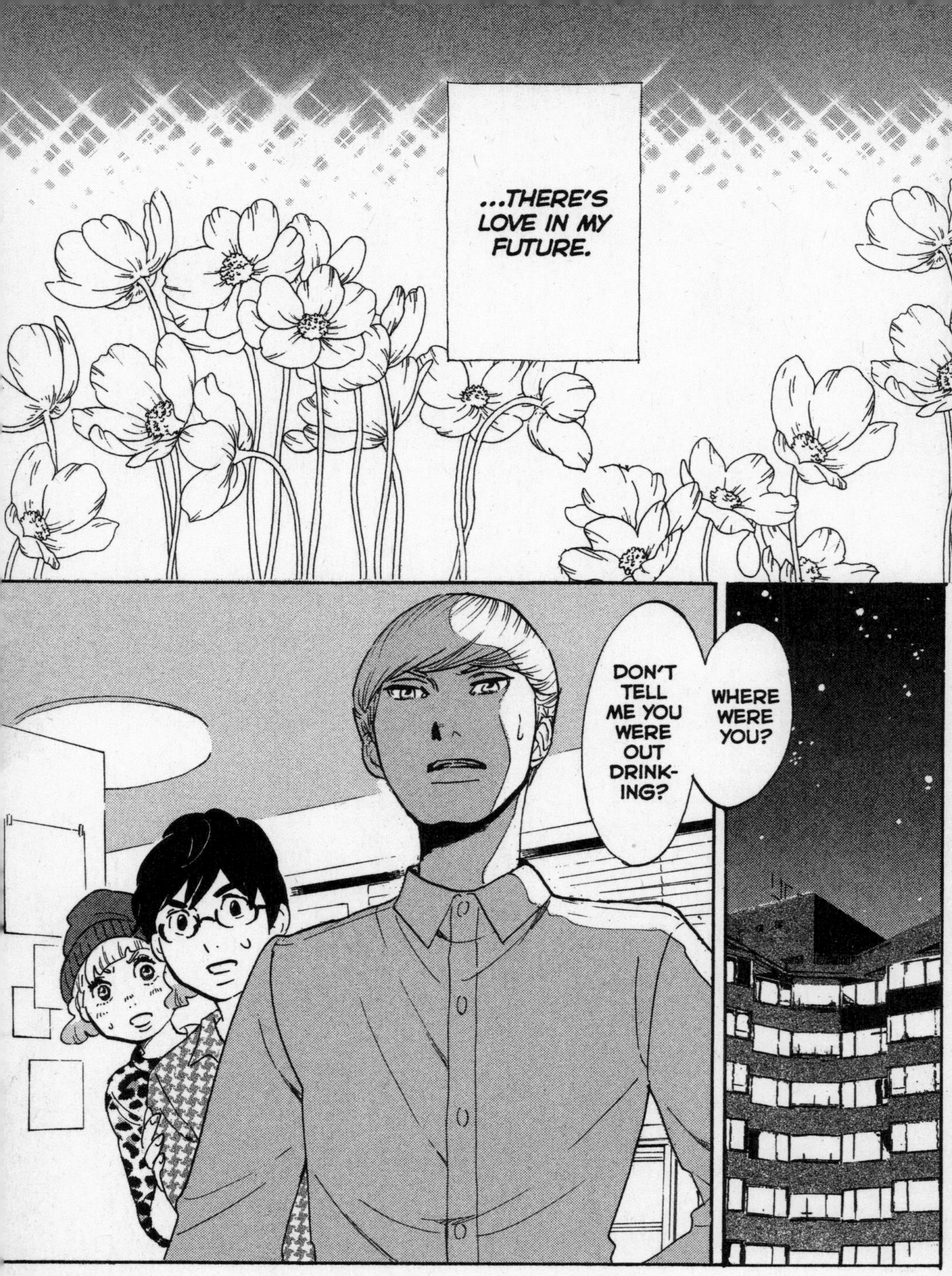
...THERE'S LOVE IN MY FUTURE.
WHERE WERE YOU?
DON'T TELL ME YOU WERE OUT DRINK-ING?

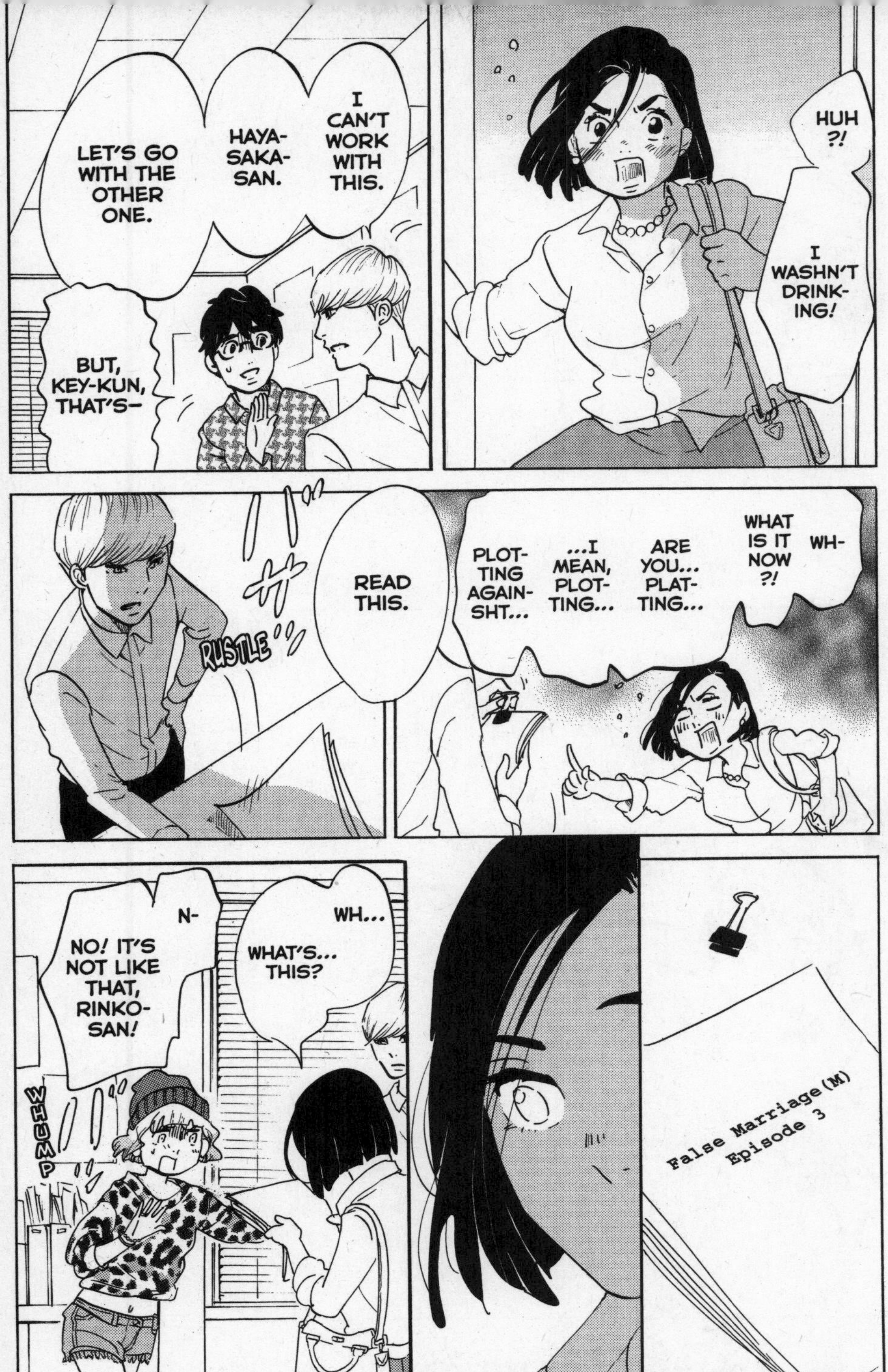
HUH?!
I WASHN'T DRINK-ING!
I CAN'T WORK WITH THIS.
HAYA-SAKA-SAN.
LET'S GO WITH THE OTHER ONE.
BUT, KEY-KUN, THAT'S—
WH-
WHAT IS IT NOW?!
ARE YOU... PLAT-TING...
...I MEAN, PLOT-TING...
PLOT-TING AGAIN-SHT...
READ THIS.
RUSTLE
False Marriage(M)
Episode 3
WH...
WHAT'S... THIS?
N-
NO! IT'S NOT LIKE THAT, RINKO-SAN!
WHUMP

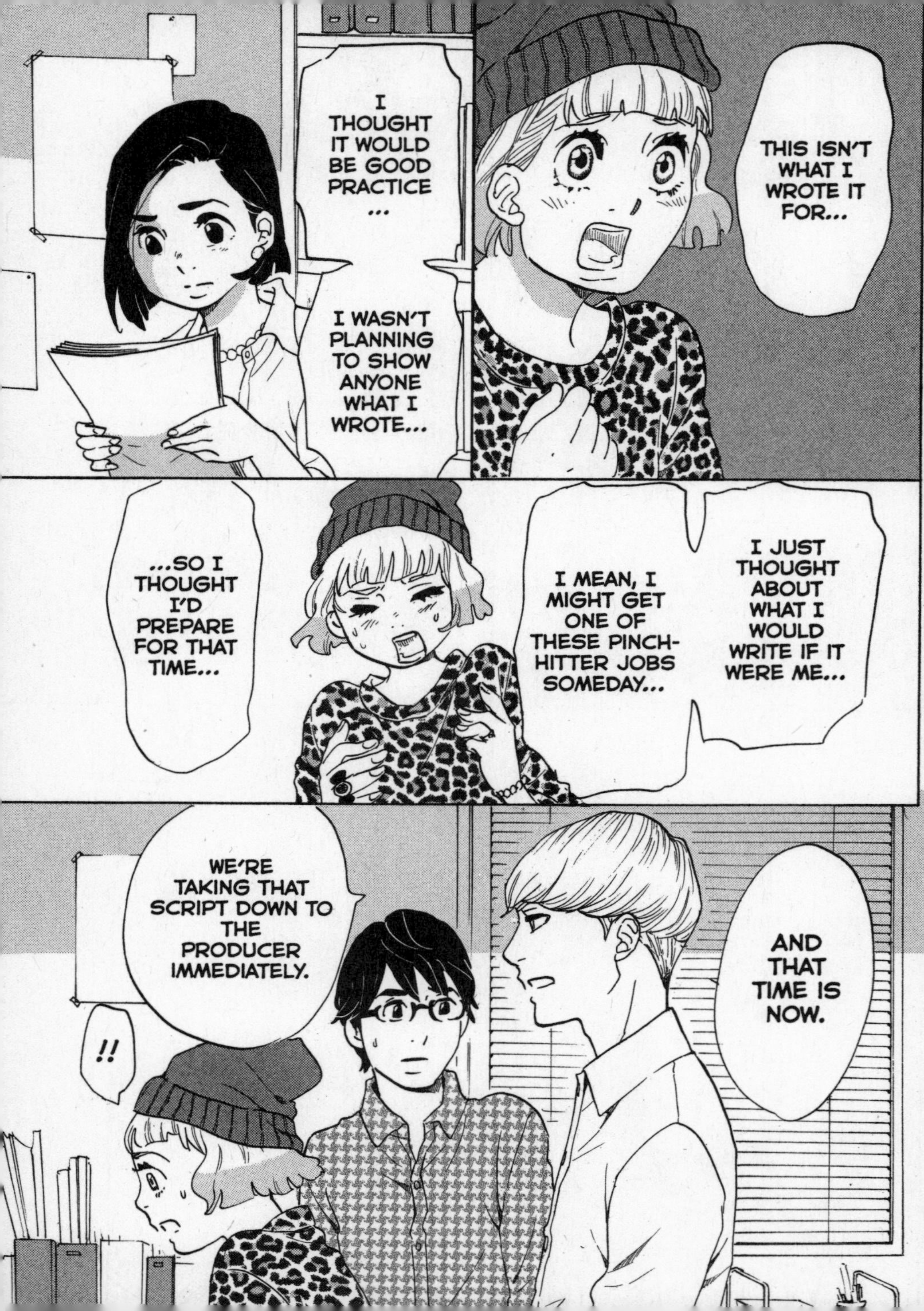
THIS ISN'T WHAT I WROTE IT FOR...
I THOUGHT IT WOULD BE GOOD PRACTICE...
I WASN'T PLANNING TO SHOW ANYONE WHAT I WROTE...
I JUST THOUGHT ABOUT WHAT I WOULD WRITE IF IT WERE ME...
I MEAN, I MIGHT GET ONE OF THESE PINCH-HITTER JOBS SOMEDAY...
...SO I THOUGHT I'D PREPARE FOR THAT TIME...
AND THAT TIME IS NOW.
WE'RE TAKING THAT SCRIPT DOWN TO THE PRODUCER IMMEDIATELY.
!!

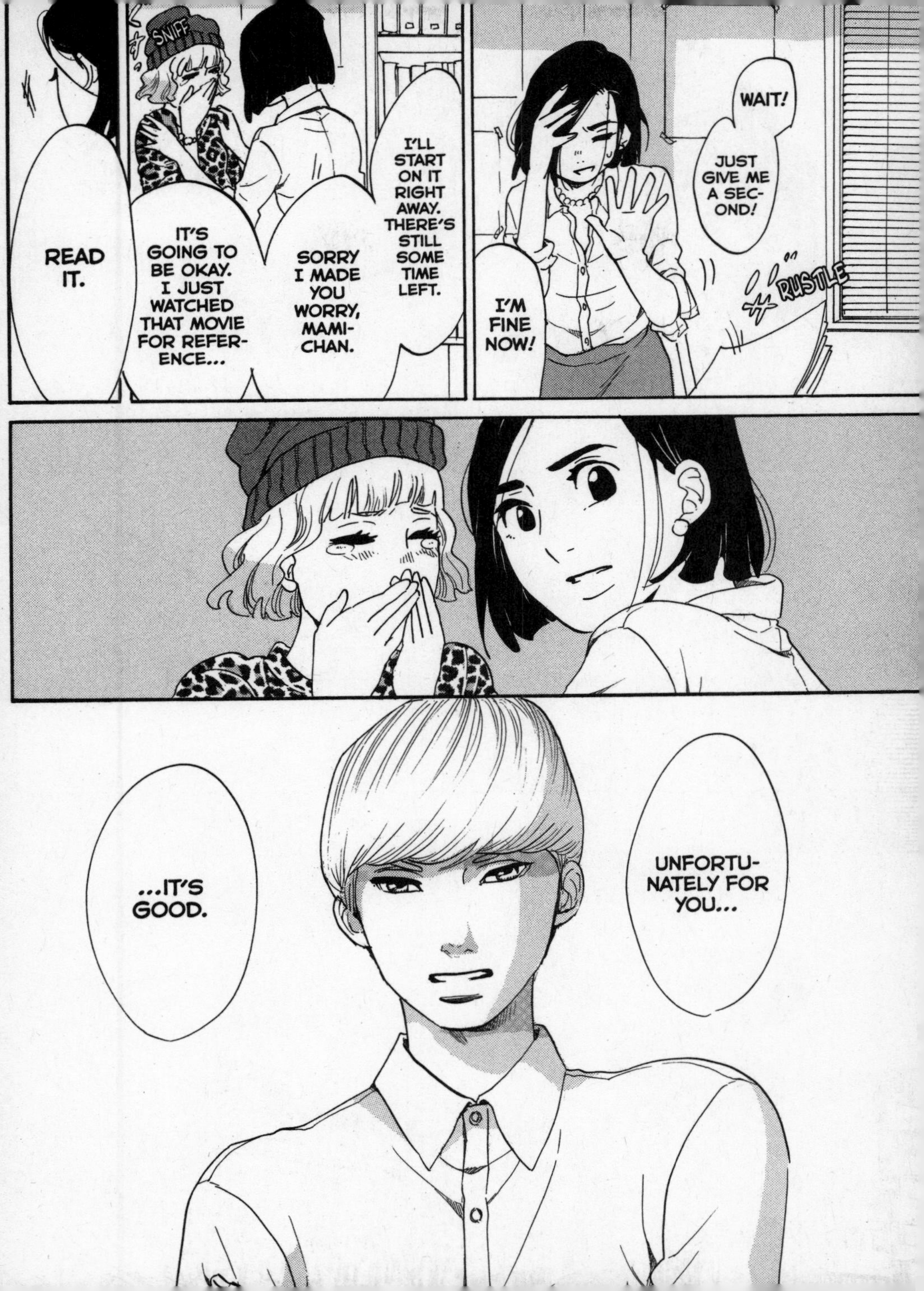
WAIT!
JUST GIVE ME A SEC-OND!
RUSTLE
I'M FINE NOW!
SNIFF
I'LL START ON IT RIGHT AWAY. THERE'S STILL SOME TIME LEFT.
SORRY I MADE YOU WORRY, MAMI-CHAN.
IT'S GOING TO BE OKAY. I JUST WATCHED THAT MOVIE FOR REFER-ENCE...
READ IT.
UNFORTU-NATELY FOR YOU...
...IT'S GOOD.

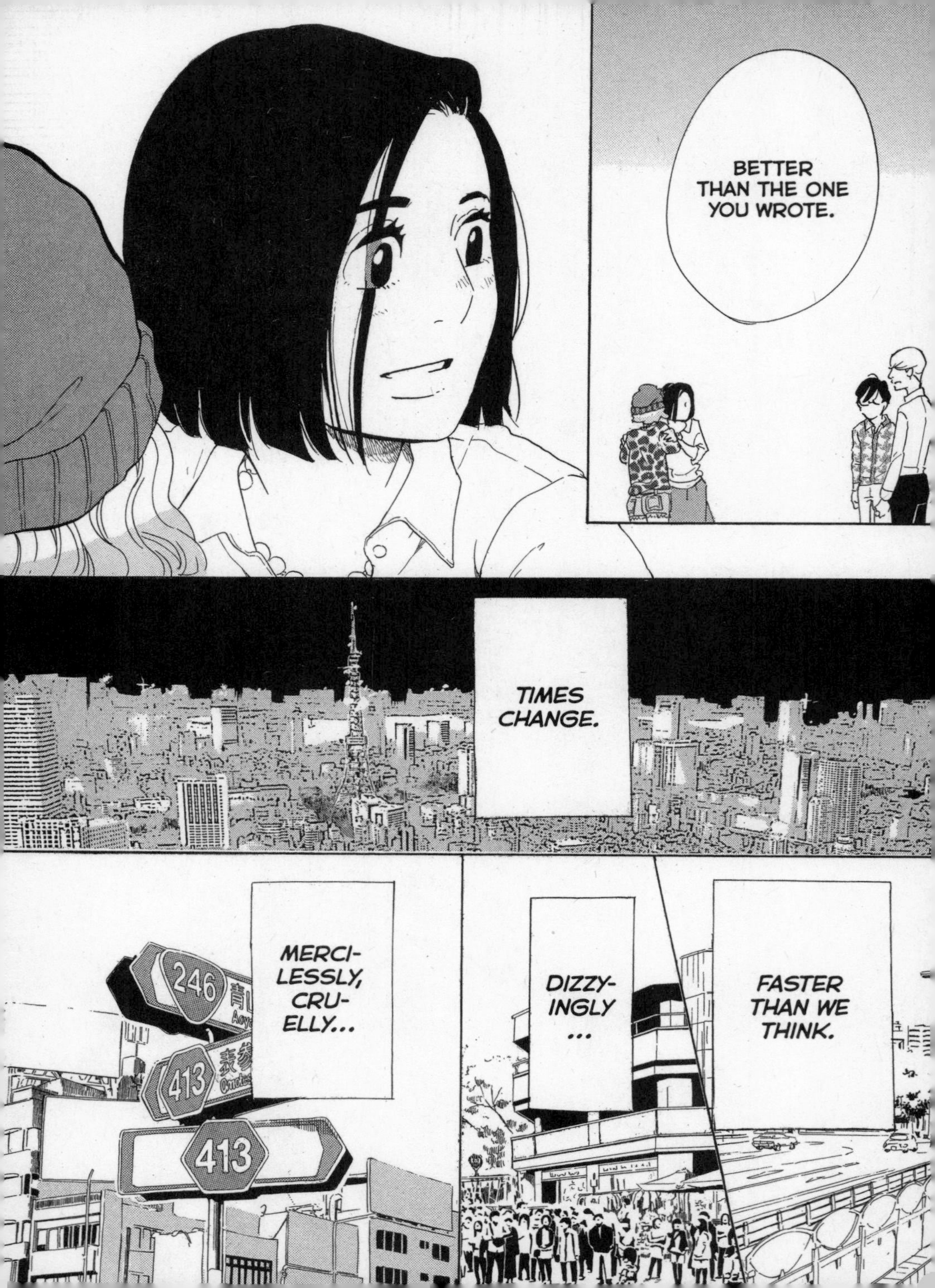
BETTER THAN THE ONE YOU WROTE.
TIMES CHANGE.
FASTER THAN WE THINK.
DIZZY-INGLY ...
MERCI-LESSLY, CRU-ELLY...
246 青山
413 表参
413

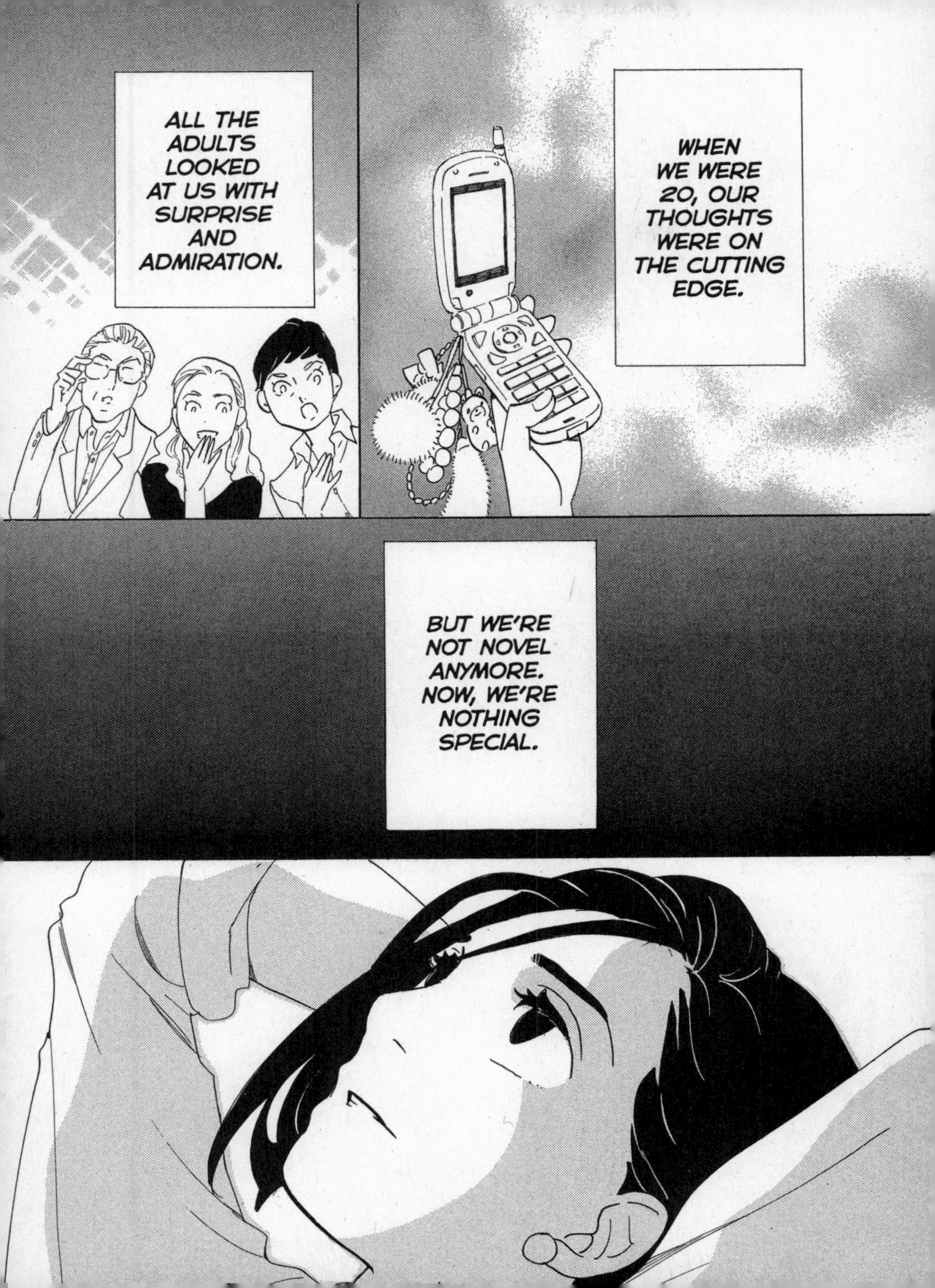
WHEN WE WERE 20, OUR THOUGHTS WERE ON THE CUTTING EDGE.
ALL THE ADULTS LOOKED AT US WITH SURPRISE AND ADMIRATION.
BUT WE'RE NOT NOVEL ANYMORE. NOW, WE'RE NOTHING SPECIAL.

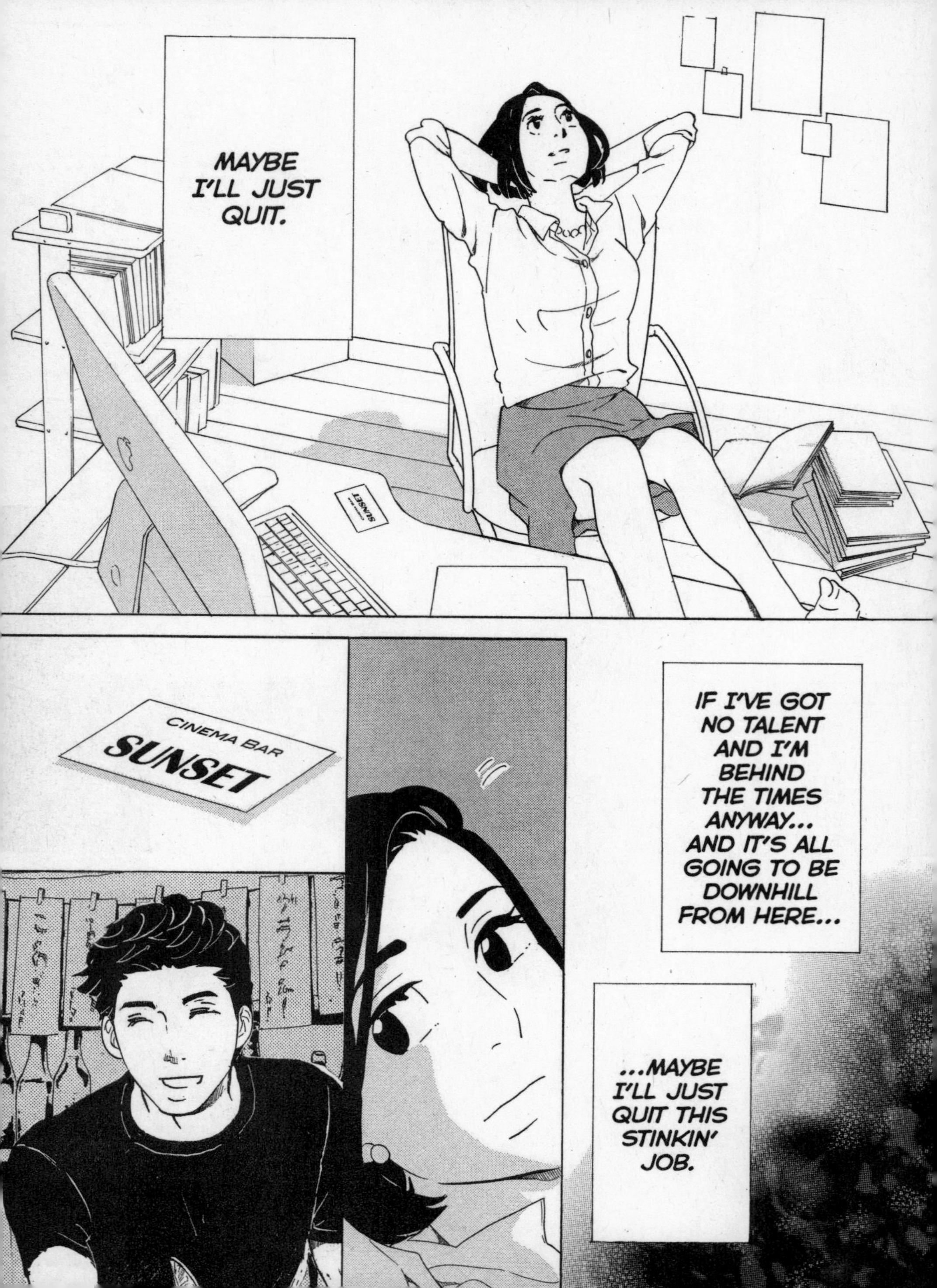
MAYBE I'LL JUST QUIT.
IF I'VE GOT NO TALENT AND I'M BEHIND THE TIMES ANYWAY... AND IT'S ALL GOING TO BE DOWNHILL FROM HERE...
...MAYBE I'LL JUST QUIT THIS STINKIN' JOB.
CINEMA BAR
SUNSET

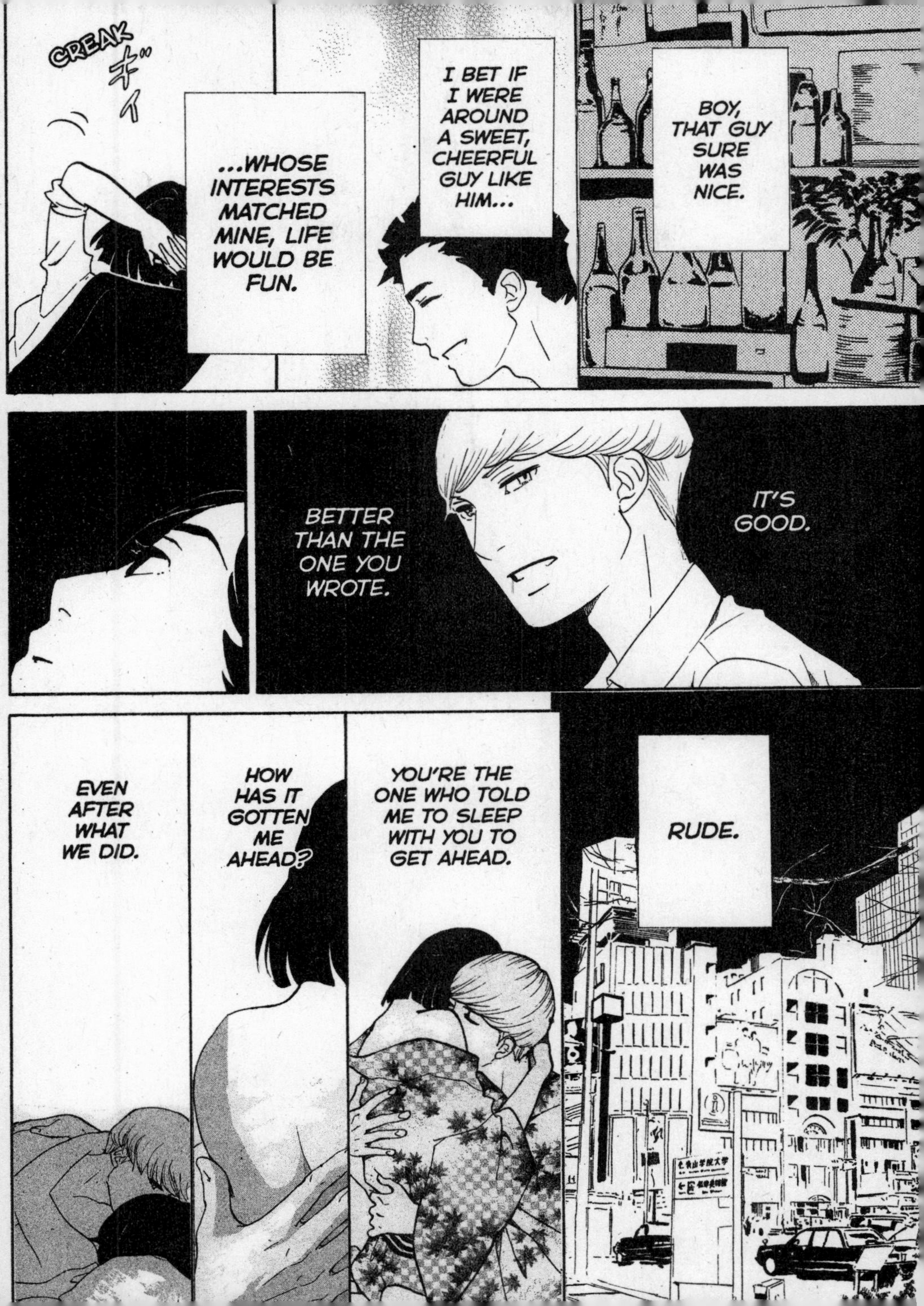
BOY, THAT GUY SURE WAS NICE.
I BET IF I WERE AROUND A SWEET, CHEERFUL GUY LIKE HIM...
...WHOSE INTERESTS MATCHED MINE, LIFE WOULD BE FUN.
CREAK
ギィ
IT'S GOOD.
BETTER THAN THE ONE YOU WROTE.
RUDE.
YOU'RE THE ONE WHO TOLD ME TO SLEEP WITH YOU TO GET AHEAD.
HOW HAS IT GOTTEN ME AHEAD?
EVEN AFTER WHAT WE DID.

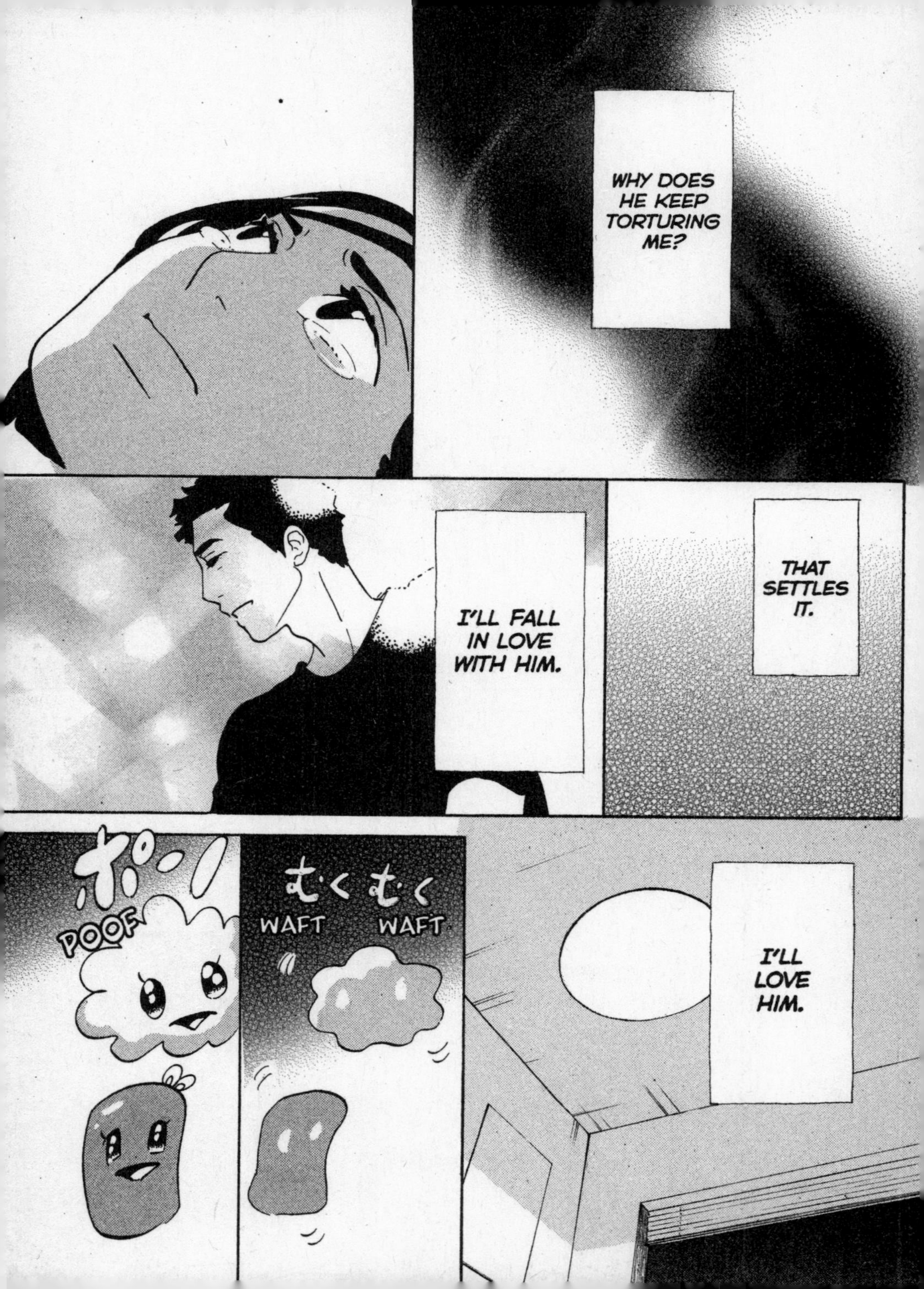
WHY DOES HE KEEP TORTURING ME?
THAT SETTLES IT.
I'LL FALL IN LOVE WITH HIM.
I'LL LOVE HIM.
むくむく
WAFT WAFT
POOF

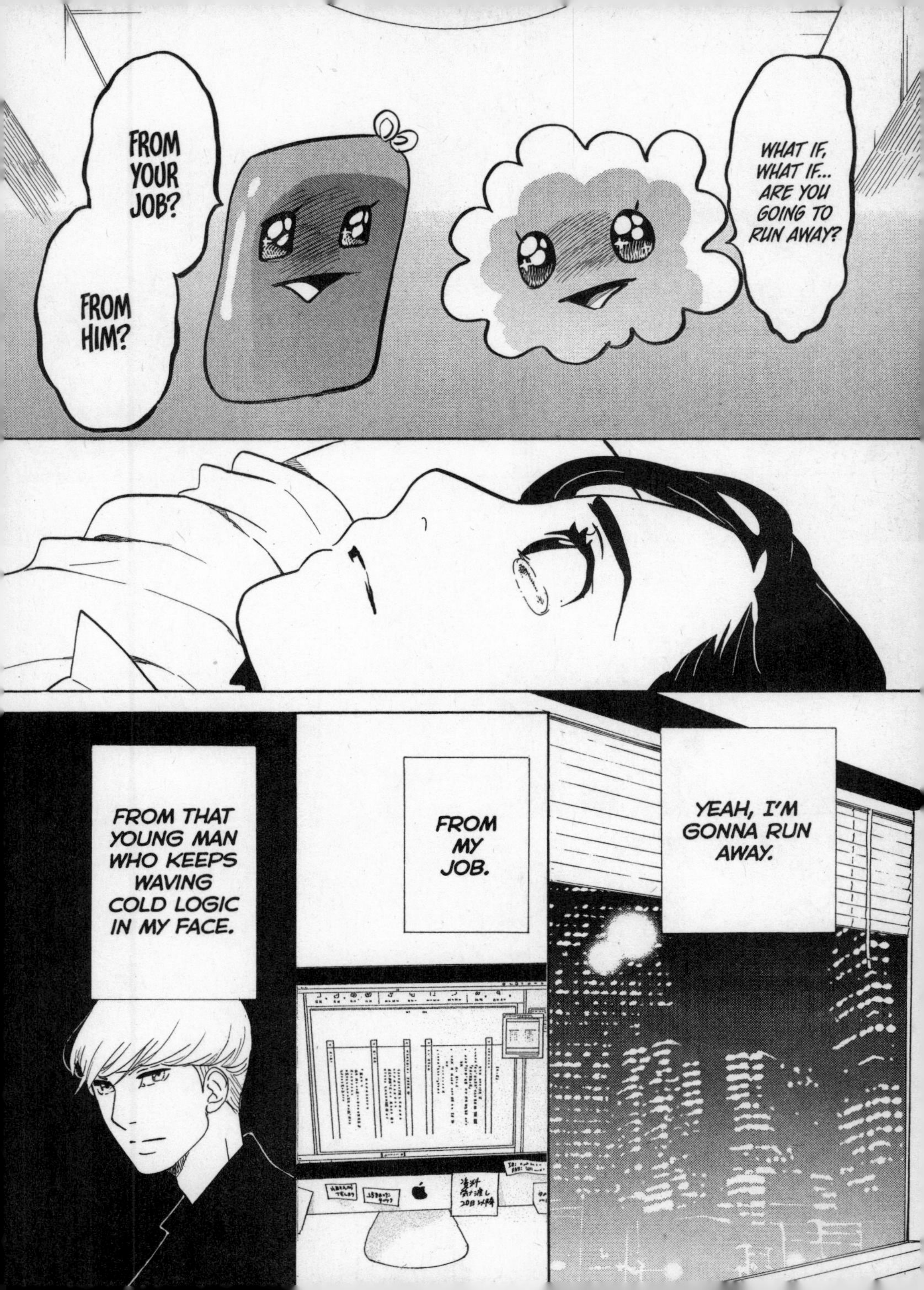

WHAT IF, WHAT IF... ARE YOU GOING TO RUN AWAY?
FROM YOUR JOB?
FROM HIM?
YEAH, I'M GONNA RUN AWAY.
FROM MY JOB.
FROM THAT YOUNG MAN WHO KEEPS WAVING COLD LOGIC IN MY FACE.

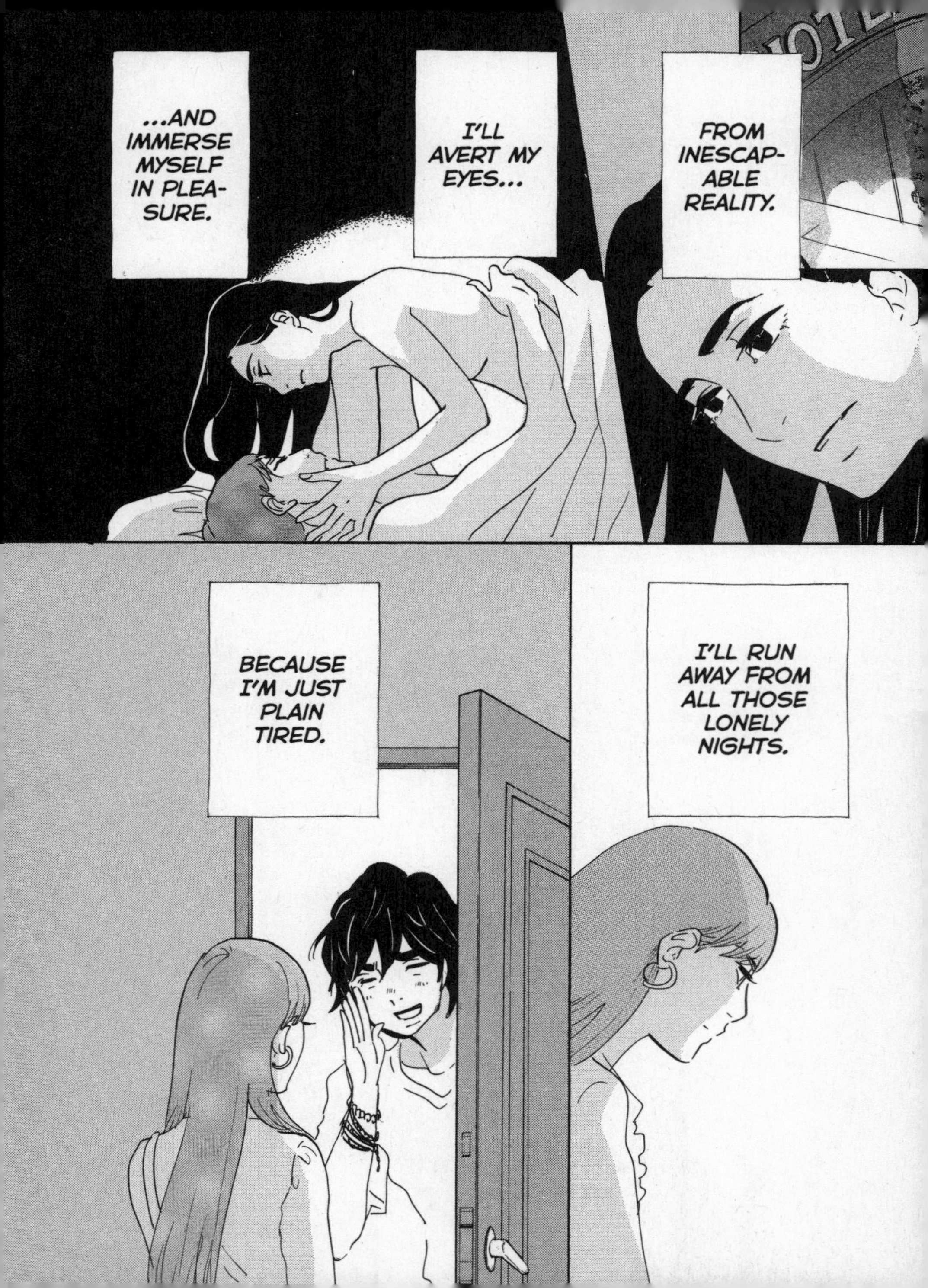

HOTEL
FROM INESCAPABLE REALITY.
I'LL AVERT MY EYES...
...AND IMMERSE MYSELF IN PLEASURE.
I'LL RUN AWAY FROM ALL THOSE LONELY NIGHTS.
BECAUSE I'M JUST PLAIN TIRED.

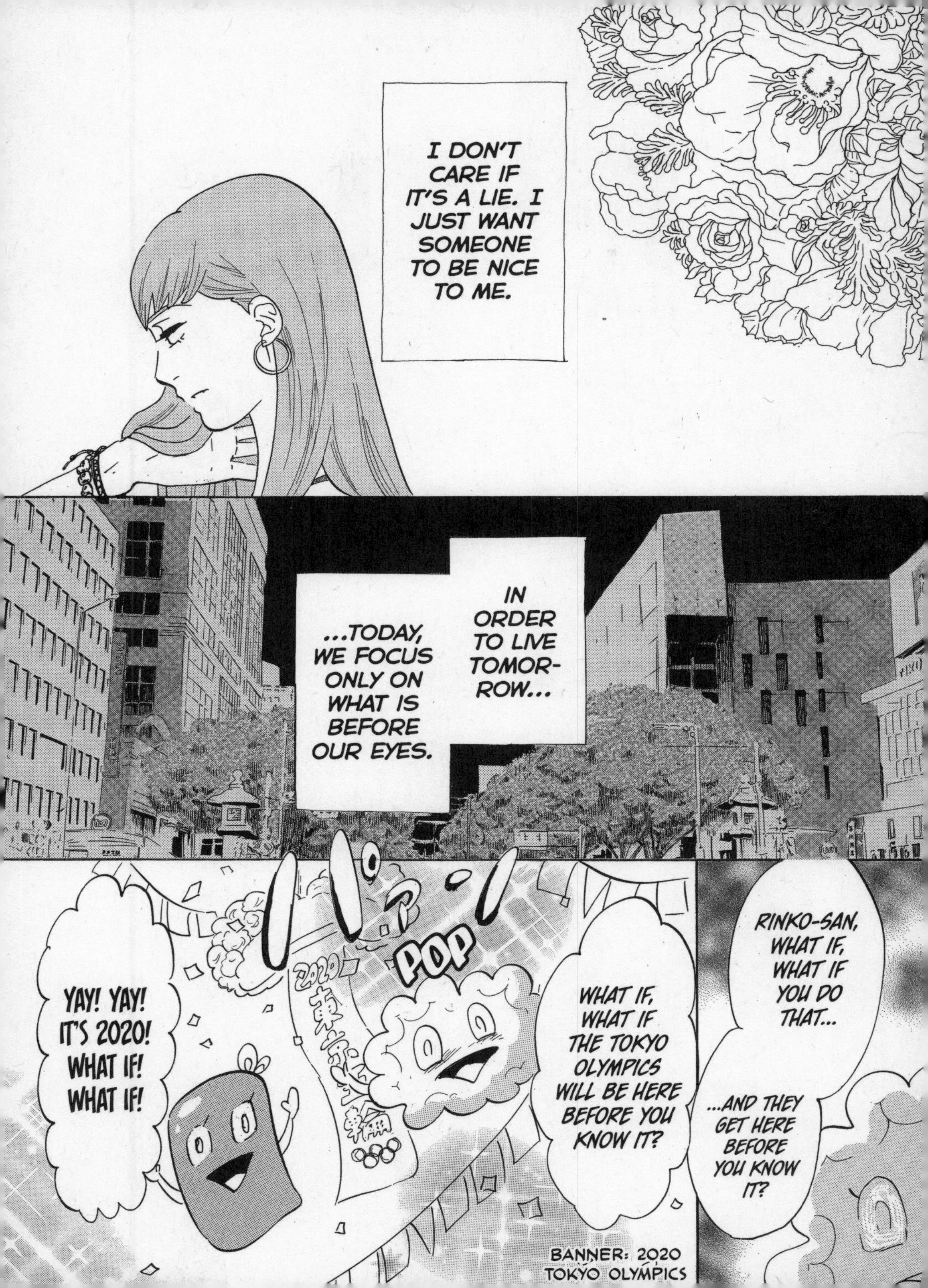
I DON'T CARE IF IT'S A LIE. I JUST WANT SOMEONE TO BE NICE TO ME.
IN ORDER TO LIVE TOMORROW...
...TODAY, WE FOCUS ONLY ON WHAT IS BEFORE OUR EYES.
RINKO-SAN, WHAT IF, WHAT IF YOU DO THAT...
...AND THEY GET HERE BEFORE YOU KNOW IT?
WHAT IF, WHAT IF THE TOKYO OLYMPICS WILL BE HERE BEFORE YOU KNOW IT?
POP
YAY! YAY! IT'S 2020! WHAT IF! WHAT IF!
BANNER: 2020 TOKYO OLYMPICS

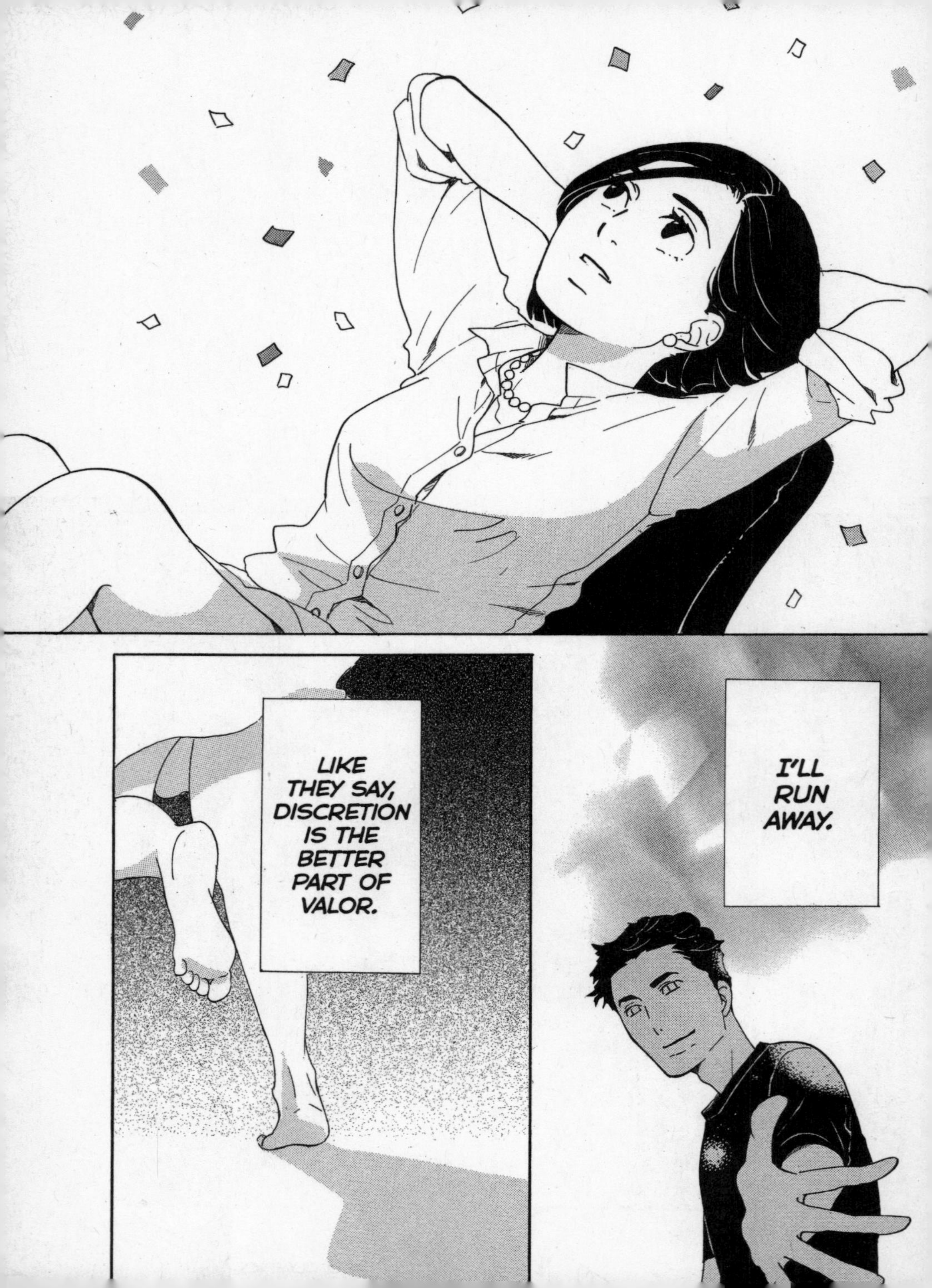
I'LL RUN AWAY.
LIKE THEY SAY, DISCRETION IS THE BETTER PART OF VALOR.

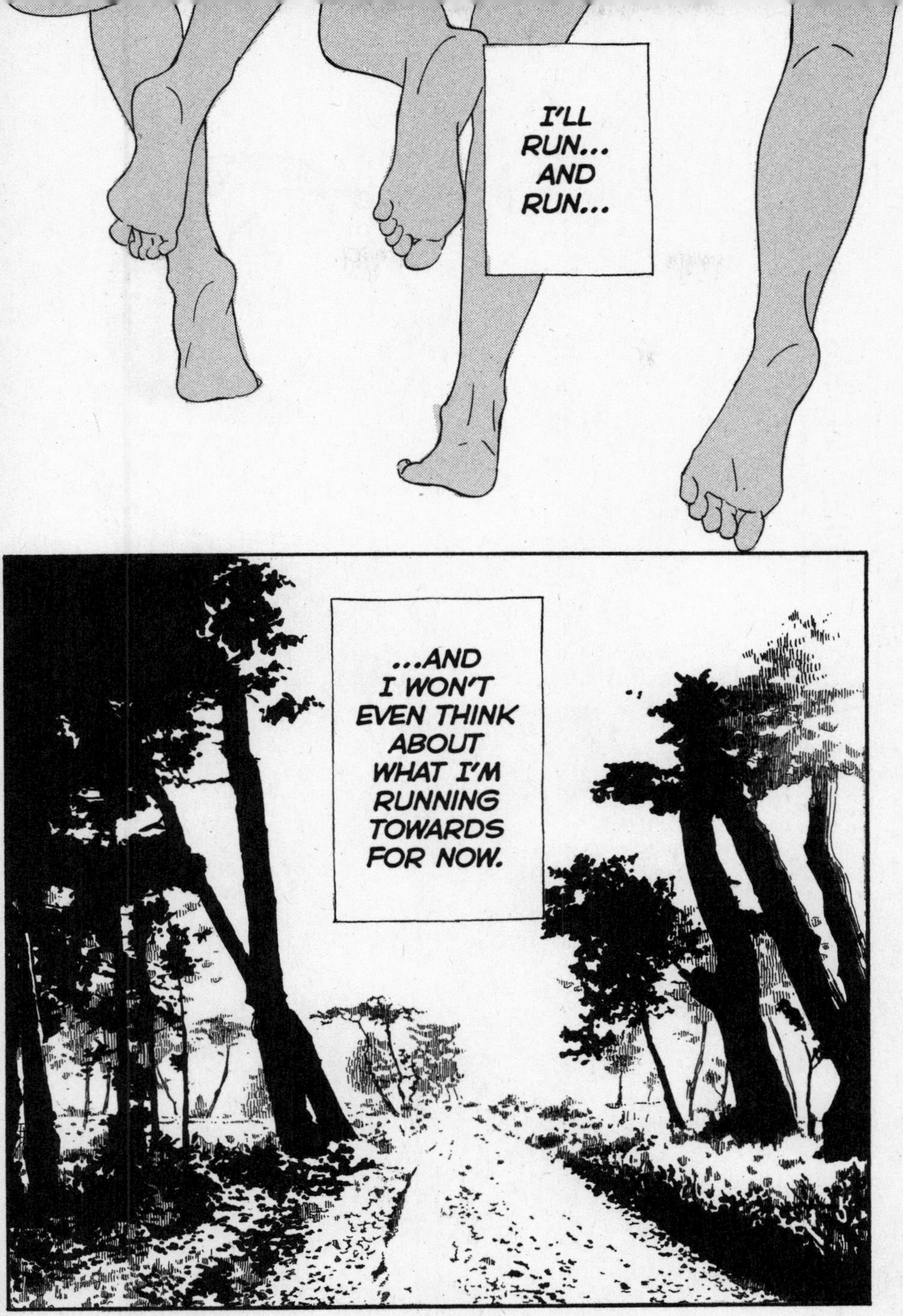
I'LL RUN... AND RUN...
...AND I WON'T EVEN THINK ABOUT WHAT I'M RUNNING TOWARDS FOR NOW.

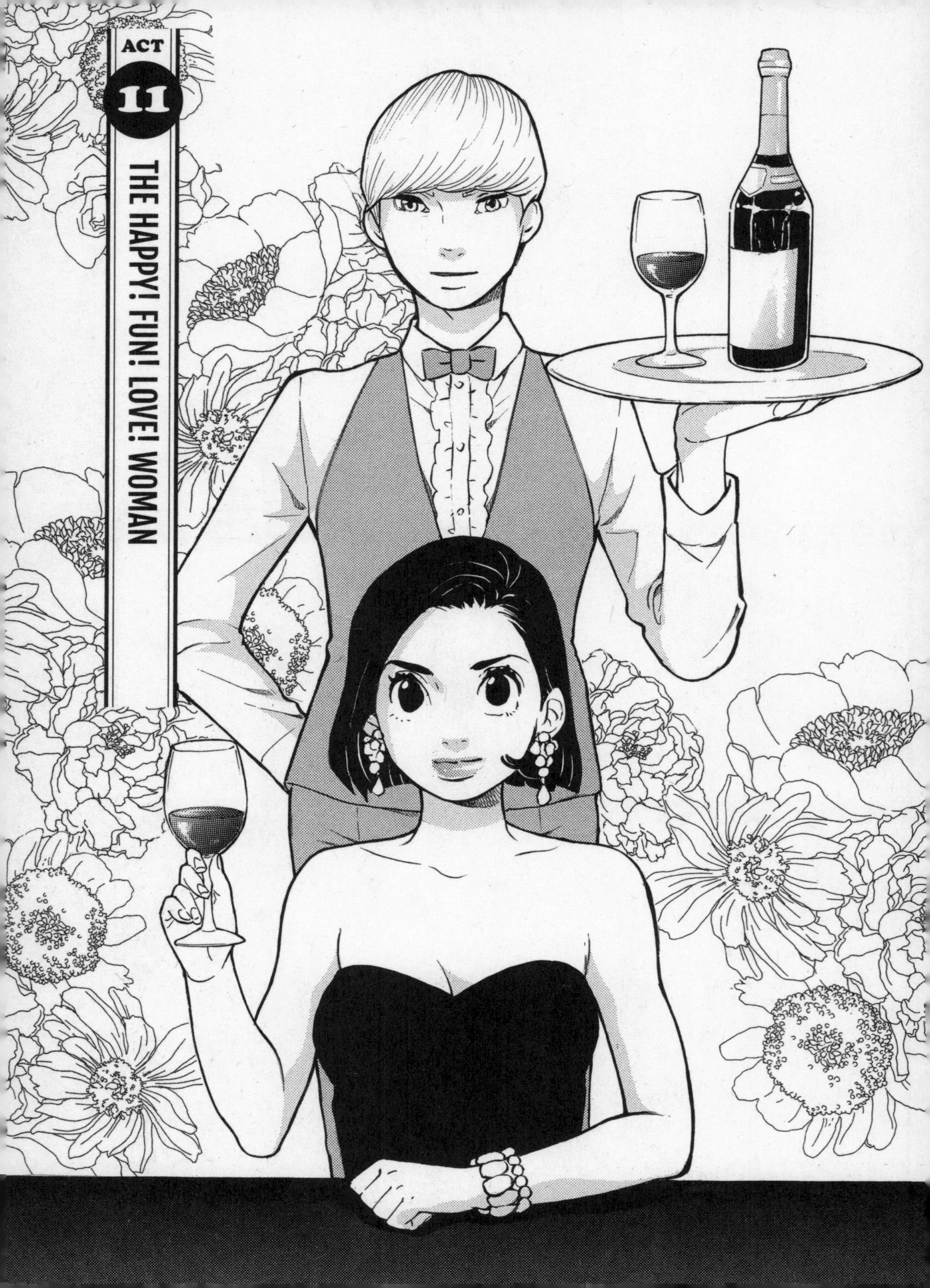
ACT
11
THE HAPPY! FUN! LOVE! WOMAN

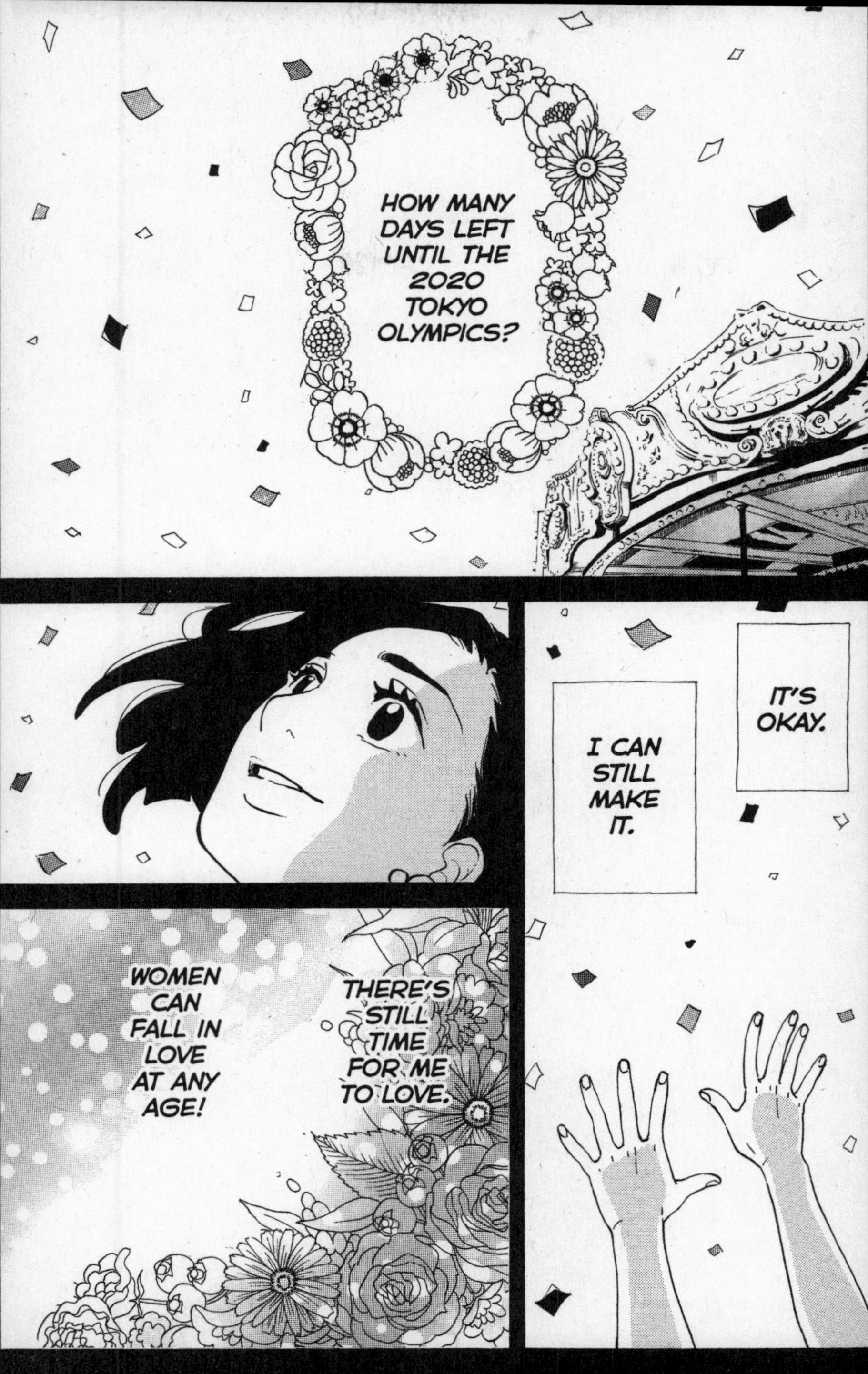
HOW MANY DAYS LEFT UNTIL THE 2020 TOKYO OLYMPICS?
IT'S OKAY.
I CAN STILL MAKE IT.
THERE'S STILL TIME FOR ME TO LOVE.
WOMEN CAN FALL IN LOVE AT ANY AGE!

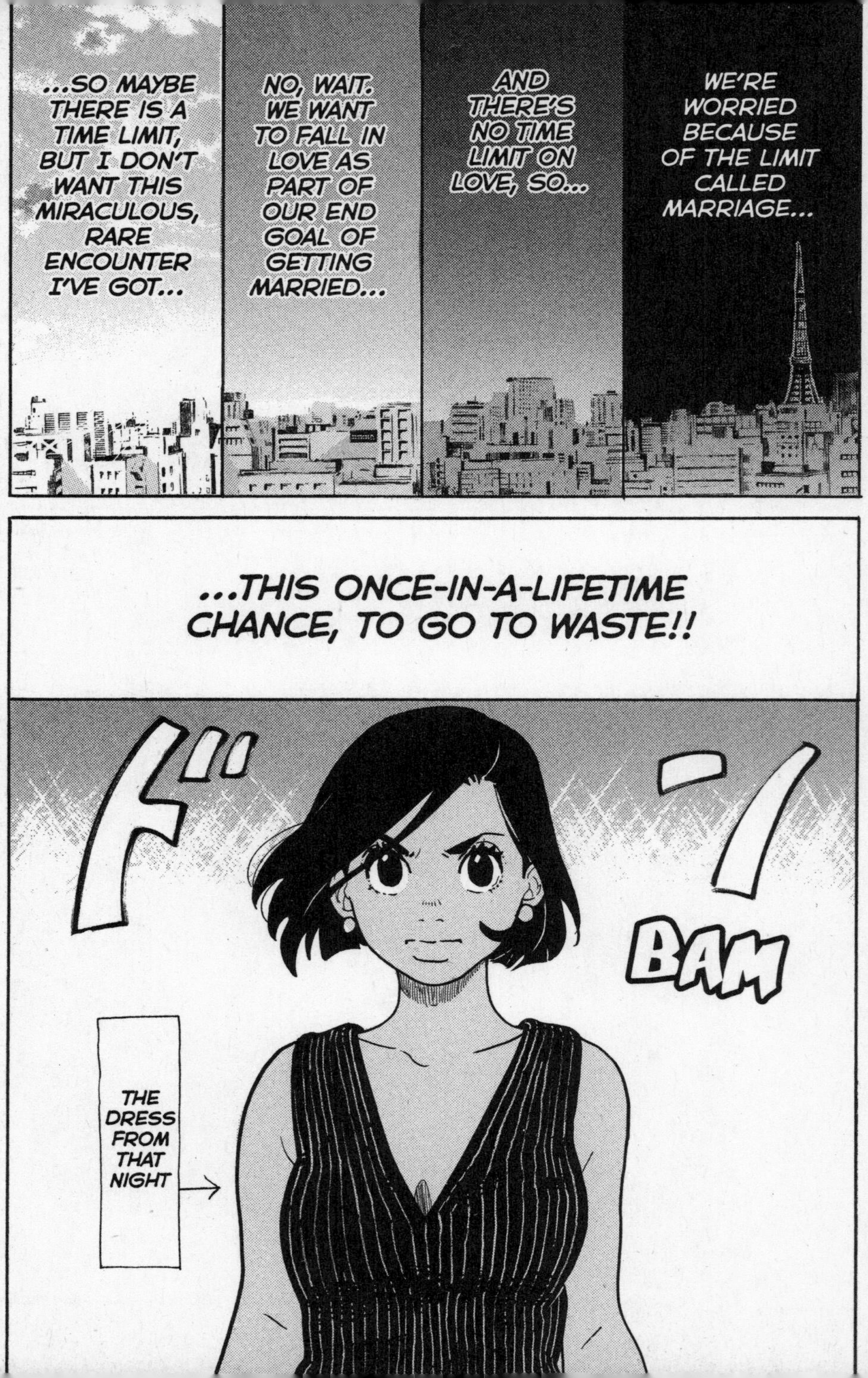
WE'RE WORRIED BECAUSE OF THE LIMIT CALLED MARRIAGE...
AND THERE'S NO TIME LIMIT ON LOVE, SO...
NO, WAIT. WE WANT TO FALL IN LOVE AS PART OF OUR END GOAL OF GETTING MARRIED...
...SO MAYBE THERE IS A TIME LIMIT, BUT I DON'T WANT THIS MIRACULOUS, RARE ENCOUNTER I'VE GOT...
...THIS ONCE-IN-A-LIFETIME CHANCE, TO GO TO WASTE!!
BAM
THE DRESS FROM THAT NIGHT

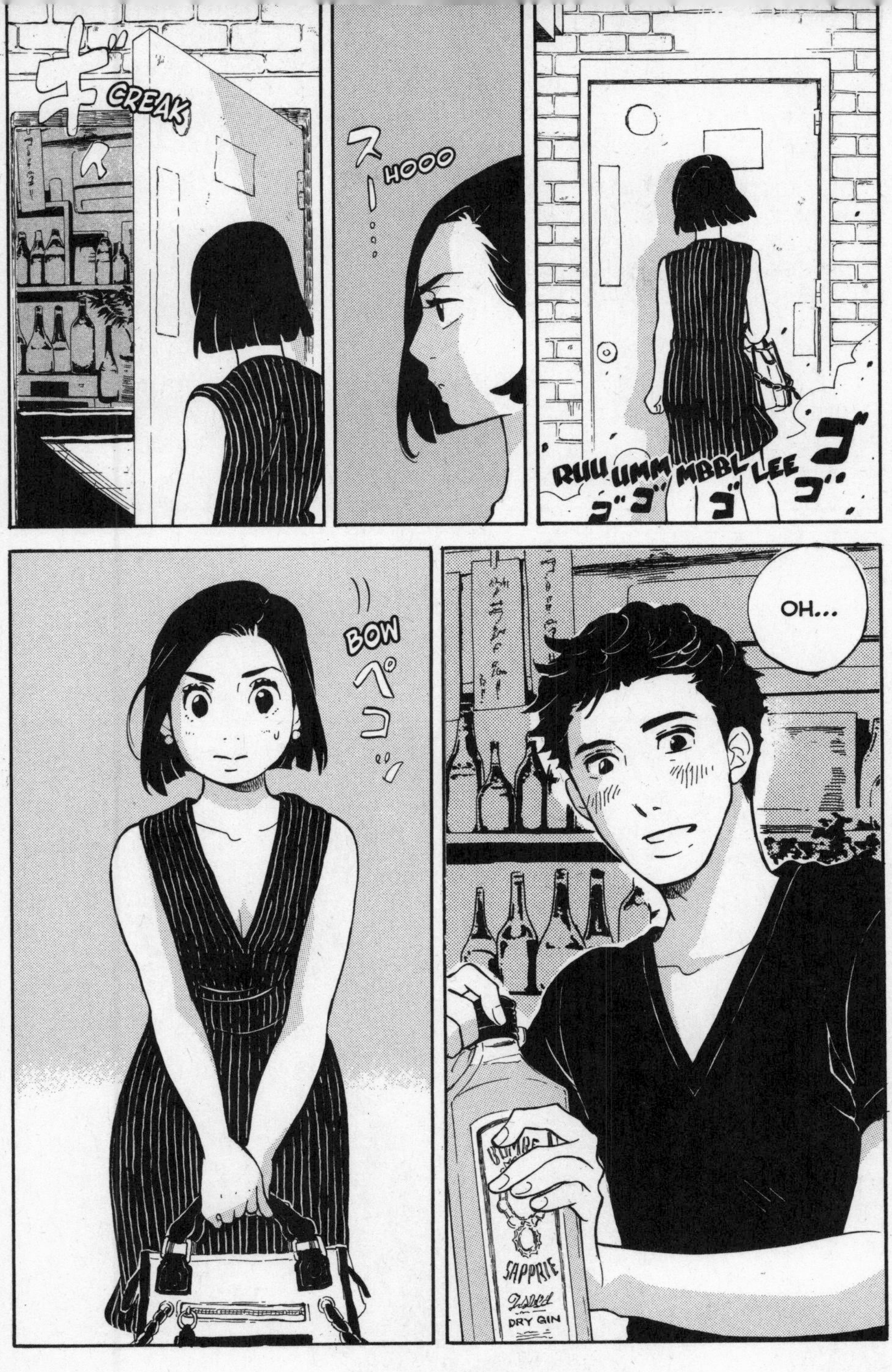
ゴゴゴゴ
RUU UMM MBBL LEE
スー。。。
HOOO
ギィ
CREAK
OH...
SAPPRIE
DRY GIN
ペコッ
BOW

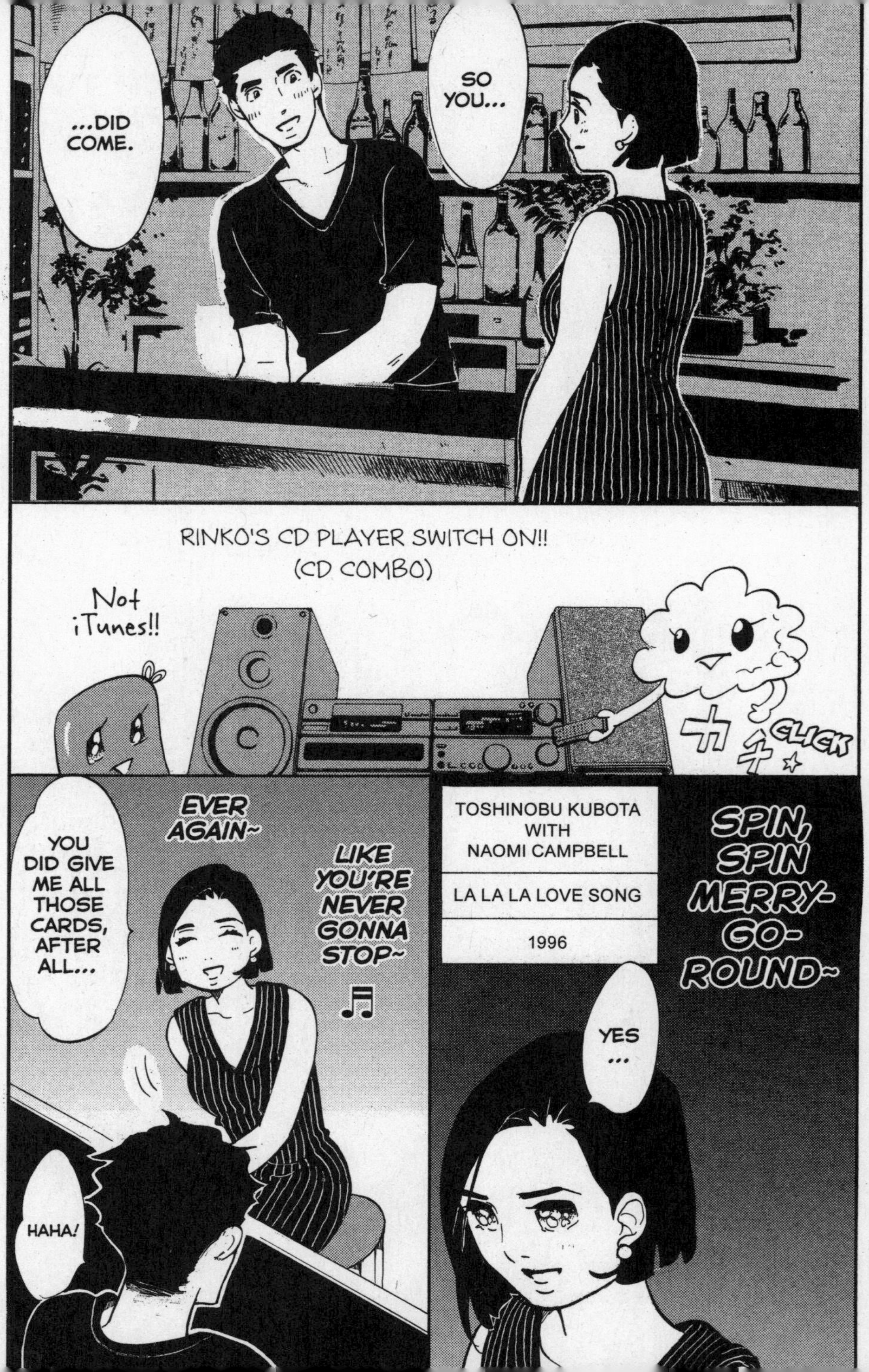
SO YOU...
...DID COME.
RINKO'S CD PLAYER SWITCH ON!!
(CD COMBO)
カチ CLICK
Not iTunes!!
SPIN, SPIN MERRY-GO-ROUND~
TOSHINOBU KUBOTA WITH NAOMI CAMPBELL
LA LA LA LOVE SONG
1996
YES ...
LIKE YOU'RE NEVER GONNA STOP~
EVER AGAIN~
YOU DID GIVE ME ALL THOSE CARDS, AFTER ALL...
HAHA!

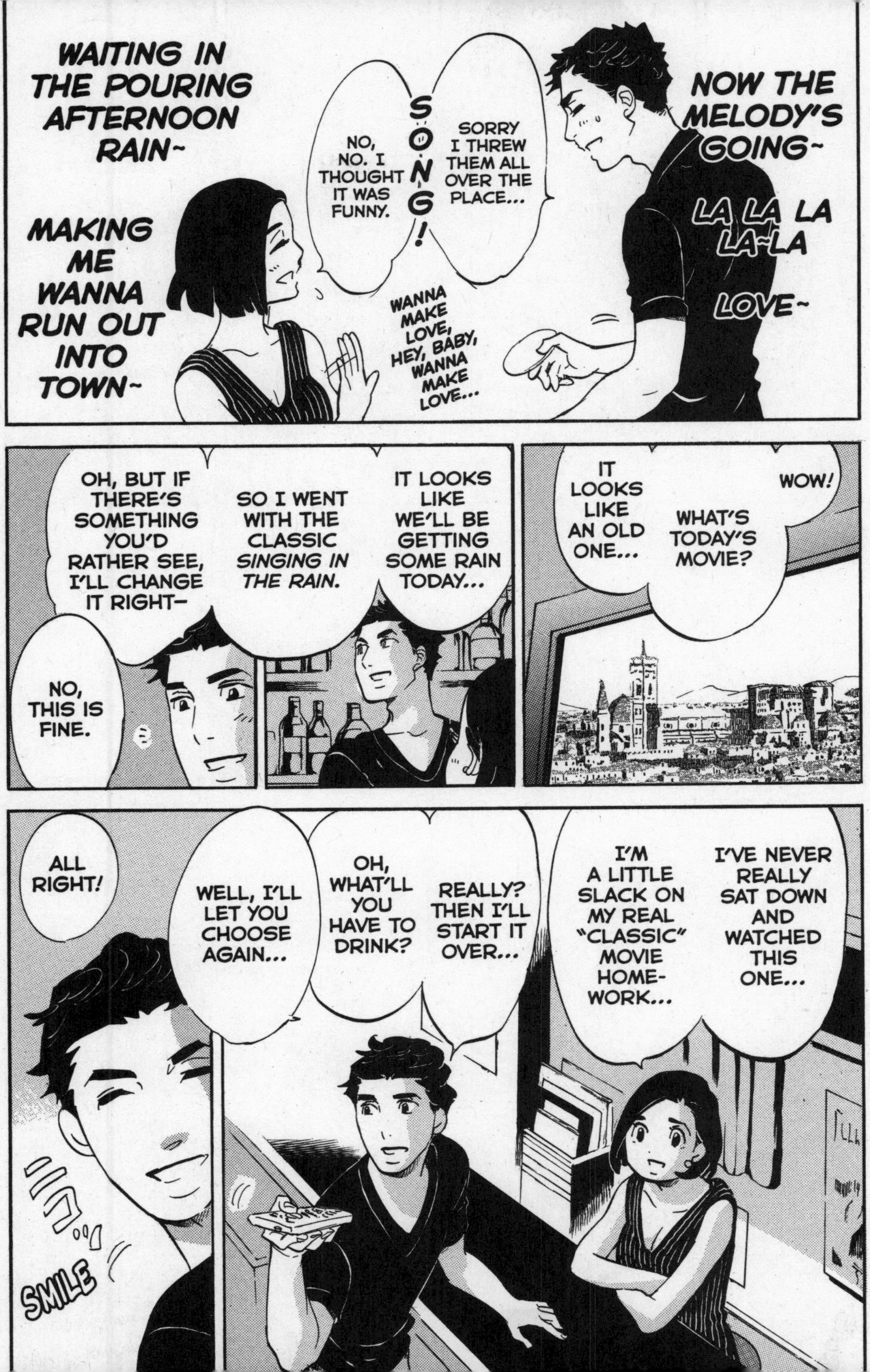
NOW THE MELODY'S GOING~
LA LA LA LA~LA
LOVE~
SORRY I THREW THEM ALL OVER THE PLACE...
SONG!
NO, NO. I THOUGHT IT WAS FUNNY.
WANNA MAKE LOVE, HEY, BABY, WANNA MAKE LOVE...
WAITING IN THE POURING AFTERNOON RAIN~
MAKING ME WANNA RUN OUT INTO TOWN~
WOW!
WHAT'S TODAY'S MOVIE?
IT LOOKS LIKE AN OLD ONE...
IT LOOKS LIKE WE'LL BE GETTING SOME RAIN TODAY...
SO I WENT WITH THE CLASSIC *SINGING IN THE RAIN.*
OH, BUT IF THERE'S SOMETHING YOU'D RATHER SEE, I'LL CHANGE IT RIGHT–
NO, THIS IS FINE.
I'VE NEVER REALLY SAT DOWN AND WATCHED THIS ONE...
I'M A LITTLE SLACK ON MY REAL "CLASSIC" MOVIE HOMEWORK...
REALLY? THEN I'LL START IT OVER...
OH, WHAT'LL YOU HAVE TO DRINK?
WELL, I'LL LET YOU CHOOSE AGAIN...
ALL RIGHT!
SMILE

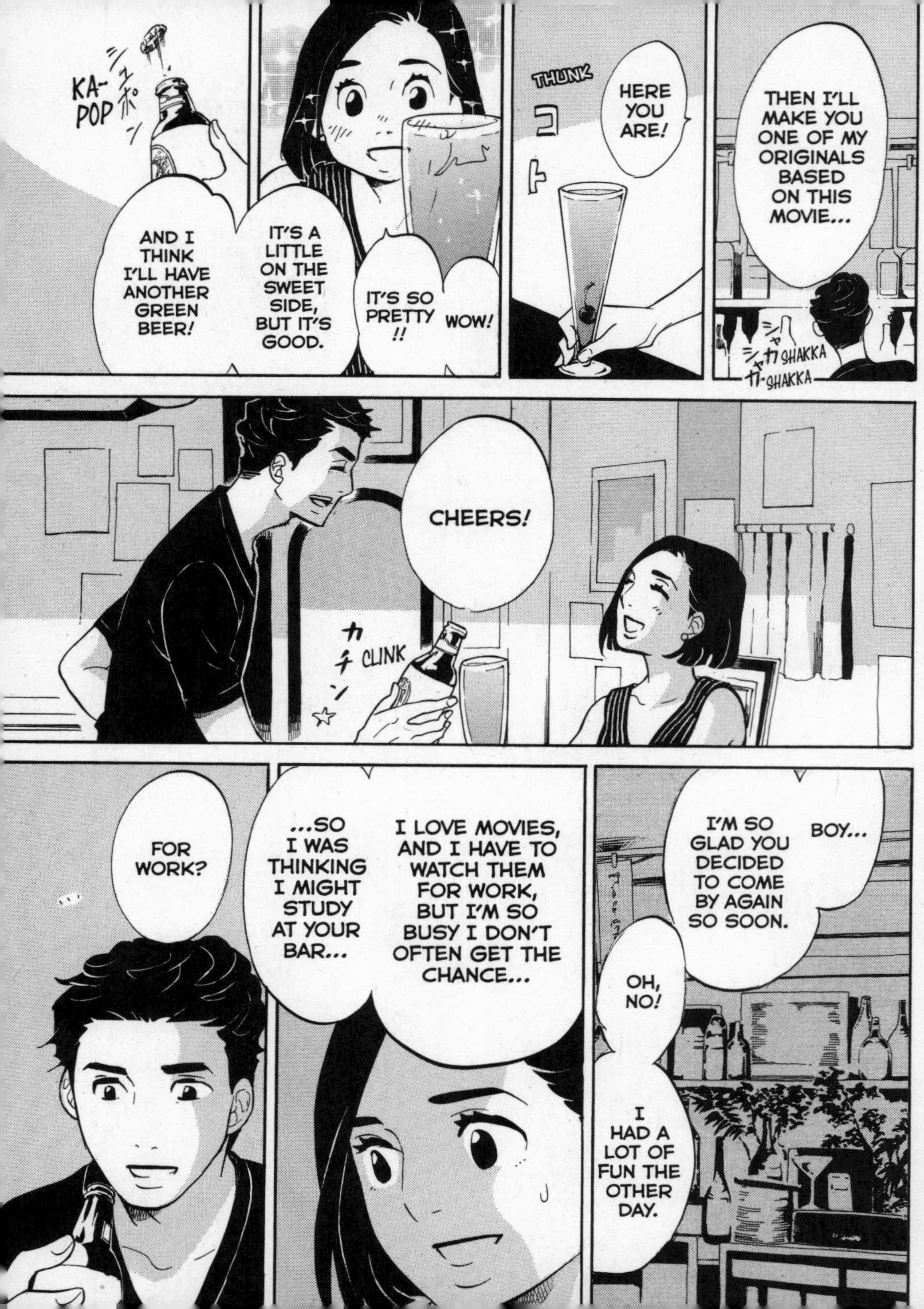
THEN I'LL MAKE YOU ONE OF MY ORIGINALS BASED ON THIS MOVIE...
シャカ SHAKKA
シャカ SHAKKA
THUNK
コト
HERE YOU ARE!
WOW!
IT'S SO PRETTY!!
IT'S A LITTLE ON THE SWEET SIDE, BUT IT'S GOOD.
KA-POP
シュポン
AND I THINK I'LL HAVE ANOTHER GREEN BEER!
CHEERS!
カチン CLINK
BOY...
I'M SO GLAD YOU DECIDED TO COME BY AGAIN SO SOON.
OH, NO!
I HAD A LOT OF FUN THE OTHER DAY.
I LOVE MOVIES, AND I HAVE TO WATCH THEM FOR WORK, BUT I'M SO BUSY I DON'T OFTEN GET THE CHANCE...
...SO I WAS THINKING I MIGHT STUDY AT YOUR BAR...
FOR WORK?

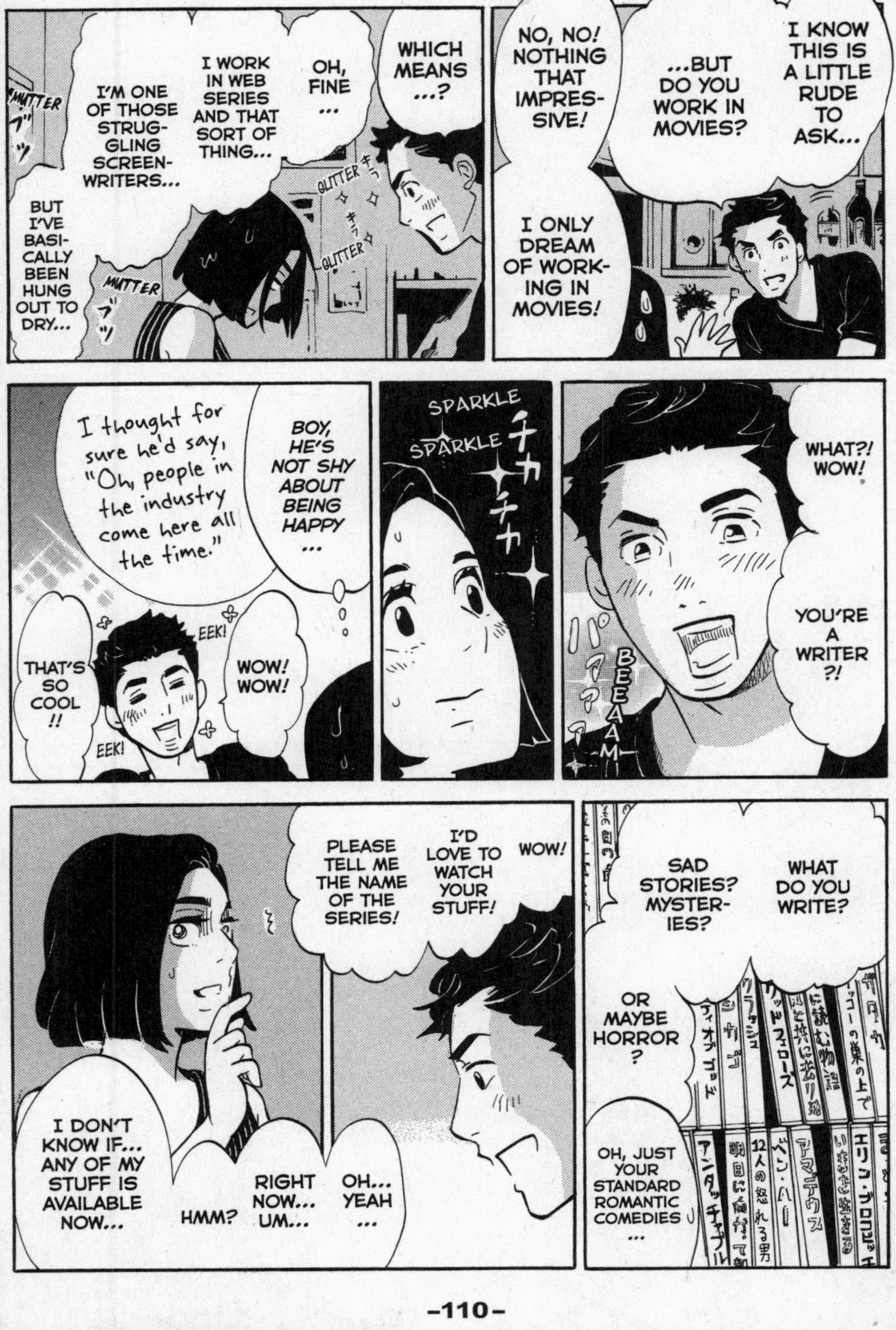
I KNOW THIS IS A LITTLE RUDE TO ASK...
...BUT DO YOU WORK IN MOVIES?
NO, NO! NOTHING THAT IMPRES-SIVE!
I ONLY DREAM OF WORK-ING IN MOVIES!
WHICH MEANS ...?
OH, FINE ...
I WORK IN WEB SERIES AND THAT SORT OF THING...
GLITTER
GLITTER
I'M ONE OF THOSE STRUG-GLING SCREEN-WRITERS...
MUTTER
BUT I'VE BASI-CALLY BEEN HUNG OUT TO DRY...
MUTTER
WHAT?! WOW!
YOU'RE A WRITER ?!
BEEEAAM
SPARKLE
SPARKLE
BOY, HE'S NOT SHY ABOUT BEING HAPPY ...
I thought for sure he'd say, "Oh, people in the industry come here all the time."
WOW! WOW!
EEK!
THAT'S SO COOL !!
EEK!
WHAT DO YOU WRITE?
SAD STORIES? MYSTER-IES?
OR MAYBE HORROR ?
OH, JUST YOUR STANDARD ROMANTIC COMEDIES ...
WOW!
I'D LOVE TO WATCH YOUR STUFF!
PLEASE TELL ME THE NAME OF THE SERIES!
OH... YEAH ...
RIGHT NOW... UM...
HMM?
I DON'T KNOW IF... ANY OF MY STUFF IS AVAILABLE NOW...

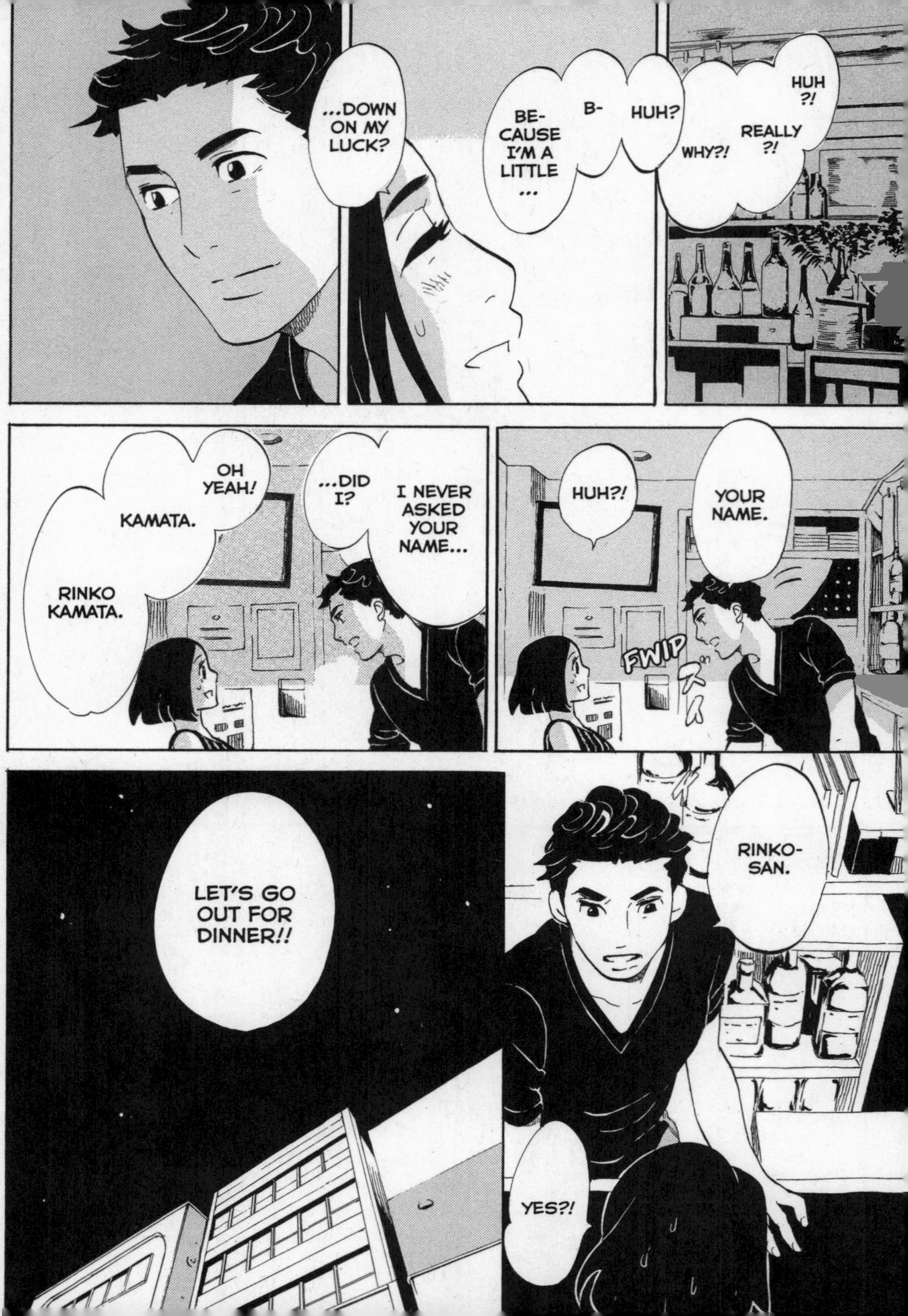
HUH ?!
REALLY ?!
WHY?!
HUH?
B-
BE-CAUSE I'M A LITTLE ...
...DOWN ON MY LUCK?
YOUR NAME.
HUH?!
FWIP
I NEVER ASKED YOUR NAME...
...DID I?
OH YEAH!
KAMATA.
RINKO KAMATA.
RINKO-SAN.
YES?!
LET'S GO OUT FOR DINNER!!

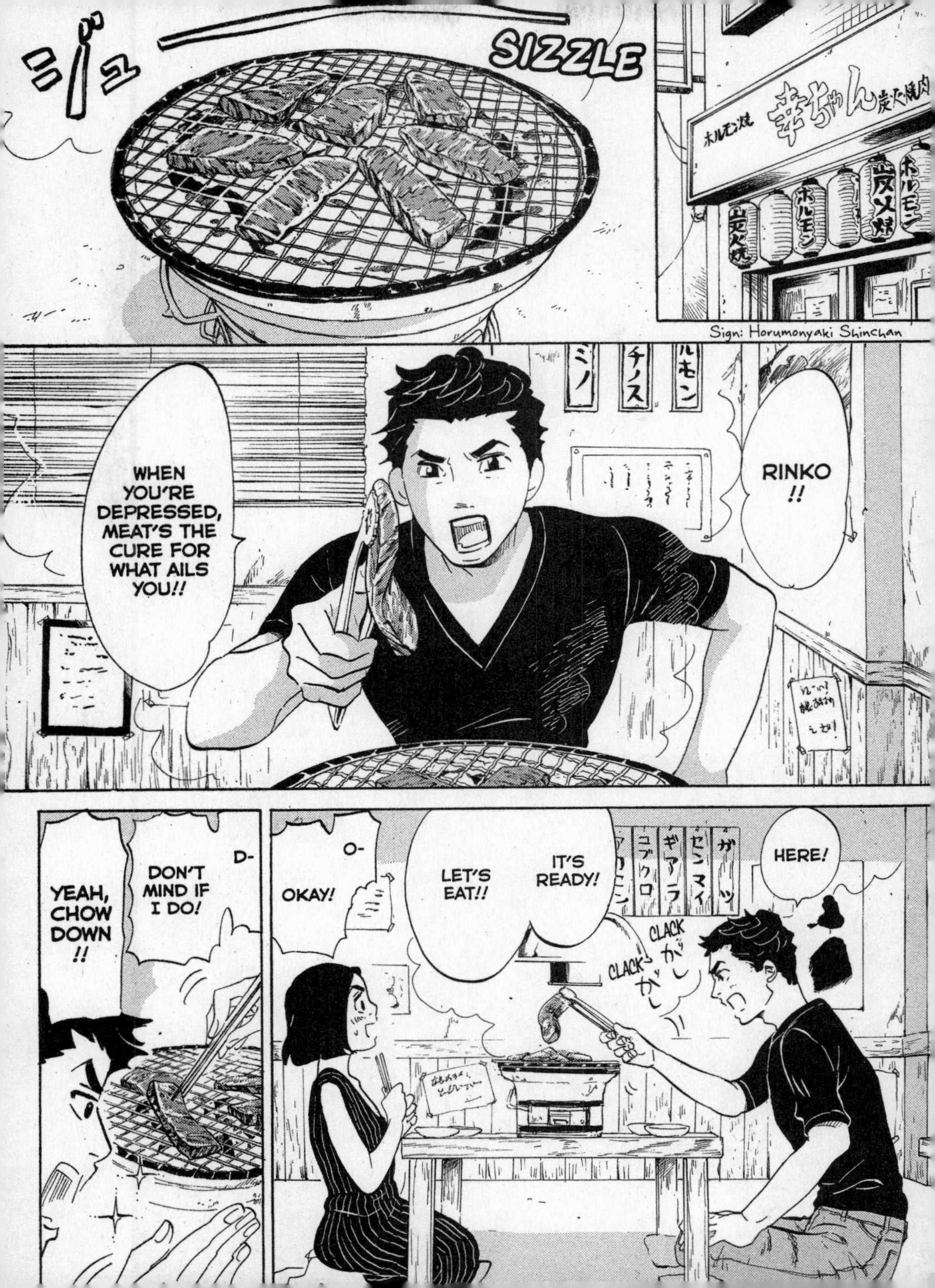
ホルモン焼 幸ちゃん 炭火焼肉
Sign: Horumonyaki Shinchan
ジュ
SIZZLE
RINKO!!
WHEN YOU'RE DEPRESSED, MEAT'S THE CURE FOR WHAT AILS YOU!!
HERE!
IT'S READY!
LET'S EAT!!
O- OKAY!
CLACK がし CLACK がし
D- DON'T MIND IF I DO!
YEAH, CHOW DOWN!!

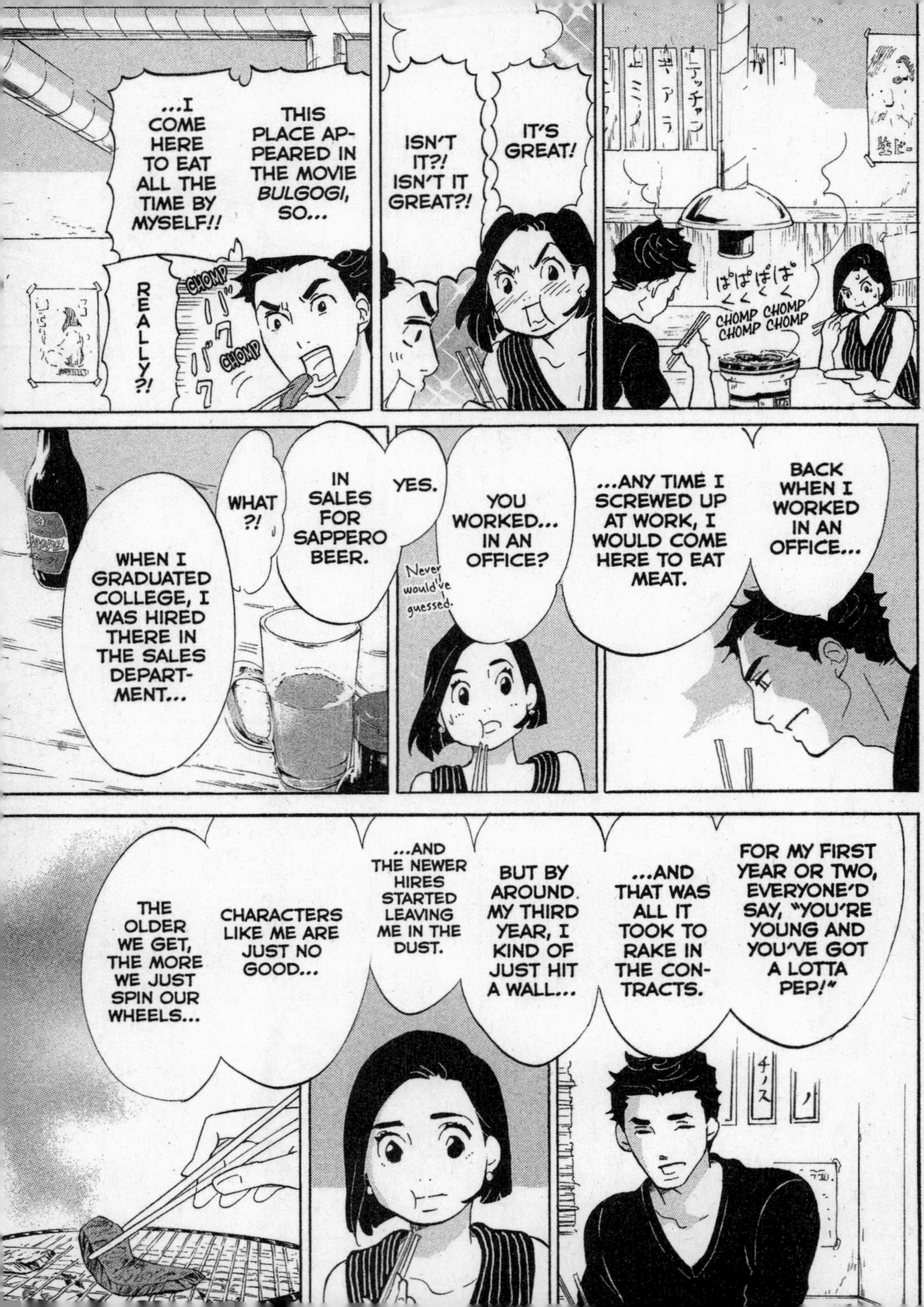

ぱくぱくぱくぱく
CHOMP CHOMP CHOMP CHOMP
IT'S GREAT!
ISN'T IT?! ISN'T IT GREAT?!
THIS PLACE APPEARED IN THE MOVIE BULGOGI, SO...
...I COME HERE TO EAT ALL THE TIME BY MYSELF!!
REALLY?!
CHOMP
CHOMP
BACK WHEN I WORKED IN AN OFFICE...
...ANY TIME I SCREWED UP AT WORK, I WOULD COME HERE TO EAT MEAT.
YOU WORKED... IN AN OFFICE?
Never would've guessed.
YES.
IN SALES FOR SAPPERO BEER.
WHAT?!
WHEN I GRADUATED COLLEGE, I WAS HIRED THERE IN THE SALES DEPARTMENT...
FOR MY FIRST YEAR OR TWO, EVERYONE'D SAY, "YOU'RE YOUNG AND YOU'VE GOT A LOTTA PEP!"
...AND THAT WAS ALL IT TOOK TO RAKE IN THE CONTRACTS.
BUT BY AROUND MY THIRD YEAR, I KIND OF JUST HIT A WALL...
...AND THE NEWER HIRES STARTED LEAVING ME IN THE DUST.
CHARACTERS LIKE ME ARE JUST NO GOOD...
THE OLDER WE GET, THE MORE WE JUST SPIN OUR WHEELS...

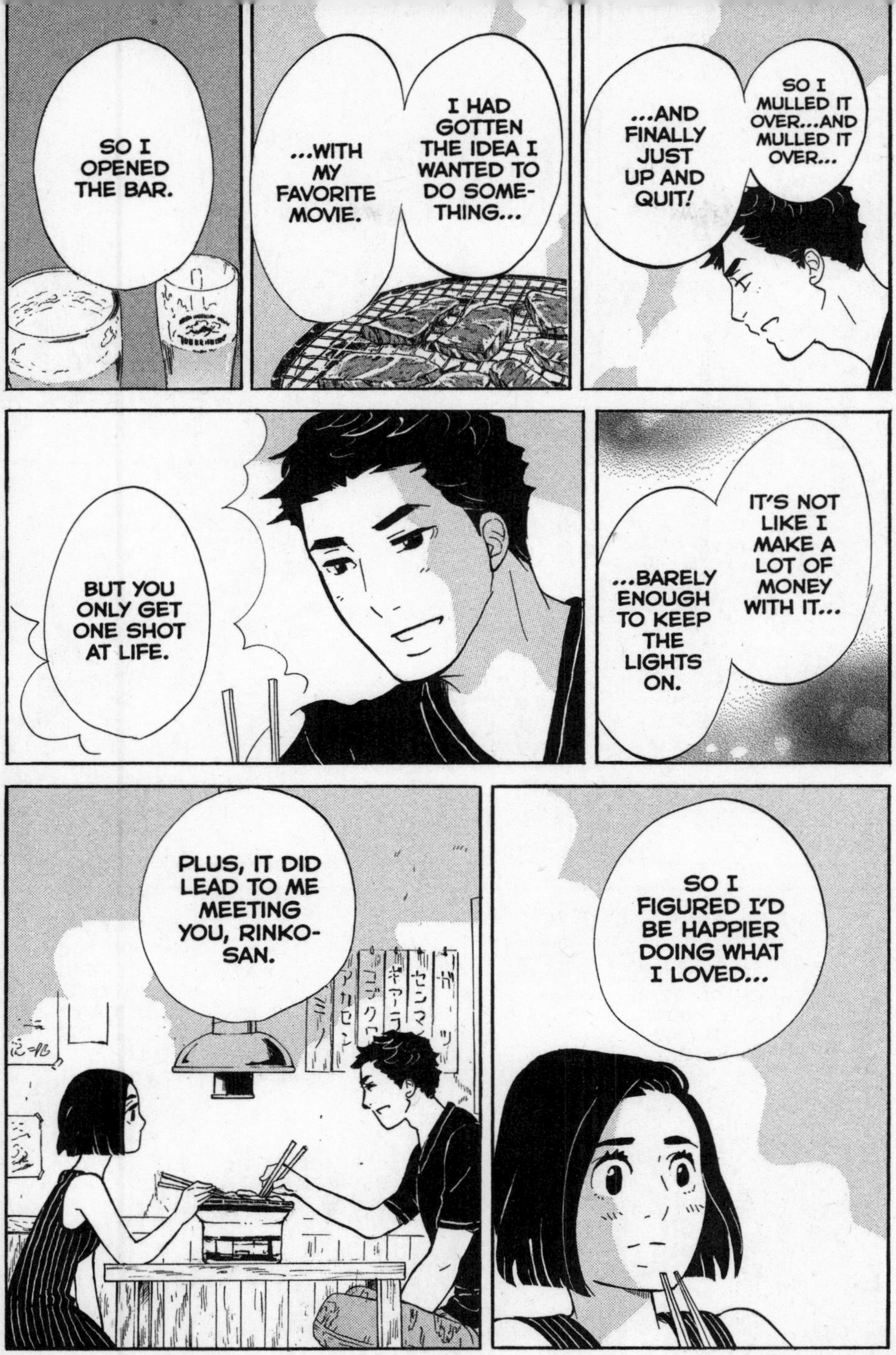
SO I MULLED IT OVER...AND MULLED IT OVER...
...AND FINALLY JUST UP AND QUIT!
I HAD GOTTEN THE IDEA I WANTED TO DO SOMETHING...
...WITH MY FAVORITE MOVIE.
SO I OPENED THE BAR.
IT'S NOT LIKE I MAKE A LOT OF MONEY WITH IT...
...BARELY ENOUGH TO KEEP THE LIGHTS ON.
BUT YOU ONLY GET ONE SHOT AT LIFE.
SO I FIGURED I'D BE HAPPIER DOING WHAT I LOVED...
PLUS, IT DID LEAD TO ME MEETING YOU, RINKO-SAN.

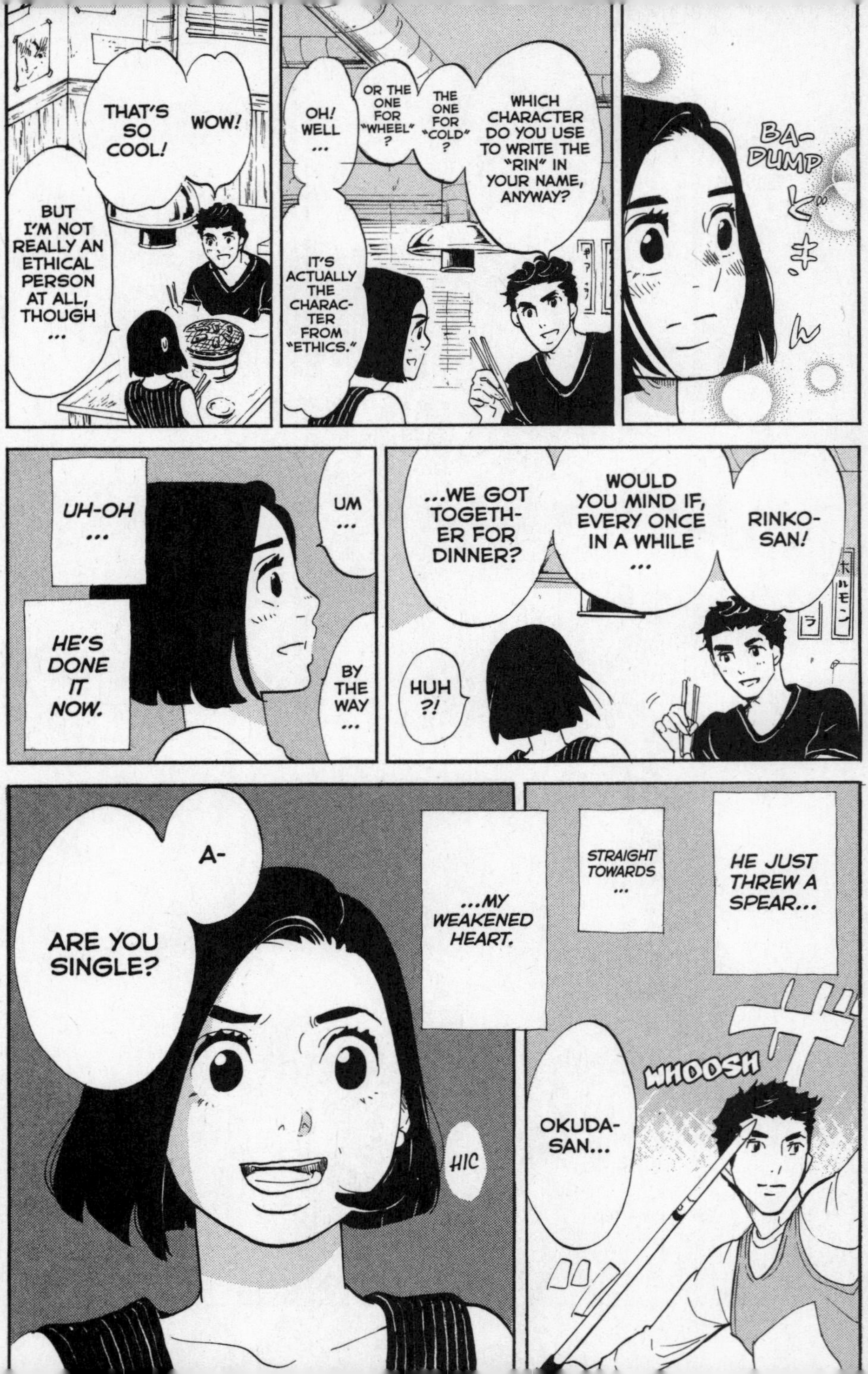
BA-DUMP
どきん
WHICH CHARACTER DO YOU USE TO WRITE THE "RIN" IN YOUR NAME, ANYWAY?
THE ONE FOR "COLD"?
OR THE ONE FOR "WHEEL"?
OH! WELL ...
IT'S ACTUALLY THE CHARACTER FROM "ETHICS."
WOW!
THAT'S SO COOL!
BUT I'M NOT REALLY AN ETHICAL PERSON AT ALL, THOUGH ...
RINKO-SAN!
WOULD YOU MIND IF, EVERY ONCE IN A WHILE ...
...WE GOT TOGETHER FOR DINNER?
ホルモン
HUH ?!
UM ...
UH-OH ...
BY THE WAY ...
HE'S DONE IT NOW.
HE JUST THREW A SPEAR...
STRAIGHT TOWARDS ...
...MY WEAKENED HEART.
ザ
WHOOSH
OKUDA-SAN...
A-
ARE YOU SINGLE?
HIC

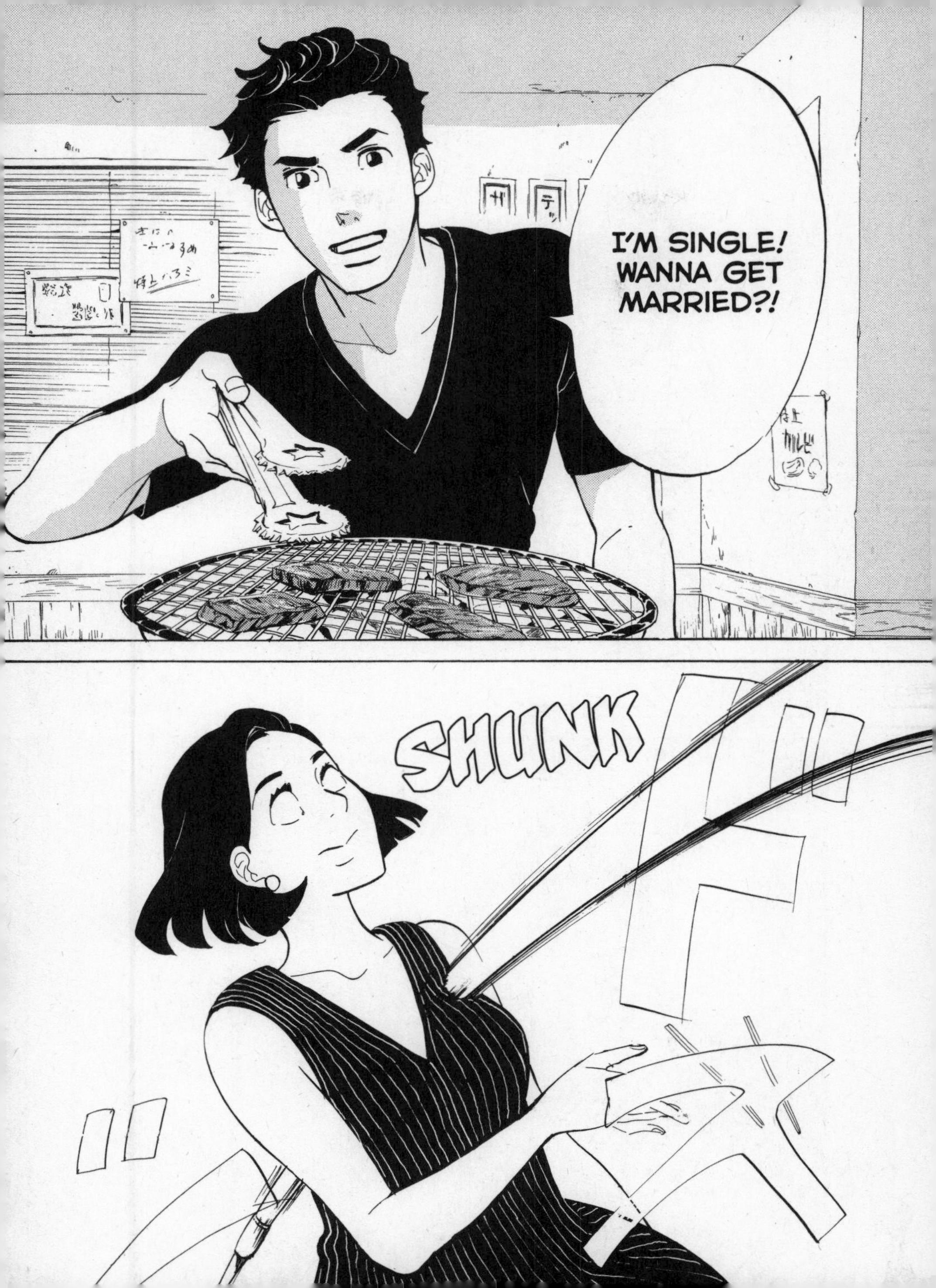
I'M SINGLE! WANNA GET MARRIED?!
SHUNK

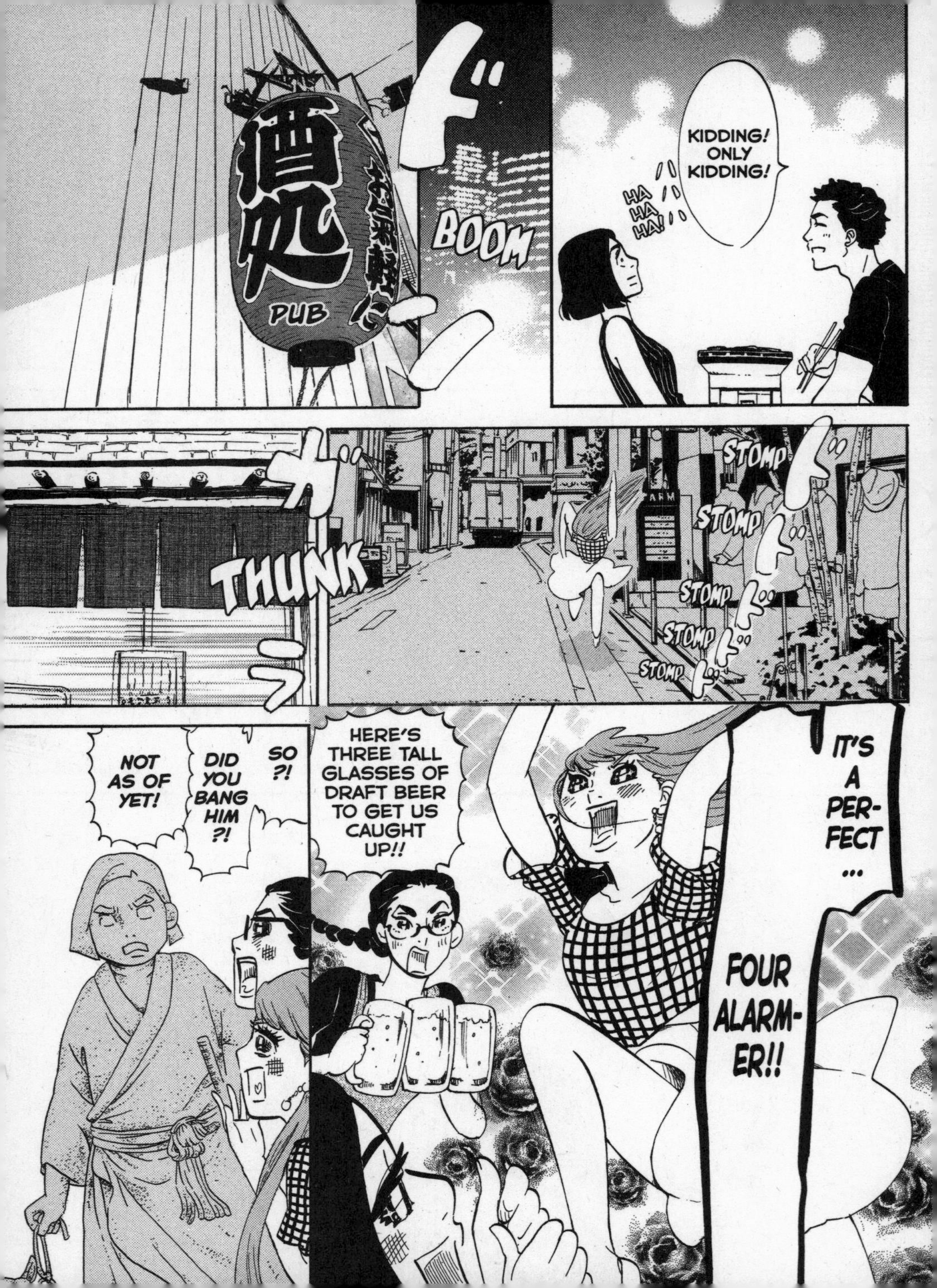
KIDDING! ONLY KIDDING!
HA HA HA!
PUB
BOOM
STOMP
STOMP
STOMP
STOMP
STOMP
THUNK
IT'S A PER-FECT...
FOUR ALARM-ER!!
HERE'S THREE TALL GLASSES OF DRAFT BEER TO GET US CAUGHT UP!!
SO?!
DID YOU BANG HIM?!
NOT AS OF YET!

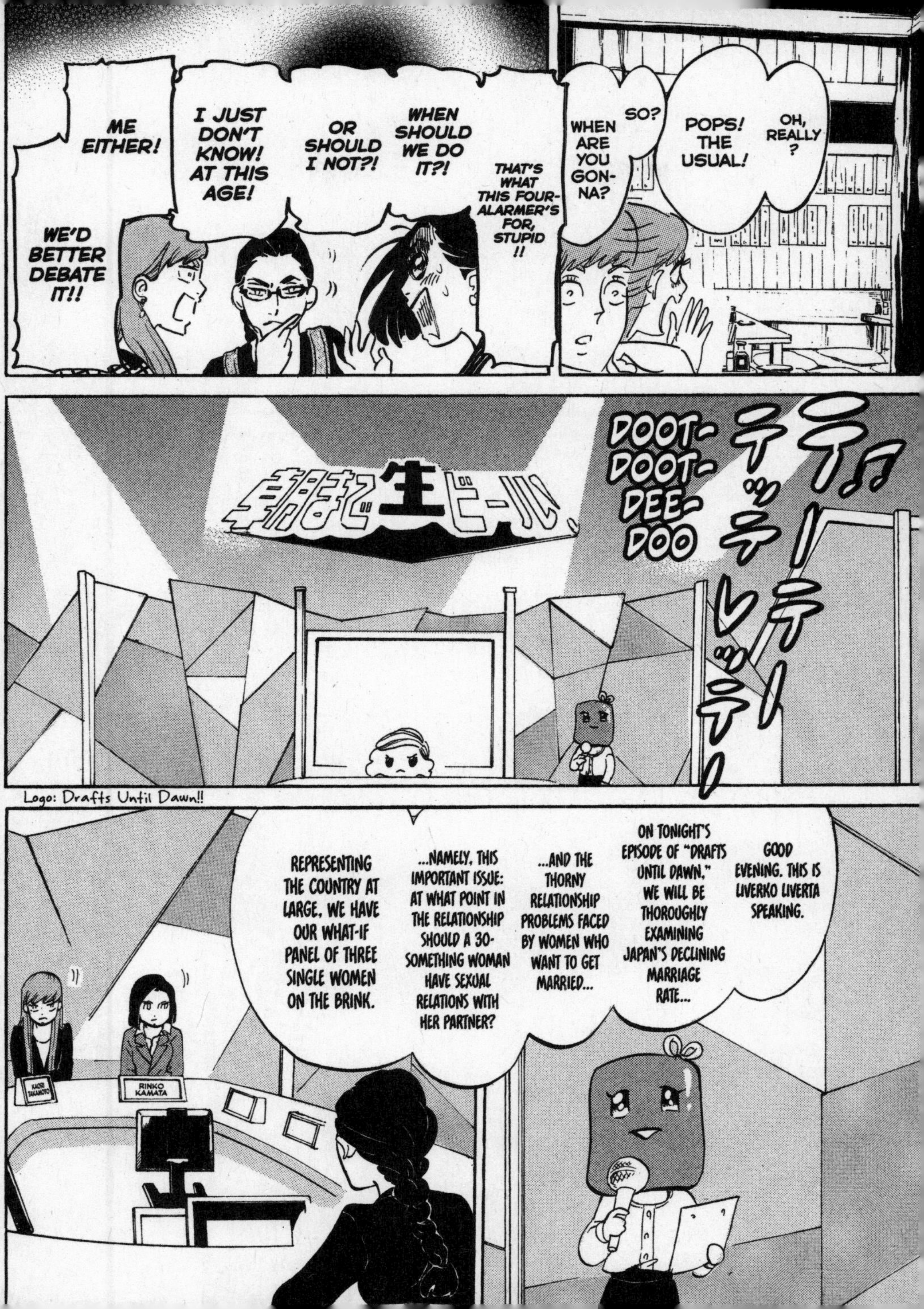
OH, REALLY?
POPS! THE USUAL!
SO?
WHEN ARE YOU GON-NA?
THAT'S WHAT THIS FOUR-ALARMER'S FOR, STUPID!!
WHEN SHOULD WE DO IT?!
OR SHOULD I NOT?!
I JUST DON'T KNOW! AT THIS AGE!
ME EITHER!
WE'D BETTER DEBATE IT!!
テ♫ーテー
テッテーレッテー
DOOT-DOOT-DEE-DOO
朝まで生ビール
GOOD EVENING. THIS IS LIVERKO LIVERTA SPEAKING.
ON TONIGHT'S EPISODE OF "DRAFTS UNTIL DAWN," WE WILL BE THOROUGHLY EXAMINING JAPAN'S DECLINING MARRIAGE RATE...
...AND THE THORNY RELATIONSHIP PROBLEMS FACED BY WOMEN WHO WANT TO GET MARRIED...
...NAMELY, THIS IMPORTANT ISSUE: AT WHAT POINT IN THE RELATIONSHIP SHOULD A 30-SOMETHING WOMAN HAVE SEXUAL RELATIONS WITH HER PARTNER?
REPRESENTING THE COUNTRY AT LARGE, WE HAVE OUR WHAT-IF PANEL OF THREE SINGLE WOMEN ON THE BRINK.
RINKO KAMATA
KAORI TAKAMOTO
Logo: Drafts Until Dawn!!

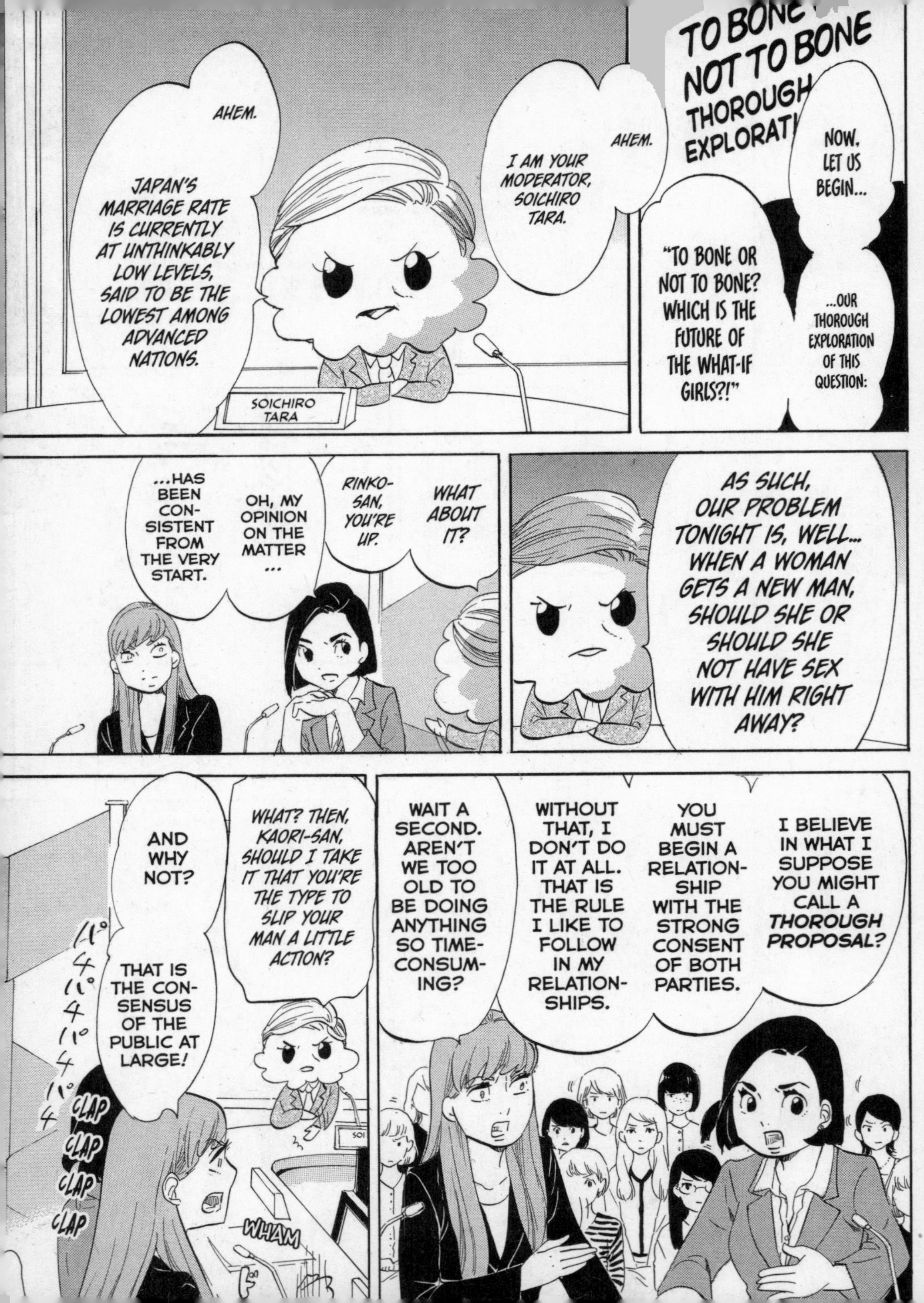
TO BONE
NOT TO BONE
THOROUGH
EXPLORAT
NOW, LET US BEGIN...
...OUR THOROUGH EXPLORATION OF THIS QUESTION:
"TO BONE OR NOT TO BONE? WHICH IS THE FUTURE OF THE WHAT-IF GIRLS?!"
AHEM.
I AM YOUR MODERATOR, SOICHIRO TARA.
AHEM.
JAPAN'S MARRIAGE RATE IS CURRENTLY AT UNTHINKABLY LOW LEVELS, SAID TO BE THE LOWEST AMONG ADVANCED NATIONS.
SOICHIRO TARA
AS SUCH, OUR PROBLEM TONIGHT IS, WELL... WHEN A WOMAN GETS A NEW MAN, SHOULD SHE OR SHOULD SHE NOT HAVE SEX WITH HIM RIGHT AWAY?
WHAT ABOUT IT?
RINKO-SAN, YOU'RE UP.
OH, MY OPINION ON THE MATTER...
...HAS BEEN CONSISTENT FROM THE VERY START.
I BELIEVE IN WHAT I SUPPOSE YOU MIGHT CALL A **THOROUGH PROPOSAL**?
YOU MUST BEGIN A RELATIONSHIP WITH THE STRONG CONSENT OF BOTH PARTIES.
WITHOUT THAT, I DON'T DO IT AT ALL. THAT IS THE RULE I LIKE TO FOLLOW IN MY RELATIONSHIPS.
WAIT A SECOND. AREN'T WE TOO OLD TO BE DOING ANYTHING SO TIME-CONSUMING?
WHAT? THEN, KAORI-SAN, SHOULD I TAKE IT THAT YOU'RE THE TYPE TO SLIP YOUR MAN A LITTLE ACTION?
AND WHY NOT?
THAT IS THE CONSENSUS OF THE PUBLIC AT LARGE!
パチパチパチパチパチ
CLAP CLAP CLAP CLAP
WHAM

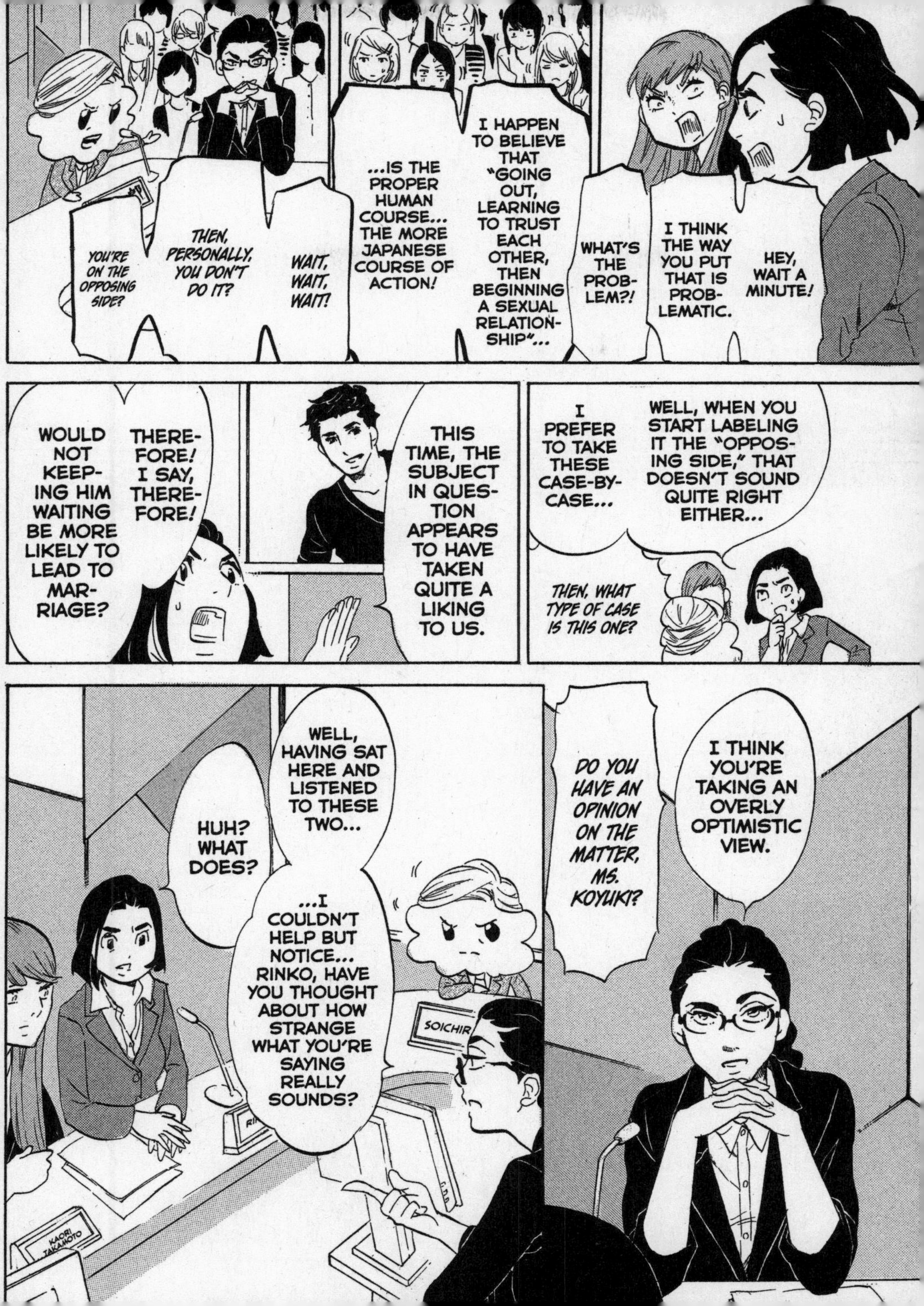
HEY, WAIT A MINUTE!
I THINK THE WAY YOU PUT THAT IS PROBLEMATIC.
WHAT'S THE PROBLEM?!
I HAPPEN TO BELIEVE THAT "GOING OUT, LEARNING TO TRUST EACH OTHER, THEN BEGINNING A SEXUAL RELATIONSHIP"...
...IS THE PROPER HUMAN COURSE... THE MORE JAPANESE COURSE OF ACTION!
WAIT, WAIT, WAIT!
THEN, PERSONALLY, YOU DON'T DO IT?
YOU'RE ON THE OPPOSING SIDE?
WELL, WHEN YOU START LABELING IT THE "OPPOSING SIDE," THAT DOESN'T SOUND QUITE RIGHT EITHER...
I PREFER TO TAKE THESE CASE-BY-CASE...
THEN, WHAT TYPE OF CASE IS THIS ONE?
THIS TIME, THE SUBJECT IN QUESTION APPEARS TO HAVE TAKEN QUITE A LIKING TO US.
THEREFORE! I SAY, THEREFORE!
WOULD NOT KEEPING HIM WAITING BE MORE LIKELY TO LEAD TO MARRIAGE?
I THINK YOU'RE TAKING AN OVERLY OPTIMISTIC VIEW.
DO YOU HAVE AN OPINION ON THE MATTER, MS. KOYUKI?
WELL, HAVING SAT HERE AND LISTENED TO THESE TWO...
HUH? WHAT DOES?
...I COULDN'T HELP BUT NOTICE... RINKO, HAVE YOU THOUGHT ABOUT HOW STRANGE WHAT YOU'RE SAYING REALLY SOUNDS?
SOICHIR
KAORI TAKAMOTO

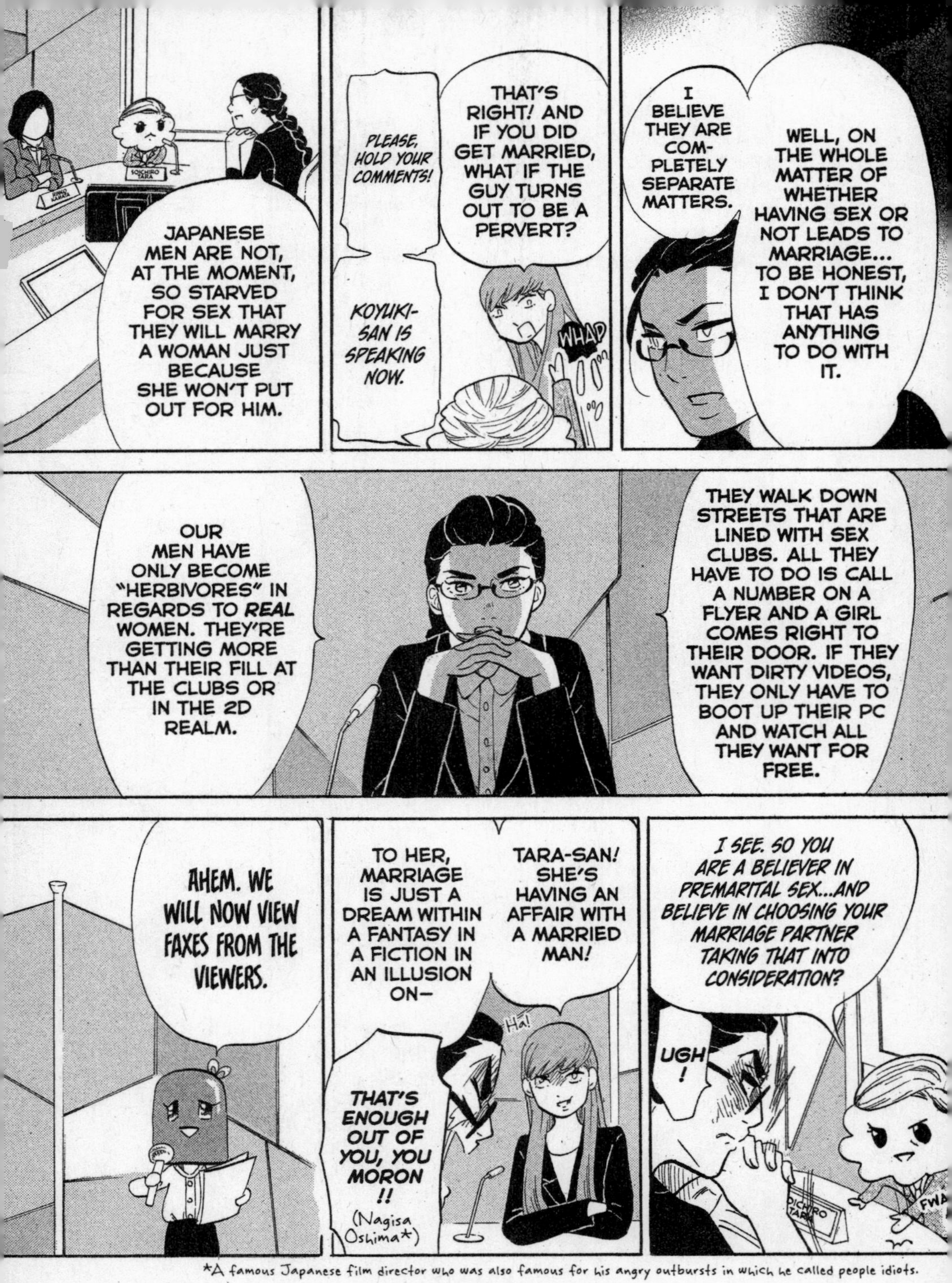
WELL, ON THE WHOLE MATTER OF WHETHER HAVING SEX OR NOT LEADS TO MARRIAGE... TO BE HONEST, I DON'T THINK THAT HAS ANYTHING TO DO WITH IT.
I BELIEVE THEY ARE COMPLETELY SEPARATE MATTERS.
THAT'S RIGHT! AND IF YOU DID GET MARRIED, WHAT IF THE GUY TURNS OUT TO BE A PERVERT?
PLEASE, HOLD YOUR COMMENTS!
KOYUKI-SAN IS SPEAKING NOW.
WHAP
JAPANESE MEN ARE NOT, AT THE MOMENT, SO STARVED FOR SEX THAT THEY WILL MARRY A WOMAN JUST BECAUSE SHE WON'T PUT OUT FOR HIM.
THEY WALK DOWN STREETS THAT ARE LINED WITH SEX CLUBS. ALL THEY HAVE TO DO IS CALL A NUMBER ON A FLYER AND A GIRL COMES RIGHT TO THEIR DOOR. IF THEY WANT DIRTY VIDEOS, THEY ONLY HAVE TO BOOT UP THEIR PC AND WATCH ALL THEY WANT FOR FREE.
OUR MEN HAVE ONLY BECOME "HERBIVORES" IN REGARDS TO REAL WOMEN. THEY'RE GETTING MORE THAN THEIR FILL AT THE CLUBS OR IN THE 2D REALM.
I SEE. SO YOU ARE A BELIEVER IN PREMARITAL SEX...AND BELIEVE IN CHOOSING YOUR MARRIAGE PARTNER TAKING THAT INTO CONSIDERATION?
UGH!
FWA
TARA-SAN! SHE'S HAVING AN AFFAIR WITH A MARRIED MAN!
TO HER, MARRIAGE IS JUST A DREAM WITHIN A FANTASY IN A FICTION IN AN ILLUSION ON—
Ha!
THAT'S ENOUGH OUT OF YOU, YOU MORON!!
(Nagisa Oshima*)
AHEM. WE WILL NOW VIEW FAXES FROM THE VIEWERS.

*A famous Japanese film director who was also famous for his angry outbursts in which he called people idiots.

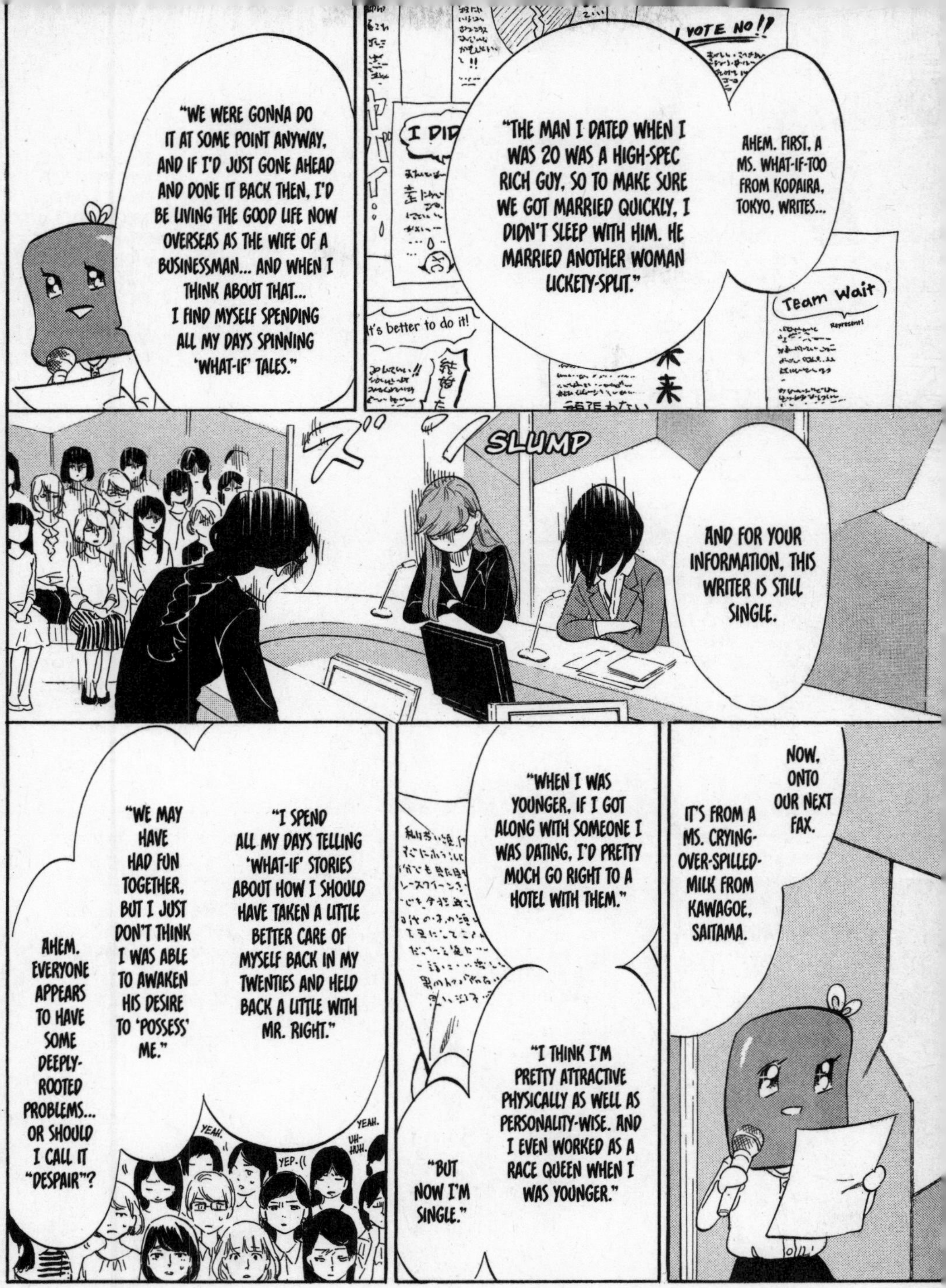
I VOTE NO!!
AHEM. FIRST, A MS. WHAT-IF-TOO FROM KODAIRA, TOKYO, WRITES...
"THE MAN I DATED WHEN I WAS 20 WAS A HIGH-SPEC RICH GUY, SO TO MAKE SURE WE GOT MARRIED QUICKLY, I DIDN'T SLEEP WITH HIM. HE MARRIED ANOTHER WOMAN LICKETY-SPLIT."
I DID
Team Wait
Represent!
it's better to do it!
"WE WERE GONNA DO IT AT SOME POINT ANYWAY, AND IF I'D JUST GONE AHEAD AND DONE IT BACK THEN, I'D BE LIVING THE GOOD LIFE NOW OVERSEAS AS THE WIFE OF A BUSINESSMAN... AND WHEN I THINK ABOUT THAT... I FIND MYSELF SPENDING ALL MY DAYS SPINNING 'WHAT-IF' TALES."
SLUMP
AND FOR YOUR INFORMATION, THIS WRITER IS STILL SINGLE.
NOW, ONTO OUR NEXT FAX.
IT'S FROM A MS. CRYING-OVER-SPILLED-MILK FROM KAWAGOE, SAITAMA.
"WHEN I WAS YOUNGER, IF I GOT ALONG WITH SOMEONE I WAS DATING, I'D PRETTY MUCH GO RIGHT TO A HOTEL WITH THEM."
"I THINK I'M PRETTY ATTRACTIVE PHYSICALLY AS WELL AS PERSONALITY-WISE. AND I EVEN WORKED AS A RACE QUEEN WHEN I WAS YOUNGER."
"BUT NOW I'M SINGLE."
"I SPEND ALL MY DAYS TELLING 'WHAT-IF' STORIES ABOUT HOW I SHOULD HAVE TAKEN A LITTLE BETTER CARE OF MYSELF BACK IN MY TWENTIES AND HELD BACK A LITTLE WITH MR. RIGHT."
"WE MAY HAVE HAD FUN TOGETHER, BUT I JUST DON'T THINK I WAS ABLE TO AWAKEN HIS DESIRE TO 'POSSESS' ME."
AHEM. EVERYONE APPEARS TO HAVE SOME DEEPLY-ROOTED PROBLEMS... OR SHOULD I CALL IT "DESPAIR"?
YEAH.
UH-HUH.
YEP.
YEAH.

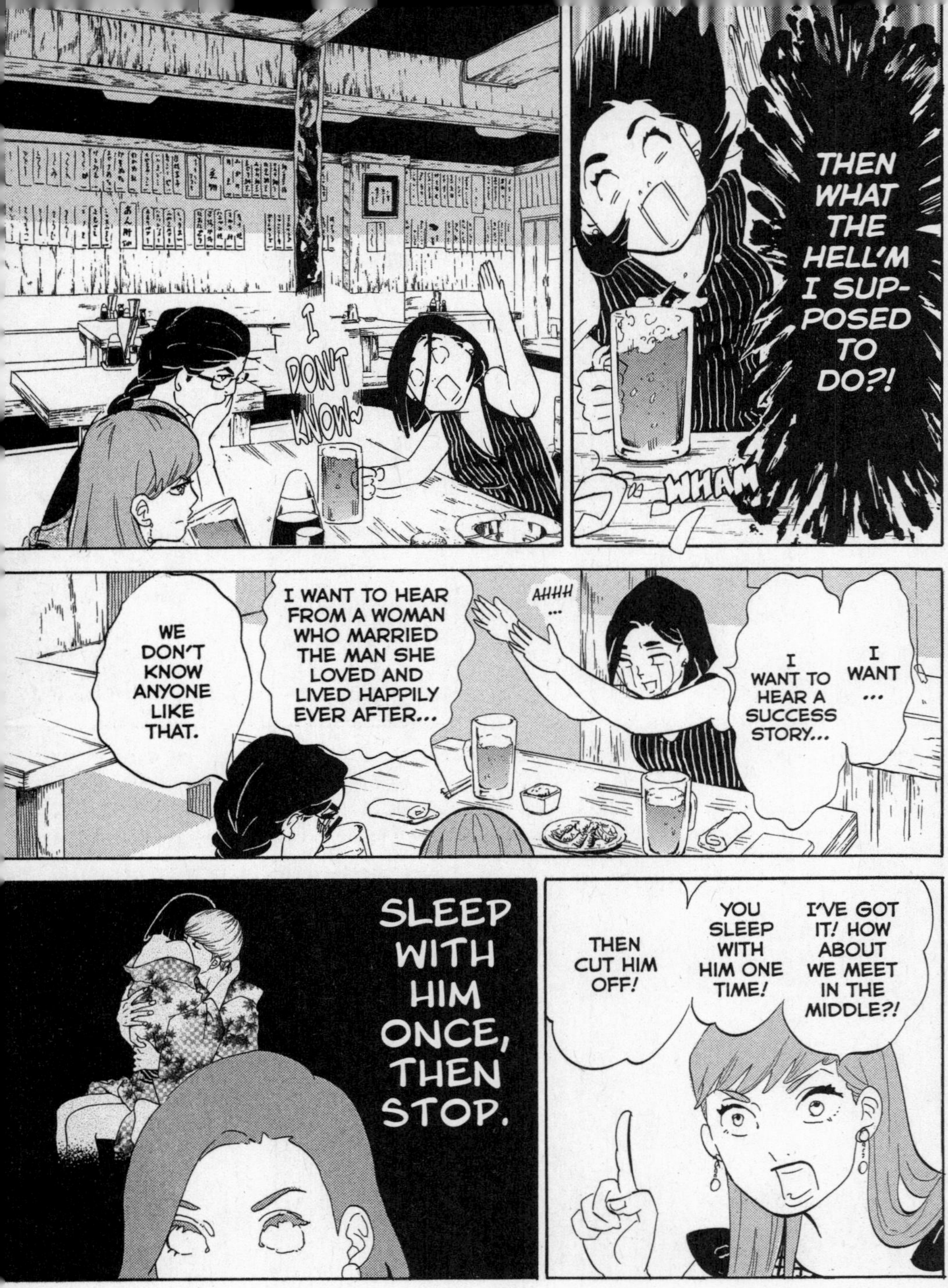
THEN WHAT THE HELL'M I SUPPOSED TO DO?!
WHAM
I DON'T KNOW~
I WANT...
I WANT TO HEAR A SUCCESS STORY...
AHHH...
I WANT TO HEAR FROM A WOMAN WHO MARRIED THE MAN SHE LOVED AND LIVED HAPPILY EVER AFTER...
WE DON'T KNOW ANYONE LIKE THAT.
I'VE GOT IT! HOW ABOUT WE MEET IN THE MIDDLE?!
YOU SLEEP WITH HIM ONE TIME!
THEN CUT HIM OFF!
SLEEP WITH HIM ONCE, THEN STOP.

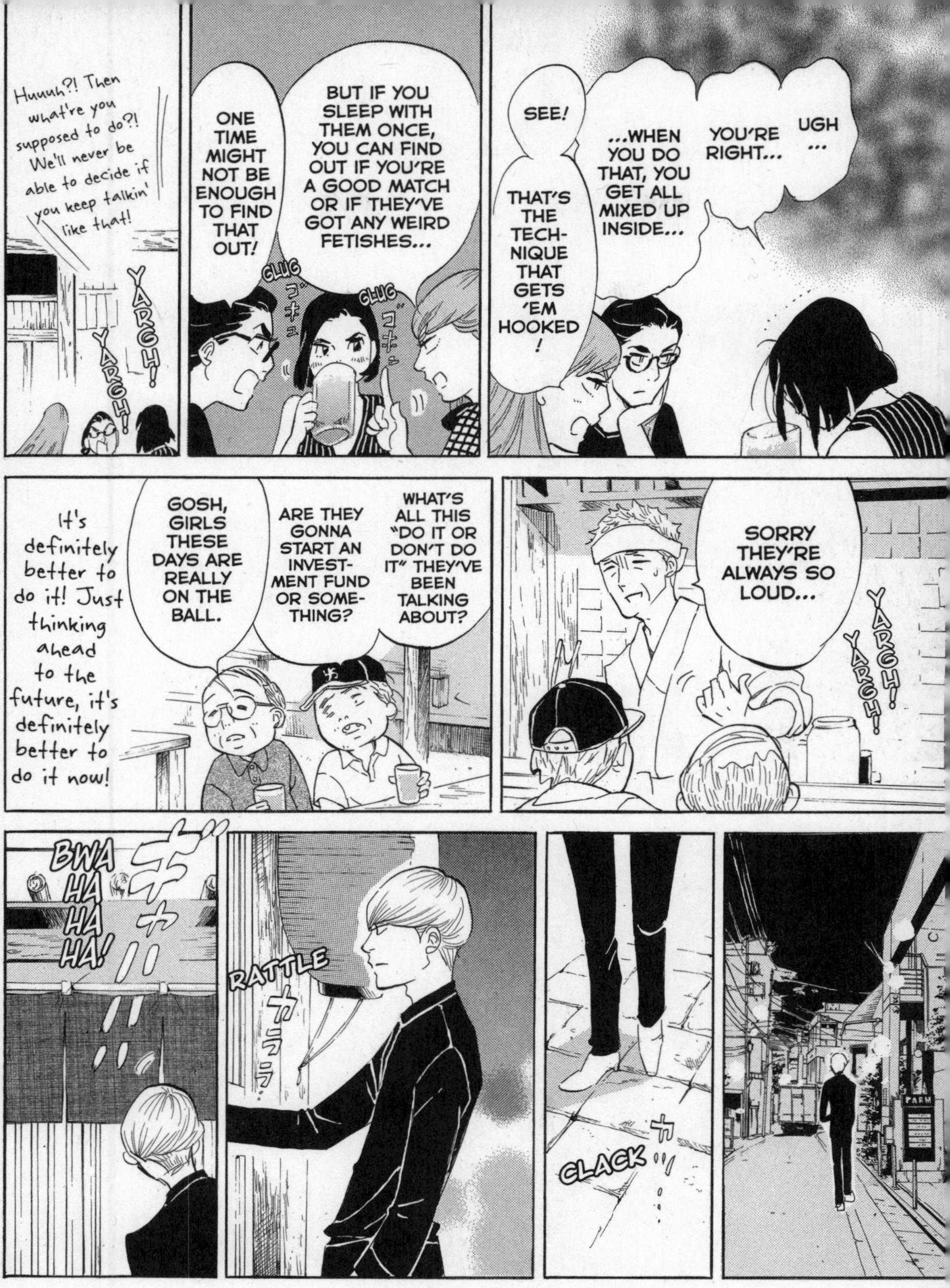
UGH ...
YOU'RE RIGHT...
...WHEN YOU DO THAT, YOU GET ALL MIXED UP INSIDE...
SEE!
THAT'S THE TECHNIQUE THAT GETS 'EM HOOKED!
BUT IF YOU SLEEP WITH THEM ONCE, YOU CAN FIND OUT IF YOU'RE A GOOD MATCH OR IF THEY'VE GOT ANY WEIRD FETISHES...
ONE TIME MIGHT NOT BE ENOUGH TO FIND THAT OUT!
GLUG
GLUG
Huuuh?! Then what're you supposed to do?! We'll never be able to decide if you keep talkin' like that!
YARGH!
YARGH!
SORRY THEY'RE ALWAYS SO LOUD...
YARGH!
YARGH!
WHAT'S ALL THIS "DO IT OR DON'T DO IT" THEY'VE BEEN TALKING ABOUT?
ARE THEY GONNA START AN INVEST-MENT FUND OR SOME-THING?
GOSH, GIRLS THESE DAYS ARE REALLY ON THE BALL.
It's definitely better to do it! Just thinking ahead to the future, it's definitely better to do it now!
CLACK
RATTLE
BWA HA HA HA HA!

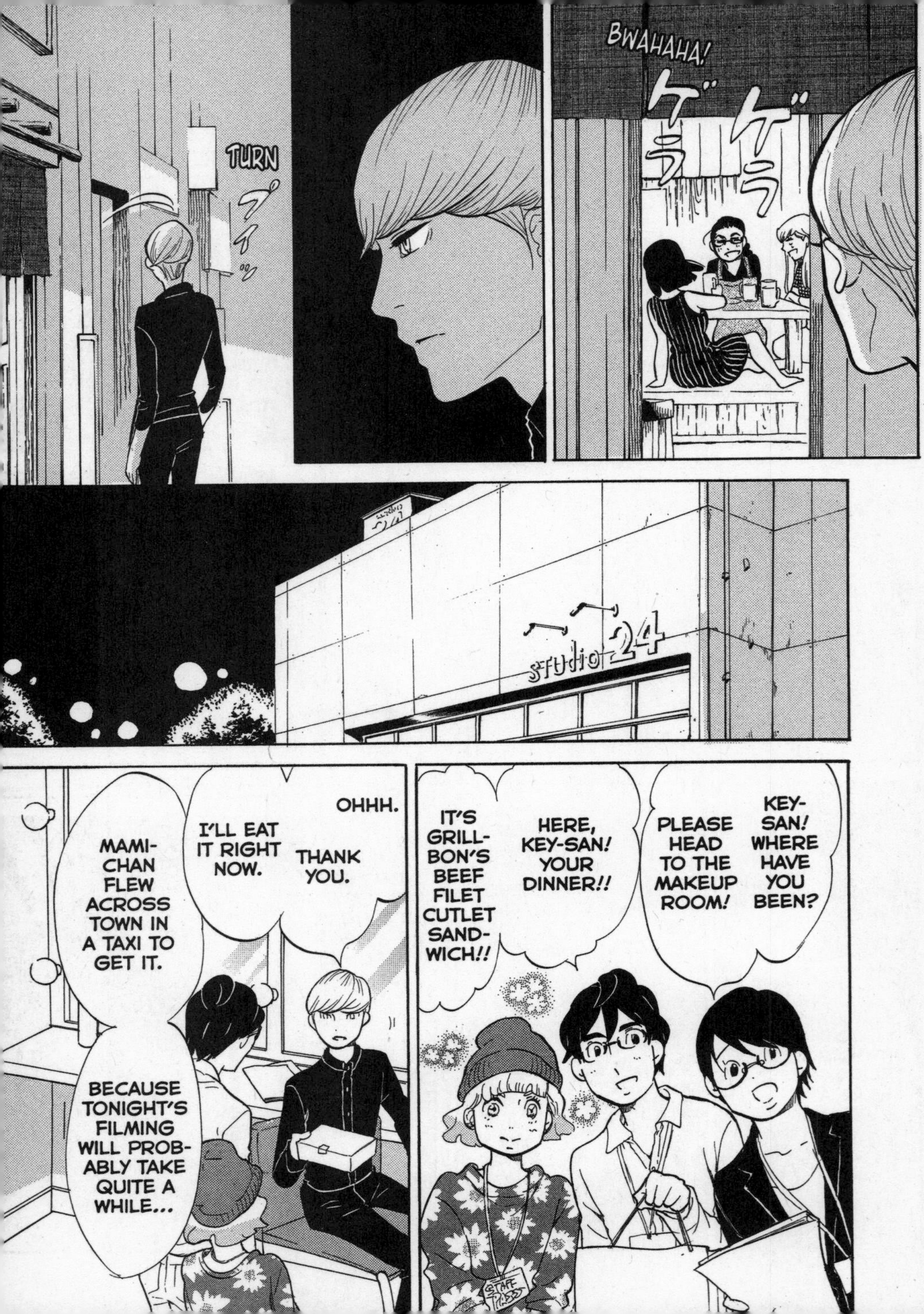
BWAHAHA!
ゲラ
ゲラ
TURN
プイッ
studio 24
KEY-SAN! WHERE HAVE YOU BEEN?
PLEASE HEAD TO THE MAKEUP ROOM!
HERE, KEY-SAN! YOUR DINNER!!
IT'S GRILL-BON'S BEEF FILET CUTLET SANDWICH!!
OHHH.
THANK YOU.
I'LL EAT IT RIGHT NOW.
MAMI-CHAN FLEW ACROSS TOWN IN A TAXI TO GET IT.
BECAUSE TONIGHT'S FILMING WILL PROBABLY TAKE QUITE A WHILE...

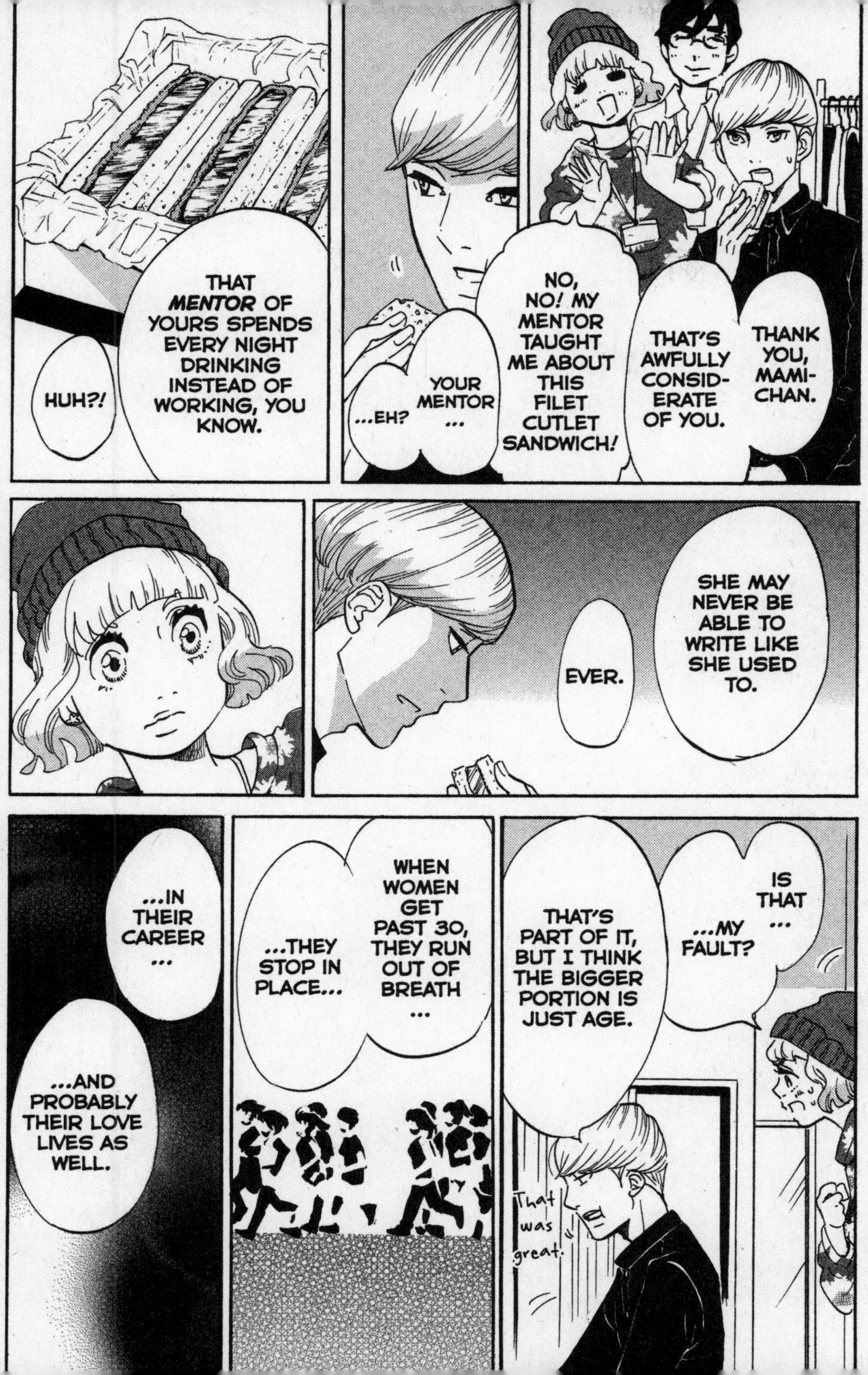
THANK YOU, MAMI-CHAN.
THAT'S AWFULLY CONSID-ERATE OF YOU.
NO, NO! MY MENTOR TAUGHT ME ABOUT THIS FILET CUTLET SANDWICH!
YOUR MENTOR ...
...EH?
THAT *MENTOR* OF YOURS SPENDS EVERY NIGHT DRINKING INSTEAD OF WORKING, YOU KNOW.
HUH?!
SHE MAY NEVER BE ABLE TO WRITE LIKE SHE USED TO.
EVER.
IS THAT ...
...MY FAULT?
THAT'S PART OF IT, BUT I THINK THE BIGGER PORTION IS JUST AGE.
That was great.
WHEN WOMEN GET PAST 30, THEY RUN OUT OF BREATH ...
...THEY STOP IN PLACE...
...IN THEIR CAREER ...
...AND PROBABLY THEIR LOVE LIVES AS WELL.

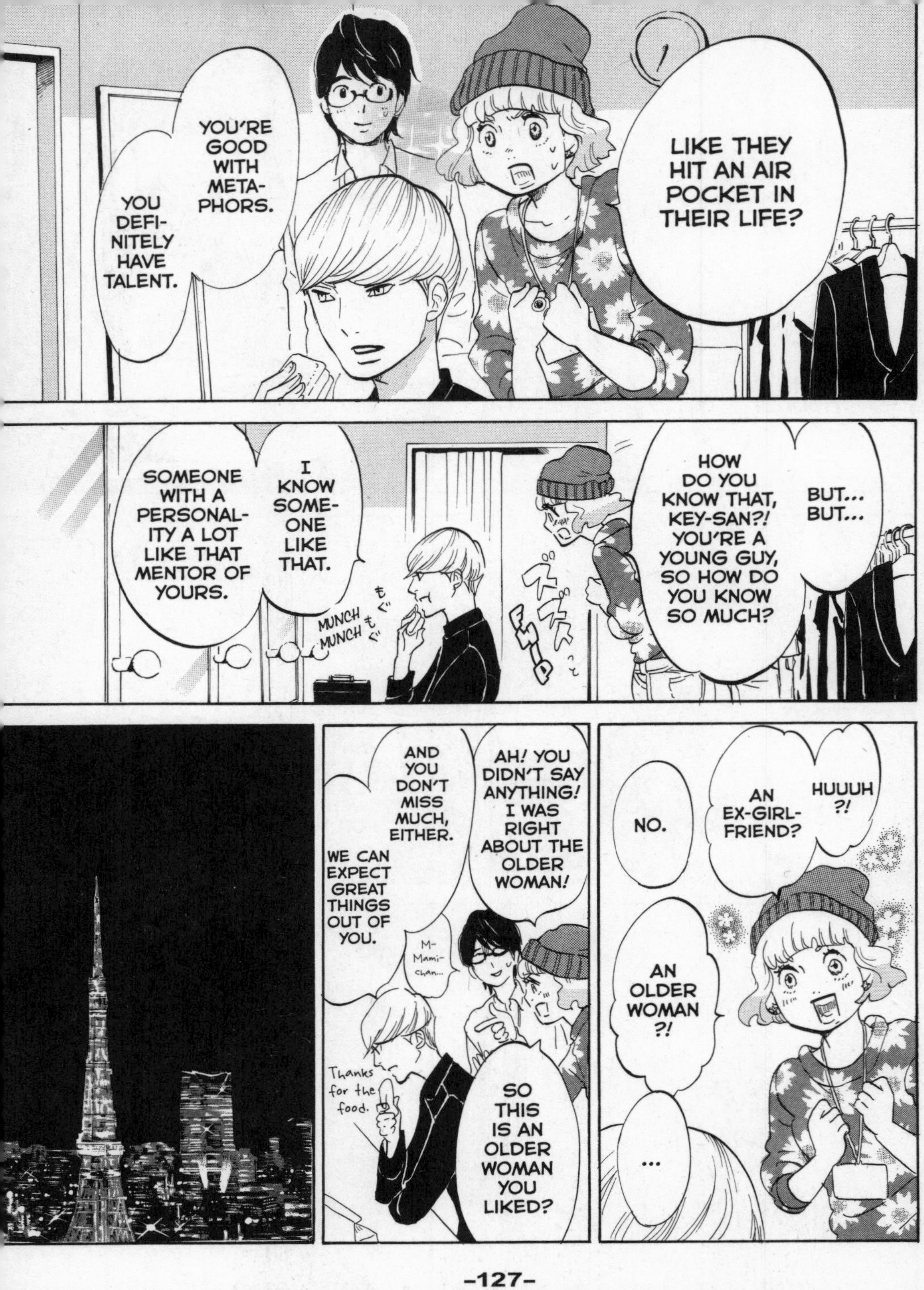
LIKE THEY HIT AN AIR POCKET IN THEIR LIFE?
YOU'RE GOOD WITH METAPHORS.
YOU DEFINITELY HAVE TALENT.
BUT... BUT...
HOW DO YOU KNOW THAT, KEY-SAN?! YOU'RE A YOUNG GUY, SO HOW DO YOU KNOW SO MUCH?
FWP
I KNOW SOMEONE LIKE THAT.
SOMEONE WITH A PERSONALITY A LOT LIKE THAT MENTOR OF YOURS.
もぐもぐ
MUNCH MUNCH
HUUUH?!
AN EX-GIRLFRIEND?
NO.
AN OLDER WOMAN?!
...
AH! YOU DIDN'T SAY ANYTHING! I WAS RIGHT ABOUT THE OLDER WOMAN!
AND YOU DON'T MISS MUCH, EITHER.
WE CAN EXPECT GREAT THINGS OUT OF YOU.
M-Mami-chan...
SO THIS IS AN OLDER WOMAN YOU LIKED?
Thanks for the food.

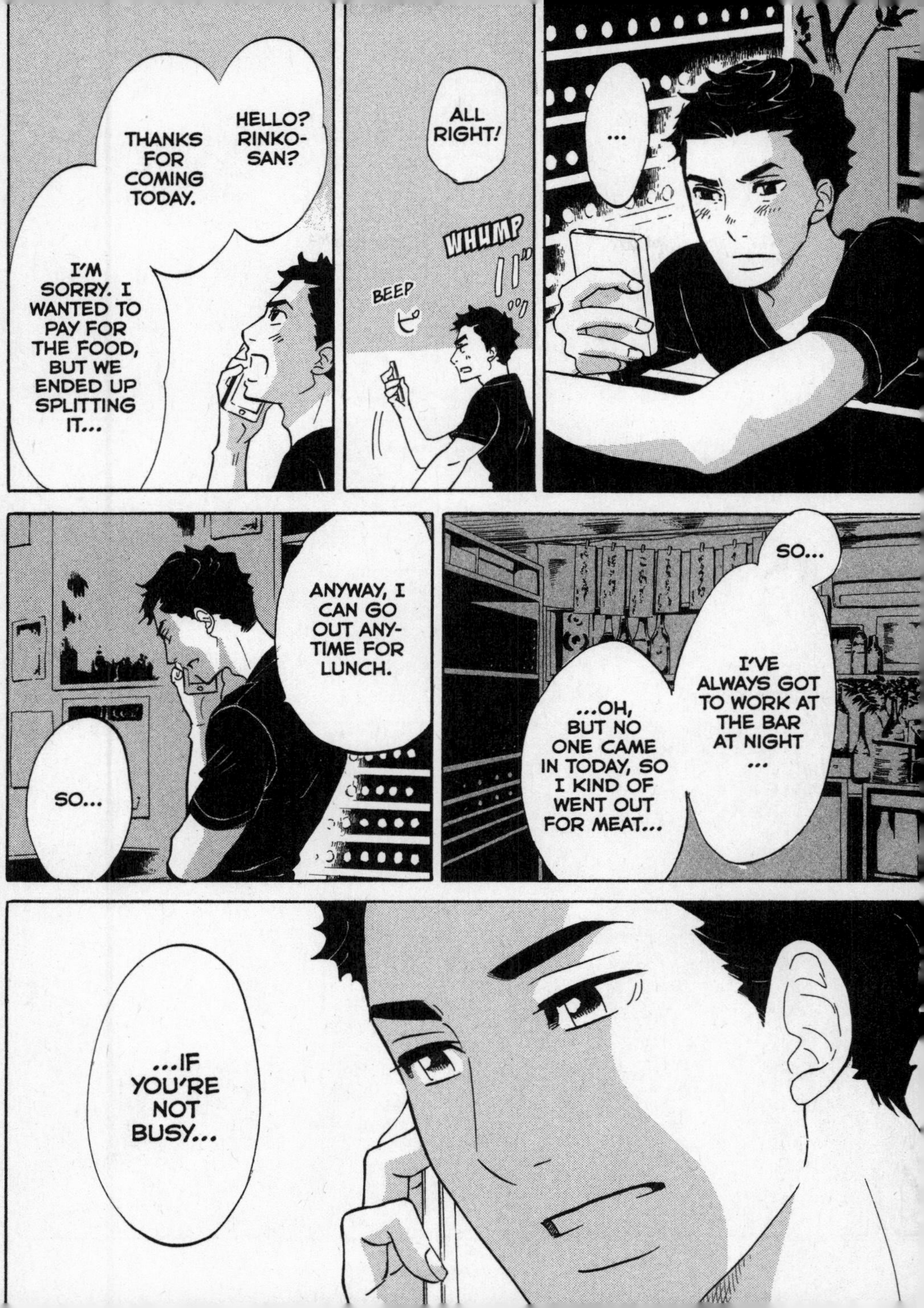
...
ALL RIGHT!
WHUMP
BEEP
ピ
HELLO? RINKO-SAN?
THANKS FOR COMING TODAY.
I'M SORRY. I WANTED TO PAY FOR THE FOOD, BUT WE ENDED UP SPLITTING IT...
SO...
I'VE ALWAYS GOT TO WORK AT THE BAR AT NIGHT...
...OH, BUT NO ONE CAME IN TODAY, SO I KIND OF WENT OUT FOR MEAT...
ANYWAY, I CAN GO OUT ANY-TIME FOR LUNCH.
SO...
...IF YOU'RE NOT BUSY...

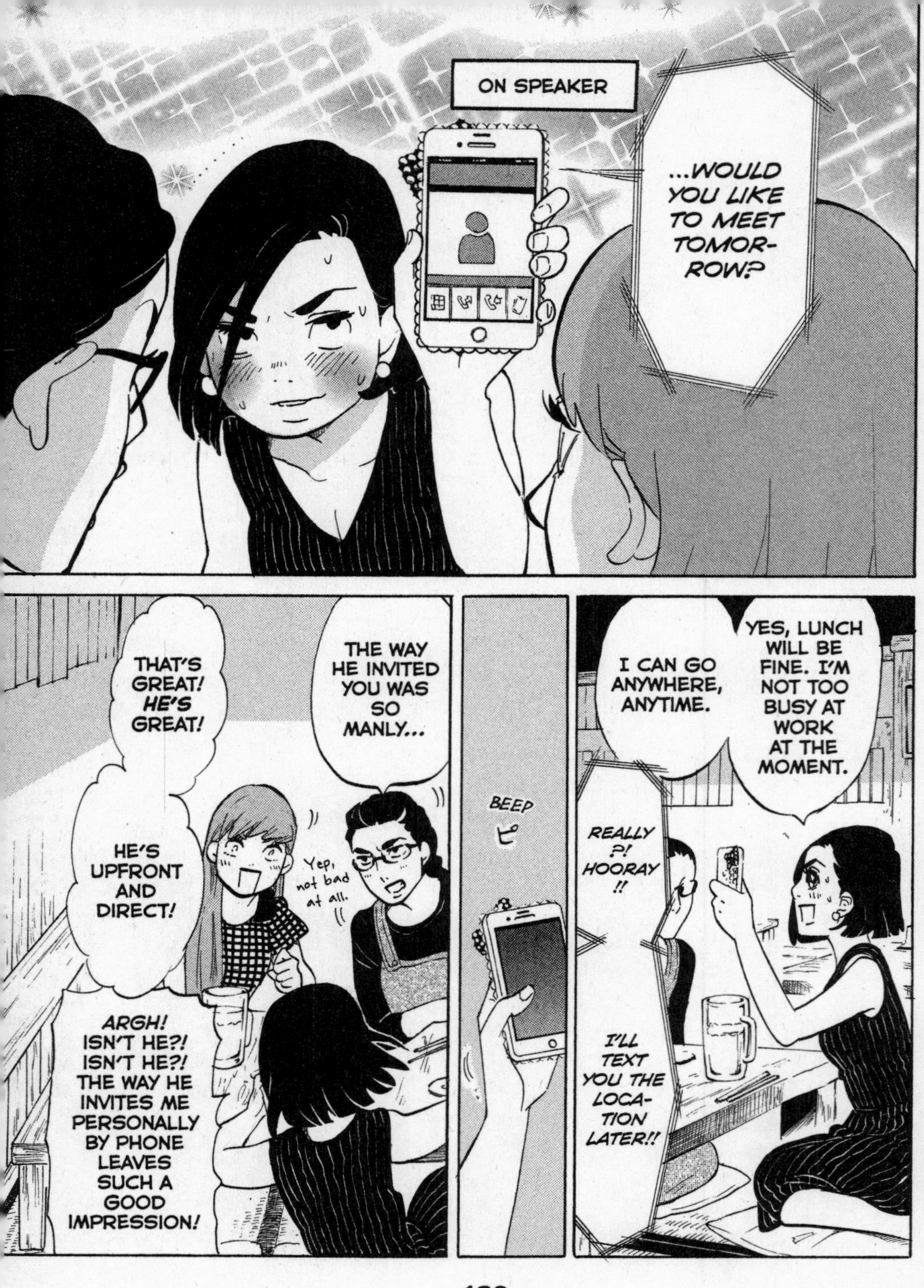
ON SPEAKER
...WOULD YOU LIKE TO MEET TOMOR-ROW?
YES, LUNCH WILL BE FINE. I'M NOT TOO BUSY AT WORK AT THE MOMENT.
I CAN GO ANYWHERE, ANYTIME.
REALLY?! HOORAY!!
I'LL TEXT YOU THE LOCA-TION LATER!!
BEEP
ピ
THE WAY HE INVITED YOU WAS SO MANLY...
THAT'S GREAT! HE'S GREAT!
Yep, not bad at all.
HE'S UPFRONT AND DIRECT!
ARGH! ISN'T HE?! ISN'T HE?! THE WAY HE INVITES ME PERSONALLY BY PHONE LEAVES SUCH A GOOD IMPRESSION!

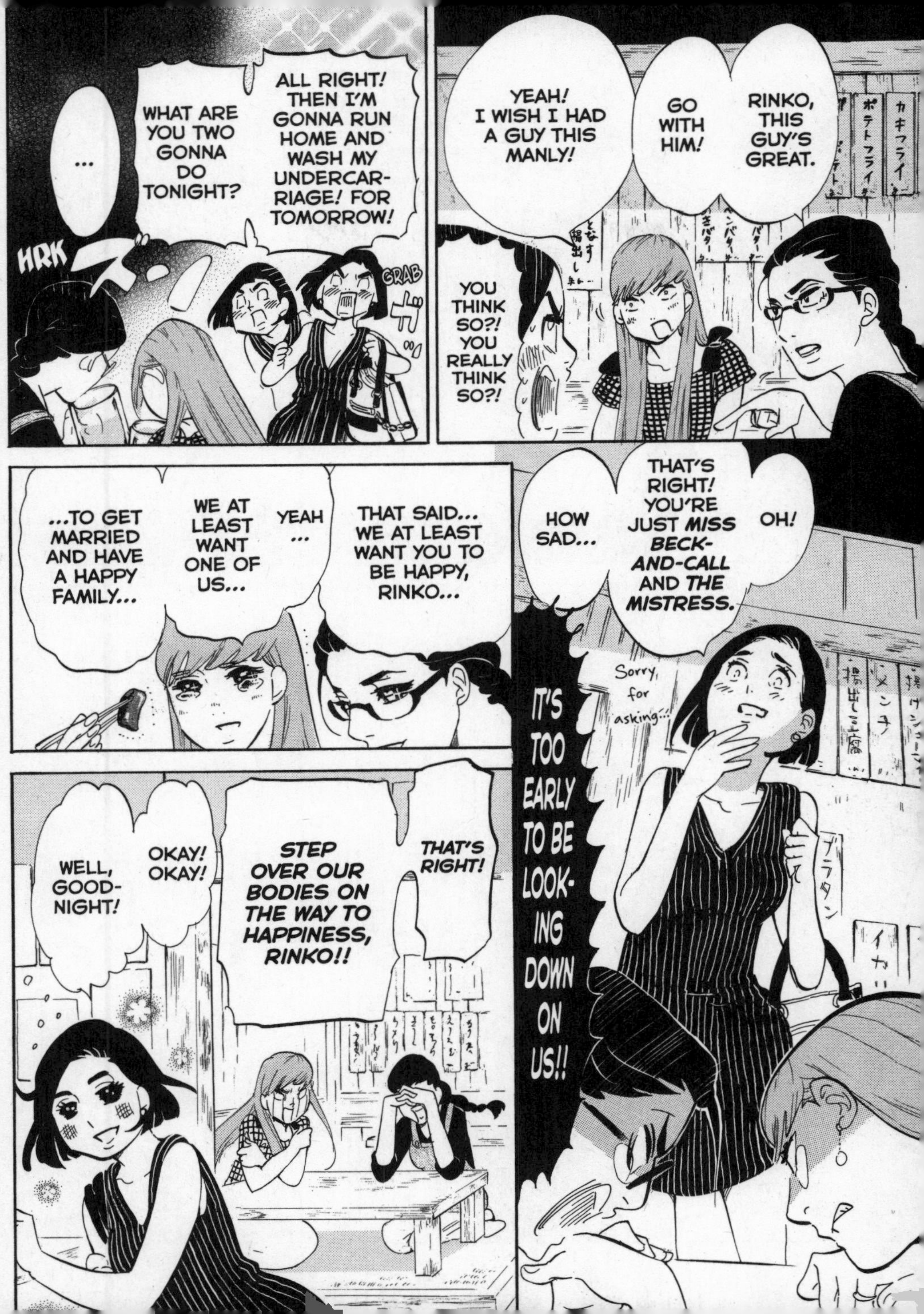
RINKO, THIS GUY'S GREAT.
GO WITH HIM!
YEAH! I WISH I HAD A GUY THIS MANLY!
YOU THINK SO?! YOU REALLY THINK SO?!
ALL RIGHT! THEN I'M GONNA RUN HOME AND WASH MY UNDERCARRIAGE! FOR TOMORROW!
WHAT ARE YOU TWO GONNA DO TONIGHT?
...
GRAB
HRK
OH!
THAT'S RIGHT! YOU'RE JUST MISS BECK-AND-CALL AND THE MISTRESS.
HOW SAD...
Sorry, for asking...
IT'S TOO EARLY TO BE LOOKING DOWN ON US!!
THAT SAID... WE AT LEAST WANT YOU TO BE HAPPY, RINKO...
YEAH ...
WE AT LEAST WANT ONE OF US...
...TO GET MARRIED AND HAVE A HAPPY FAMILY...
THAT'S RIGHT!
STEP OVER OUR BODIES ON THE WAY TO HAPPINESS, RINKO!!
OKAY! OKAY!
WELL, GOOD-NIGHT!

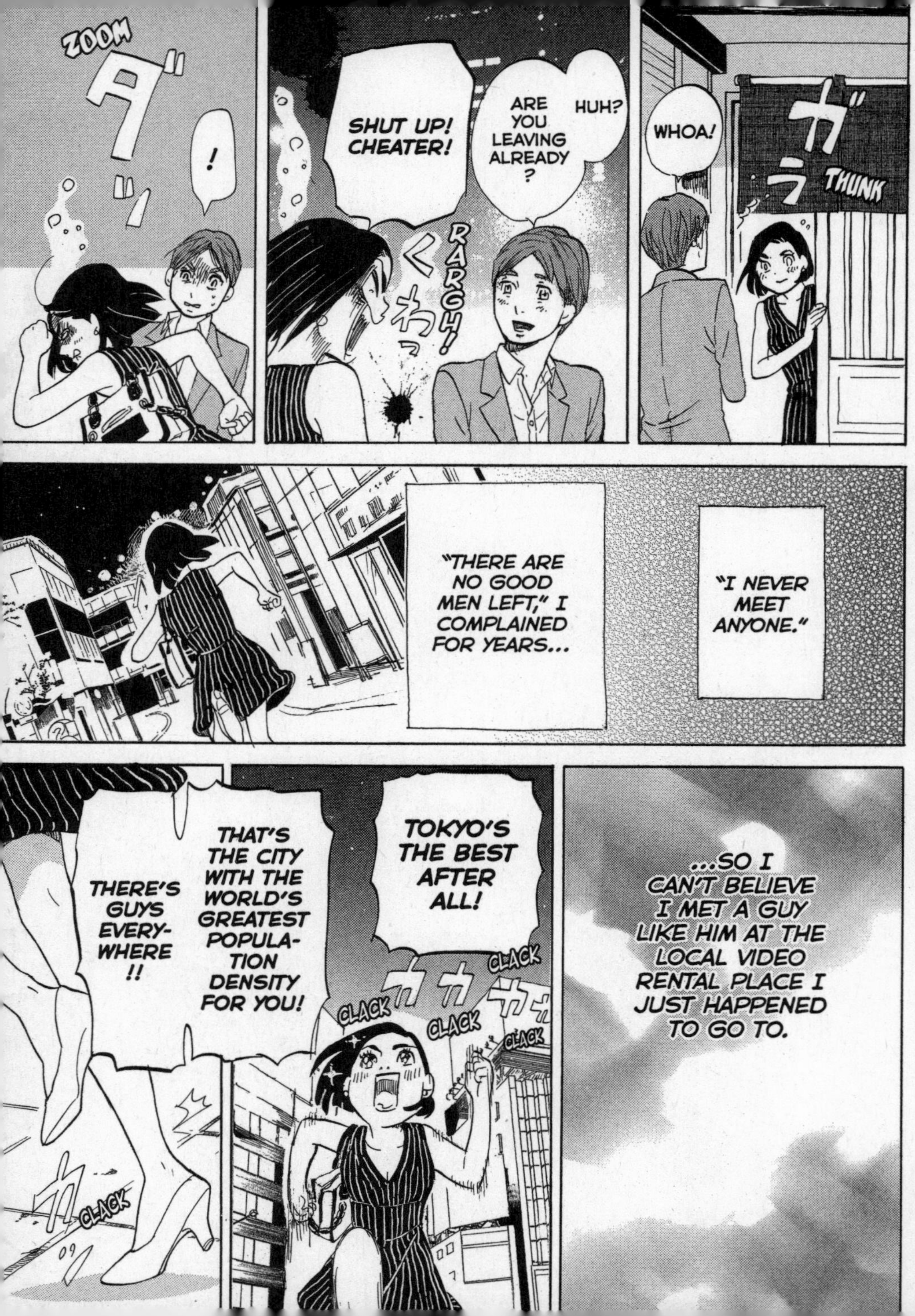

WHOA!
THUNK
HUH?
ARE YOU LEAVING ALREADY?
SHUT UP! CHEATER!
RARGH!
ZOOM
!
"I NEVER MEET ANYONE."
"THERE ARE NO GOOD MEN LEFT," I COMPLAINED FOR YEARS...
...SO I CAN'T BELIEVE I MET A GUY LIKE HIM AT THE LOCAL VIDEO RENTAL PLACE I JUST HAPPENED TO GO TO.
TOKYO'S THE BEST AFTER ALL!
THAT'S THE CITY WITH THE WORLD'S GREATEST POPULATION DENSITY FOR YOU!
CLACK
CLACK
CLACK
CLACK
THERE'S GUYS EVERYWHERE!!
CLACK

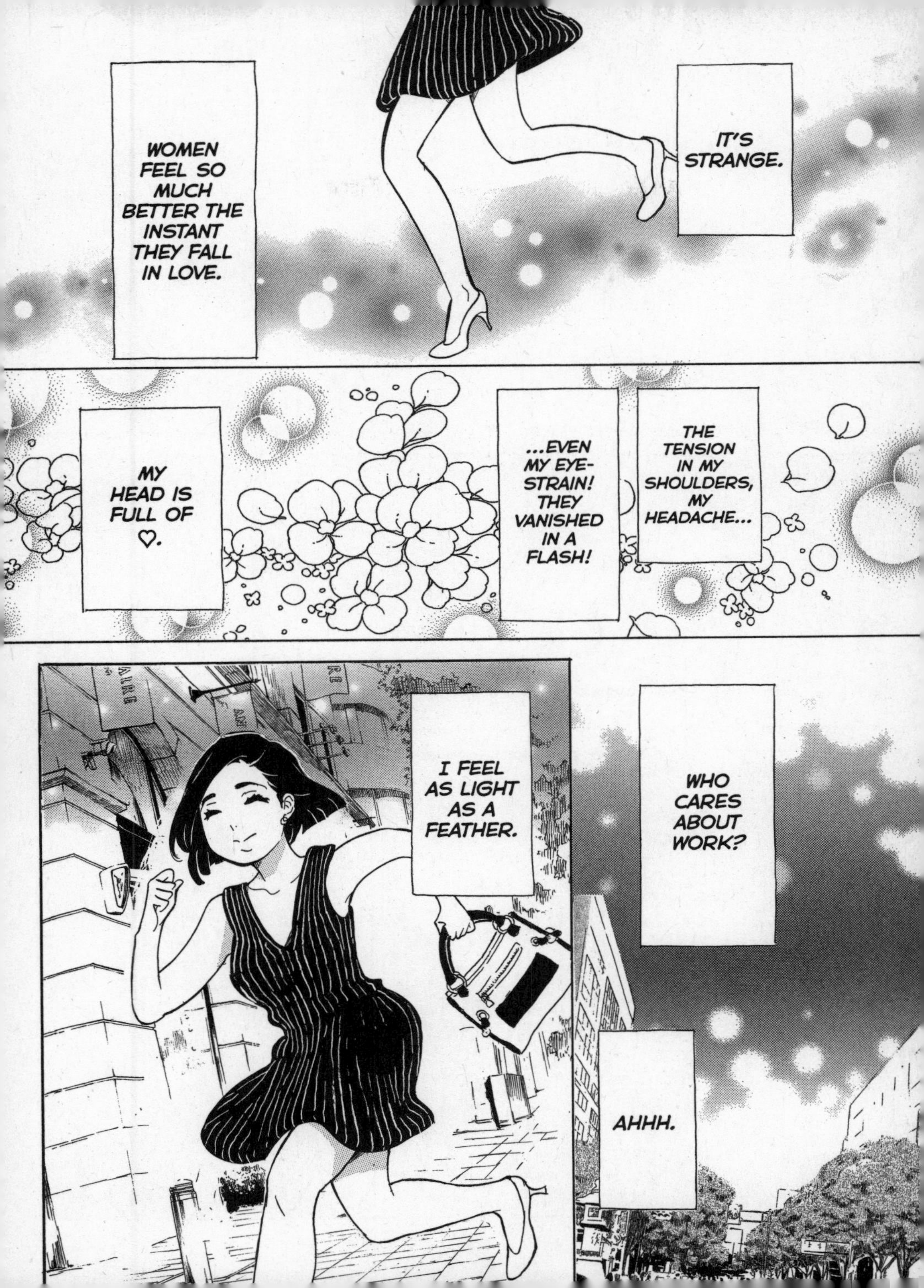
IT'S STRANGE.
WOMEN FEEL SO MUCH BETTER THE INSTANT THEY FALL IN LOVE.
THE TENSION IN MY SHOULDERS, MY HEADACHE...
...EVEN MY EYE-STRAIN! THEY VANISHED IN A FLASH!
MY HEAD IS FULL OF ♡.
WHO CARES ABOUT WORK?
AHHH.
I FEEL AS LIGHT AS A FEATHER.

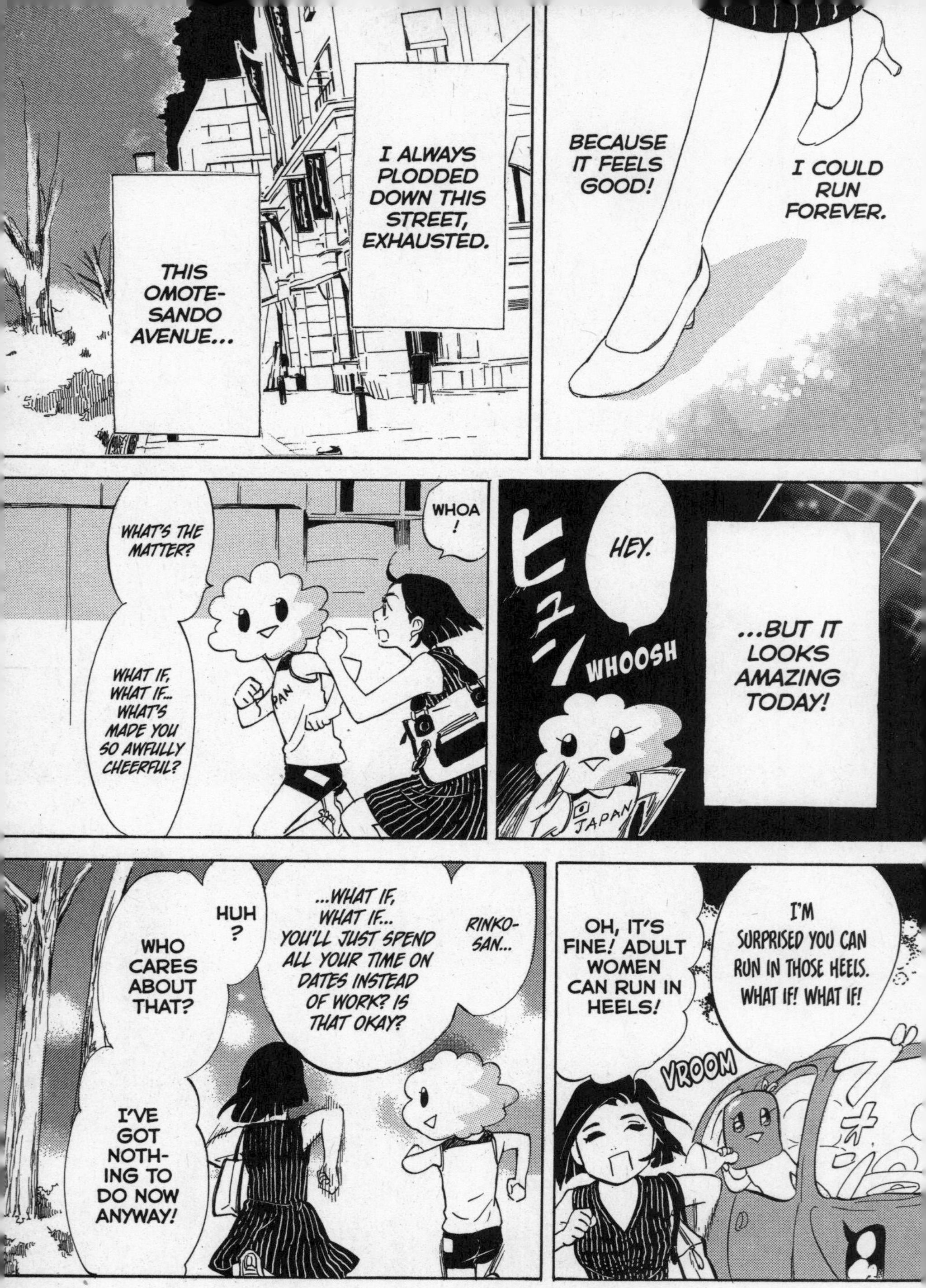
I COULD RUN FOREVER.
BECAUSE IT FEELS GOOD!
I ALWAYS PLODDED DOWN THIS STREET, EXHAUSTED.
THIS OMOTE-SANDO AVENUE...
...BUT IT LOOKS AMAZING TODAY!
HEY.
ヒュン
WHOOSH
WHOA!
WHAT'S THE MATTER?
WHAT IF, WHAT IF... WHAT'S MADE YOU SO AWFULLY CHEERFUL?
I'M SURPRISED YOU CAN RUN IN THOSE HEELS. WHAT IF! WHAT IF!
OH, IT'S FINE! ADULT WOMEN CAN RUN IN HEELS!
VROOM
RINKO-SAN...
...WHAT IF, WHAT IF... YOU'LL JUST SPEND ALL YOUR TIME ON DATES INSTEAD OF WORK? IS THAT OKAY?
HUH?
WHO CARES ABOUT THAT?
I'VE GOT NOTHING TO DO NOW ANYWAY!

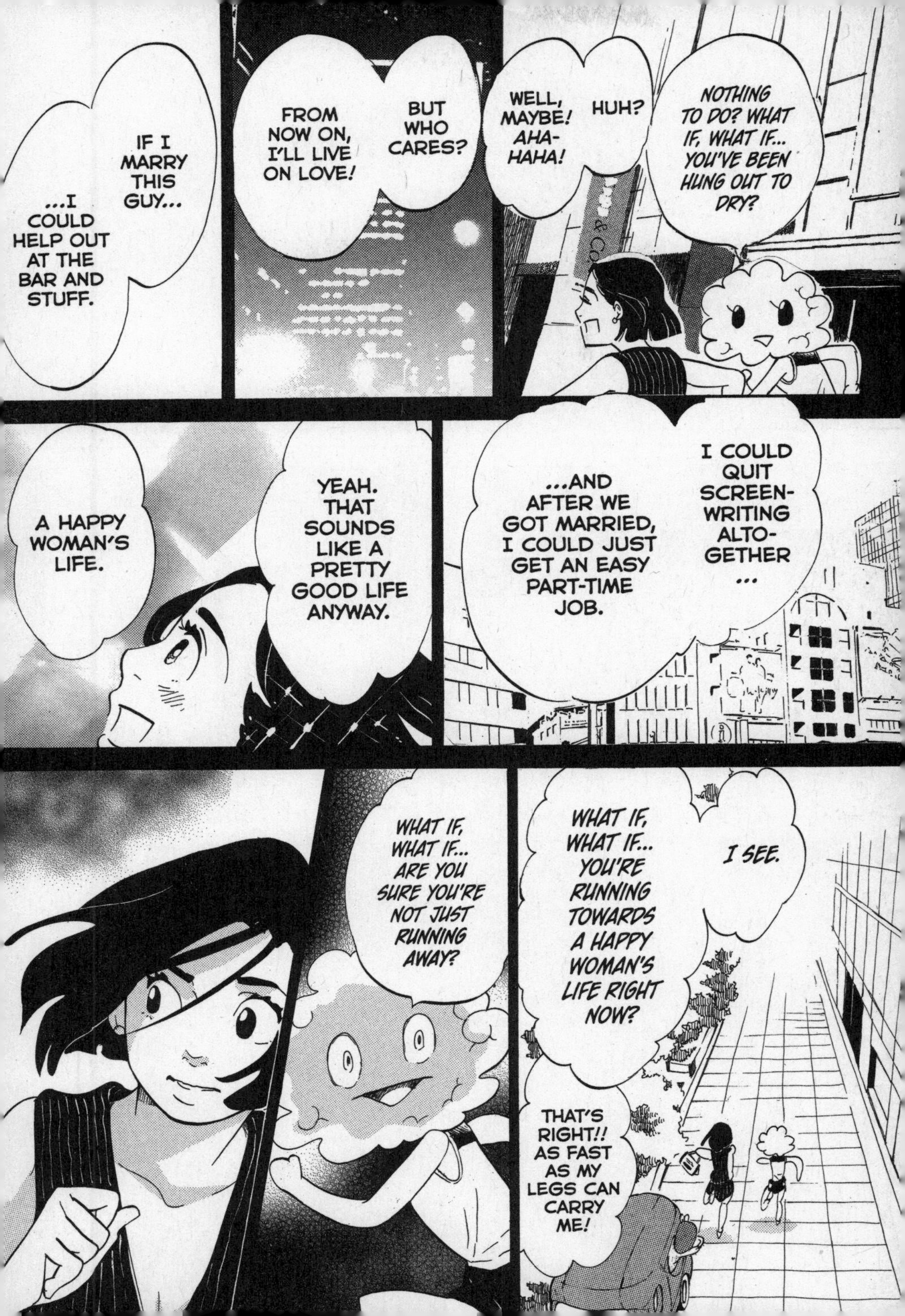
NOTHING TO DO? WHAT IF, WHAT IF... YOU'VE BEEN HUNG OUT TO DRY?
HUH?
WELL, MAYBE! AHA-HAHA!
BUT WHO CARES?
FROM NOW ON, I'LL LIVE ON LOVE!
IF I MARRY THIS GUY...
...I COULD HELP OUT AT THE BAR AND STUFF.
I COULD QUIT SCREEN-WRITING ALTO-GETHER...
...AND AFTER WE GOT MARRIED, I COULD JUST GET AN EASY PART-TIME JOB.
YEAH. THAT SOUNDS LIKE A PRETTY GOOD LIFE ANYWAY.
A HAPPY WOMAN'S LIFE.
I SEE.
WHAT IF, WHAT IF... YOU'RE RUNNING TOWARDS A HAPPY WOMAN'S LIFE RIGHT NOW?
THAT'S RIGHT!! AS FAST AS MY LEGS CAN CARRY ME!
WHAT IF, WHAT IF... ARE YOU SURE YOU'RE NOT JUST RUNNING AWAY?

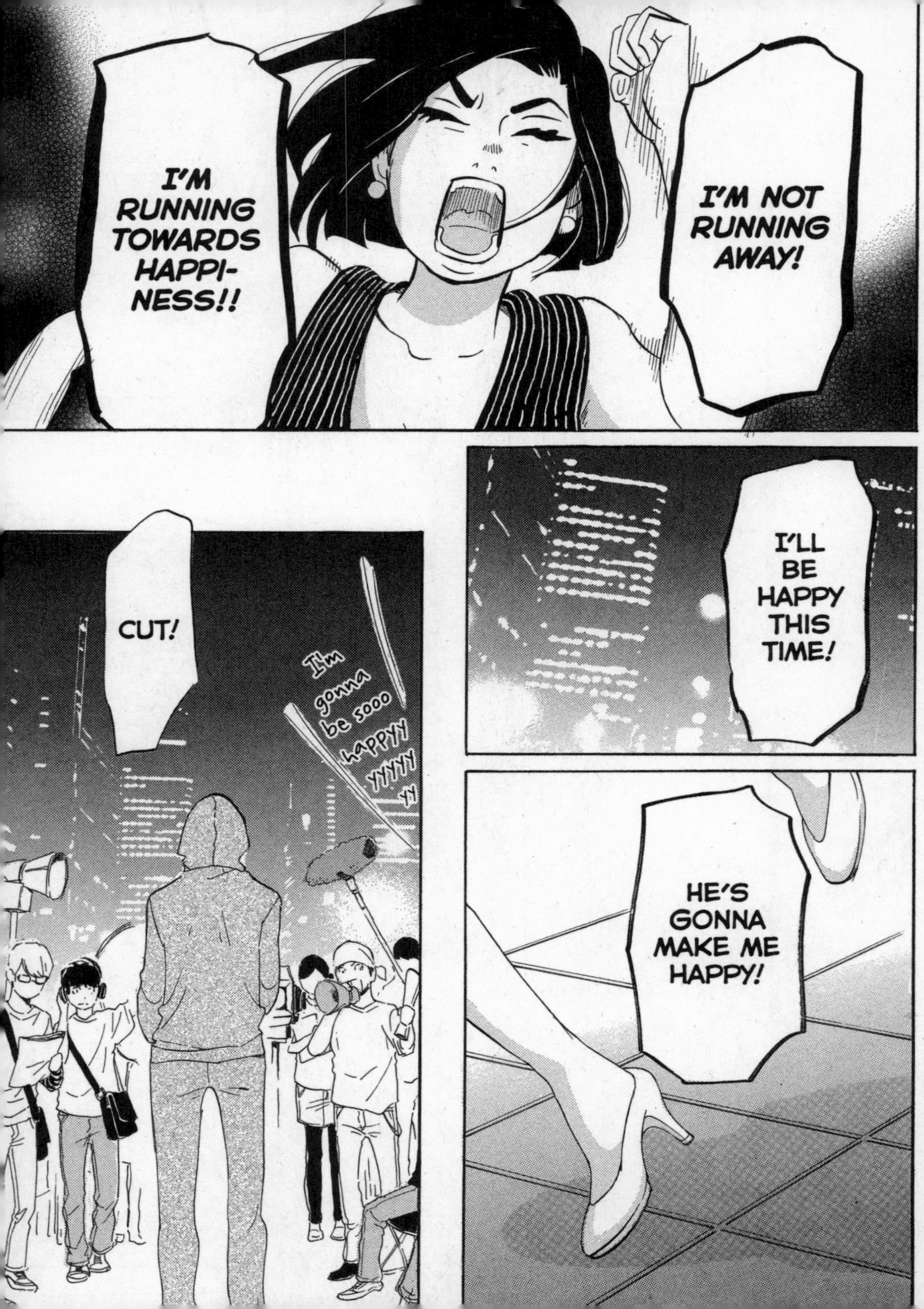
I'M NOT RUNNING AWAY!
I'M RUNNING TOWARDS HAPPI-NESS!!
I'LL BE HAPPY THIS TIME!
HE'S GONNA MAKE ME HAPPY!
I'm gonna be sooo happyyyyyyyyy
CUT!

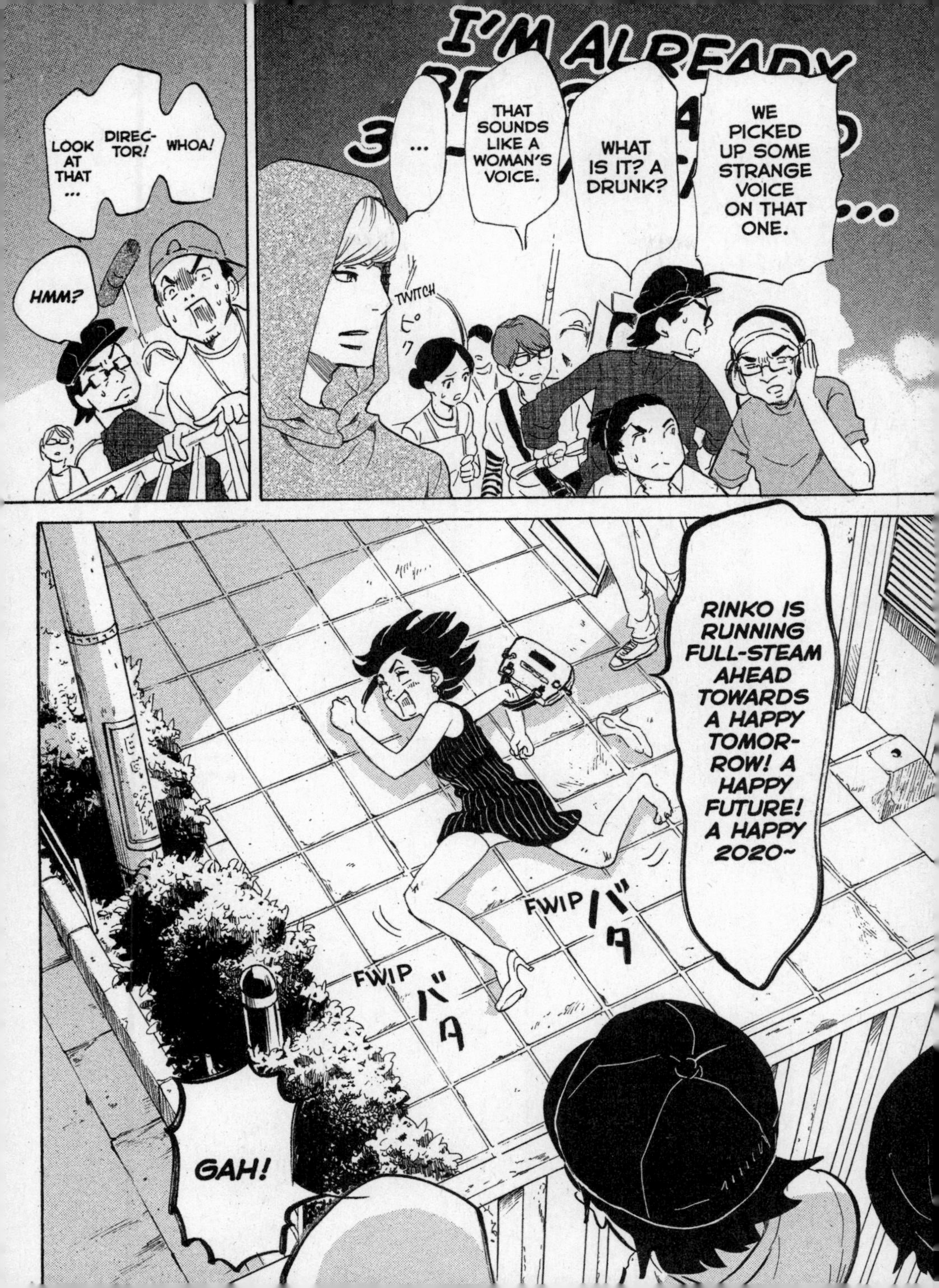
I'M ALREADY
WE PICKED UP SOME STRANGE VOICE ON THAT ONE.
WHAT IS IT? A DRUNK?
THAT SOUNDS LIKE A WOMAN'S VOICE.
...
TWITCH ピク
WHOA!
DIREC-TOR!
LOOK AT THAT ...
HMM?
RINKO IS RUNNING FULL-STEAM AHEAD TOWARDS A HAPPY TOMOR-ROW! A HAPPY FUTURE! A HAPPY 2020~
FWIP バタ
FWIP バタ
GAH!

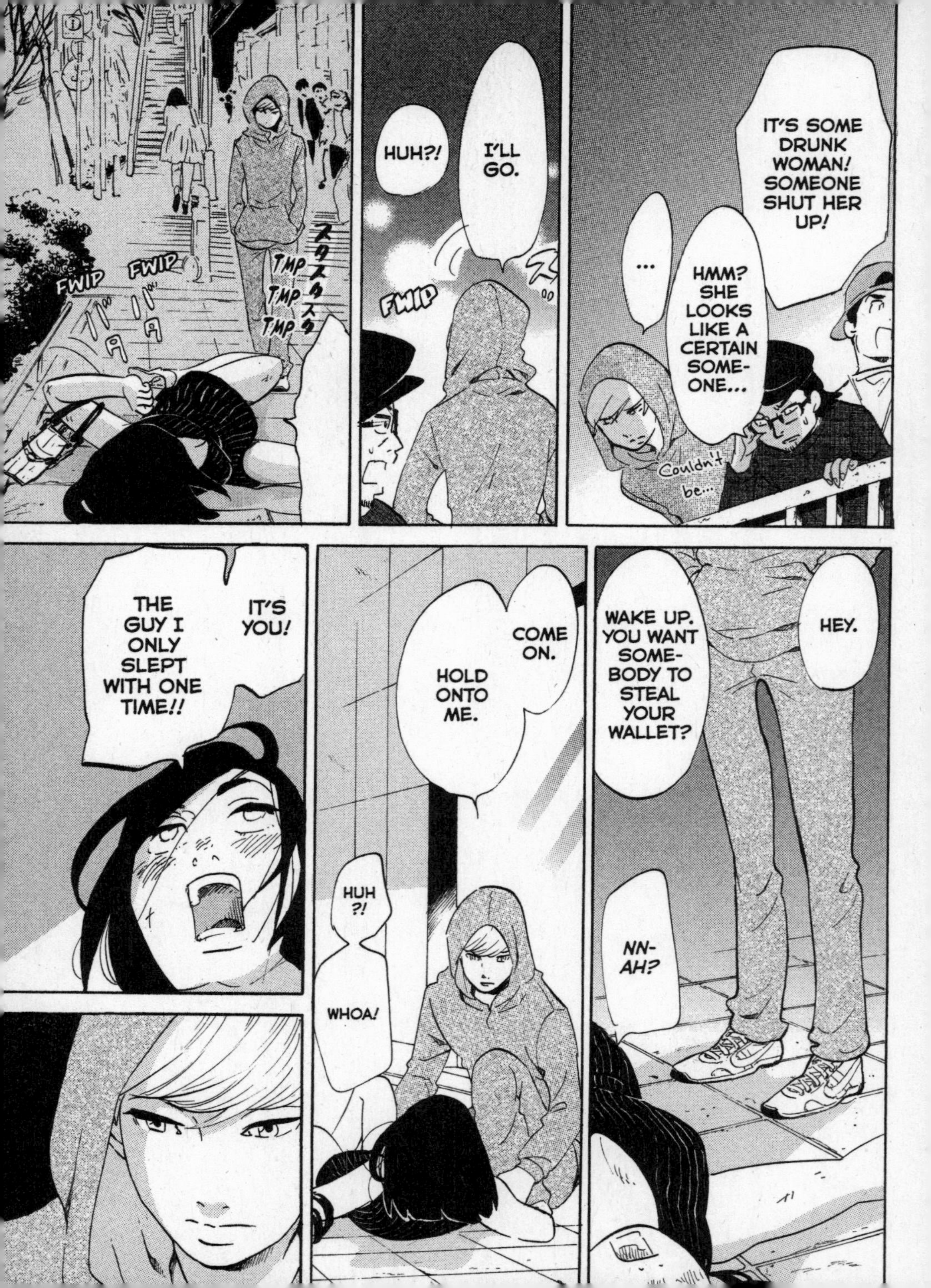
IT'S SOME DRUNK WOMAN! SOMEONE SHUT HER UP!
HMM? SHE LOOKS LIKE A CERTAIN SOME-ONE...
...
Couldn't be...
I'LL GO.
HUH?!
FWIP
FWIP
FWIP
TMP
TMP
TMP
HEY.
WAKE UP. YOU WANT SOME-BODY TO STEAL YOUR WALLET?
NN-AH?
COME ON.
HOLD ONTO ME.
HUH ?!
WHOA!
IT'S YOU!
THE GUY I ONLY SLEPT WITH ONE TIME!!

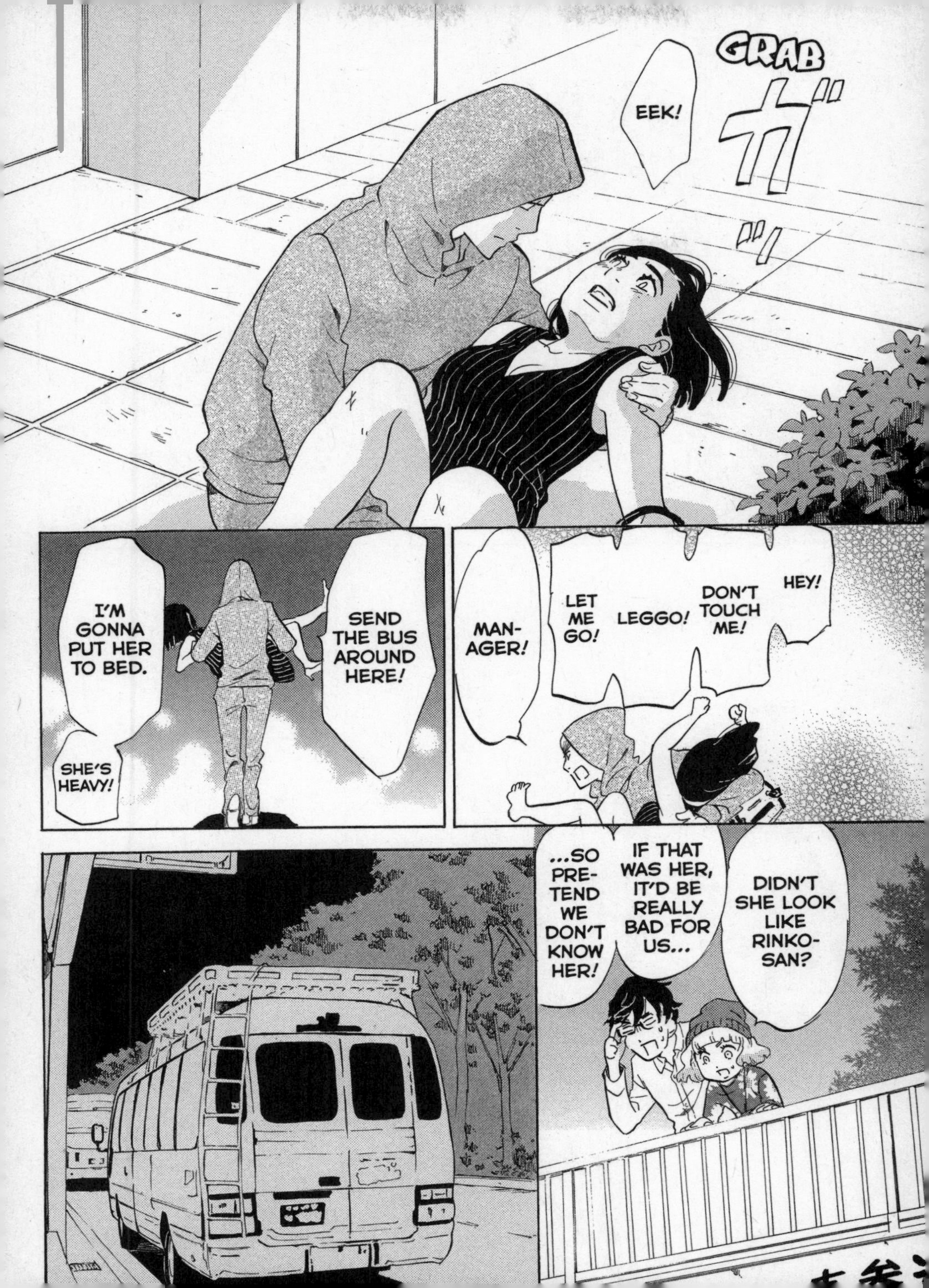
GRAB
EEK!
HEY!
DON'T TOUCH ME!
LEGGO!
LET ME GO!
MAN-AGER!
SEND THE BUS AROUND HERE!
I'M GONNA PUT HER TO BED.
SHE'S HEAVY!
DIDN'T SHE LOOK LIKE RINKO-SAN?
IF THAT WAS HER, IT'D BE REALLY BAD FOR US...
...SO PRETEND WE DON'T KNOW HER!

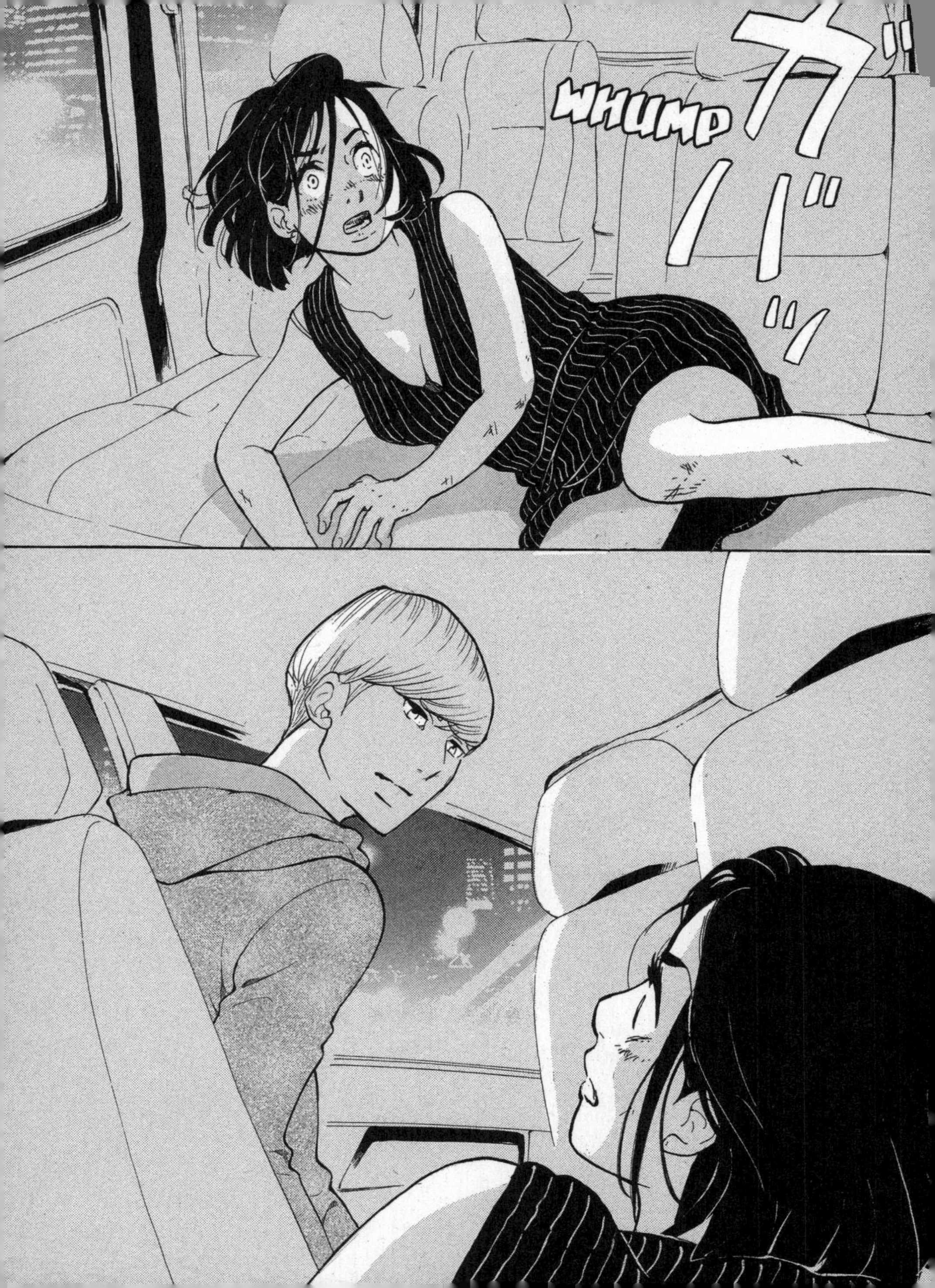
WHUMP
ガバッ

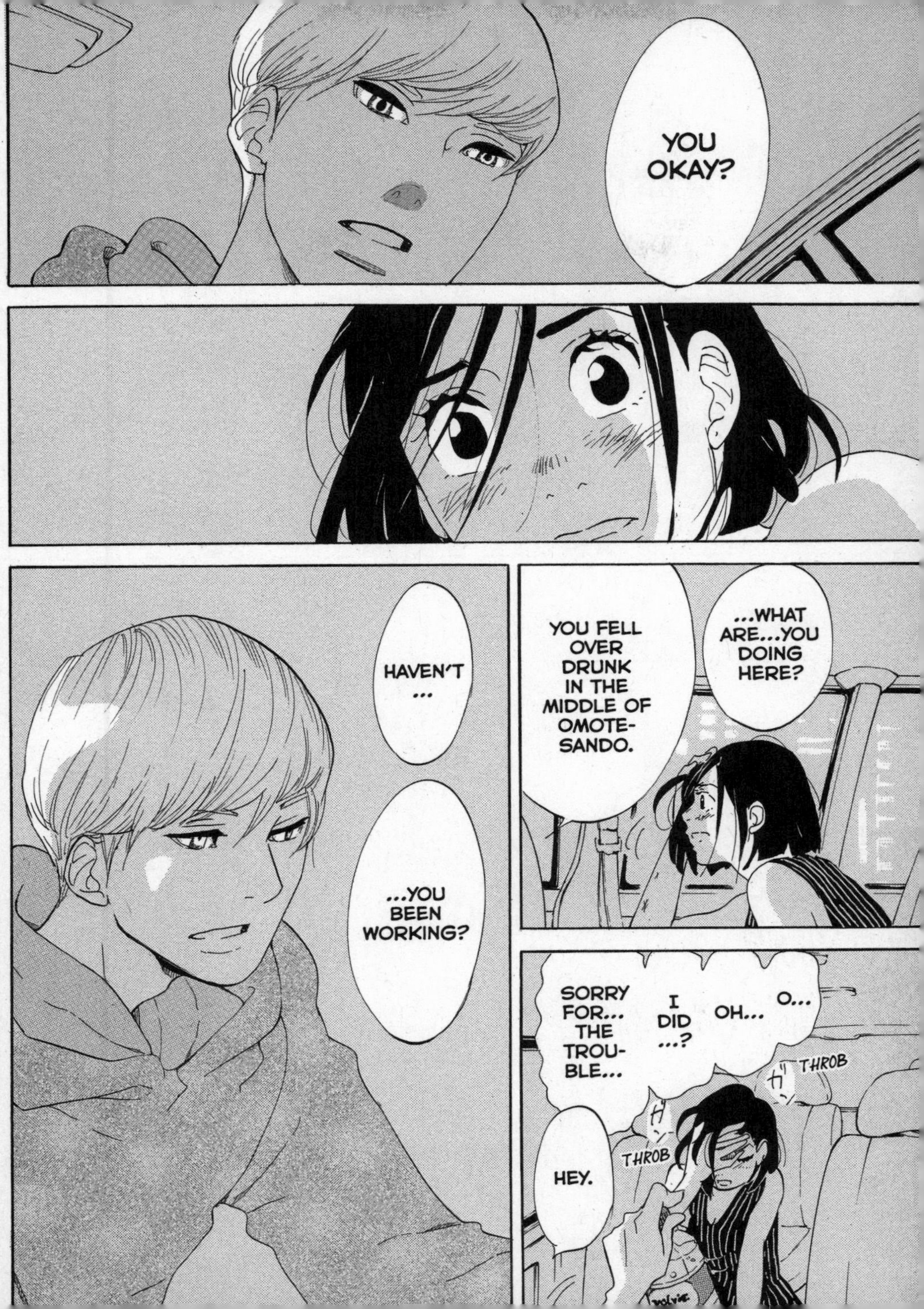
YOU OKAY?
...WHAT ARE...YOU DOING HERE?
YOU FELL OVER DRUNK IN THE MIDDLE OF OMOTE-SANDO.
O...
OH...
I DID ...?
SORRY FOR... THE TROUBLE...
THROB
THROB
HEY.
HAVEN'T ...
...YOU BEEN WORKING?

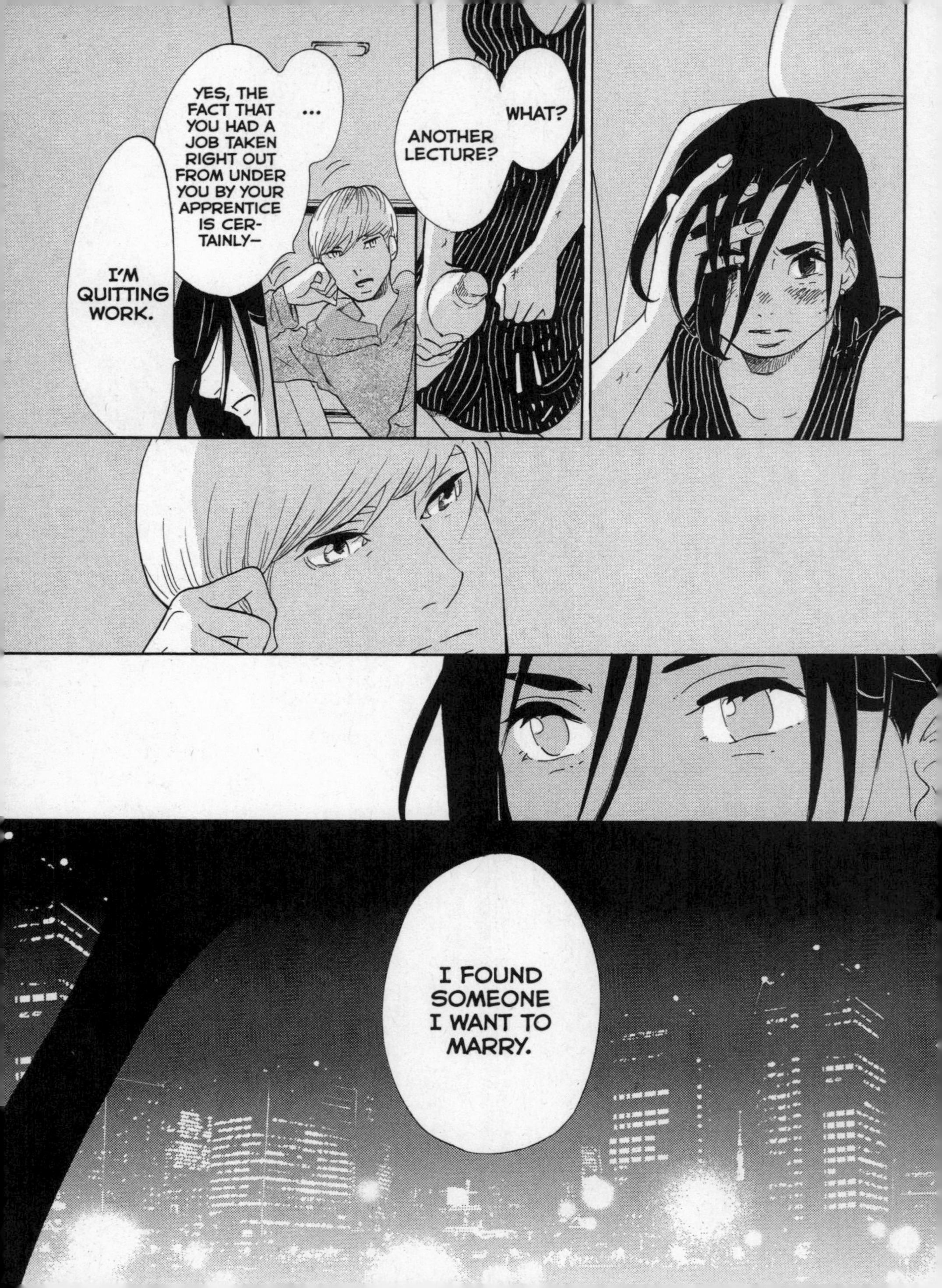
WHAT?
ANOTHER LECTURE?
...
YES, THE FACT THAT YOU HAD A JOB TAKEN RIGHT OUT FROM UNDER YOU BY YOUR APPRENTICE IS CER-TAINLY—
I'M QUITTING WORK.
I FOUND SOMEONE I WANT TO MARRY.

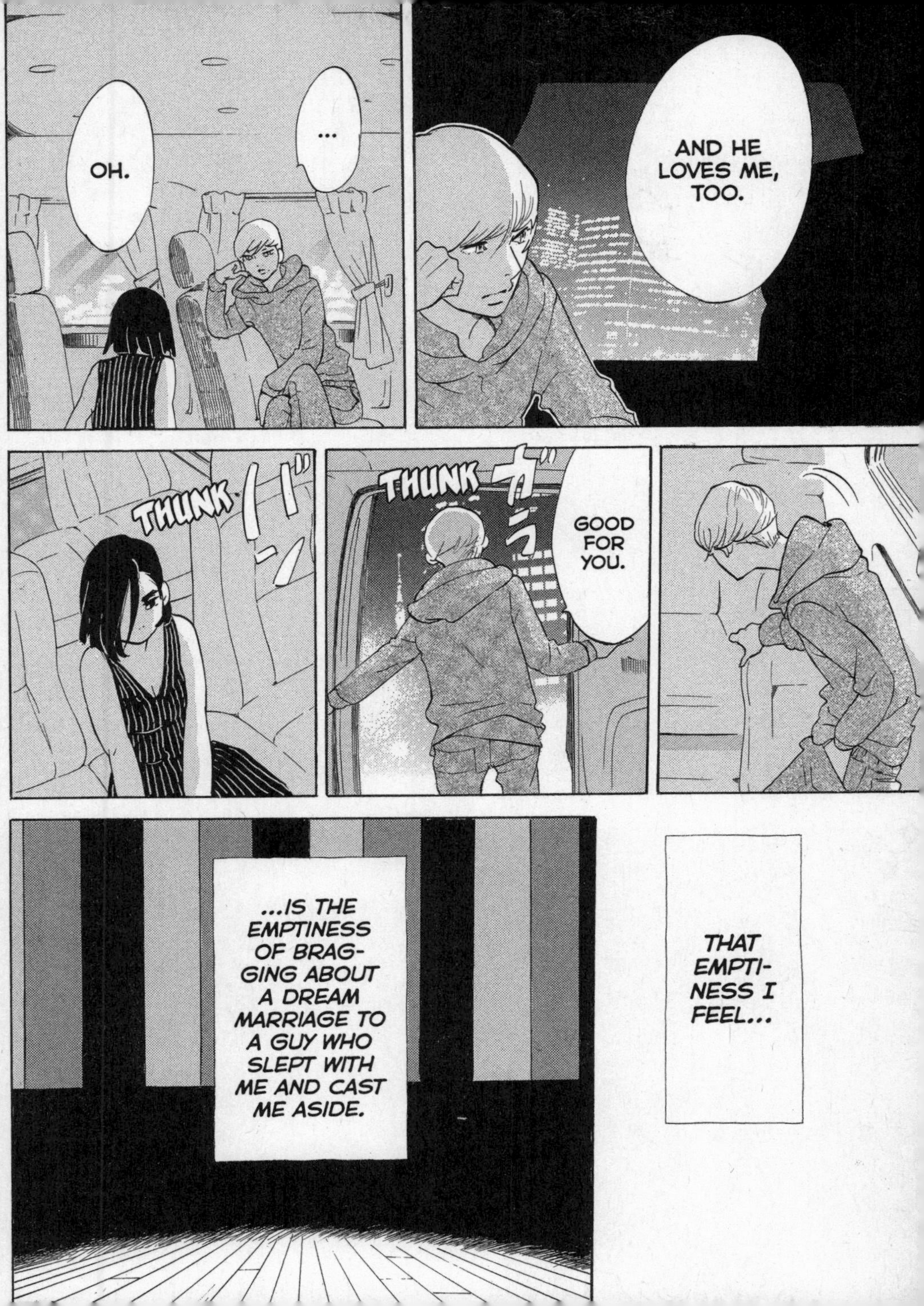
AND HE LOVES ME, TOO.
...
OH.
GOOD FOR YOU.
THUNK
THUNK
THAT EMPTINESS I FEEL...
...IS THE EMPTINESS OF BRAGGING ABOUT A DREAM MARRIAGE TO A GUY WHO SLEPT WITH ME AND CAST ME ASIDE.

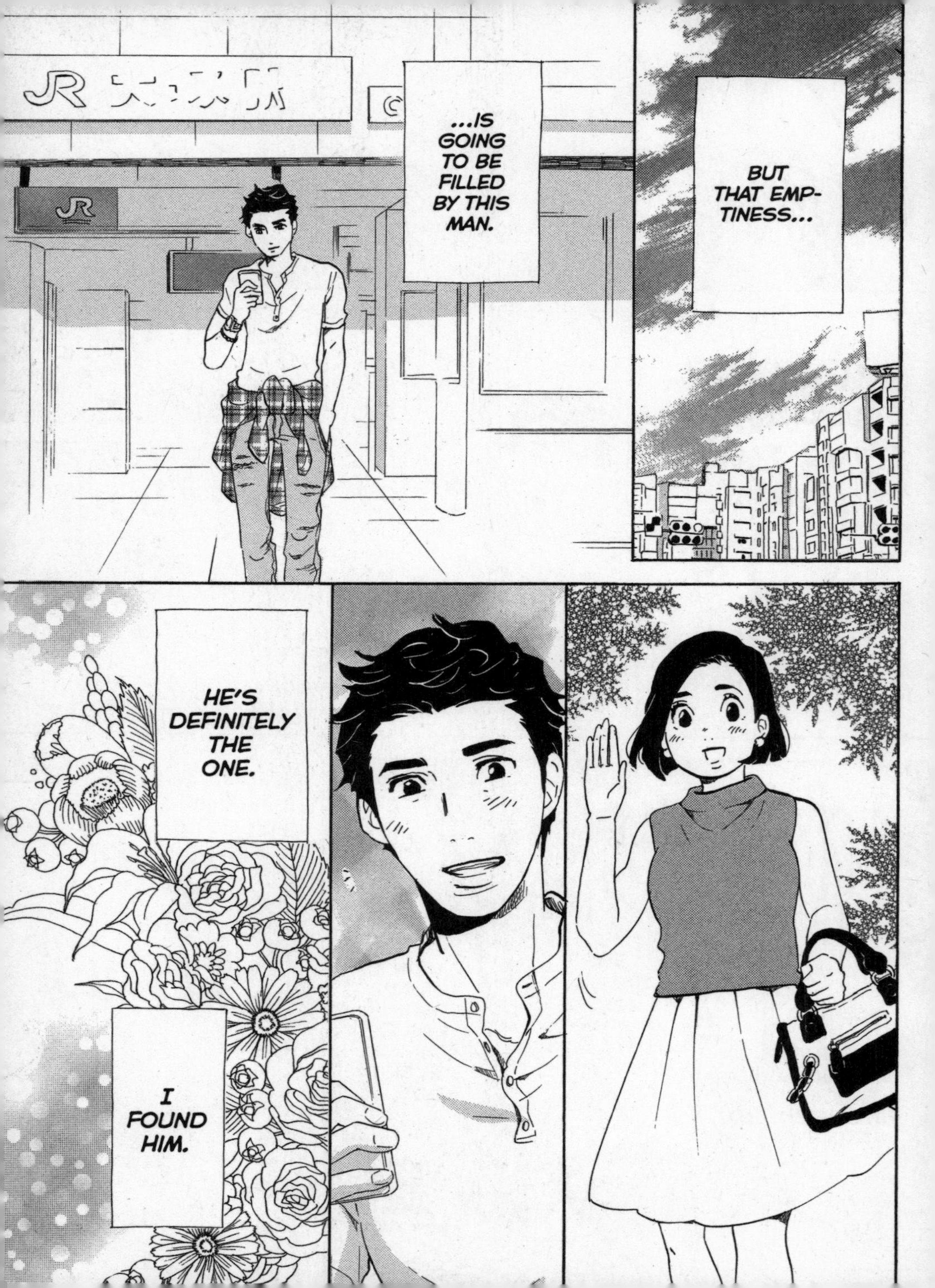
BUT THAT EMPTINESS...
...IS GOING TO BE FILLED BY THIS MAN.
HE'S DEFINITELY THE ONE.
I FOUND HIM.

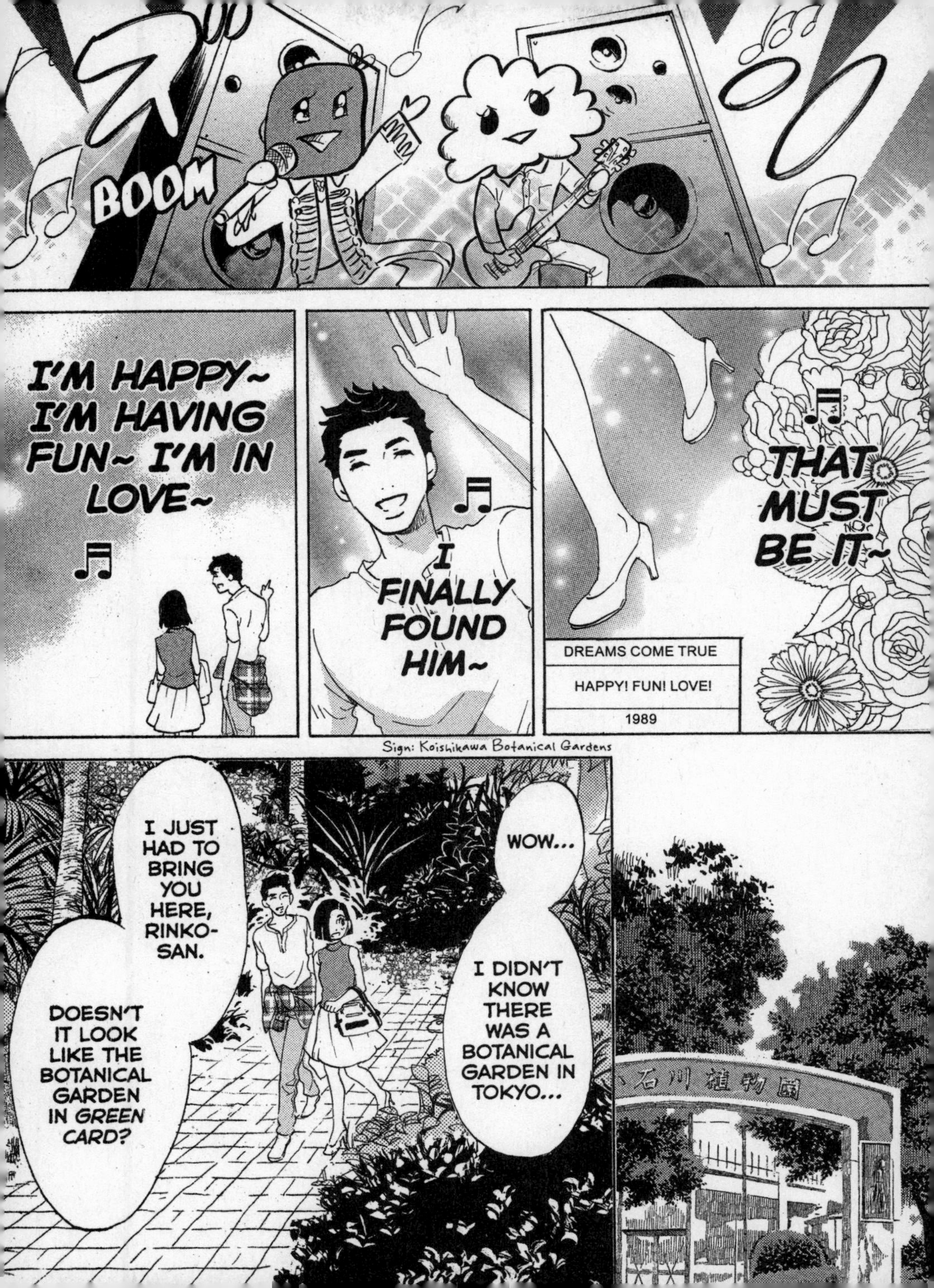
BOOM
THAT MUST BE IT~
DREAMS COME TRUE
HAPPY! FUN! LOVE!
1989
I FINALLY FOUND HIM~
I'M HAPPY~ I'M HAVING FUN~ I'M IN LOVE~
Sign: Koishikawa Botanical Gardens
WOW...
I DIDN'T KNOW THERE WAS A BOTANICAL GARDEN IN TOKYO...
I JUST HAD TO BRING YOU HERE, RINKO-SAN.
DOESN'T IT LOOK LIKE THE BOTANICAL GARDEN IN *GREEN CARD*?

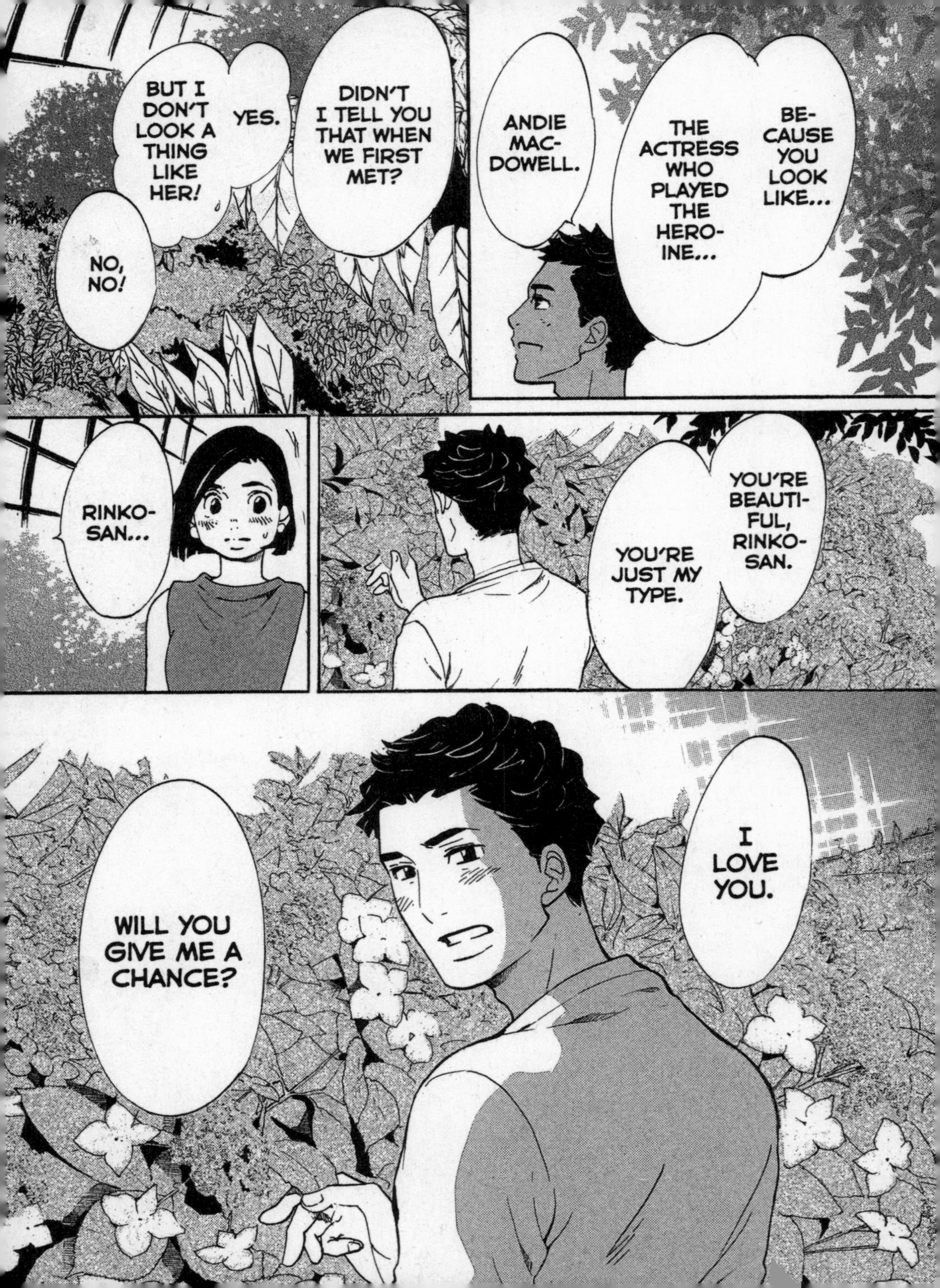
BECAUSE YOU LOOK LIKE...
THE ACTRESS WHO PLAYED THE HEROINE...
ANDIE MACDOWELL.
DIDN'T I TELL YOU THAT WHEN WE FIRST MET?
YES.
BUT I DON'T LOOK A THING LIKE HER!
NO, NO!
YOU'RE BEAUTIFUL, RINKO-SAN.
YOU'RE JUST MY TYPE.
RINKO-SAN...
I LOVE YOU.
WILL YOU GIVE ME A CHANCE?

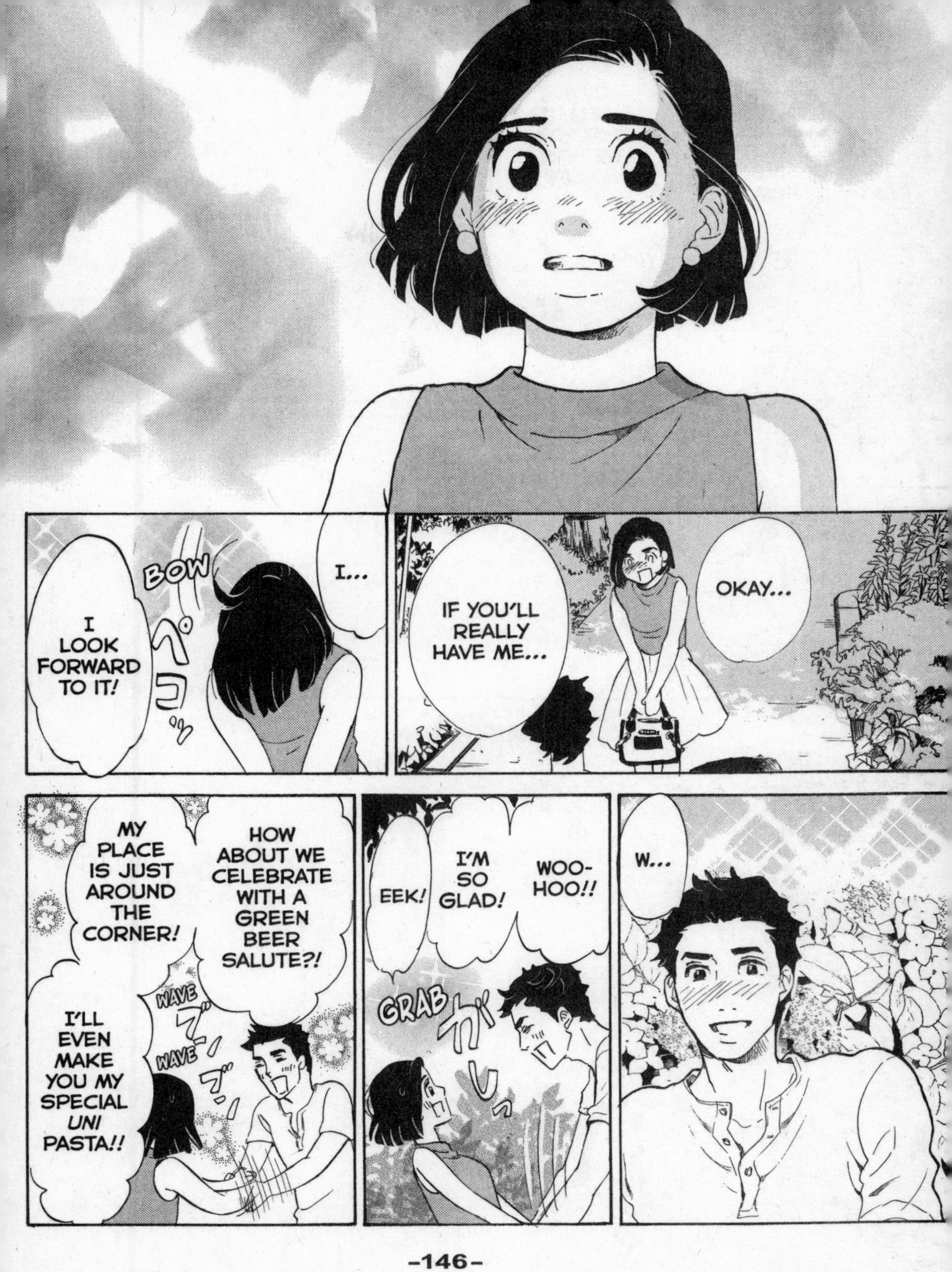
OKAY...
IF YOU'LL REALLY HAVE ME...
I...
BOW
ペコッ
I LOOK FORWARD TO IT!
W...
WOO-HOO!!
I'M SO GLAD!
EEK!
GRAB
HOW ABOUT WE CELEBRATE WITH A GREEN BEER SALUTE?!
MY PLACE IS JUST AROUND THE CORNER!
WAVE
WAVE
I'LL EVEN MAKE YOU MY SPECIAL *UNI* PASTA!!

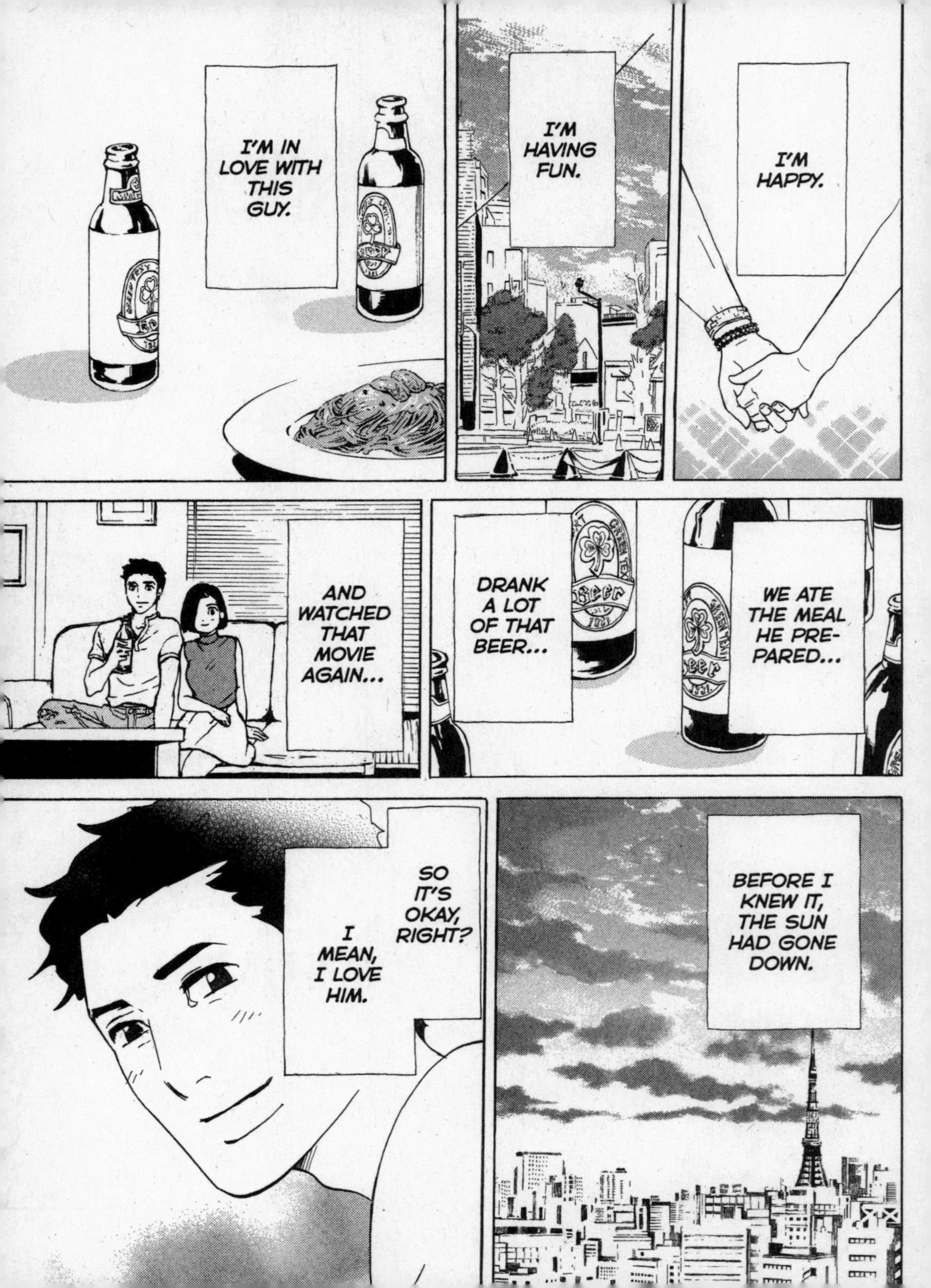
I'M HAPPY.
I'M HAVING FUN.
I'M IN LOVE WITH THIS GUY.
WE ATE THE MEAL HE PRE-PARED...
DRANK A LOT OF THAT BEER...
AND WATCHED THAT MOVIE AGAIN...
BEFORE I KNEW IT, THE SUN HAD GONE DOWN.
SO IT'S OKAY, RIGHT?
I MEAN, I LOVE HIM.

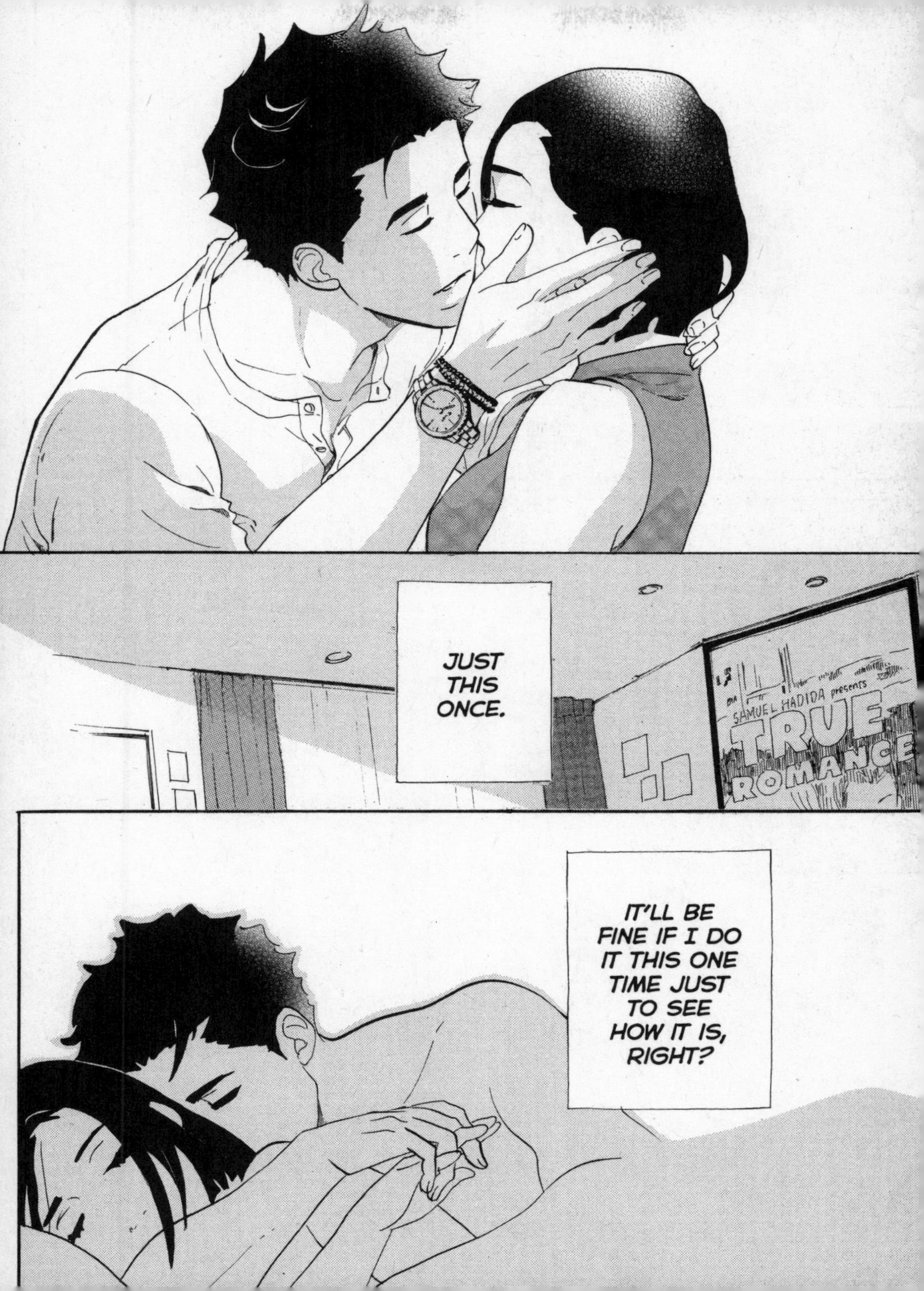
SAMUEL HADIDA presents
TRUE ROMANCE
JUST THIS ONCE.
IT'LL BE FINE IF I DO IT THIS ONE TIME JUST TO SEE HOW IT IS, RIGHT?

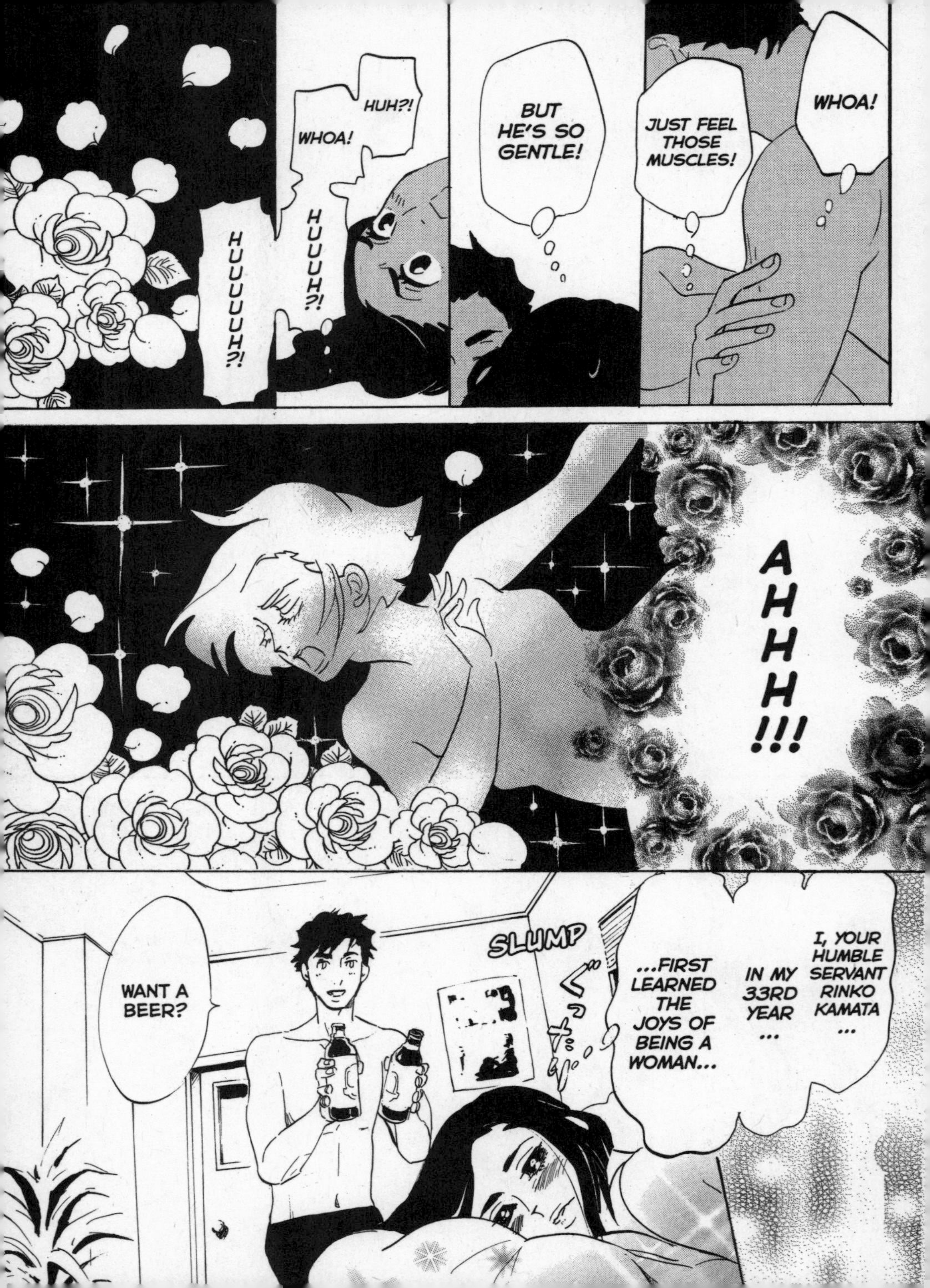
WHOA!
JUST FEEL THOSE MUSCLES!
BUT HE'S SO GENTLE!
HUH?!
WHOA!
HUUUUH?!
HUUUUUUH?!
AHHH!!!
I, YOUR HUMBLE SERVANT RINKO KAMATA ...
IN MY 33RD YEAR ...
...FIRST LEARNED THE JOYS OF BEING A WOMAN...
SLUMP
WANT A BEER?

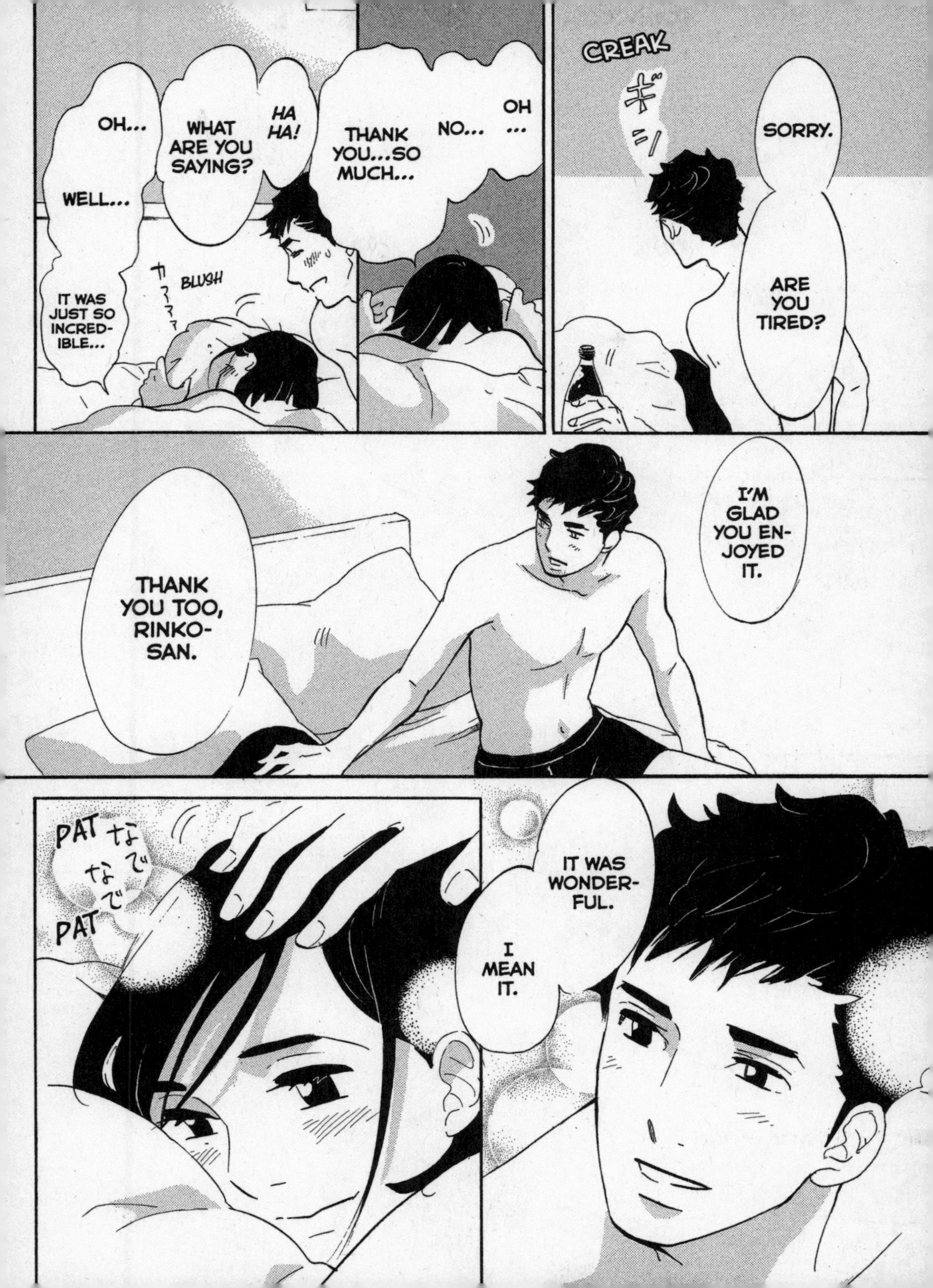
CREAK
ギシ
SORRY.
ARE YOU TIRED?
OH ...
NO...
THANK YOU...SO MUCH...
HA HA!
WHAT ARE YOU SAYING?
OH...
WELL...
IT WAS JUST SO INCREDIBLE...
BLUSH
I'M GLAD YOU ENJOYED IT.
THANK YOU TOO, RINKO-SAN.
IT WAS WONDERFUL.
I MEAN IT.
PAT なで
なで PAT

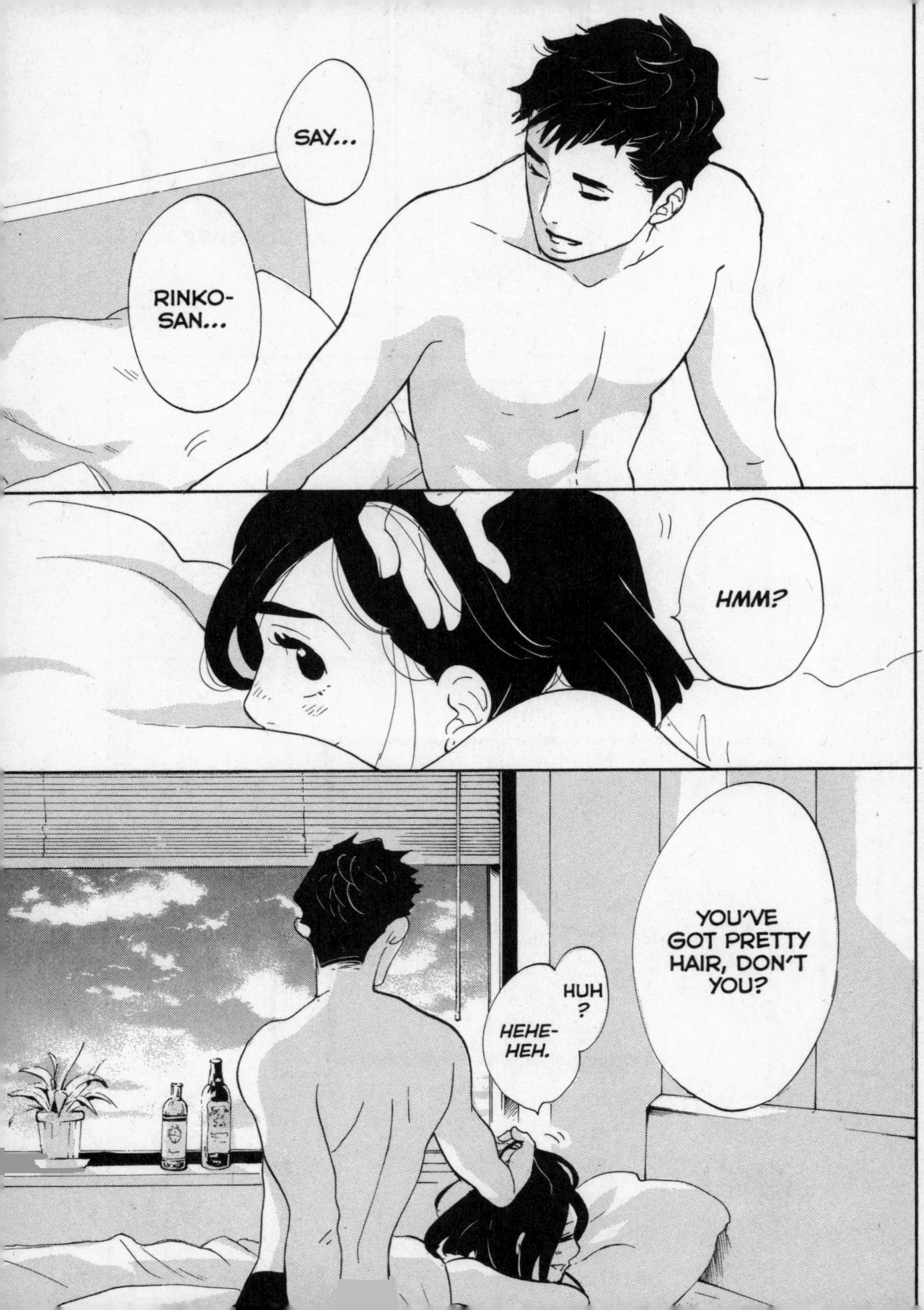
SAY...
RINKO-SAN...
HMM?
YOU'VE GOT PRETTY HAIR, DON'T YOU?
HUH? HEHE-HEH.

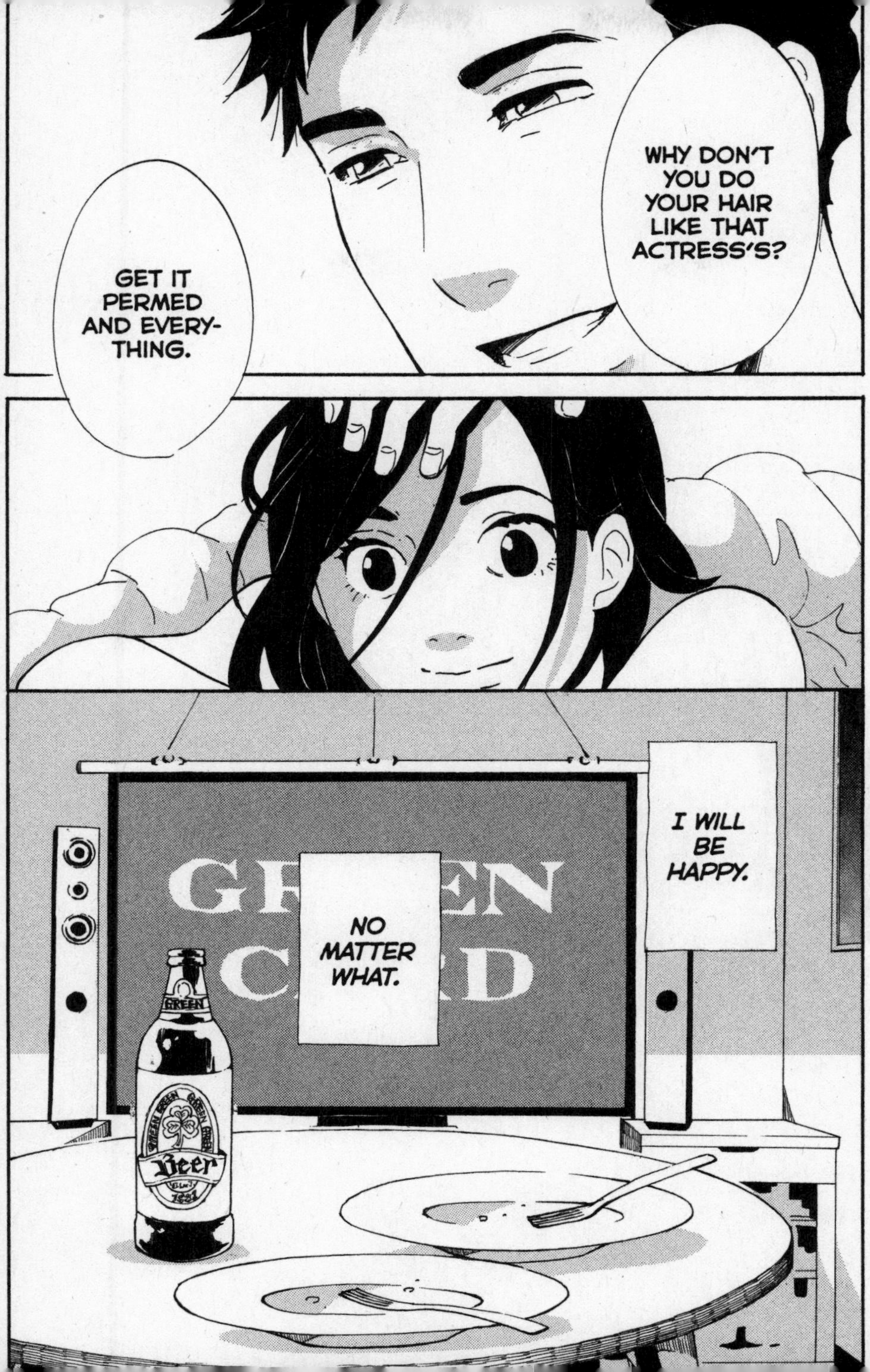
WHY DON'T YOU DO YOUR HAIR LIKE THAT ACTRESS'S?
GET IT PERMED AND EVERY-THING.
I WILL BE HAPPY.
NO MATTER WHAT.

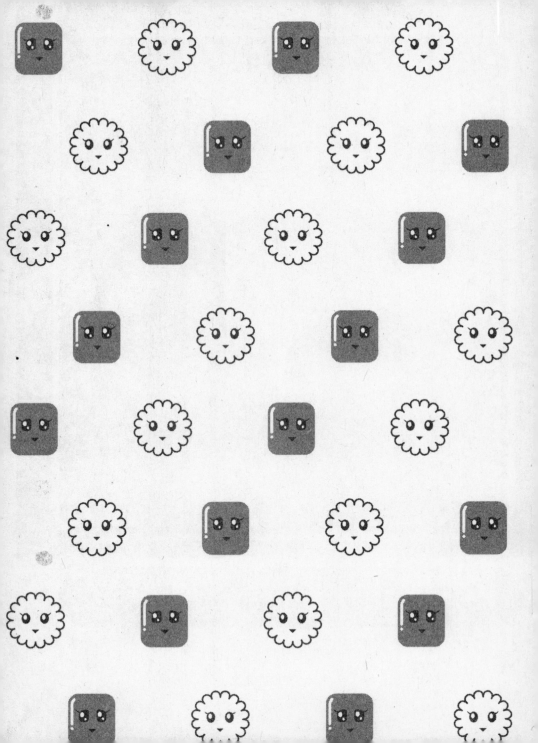

TOKYO TARAREBA GIRLS
(SIDE STORY)

Tarare-Bar

IN THE FOLLOWING SIDE STORY, "TARARE-BAR," WE PUBLISH PROBLEMS SUBMITTED BY READERS FROM ACROSS THE COUNTRY.

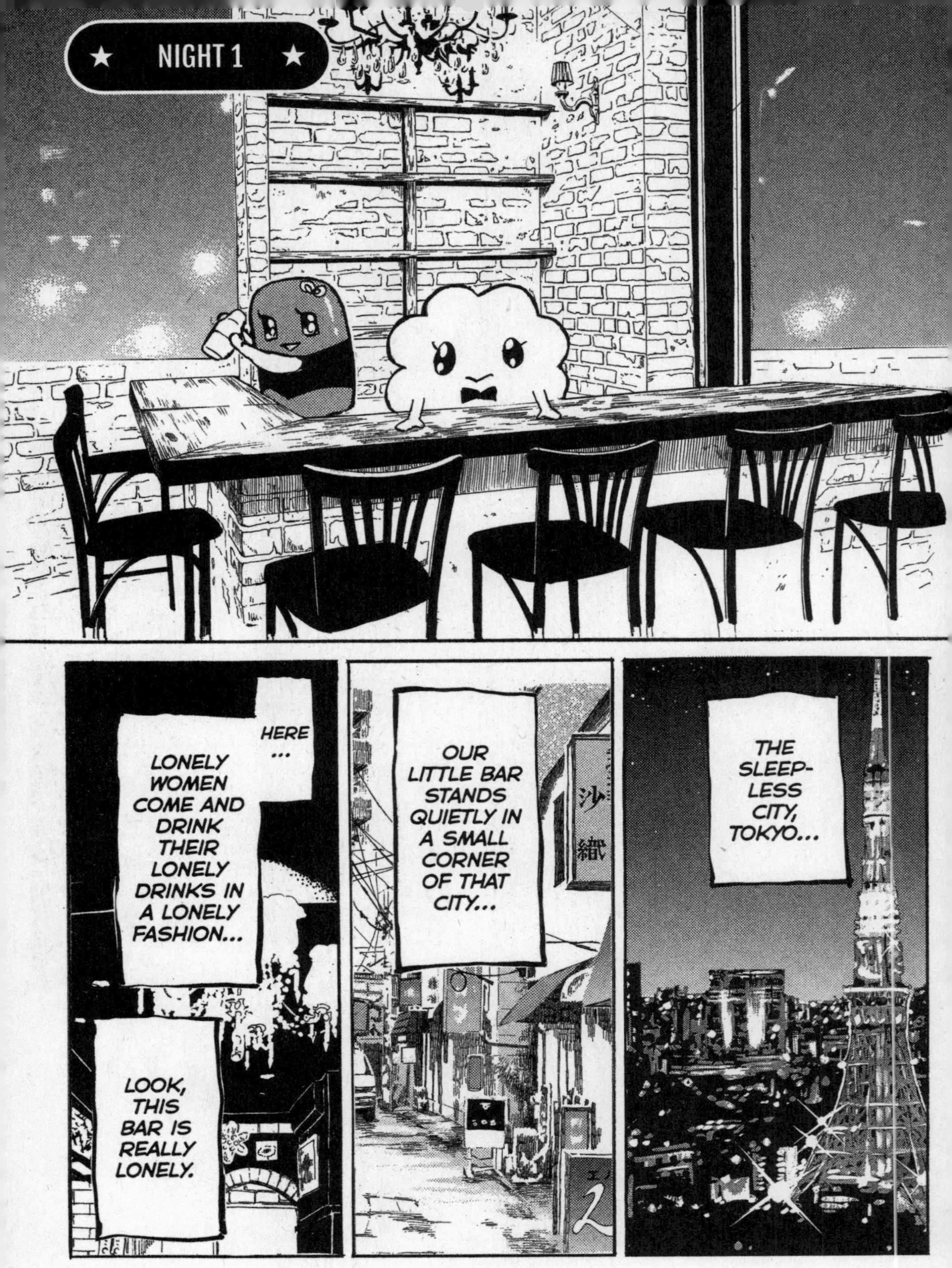
NIGHT 1
THE SLEEPLESS CITY, TOKYO...
OUR LITTLE BAR STANDS QUIETLY IN A SMALL CORNER OF THAT CITY...
HERE...
LONELY WOMEN COME AND DRINK THEIR LONELY DRINKS IN A LONELY FASHION...
LOOK, THIS BAR IS REALLY LONELY.

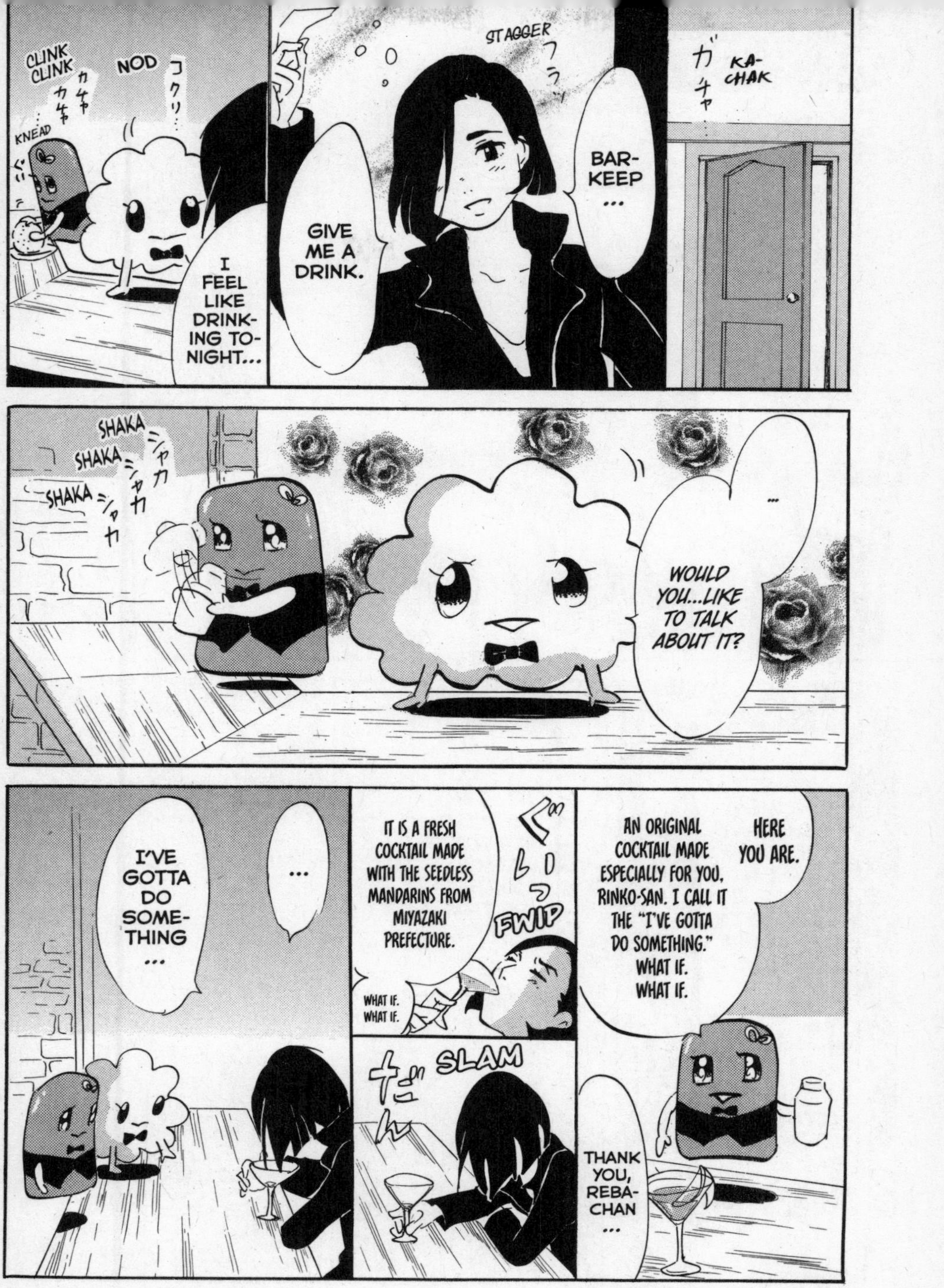
ガチャ
KA-CHAK
STAGGER
フラッ
BAR-KEEP...
GIVE ME A DRINK.
I FEEL LIKE DRINKING TONIGHT...
コクリ…
NOD
CLINK CLINK
カチャカチャ
KNEAD
...
WOULD YOU...LIKE TO TALK ABOUT IT?
SHAKA シャカ
SHAKA シャカ
SHAKA シャカ
HERE YOU ARE.
AN ORIGINAL COCKTAIL MADE ESPECIALLY FOR YOU, RINKO-SAN. I CALL IT THE "I'VE GOTTA DO SOMETHING." WHAT IF. WHAT IF.
THANK YOU, REBA-CHAN...
FWIP
IT IS A FRESH COCKTAIL MADE WITH THE SEEDLESS MANDARINS FROM MIYAZAKI PREFECTURE.
WHAT IF. WHAT IF.
SLAM
...
I'VE GOTTA DO SOMETHING...

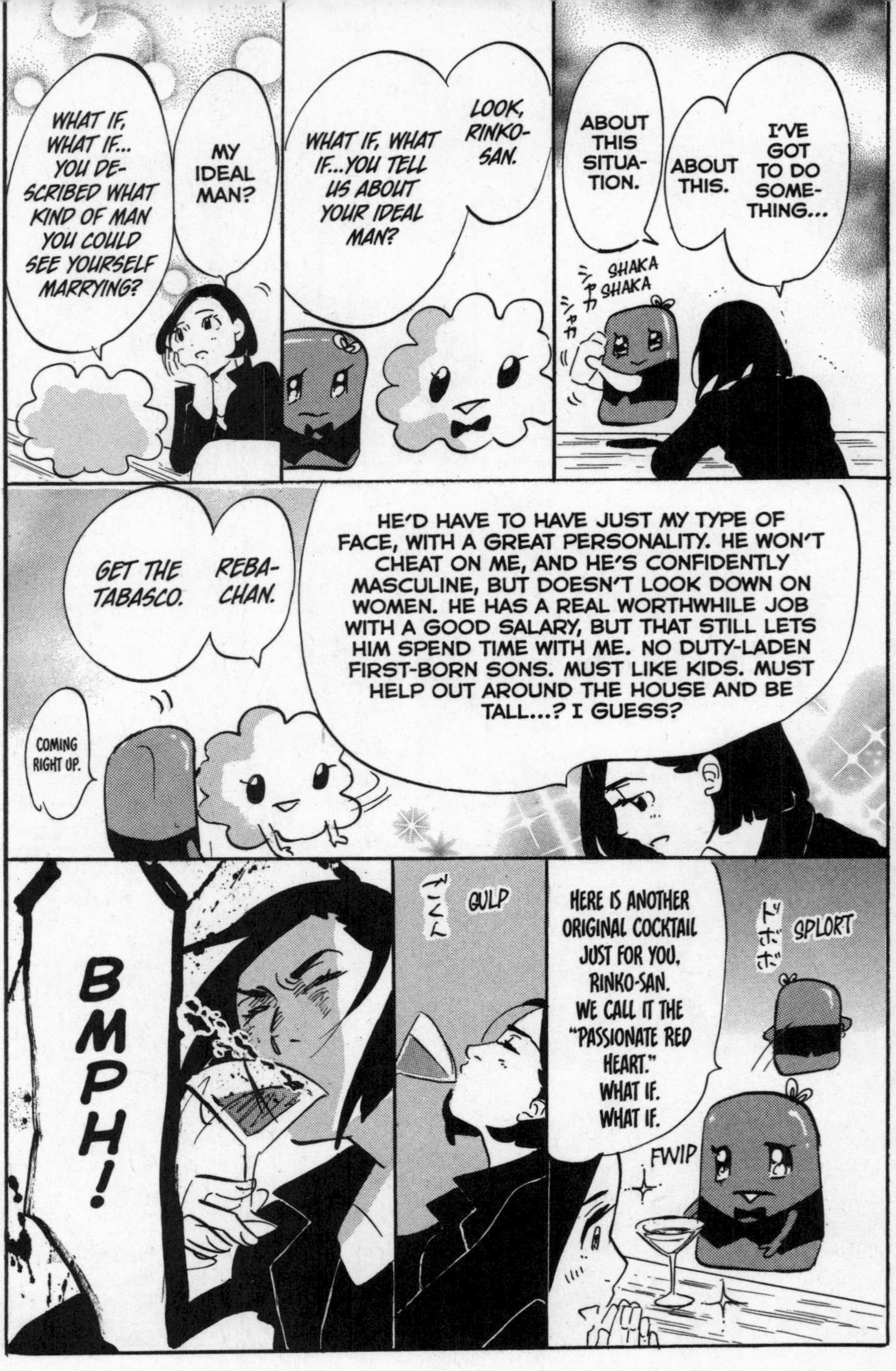
I'VE GOT TO DO SOMETHING...
ABOUT THIS.
ABOUT THIS SITUATION.
シャカシャカ
SHAKA SHAKA
LOOK, RINKO-SAN.
WHAT IF, WHAT IF...YOU TELL US ABOUT YOUR IDEAL MAN?
MY IDEAL MAN?
WHAT IF, WHAT IF... YOU DESCRIBED WHAT KIND OF MAN YOU COULD SEE YOURSELF MARRYING?
HE'D HAVE TO HAVE JUST MY TYPE OF FACE, WITH A GREAT PERSONALITY. HE WON'T CHEAT ON ME, AND HE'S CONFIDENTLY MASCULINE, BUT DOESN'T LOOK DOWN ON WOMEN. HE HAS A REAL WORTHWHILE JOB WITH A GOOD SALARY, BUT THAT STILL LETS HIM SPEND TIME WITH ME. NO DUTY-LADEN FIRST-BORN SONS. MUST LIKE KIDS. MUST HELP OUT AROUND THE HOUSE AND BE TALL...? I GUESS?
REBA-CHAN.
GET THE TABASCO.
COMING RIGHT UP.
ドボボ
SPLORT
HERE IS ANOTHER ORIGINAL COCKTAIL JUST FOR YOU, RINKO-SAN. WE CALL IT THE "PASSIONATE RED HEART." WHAT IF. WHAT IF.
FWIP
ごくん
GULP
BMPH!

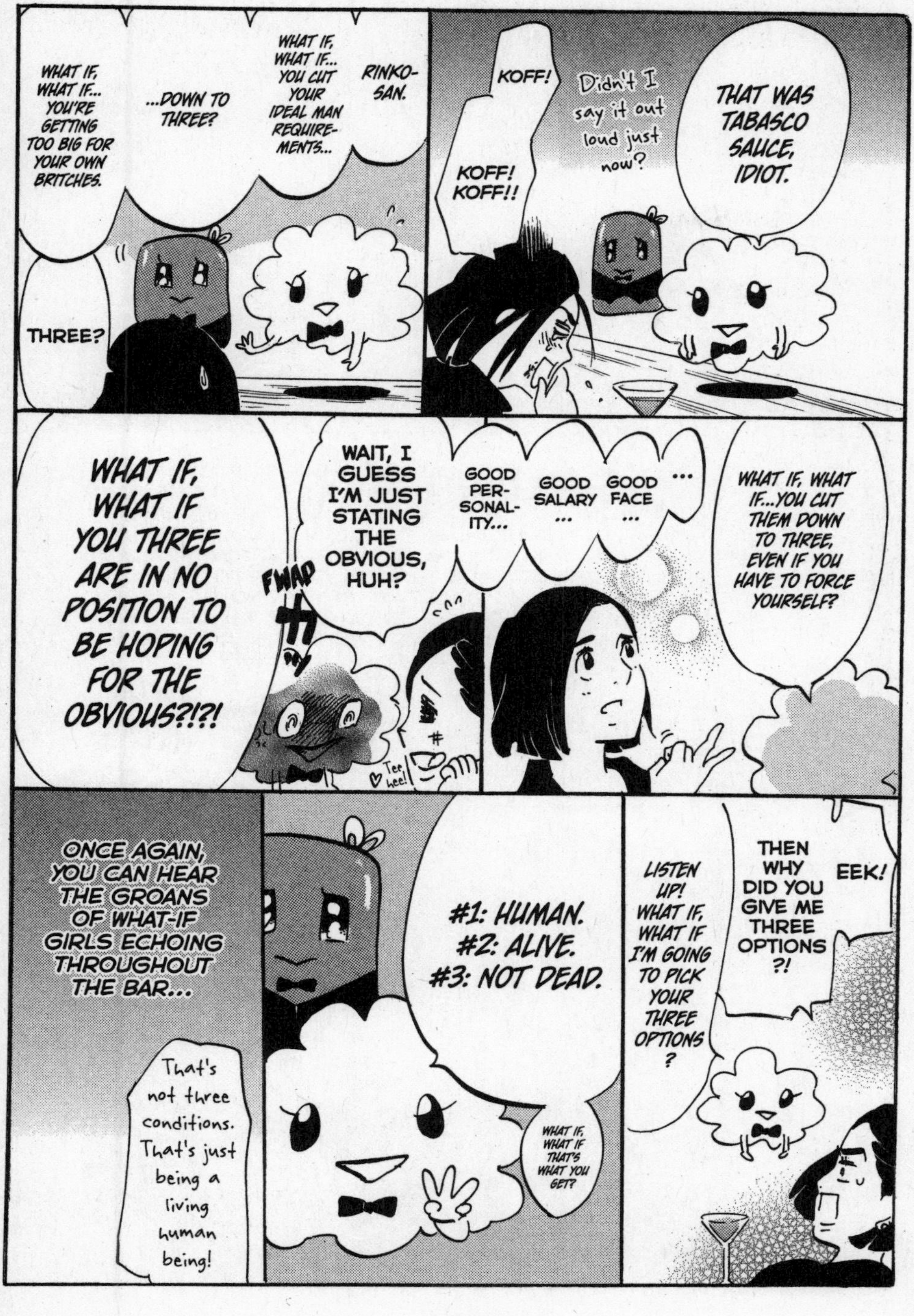
THAT WAS TABASCO SAUCE, IDIOT.
Didn't I say it out loud just now?
KOFF!
KOFF! KOFF!!
RINKO-SAN.
WHAT IF, WHAT IF... YOU CUT YOUR IDEAL MAN REQUIREMENTS...
...DOWN TO THREE?
WHAT IF, WHAT IF... YOU'RE GETTING TOO BIG FOR YOUR OWN BRITCHES.
THREE?
WHAT IF, WHAT IF...YOU CUT THEM DOWN TO THREE, EVEN IF YOU HAVE TO FORCE YOURSELF?
...
GOOD FACE ...
GOOD SALARY ...
GOOD PERSONALITY...
WAIT, I GUESS I'M JUST STATING THE OBVIOUS, HUH?
FWAP
Tee hee!
WHAT IF, WHAT IF YOU THREE ARE IN NO POSITION TO BE HOPING FOR THE OBVIOUS?!?!
EEK!
THEN WHY DID YOU GIVE ME THREE OPTIONS?!
LISTEN UP! WHAT IF, WHAT IF I'M GOING TO PICK YOUR THREE OPTIONS?
#1: HUMAN. #2: ALIVE. #3: NOT DEAD.
WHAT IF, WHAT IF THAT'S WHAT YOU GET?
That's not three conditions. That's just being a living human being!
ONCE AGAIN, YOU CAN HEAR THE GROANS OF WHAT-IF GIRLS ECHOING THROUGHOUT THE BAR...

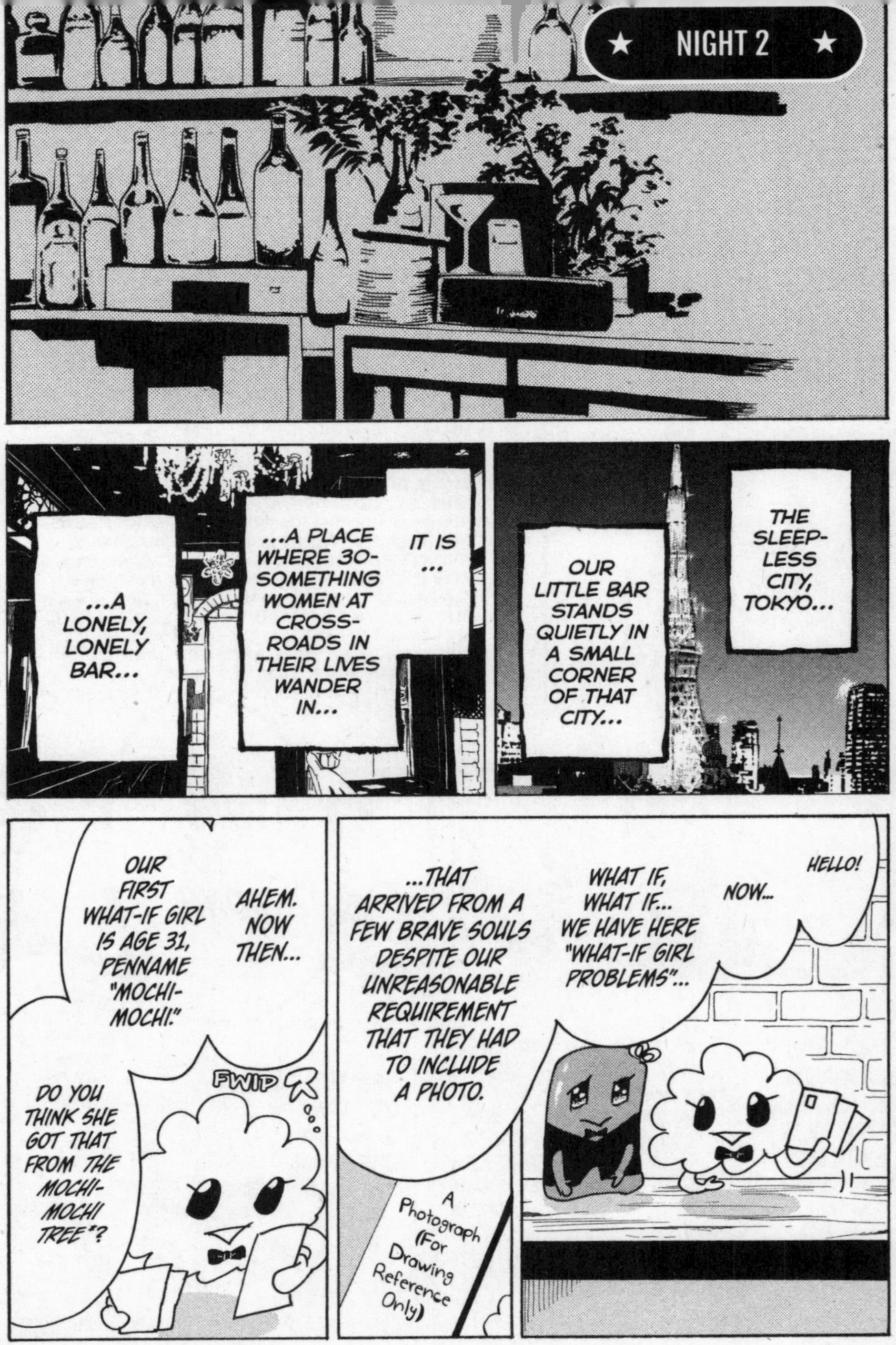
NIGHT 2
THE SLEEPLESS CITY, TOKYO...
OUR LITTLE BAR STANDS QUIETLY IN A SMALL CORNER OF THAT CITY...
IT IS ...
...A PLACE WHERE 30-SOMETHING WOMEN AT CROSSROADS IN THEIR LIVES WANDER IN...
...A LONELY, LONELY BAR...
HELLO!
NOW...
WHAT IF, WHAT IF... WE HAVE HERE "WHAT-IF GIRL PROBLEMS"...
...THAT ARRIVED FROM A FEW BRAVE SOULS DESPITE OUR UNREASONABLE REQUIREMENT THAT THEY HAD TO INCLUDE A PHOTO.
A Photograph (For Drawing Reference Only)
AHEM. NOW THEN...
OUR FIRST WHAT-IF GIRL IS AGE 31, PENNAME "MOCHI-MOCHI."
FWIP
DO YOU THINK SHE GOT THAT FROM THE MOCHI-MOCHI TREE*?

*The Mochi-Mochi Tree is a children's book that was released in 1971.

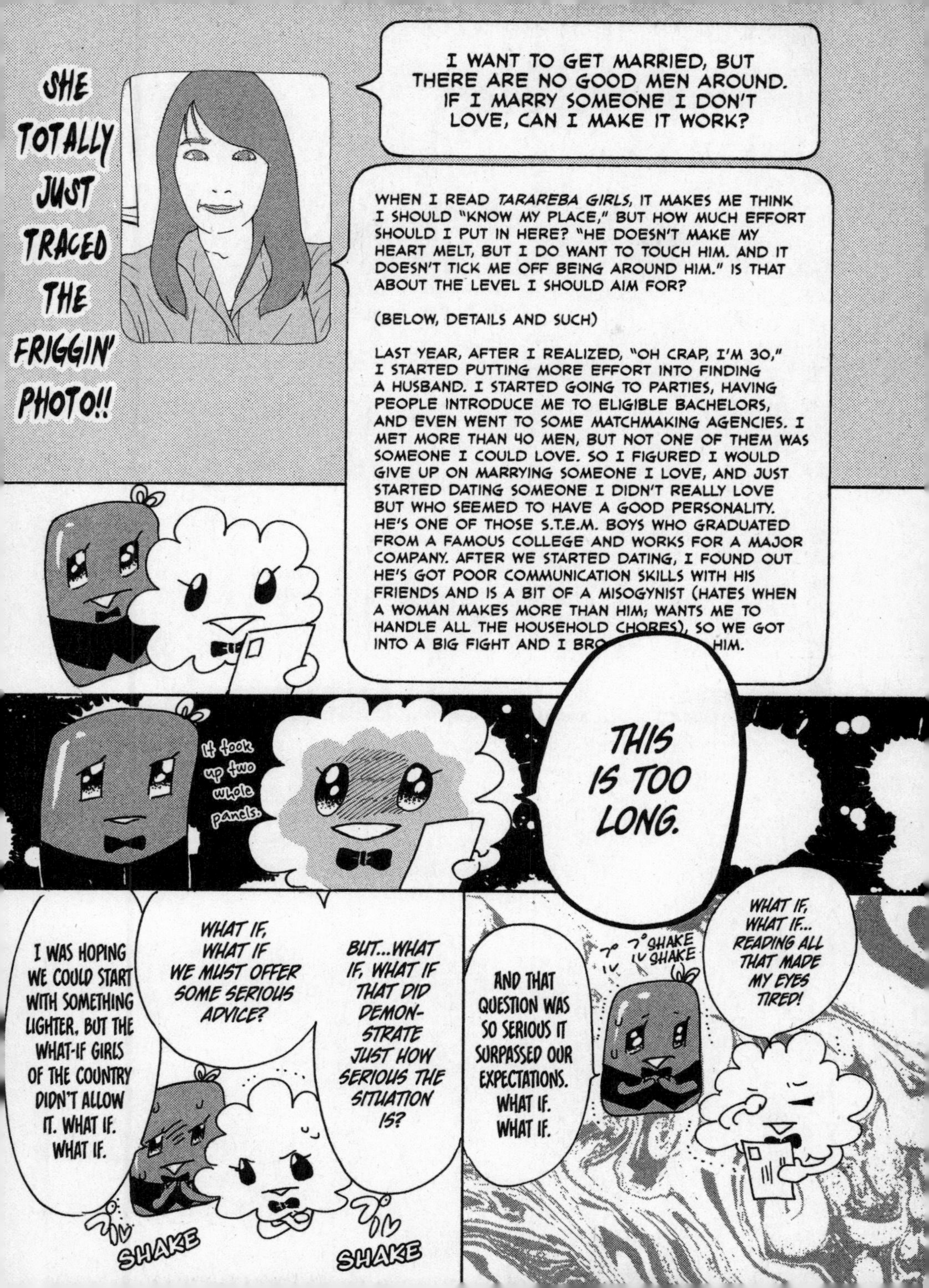
I WANT TO GET MARRIED, BUT THERE ARE NO GOOD MEN AROUND. IF I MARRY SOMEONE I DON'T LOVE, CAN I MAKE IT WORK?
WHEN I READ *TARAREBA GIRLS*, IT MAKES ME THINK I SHOULD "KNOW MY PLACE," BUT HOW MUCH EFFORT SHOULD I PUT IN HERE? "HE DOESN'T MAKE MY HEART MELT, BUT I DO WANT TO TOUCH HIM. AND IT DOESN'T TICK ME OFF BEING AROUND HIM." IS THAT ABOUT THE LEVEL I SHOULD AIM FOR?
(BELOW, DETAILS AND SUCH)
LAST YEAR, AFTER I REALIZED, "OH CRAP, I'M 30," I STARTED PUTTING MORE EFFORT INTO FINDING A HUSBAND. I STARTED GOING TO PARTIES, HAVING PEOPLE INTRODUCE ME TO ELIGIBLE BACHELORS, AND EVEN WENT TO SOME MATCHMAKING AGENCIES. I MET MORE THAN 40 MEN, BUT NOT ONE OF THEM WAS SOMEONE I COULD LOVE. SO I FIGURED I WOULD GIVE UP ON MARRYING SOMEONE I LOVE, AND JUST STARTED DATING SOMEONE I DIDN'T REALLY LOVE BUT WHO SEEMED TO HAVE A GOOD PERSONALITY. HE'S ONE OF THOSE S.T.E.M. BOYS WHO GRADUATED FROM A FAMOUS COLLEGE AND WORKS FOR A MAJOR COMPANY. AFTER WE STARTED DATING, I FOUND OUT HE'S GOT POOR COMMUNICATION SKILLS WITH HIS FRIENDS AND IS A BIT OF A MISOGYNIST (HATES WHEN A WOMAN MAKES MORE THAN HIM; WANTS ME TO HANDLE ALL THE HOUSEHOLD CHORES), SO WE GOT INTO A BIG FIGHT AND I BRO HIM.
SHE TOTALLY JUST TRACED THE FRIGGIN' PHOTO!!
THIS IS TOO LONG.
It took up two whole panels.
WHAT IF, WHAT IF... READING ALL THAT MADE MY EYES TIRED!
SHAKE SHAKE
AND THAT QUESTION WAS SO SERIOUS IT SURPASSED OUR EXPECTATIONS. WHAT IF. WHAT IF.
BUT...WHAT IF, WHAT IF THAT DID DEMON-STRATE JUST HOW SERIOUS THE SITUATION IS?
WHAT IF, WHAT IF WE MUST OFFER SOME SERIOUS ADVICE?
I WAS HOPING WE COULD START WITH SOMETHING LIGHTER, BUT THE WHAT-IF GIRLS OF THE COUNTRY DIDN'T ALLOW IT. WHAT IF. WHAT IF.
SHAKE
SHAKE

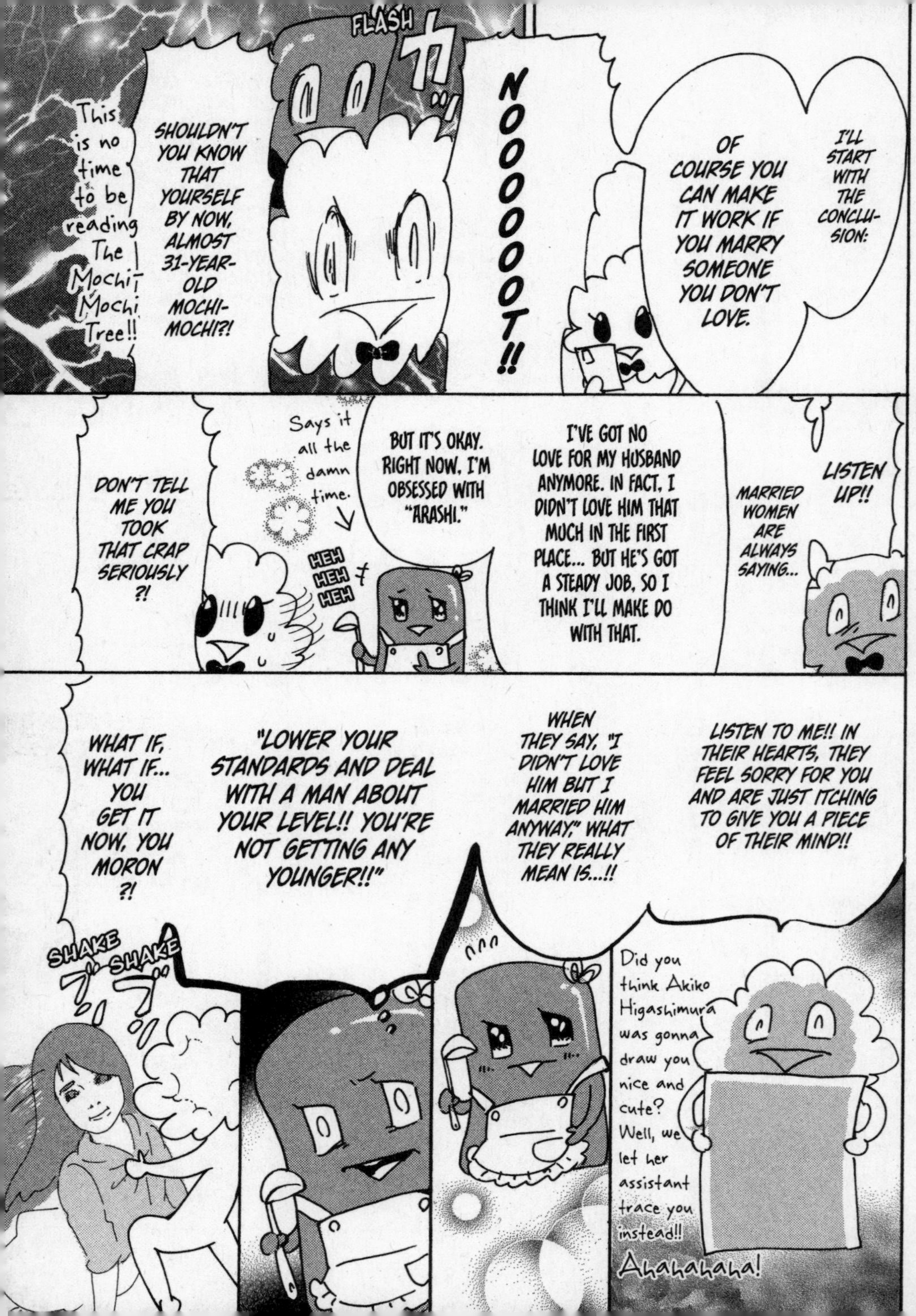
I'LL START WITH THE CONCLUSION:
OF COURSE YOU CAN MAKE IT WORK IF YOU MARRY SOMEONE YOU DON'T LOVE.
FLASH
NOOOOOOOT!!
SHOULDN'T YOU KNOW THAT YOURSELF BY NOW, ALMOST 31-YEAR-OLD MOCHI-MOCHI?!
This is no time to be reading The Mochi Mochi Tree!!
LISTEN UP!!
MARRIED WOMEN ARE ALWAYS SAYING...
I'VE GOT NO LOVE FOR MY HUSBAND ANYMORE. IN FACT, I DIDN'T LOVE HIM THAT MUCH IN THE FIRST PLACE... BUT HE'S GOT A STEADY JOB, SO I THINK I'LL MAKE DO WITH THAT.
BUT IT'S OKAY. RIGHT NOW, I'M OBSESSED WITH "ARASHI."
Says it all the damn time.
HEH HEH HEH
DON'T TELL ME YOU TOOK THAT CRAP SERIOUSLY?!
LISTEN TO ME!! IN THEIR HEARTS, THEY FEEL SORRY FOR YOU AND ARE JUST ITCHING TO GIVE YOU A PIECE OF THEIR MIND!!
WHEN THEY SAY, "I DIDN'T LOVE HIM BUT I MARRIED HIM ANYWAY," WHAT THEY REALLY MEAN IS...!!
"LOWER YOUR STANDARDS AND DEAL WITH A MAN ABOUT YOUR LEVEL!! YOU'RE NOT GETTING ANY YOUNGER!!"
WHAT IF, WHAT IF... YOU GET IT NOW, YOU MORON?!
Did you think Akiko Higashimura was gonna draw you nice and cute? Well, we let her assistant trace you instead!!
Ahahahaha!
SHAKE SHAKE

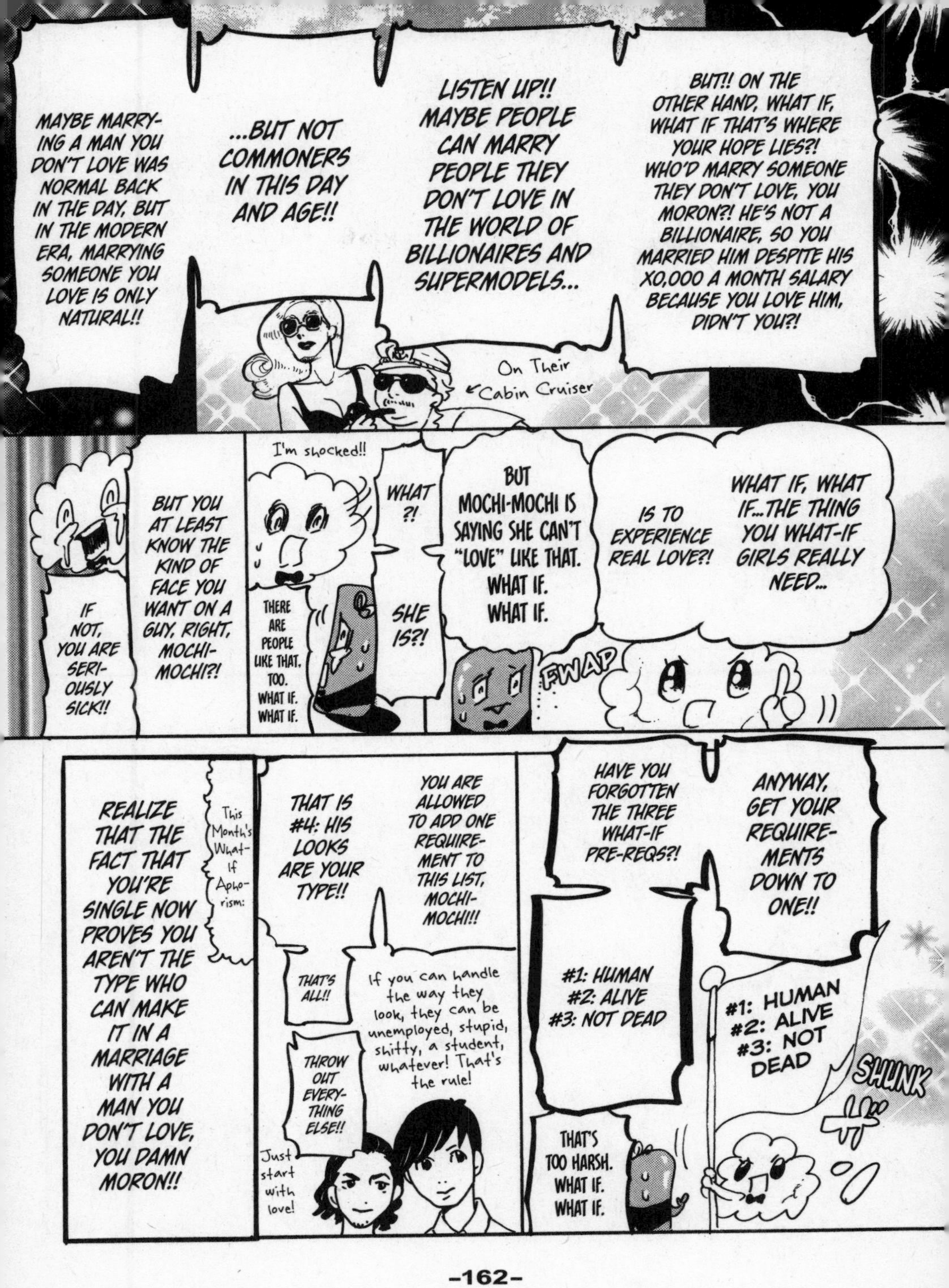

BUT!! ON THE OTHER HAND, WHAT IF, WHAT IF THAT'S WHERE YOUR HOPE LIES?! WHO'D MARRY SOMEONE THEY DON'T LOVE, YOU MORON?! HE'S NOT A BILLIONAIRE, SO YOU MARRIED HIM DESPITE HIS XO,000 A MONTH SALARY BECAUSE YOU LOVE HIM, DIDN'T YOU?!
LISTEN UP!! MAYBE PEOPLE CAN MARRY PEOPLE THEY DON'T LOVE IN THE WORLD OF BILLIONAIRES AND SUPERMODELS...
...BUT NOT COMMONERS IN THIS DAY AND AGE!!
MAYBE MARRYING A MAN YOU DON'T LOVE WAS NORMAL BACK IN THE DAY, BUT IN THE MODERN ERA, MARRYING SOMEONE YOU LOVE IS ONLY NATURAL!!
On Their Cabin Cruiser
WHAT IF, WHAT IF...THE THING YOU WHAT-IF GIRLS REALLY NEED...
IS TO EXPERIENCE REAL LOVE?!
FWAP
BUT MOCHI-MOCHI IS SAYING SHE CAN'T "LOVE" LIKE THAT. WHAT IF. WHAT IF.
WHAT?!
SHE IS?!
I'm shocked!!
THERE ARE PEOPLE LIKE THAT, TOO. WHAT IF. WHAT IF.
BUT YOU AT LEAST KNOW THE KIND OF FACE YOU WANT ON A GUY, RIGHT, MOCHI-MOCHI?!
IF NOT, YOU ARE SERIOUSLY SICK!!
ANYWAY, GET YOUR REQUIREMENTS DOWN TO ONE!!
HAVE YOU FORGOTTEN THE THREE WHAT-IF PRE-REQS?!
#1: HUMAN #2: ALIVE #3: NOT DEAD
#1: HUMAN #2: ALIVE #3: NOT DEAD
SHUNK
THAT'S TOO HARSH. WHAT IF. WHAT IF.
YOU ARE ALLOWED TO ADD ONE REQUIREMENT TO THIS LIST, MOCHI-MOCHI!!!
THAT IS #4: HIS LOOKS ARE YOUR TYPE!!
If you can handle the way they look, they can be unemployed, stupid, shitty, a student, whatever! That's the rule!
THAT'S ALL!!
THROW OUT EVERYTHING ELSE!!
Just start with love!
This Month's What-If Aphorism:
REALIZE THAT THE FACT THAT YOU'RE SINGLE NOW PROVES YOU AREN'T THE TYPE WHO CAN MAKE IT IN A MARRIAGE WITH A MAN YOU DON'T LOVE, YOU DAMN MORON!!

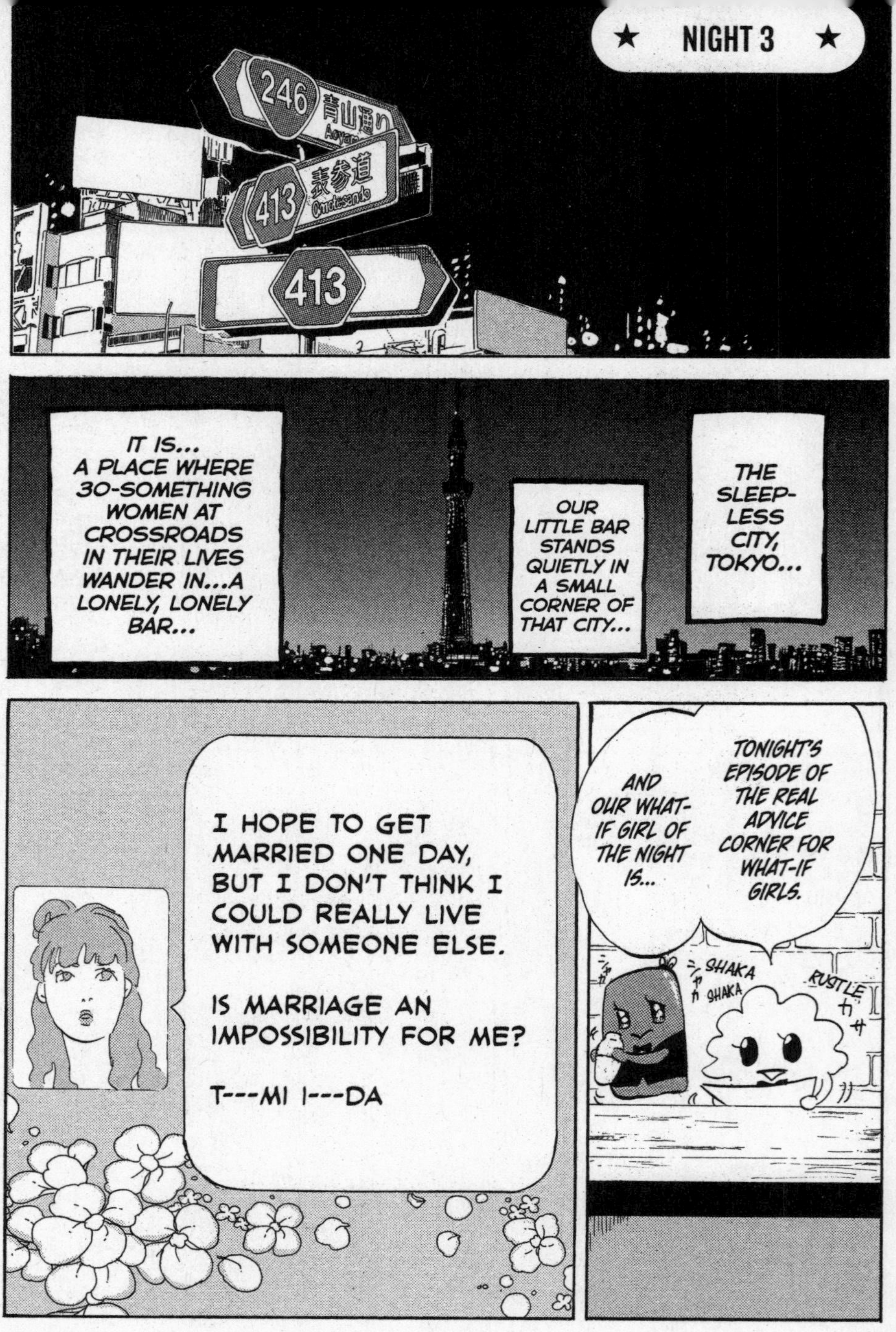
★ NIGHT 3 ★
246
青山通り
413
表参道
Omotesando
413
THE SLEEPLESS CITY, TOKYO...
OUR LITTLE BAR STANDS QUIETLY IN A SMALL CORNER OF THAT CITY...
IT IS... A PLACE WHERE 30-SOMETHING WOMEN AT CROSSROADS IN THEIR LIVES WANDER IN...A LONELY, LONELY BAR...
TONIGHT'S EPISODE OF THE REAL ADVICE CORNER FOR WHAT-IF GIRLS.
AND OUR WHAT-IF GIRL OF THE NIGHT IS...
SHAKA SHAKA
RUSTLE
I HOPE TO GET MARRIED ONE DAY, BUT I DON'T THINK I COULD REALLY LIVE WITH SOMEONE ELSE.
IS MARRIAGE AN IMPOSSIBILITY FOR ME?
T---MI I---DA

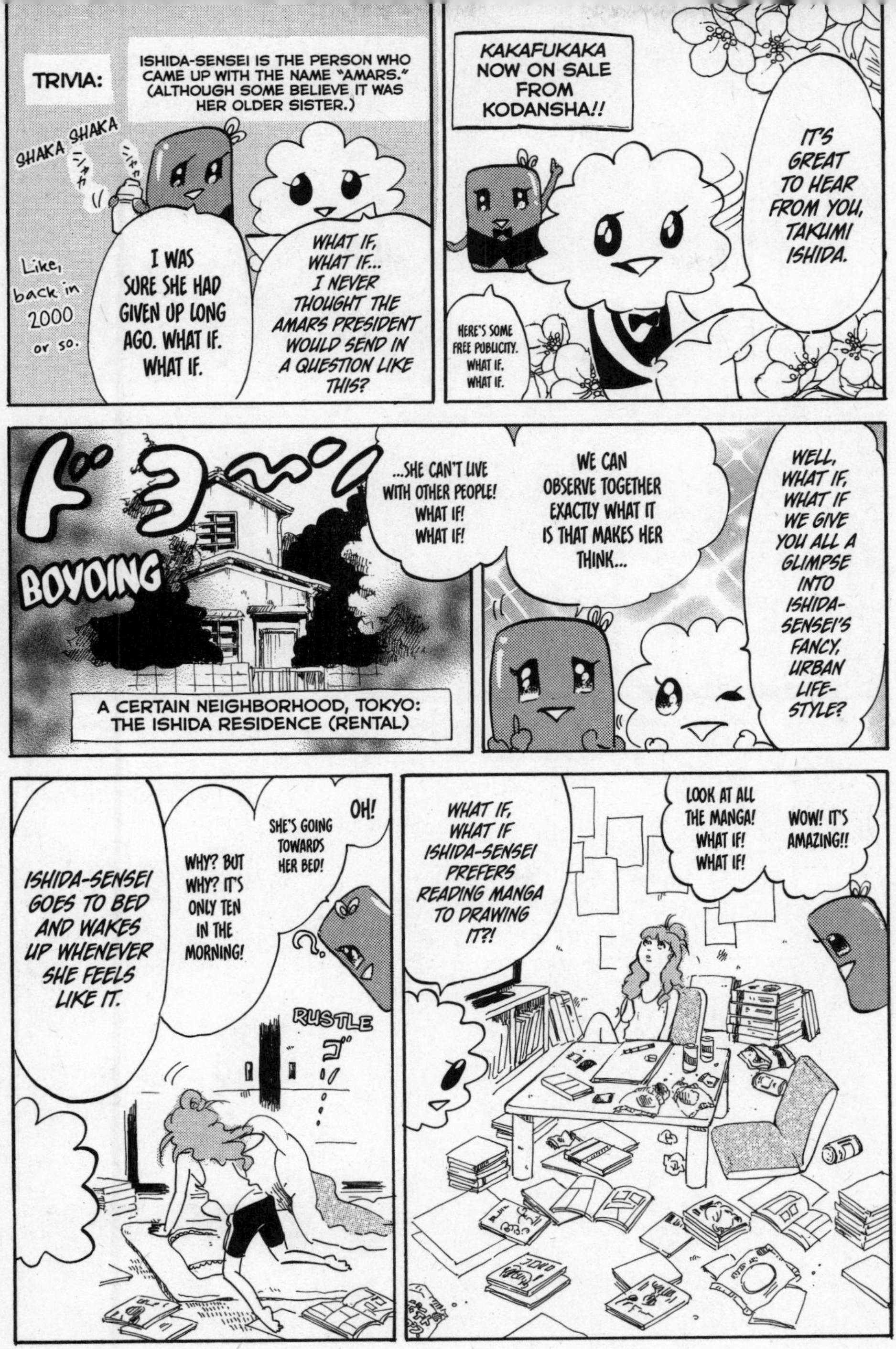
KAKAFUKAKA NOW ON SALE FROM KODANSHA!!
IT'S GREAT TO HEAR FROM YOU, TAKUMI ISHIDA.
HERE'S SOME FREE PUBLICITY. WHAT IF, WHAT IF.
TRIVIA:
ISHIDA-SENSEI IS THE PERSON WHO CAME UP WITH THE NAME "AMARS." (ALTHOUGH SOME BELIEVE IT WAS HER OLDER SISTER.)
SHAKA SHAKA
WHAT IF, WHAT IF... I NEVER THOUGHT THE AMARS PRESIDENT WOULD SEND IN A QUESTION LIKE THIS?
I WAS SURE SHE HAD GIVEN UP LONG AGO. WHAT IF. WHAT IF.
Like, back in 2000 or so.
WELL, WHAT IF, WHAT IF WE GIVE YOU ALL A GLIMPSE INTO ISHIDA-SENSEI'S FANCY, URBAN LIFE-STYLE?
WE CAN OBSERVE TOGETHER EXACTLY WHAT IT IS THAT MAKES HER THINK...
...SHE CAN'T LIVE WITH OTHER PEOPLE! WHAT IF! WHAT IF!
BOYOING
A CERTAIN NEIGHBORHOOD, TOKYO: THE ISHIDA RESIDENCE (RENTAL)
WOW! IT'S AMAZING!!
LOOK AT ALL THE MANGA! WHAT IF! WHAT IF!
WHAT IF, WHAT IF ISHIDA-SENSEI PREFERS READING MANGA TO DRAWING IT?!
OH!
SHE'S GOING TOWARDS HER BED!
WHY? BUT WHY? IT'S ONLY TEN IN THE MORNING!
ISHIDA-SENSEI GOES TO BED AND WAKES UP WHENEVER SHE FEELS LIKE IT.
RUSTLE

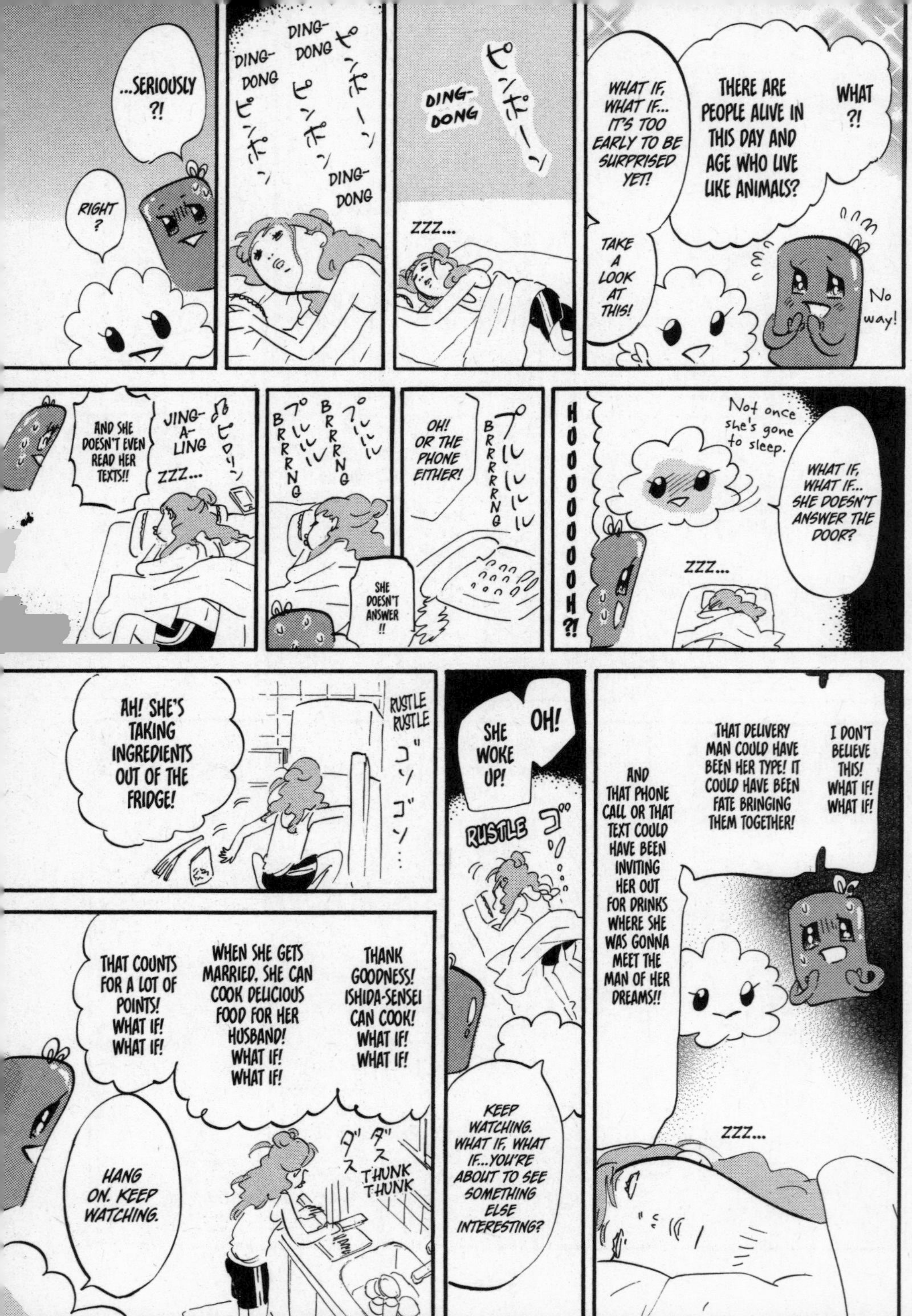
WHAT ?!
THERE ARE PEOPLE ALIVE IN THIS DAY AND AGE WHO LIVE LIKE ANIMALS?
WHAT IF, WHAT IF... IT'S TOO EARLY TO BE SURPRISED YET!
No way!
TAKE A LOOK AT THIS!
ピンポーン
DING-DONG
ZZZ...
DING-DONG ピンポーン
DING-DONG ピンポーン
DING-DONG ピンポーン
DING-DONG
...SERIOUSLY ?!
RIGHT ?
Not once she's gone to sleep.
WHAT IF, WHAT IF... SHE DOESN'T ANSWER THE DOOR?
HUUUUUUUH?!
ZZZ...
プルルル
BRRRRRNG
OH! OR THE PHONE EITHER!
SHE DOESN'T ANSWER!!
プルルル BRRRNG
プルルル BRRRNG
ピロリン
JING-A-LING
AND SHE DOESN'T EVEN READ HER TEXTS!!
ZZZ...
I DON'T BELIEVE THIS! WHAT IF! WHAT IF!
THAT DELIVERY MAN COULD HAVE BEEN HER TYPE! IT COULD HAVE BEEN FATE BRINGING THEM TOGETHER!
AND THAT PHONE CALL OR THAT TEXT COULD HAVE BEEN INVITING HER OUT FOR DRINKS WHERE SHE WAS GONNA MEET THE MAN OF HER DREAMS!!
ZZZ...
OH!
SHE WOKE UP!
ゴソ
RUSTLE
RUSTLE RUSTLE
ゴソゴソ...
AH! SHE'S TAKING INGREDIENTS OUT OF THE FRIDGE!
KEEP WATCHING. WHAT IF, WHAT IF...YOU'RE ABOUT TO SEE SOMETHING ELSE INTERESTING?
THANK GOODNESS! ISHIDA-SENSEI CAN COOK! WHAT IF! WHAT IF!
WHEN SHE GETS MARRIED, SHE CAN COOK DELICIOUS FOOD FOR HER HUSBAND! WHAT IF! WHAT IF!
THAT COUNTS FOR A LOT OF POINTS! WHAT IF! WHAT IF!
ダスダス
THUNK THUNK
HANG ON. KEEP WATCHING.

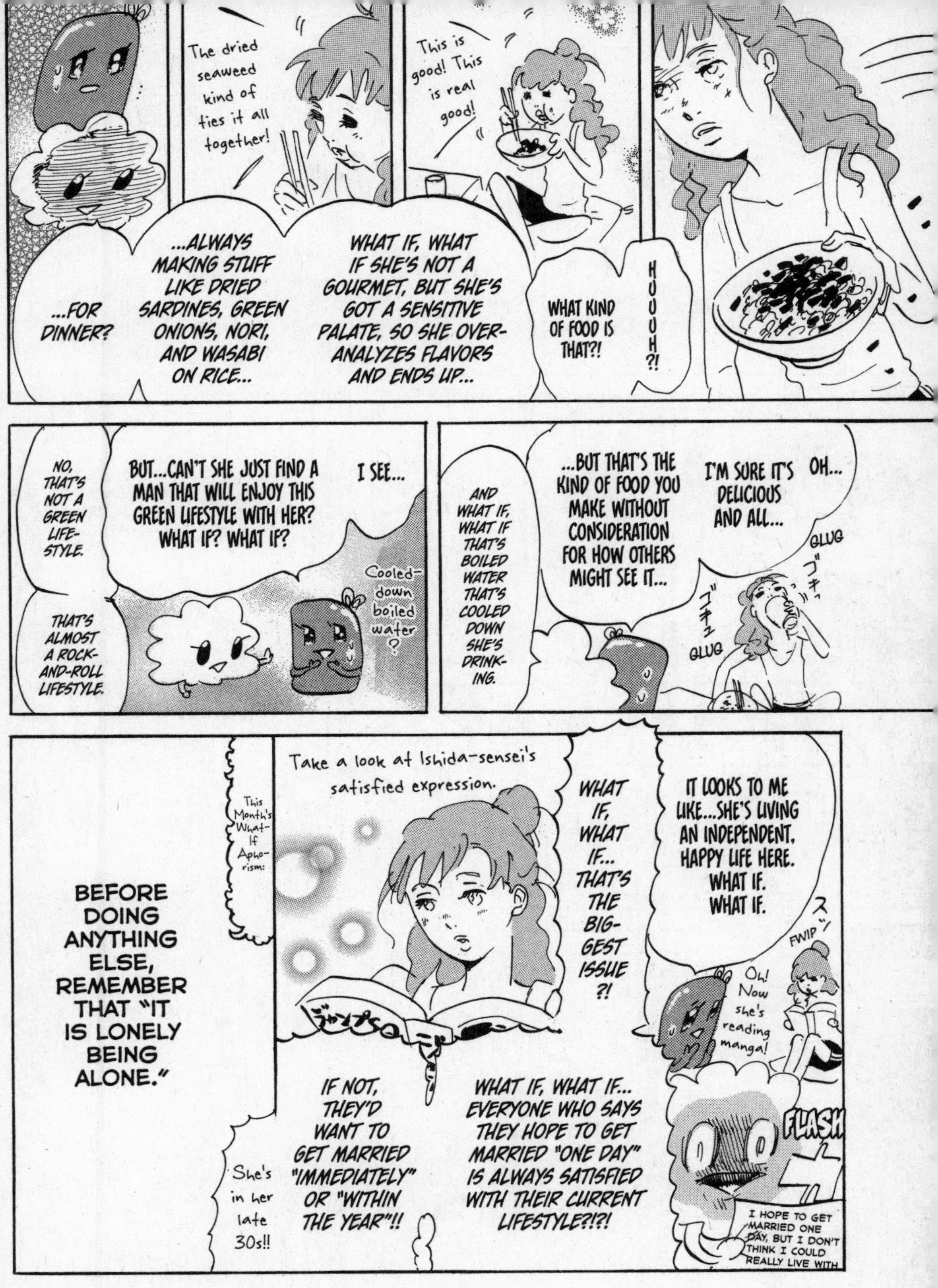
HUUUUH?!
WHAT KIND OF FOOD IS THAT?!
This is good! This is real good!
The dried seaweed kind of ties it all together!
WHAT IF, WHAT IF SHE'S NOT A GOURMET, BUT SHE'S GOT A SENSITIVE PALATE, SO SHE OVER-ANALYZES FLAVORS AND ENDS UP...
...ALWAYS MAKING STUFF LIKE DRIED SARDINES, GREEN ONIONS, NORI, AND WASABI ON RICE...
...FOR DINNER?
OH...
I'M SURE IT'S DELICIOUS AND ALL...
...BUT THAT'S THE KIND OF FOOD YOU MAKE WITHOUT CONSIDERATION FOR HOW OTHERS MIGHT SEE IT...
GLUG
GLUG
AND WHAT IF, WHAT IF THAT'S BOILED WATER THAT'S COOLED DOWN SHE'S DRINKING.
I SEE...
BUT...CAN'T SHE JUST FIND A MAN THAT WILL ENJOY THIS GREEN LIFESTYLE WITH HER? WHAT IF? WHAT IF?
Cooled-down boiled water?
NO, THAT'S NOT A GREEN LIFE-STYLE.
THAT'S ALMOST A ROCK-AND-ROLL LIFESTYLE.
IT LOOKS TO ME LIKE...SHE'S LIVING AN INDEPENDENT, HAPPY LIFE HERE. WHAT IF. WHAT IF.
FWIP
Oh! Now she's reading manga!
WHAT IF, WHAT IF... THAT'S THE BIG-GEST ISSUE?!
Take a look at Ishida-sensei's satisfied expression.
FLASH
I HOPE TO GET MARRIED ONE DAY, BUT I DON'T THINK I COULD REALLY LIVE WITH
WHAT IF, WHAT IF... EVERYONE WHO SAYS THEY HOPE TO GET MARRIED "ONE DAY" IS ALWAYS SATISFIED WITH THEIR CURRENT LIFESTYLE?!?!
IF NOT, THEY'D WANT TO GET MARRIED "IMMEDIATELY" OR "WITHIN THE YEAR"!!
She's in her late 30s!!
This Month's What-If Apho-rism:
BEFORE DOING ANYTHING ELSE, REMEMBER THAT "IT IS LONELY BEING ALONE."

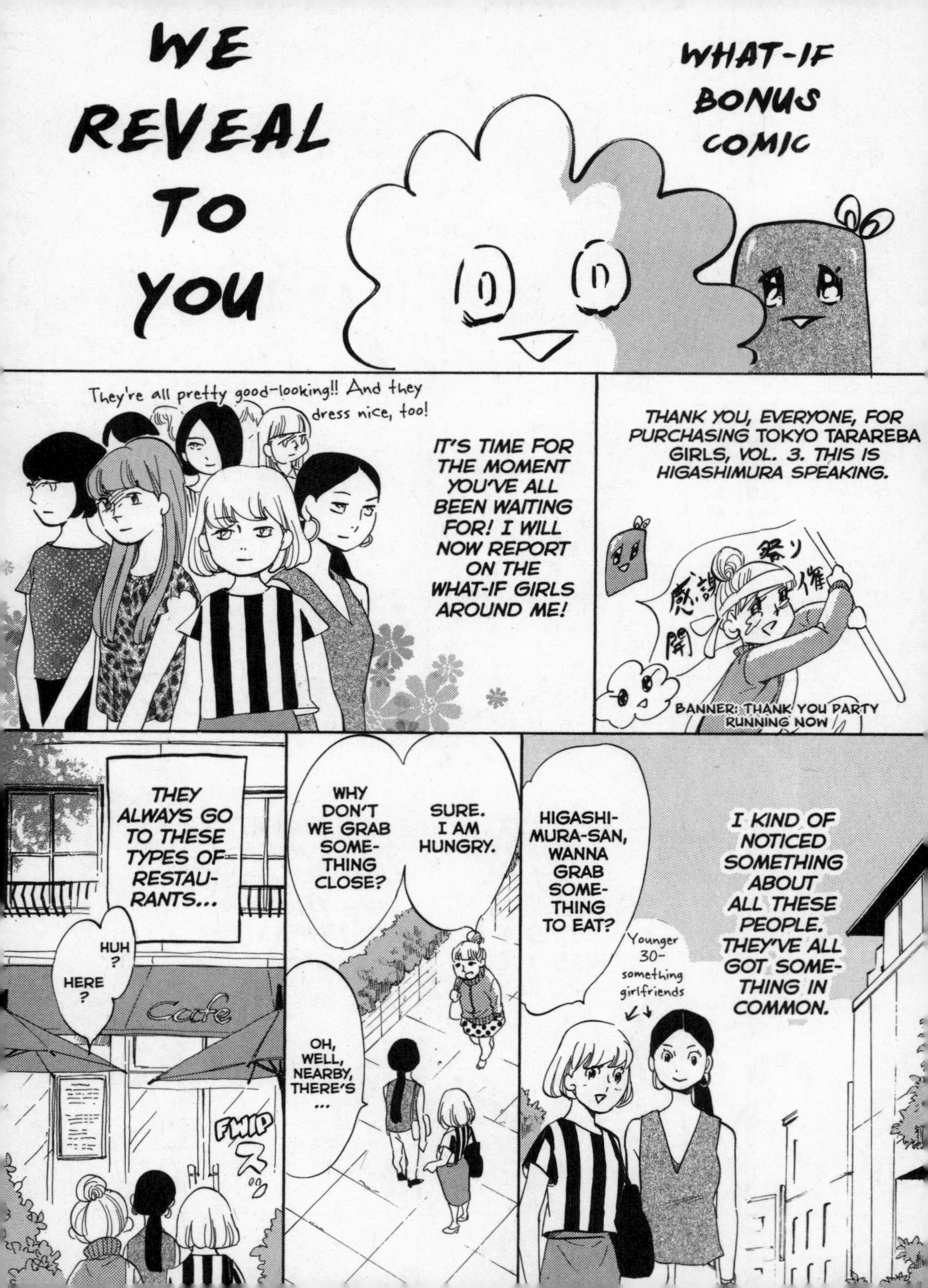
WHAT-IF BONUS COMIC
WE REVEAL TO YOU
THANK YOU, EVERYONE, FOR PURCHASING TOKYO TARAREBA GIRLS, VOL. 3. THIS IS HIGASHIMURA SPEAKING.
BANNER: THANK YOU PARTY RUNNING NOW
IT'S TIME FOR THE MOMENT YOU'VE ALL BEEN WAITING FOR! I WILL NOW REPORT ON THE WHAT-IF GIRLS AROUND ME!
They're all pretty good-looking!! And they dress nice, too!
I KIND OF NOTICED SOMETHING ABOUT ALL THESE PEOPLE. THEY'VE ALL GOT SOMETHING IN COMMON.
HIGASHIMURA-SAN, WANNA GRAB SOMETHING TO EAT?
Younger 30-something girlfriends
SURE. I AM HUNGRY.
WHY DON'T WE GRAB SOMETHING CLOSE?
OH, WELL, NEARBY, THERE'S ...
THEY ALWAYS GO TO THESE TYPES OF RESTAURANTS...
HUH?
HERE?
Cafe
FWIP
ス

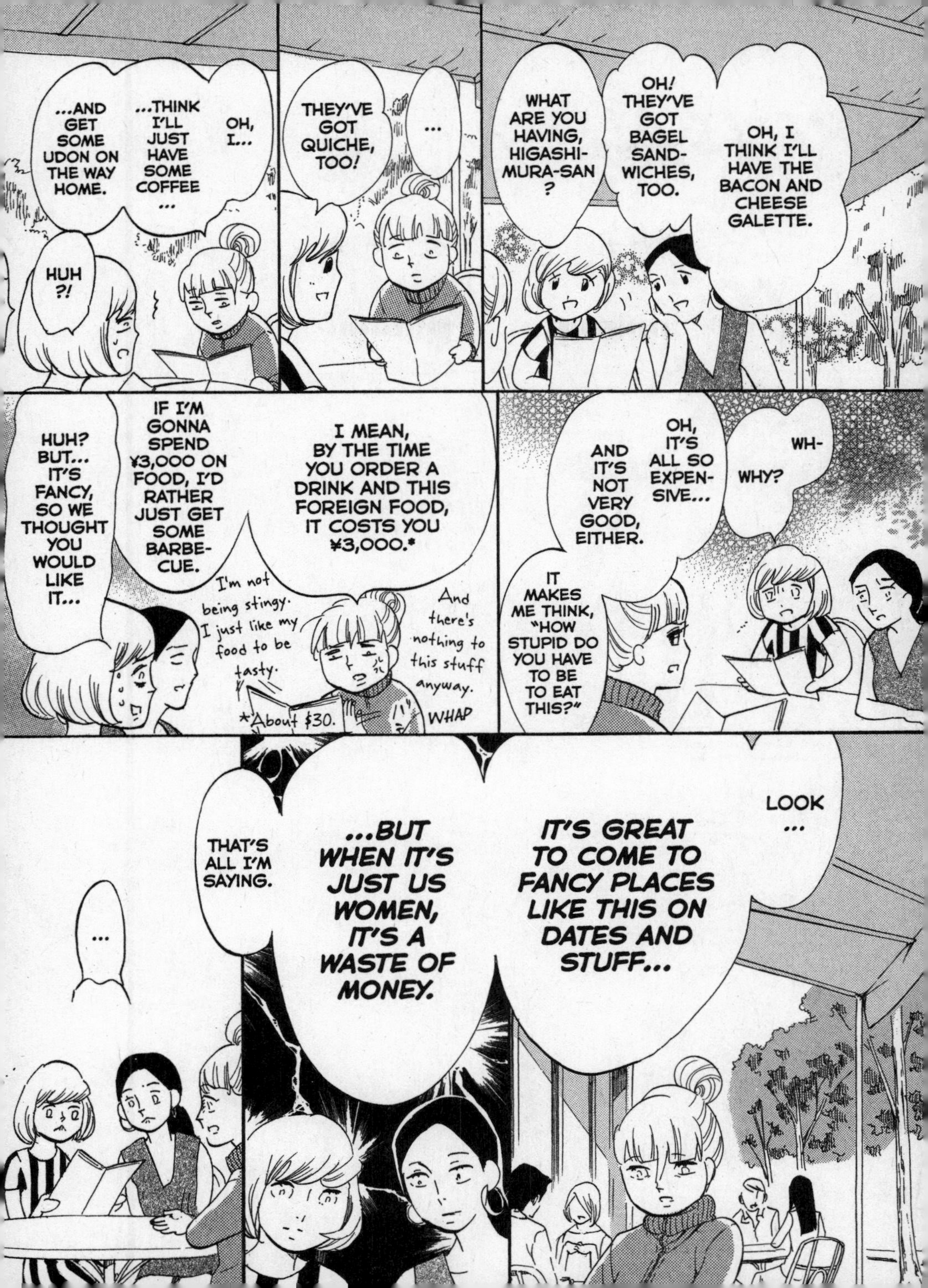
OH, I THINK I'LL HAVE THE BACON AND CHEESE GALETTE.
OH! THEY'VE GOT BAGEL SANDWICHES, TOO.
WHAT ARE YOU HAVING, HIGASHIMURA-SAN?
...
THEY'VE GOT QUICHE, TOO!
OH, I...
...THINK I'LL JUST HAVE SOME COFFEE...
...AND GET SOME UDON ON THE WAY HOME.
HUH?!
WH- WHY?
OH, IT'S ALL SO EXPENSIVE...
AND IT'S NOT VERY GOOD, EITHER.
IT MAKES ME THINK, "HOW STUPID DO YOU HAVE TO BE TO EAT THIS?"
I MEAN, BY THE TIME YOU ORDER A DRINK AND THIS FOREIGN FOOD, IT COSTS YOU ¥3,000.*
IF I'M GONNA SPEND ¥3,000 ON FOOD, I'D RATHER JUST GET SOME BARBECUE.
HUH? BUT... IT'S FANCY, SO WE THOUGHT YOU WOULD LIKE IT...
And there's nothing to this stuff anyway.
I'm not being stingy. I just like my food to be tasty.
WHAP
*About $30.
LOOK...
IT'S GREAT TO COME TO FANCY PLACES LIKE THIS ON DATES AND STUFF...
...BUT WHEN IT'S JUST US WOMEN, IT'S A WASTE OF MONEY.
THAT'S ALL I'M SAYING.
...

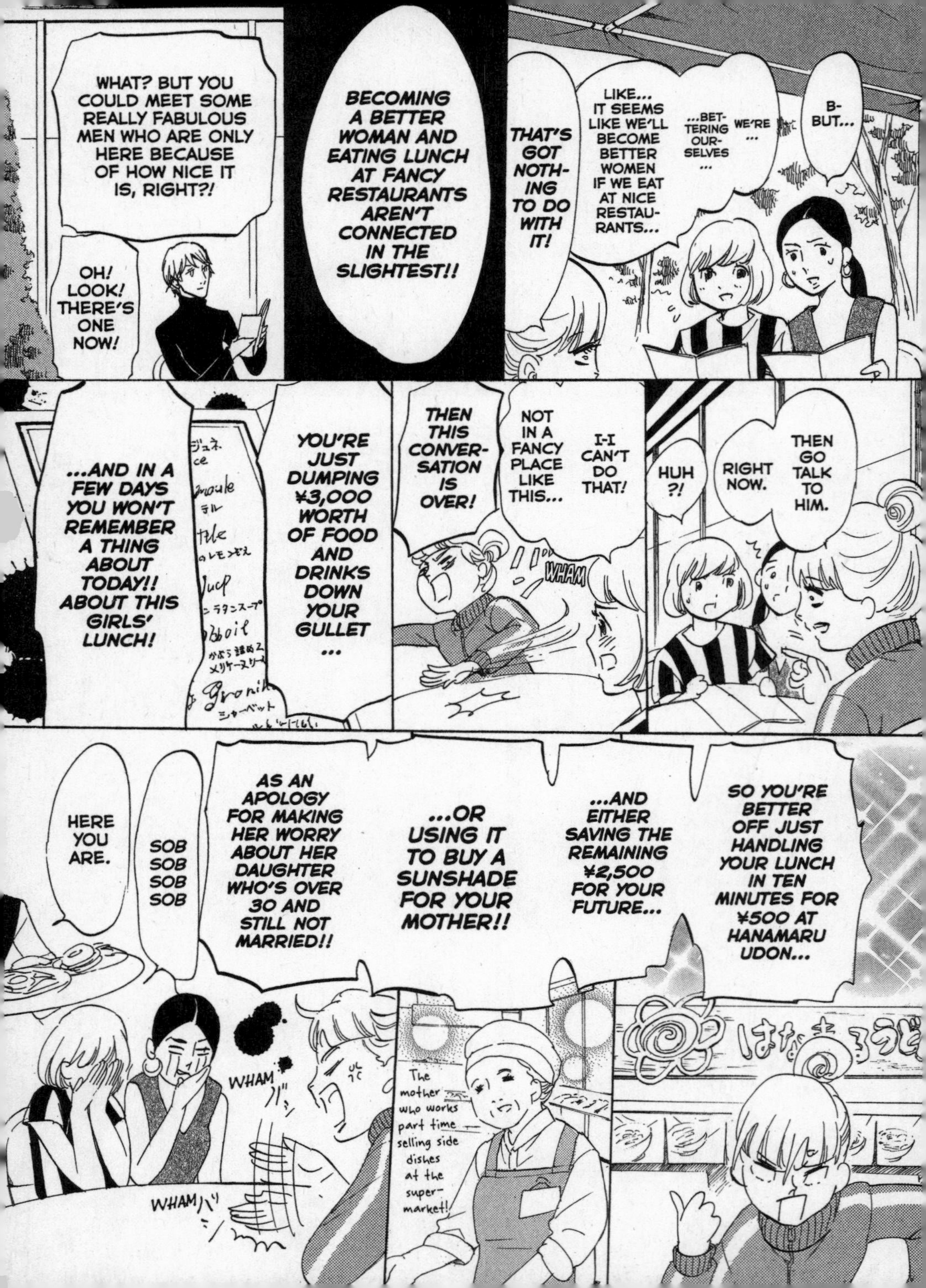
B- BUT...
WE'RE ...
...BETTERING OURSELVES ...
LIKE... IT SEEMS LIKE WE'LL BECOME BETTER WOMEN IF WE EAT AT NICE RESTAURANTS...
THAT'S GOT NOTHING TO DO WITH IT!
BECOMING A BETTER WOMAN AND EATING LUNCH AT FANCY RESTAURANTS AREN'T CONNECTED IN THE SLIGHTEST!!
WHAT? BUT YOU COULD MEET SOME REALLY FABULOUS MEN WHO ARE ONLY HERE BECAUSE OF HOW NICE IT IS, RIGHT?!
OH! LOOK! THERE'S ONE NOW!
THEN GO TALK TO HIM.
RIGHT NOW.
HUH ?!
I-I CAN'T DO THAT!
NOT IN A FANCY PLACE LIKE THIS...
THEN THIS CONVERSATION IS OVER!
WHAM
YOU'RE JUST DUMPING ¥3,000 WORTH OF FOOD AND DRINKS DOWN YOUR GULLET ...
...AND IN A FEW DAYS YOU WON'T REMEMBER A THING ABOUT TODAY!! ABOUT THIS GIRLS' LUNCH!
SO YOU'RE BETTER OFF JUST HANDLING YOUR LUNCH IN TEN MINUTES FOR ¥500 AT HANAMARU UDON...
...AND EITHER SAVING THE REMAINING ¥2,500 FOR YOUR FUTURE...
...OR USING IT TO BUY A SUNSHADE FOR YOUR MOTHER!!
AS AN APOLOGY FOR MAKING HER WORRY ABOUT HER DAUGHTER WHO'S OVER 30 AND STILL NOT MARRIED!!
The mother who works part time selling side dishes at the super-market!
WHAM
WHAM
SOB SOB SOB SOB
HERE YOU ARE.

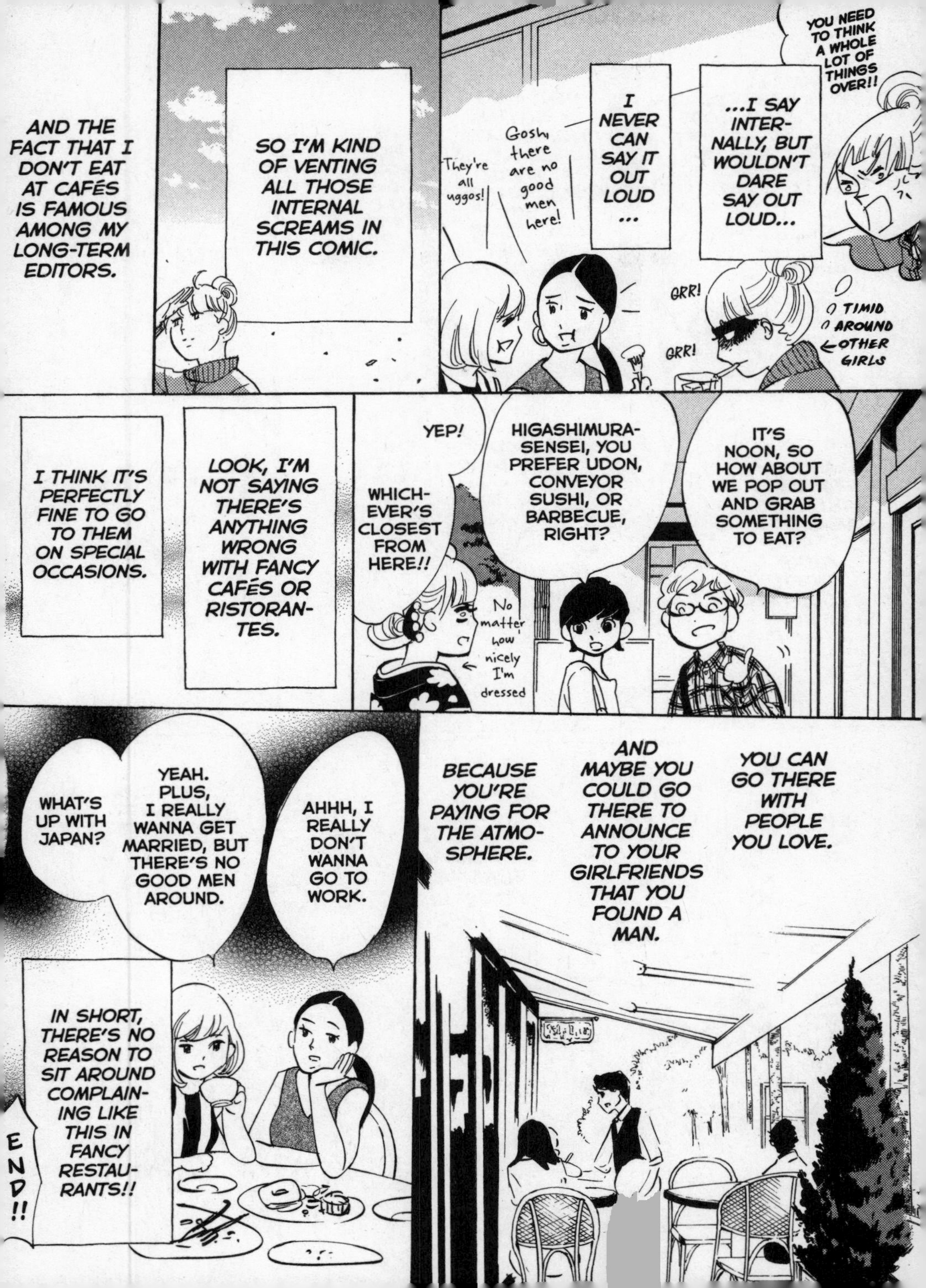
YOU NEED TO THINK A WHOLE LOT OF THINGS OVER!!
...I SAY INTERNALLY, BUT WOULDN'T DARE SAY OUT LOUD...
I NEVER CAN SAY IT OUT LOUD ...
Gosh, there are no good men here!
They're all uggos!
GRR!
GRR!
TIMID AROUND OTHER GIRLS
SO I'M KIND OF VENTING ALL THOSE INTERNAL SCREAMS IN THIS COMIC.
AND THE FACT THAT I DON'T EAT AT CAFÉS IS FAMOUS AMONG MY LONG-TERM EDITORS.
IT'S NOON, SO HOW ABOUT WE POP OUT AND GRAB SOMETHING TO EAT?
HIGASHIMURA-SENSEI, YOU PREFER UDON, CONVEYOR SUSHI, OR BARBECUE, RIGHT?
YEP!
WHICHEVER'S CLOSEST FROM HERE!!
No matter how nicely I'm dressed
LOOK, I'M NOT SAYING THERE'S ANYTHING WRONG WITH FANCY CAFÉS OR RISTORANTES.
I THINK IT'S PERFECTLY FINE TO GO TO THEM ON SPECIAL OCCASIONS.
YOU CAN GO THERE WITH PEOPLE YOU LOVE.
AND MAYBE YOU COULD GO THERE TO ANNOUNCE TO YOUR GIRLFRIENDS THAT YOU FOUND A MAN.
BECAUSE YOU'RE PAYING FOR THE ATMOSPHERE.
AHHH, I REALLY DON'T WANNA GO TO WORK.
YEAH. PLUS, I REALLY WANNA GET MARRIED, BUT THERE'S NO GOOD MEN AROUND.
WHAT'S UP WITH JAPAN?
IN SHORT, THERE'S NO REASON TO SIT AROUND COMPLAINING LIKE THIS IN FANCY RESTAURANTS!!
END!!

TOKYO
TARAREBA
GIRLS

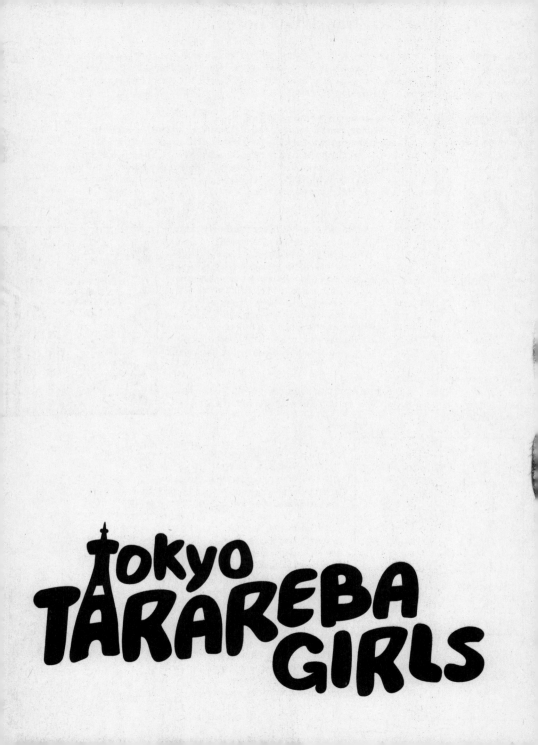

Tokyo Tarareba Girls Translation notes

Tokyo Tarareba Girls: *"Tarareba"* means "What-if," like the "What-if" stories you tell yourself about what could be or could have been. The name is also taken from the names of the two food characters in the series, *tara* (codfish milt) and *reba* (liver) who always say *"tara"* and *"reba"* respectively at the end of their sentences in Japanese, referencing the "what-if" meaning of *"tarareba."*

I'm gonna go see how he's doing, so come with me.
じゃんがら
全部入り
HUH?!
WHY DO WE HAVE TO GO, TOO?!
Sign: Jangara with Everything!

Jangara with everything, page 6
Kyushu Jangara Ramen is a popular, if small, ramen chain in Tokyo. There's one in Omotesando, which may be the one Rinko is at! Their most popular item is the Kyushu Jangara ramen, which boasts a soup base made from *tonkotsu* (pork bone) broth mixed with chicken and vegetable broth. If you get it "with everything," it will include chunks of marinated pork, seasoned cod roe, and a flavored boiled egg. Yum!

With a gift box from a confectionery, page 7
Gift giving is important in Japanese culture, and is often seen as a way to show good intentions when making business deals or establishing personal relationships. In many cases, these gifts are in the form of food, often desserts or fruit (which can be quite expensive in Japan, and thus a high-quality gift). Ginza Sembikiya specializes in fresh fruit and fruit-based desserts, which means only one thing: The producers have come to beg Rinko's forgiveness.

FOR SOME REASON, HAYASAKA-SAN IS HERE WITH THE WHOLE GANG THAT DROPPED YOU FROM THAT PROJECT!
WITH A GIFT BOX FROM A CONFECTIONERY !!
IT'S IN THAT ROSE WRAPPING PAPER FROM THE GINZA SEMBIKIYA!

Skip the seconds, page 8
At many ramen shops, you can order more noodles to add to your remaining ramen broth once you finish your first portion. Seems like Rinko has a habit of doing just that.

旬搾り
チューハイ
ラ・フランス
チューハイ

Chu-Hi, page 54
Chu-Hi is an alcoholic cocktail (an abbreviation of *"shochu* highball"), often sold canned in supermarkets and liquor stores. It's made by mixing *shochu*, a Japanese liquor, with carbonated, flavored water. The most popular year-round flavors are lemon, cherry, and grapefruit, but other seasonal flavors can include apple, pineapple, and pear.

Cinema Bar Sunset's Movie Collection, page 110
Okuda-san has a fantastic, wide library of mostly foreign films, including *Gattica*, *The Notebook*, *Ben Hur*, *Amadeus*, *Goodfellas*, *Erin Brockovich*, and *Butch Cassidy and the Sundance Kid*.

WHAT DO YOU WRITE?
SAD STORIES? MYSTERIES?
OR MAYBE HORROR ?
OH, JUST YOUR STANDARD ROMANTIC COMEDIES ...

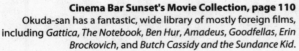